Communities of Journalism

THE HISTORY OF COMMUNICATION

Robert W. McChesney and John C. Nerone, editors

A list of books in the series appears at the end of this book.

Communities of Journalism

*A History of American Newspapers
and Their Readers*

DAVID PAUL NORD

University of Illinois Press

URBANA AND CHICAGO

Library of Congress Cataloging-in-Publication Data
Nord, David Paul.
Communities of journalism : a history of American newspapers
and their readers / David Paul Nord.
p.   cm. — (The History of communication)
Includes bibliographical references and index.
ISBN 0-252-02671-3 (alk. paper)
1. Journalism—United States—History.
2. American newspapers—History.
I. Title. II. Series.
PN4855.N67   2001
071'.3'09—dc21   2001000370

For Martha

Contents

Acknowledgments

EACH ESSAY IN this book has its own genealogy, and each deserves—but, alas, cannot have—its own page of acknowledgments. In twenty years of reading, thinking, and writing about American journalism, I have accumulated so much intellectual debt that I cannot recall all my creditors, much less repay or even acknowledge them. But I will name a few. Most of all I am indebted to the libraries (the institutions and their staffs) that helped me find and use the materials on which these essays are based: the American Antiquarian Society, Newberry Library, Chicago Historical Society, State Historical Society of Wisconsin, New-York Historical Society, New York Public Library, Library Company of Philadelphia, Historical Society of Pennsylvania, American Philosophical Society, and the libraries of Indiana University, Columbia University, the University of Chicago, and the University of Wisconsin. I am grateful for financial support from the University of Wisconsin, Indiana University, and the American Antiquarian Society.

As a former journal editor, I am particularly thankful to those editors who took a chance on these articles and accepted them for publication in their journals and books: Blaine Brownell, Steve Chaffee, Cathy Davidson, J. Worth Estes, Paul H. Hass, John Hench, Susan Henry, Craig Klugman, Mark Levy, Janice Radway, Donald Shaw, Billy G. Smith, Guido Stempel III, and David Thelen. I also appreciate the fine editorial work of the University of Illinois Press, especially the skill, grace, and good humor of the managing editor, Theresa L. Sears.

Working as a historian outside a history department has its perils but also its pleasures. The greatest pleasure for me has been the wonderful intellectual and personal friendships that I have had with colleagues who play roles similar to mine in other schools and departments of journalism and mass communication, especially Gerald Baldasty, James Baughman, James Carey, Thomas Leonard, John Nerone, Michael Schudson, and Jeffery Smith. In working on these essays I have also had the support and encouragement of scholars outside the realm of journalism history, most notably David D. Hall, Carl Kaestle, Sally Griffith, Robert Gross, and David Thelen. So long in preparation, this book will never be seen by five supportive colleagues and friends: Catherine Covert, Edwin Emery, Bill Gilmore-Lehne, Richard Gray, and Harold Nelson.

Finally, I thank my family—Martha, Molly, Paul, and Cherry—who love me.

*   *   *

The chapters in this book were first published in the following publications and are reprinted here, in slightly revised form, with permission:

Chapter 1: "Teleology and News: The Religious Roots of American Journalism, 1630–1730," *Journal of American History* 77 (June 1990): 9–38. Reprinted by permission of the Organization of American Historians.

Chapter 2: "The Authority of Truth: Religion and the John Peter Zenger Case," *Journalism Quarterly* 62 (Summer 1985): 227–35. Reprinted by permission of the Association for Education in Journalism and Mass Communication.

Chapter 3: "Newspapers and American Nationhood, 1776–1826," *Proceedings of the American Antiquarian Society* 100 (Oct. 1990): 391–405. Reprinted by permission of the Society. This chapter originally was a lecture, delivered at the American Antiquarian Society in October 1990, the second in the series "Three Hundred Years of the American Newspaper," a program made possible by a grant from the Gannett Foundation.

Chapter 4: "Tocqueville, Garrison, and the Perfection of Journalism," *Journalism History* 13 (Summer 1986): 56–63. Reprinted by permission of *Journalism History.*

Chapter 5: "The Public Community: The Urbanization of Journalism in Chicago," *Journal of Urban History* 11 (Aug. 1985): 411–41. © 1985 by Sage Publications. Reprinted by permission of Sage Publications.

Chapter 6: "The Business Values of American Newspapers: The Nineteenth-Century Watershed in Chicago," *Journalism Quarterly* 61 (Summer 1984): 265–73. Reprinted by permission of the Association for Education in Journalism and Mass Communication.

Chapter 7: "The Paradox of Municipal Reform in the Late Nineteenth Century," *Wisconsin Magazine of History* 66 (Winter 1982–83): 128–42. Reprinted by permission of the State Historical Society of Wisconsin.

Chapter 8: "A Republican Literature: A Study of Magazine Readers and Reading in Late Eighteenth-Century New York," *American Quarterly* 40 (Mar. 1988): 42–64. Reprinted by permission of Johns Hopkins University Press.

Chapter 9: "Readership as Citizenship in Late Eighteenth-Century Philadelphia," in *"A Melancholy Scene of Devastation": The Public Response to the 1793 Philadelphia Yellow Fever Epidemic,* ed. Billy G. Smith and J. Worth Estes (Canton, Mass.: Science History Publications, 1997), 19–44. Reprinted by permission of the Library Company of Philadelphia and the College of Physicians of Philadelphia.

Chapter 10: "Working-Class Readers: Family, Community, and Reading in Late Nineteenth-Century America," *Communication Research* 11 (Apr. 1986): 156–81. © 1986 by Sage Publications. Reprinted by permission of Sage Publications.

Chapter 11: "Reading the Newspaper: Strategies and Politics of Reader Response, Chicago, 1912–1917," *Journal of Communication* 45 (Summer 1995): 66–93. Reprinted by permission of Oxford University Press.

Chapter 12: "Readers Love to Argue about the News—But Not in Newspapers," *ASNE Bulletin* (Apr. 1992): 24–27. Reprinted by permission of the *American Society of Newspaper Editors Bulletin.*

Communities of Journalism

Introduction:
Communication and Community

Thus stands the cause between God and us: we are entered into
covenant with Him for this work; . . . we must be knit together in
this work as one man; . . . we must delight in each other, make
others' conditions our own, rejoice together, mourn together, labor
and suffer together, always having before our eyes our commission
and community in the work, our community as members of the
same body.
—John Winthrop to the Puritan settlers of Boston, 1630[1]

Sir, you are mistaken: you think you are preaching to the people at
the Bay; our main end was to catch fish.
—New England fisherman a few years later[2]

AMERICA BEGAN in the quest for community. At Massachusetts Bay, John
Winthrop hoped to build a city on a hill, a single community, a unified people. But it was not to be.[3] Some came to New England not to serve God or
man but to catch fish. Others shared Winthrop's dream but embraced it differently, drifting into dissent and schism and, in some cases, into Rhode Island, where, it was said at the time, people thought otherwise. So it has been
throughout American history. Communities were built; communities were
fractured; new communities were formed inside, outside, and in opposition
to the old. Standard story lines of American history typically highlight tensions—between social solidarity and individualism, republican virtue and
laissez-faire liberalism, authority and heresy, tradition and modernity, community and liberty. My story line traces those tensions as well, but I see elements of community on all sides, at every turn. From neighborhood to nation state, Americans have been driven by desire for more unified, more true
community experience, though the outcome of their desire has been to fragment community as well as to solidify it.

The pervasiveness of the community ideal in American life may grow from
the formal, self-conscious, organized nature of the community-building

enterprise in the New World. Early settlers and later immigrants brought with them ancient customs, but here they had to build anew. Even those who arrived at Boston in 1630 were as much strangers to each other as to the land. For them, formal institutions—church and meeting—were the incubators of communal solidarity. Historians have often noted the tendency of Americans to seek community in the public sphere—that is, to seek identity, mutuality, sympathy, and camaraderie in the realm of contract, interest, and government. Americans have routinely carried community values and aspirations into public life and, conversely, have drawn out of public life the cultural materials from which they fashioned face-to-face relationships. Scholars have criticized this tendency to confuse the public and the communal as utopian and destructive of both.[4] But, for good or ill, that is the way it has worked in this country.

Communities are built, maintained, and wrecked in communication. In static communities the most potent forms of communication are traditions—religion, myth, ritual, and habit. Such traditional forms of communication certainly helped to shape American society. But when community building is an active, conscious act, as it often has been in American history, communication becomes more conscious, more formal, more organized. John Winthrop could easily preach to his small flock crowded aboard the *Arbella,* but when the ship landed, the group had to make formal arrangements for public meetings and public communication, including, very soon, a printing press.[5] So it has been ever since. Americans have been active builders of communications media as well as communities. They have been avid producers and consumers of charters, constitutions, declarations, contracts, books, pamphlets, newsletters, newspapers, magazines, telegraph dispatches, radio programs, and Internet Web sites. Traditional forms of communication have been important. But at the vortex of many collective efforts to build community or to undermine it has been formal, public, printed communication, including journalism.

This book is about journalism in American community life. Although I wrote the chapters as free-standing articles over a span of twenty years, a theme runs through them. In all of them I have been interested in what I have sometimes called *public communities.* I first used that term explicitly in chapter 5 to describe the urban culture I saw developing in Chicago in the late nineteenth century: a linking of community values of interdependence, sentiment, and sympathy with formal, public institutions, including the metropolitan daily newspaper. A similar idea lurks in the other chapters as well. Through the work of formal institutions and the press, a variety of public communities have been constructed, including religious elites, political factions, reform associations, ethnic groups, cultural interest groups, people who live in cities, and people who form a nation. Journalism is by nature pub-lic—*publication* means to make public—yet the role that journalism has played in American society has not been contained in the purely public realm.

Does it matter that the communication medium of community has often been *print*? Yes, it does—and that is a central theme of this book. In any so-ciety those who hold power and authority always seek to control communi-cation, and printed communication would seem especially susceptible to control. The technological nature of the printing press clearly favored cen-tralized, one-way, point-to-mass dissemination. But control of print has al-ways been tenuous. In the long history of printing, technological and busi-ness changes—and the forces that drove them—gradually undermined centralization. New players intruded on the stage of print.[6] That is a theme in the chapters that follow. More important, the nature of print itself makes control of meaning elusive. Though the words on a printed page are immu-table, their meaning is revealed in the context in which they are read, not the context in which they were written or printed. Much to the dismay of elites and authorities, heresy runs rampant among the readers of all forms of print, from Bibles to newspapers.[7] That is another theme in this book.

When John Winthrop and his band of sojourners arrived at Massachusetts Bay in 1630, they set up a church and a town and, not long after that, a college and a printing press. They built public institutions and, through them, a com-munity. From the beginning the printed word helped to tie that community together—and later to split it apart. Since 1630 there have been many churches, towns, colleges, organizations, and myriad other forms of public communi-ties. And there have been many printing presses, books, pamphlets, magazines, and newspapers. This book tells stories of some of those communities and their members, some of those newspapers and their readers.

* * *

> The function of a newspaper in a well-ordered society is to control
> the state through the authority of facts.
> —Delos Wilcox, 1900[8]

> . . . the job of the press is to encourage debate, not to supply the
> public with information.
> —Christopher Lasch, 1990[9]

How does journalism do its community work? How do reporters, editors, and publishers make newspapers? How do readers use them? In short, what is the function of a newspaper? Those are the kinds of process questions that drew me into the study of American journalism. As a historian, I hoped to see not only through my own eyes but through the eyes of the people who had lived with journalism in the past. I saw—and I believe they saw—a twofold function of the press: facts and forum.

In the 1970s I migrated to the study of journalism history from urban history, and I brought along with me a historical figure I knew from the progressive era, Delos Wilcox, a man who appears not at all in standard journalism histories. Wilcox was a quintessential progressive, a municipal reformer and public utility expert with a social conscience and a doctoral degree. Like many progressives, Wilcox sensed the challenge and the opportunity of what Daniel Rodgers has recently called "the collectivism of urban life" in late nineteenth-century cities. The new industrial city was an impersonal marketplace driven by individual desire and private decision, yet it was also "a vast network of mutually dependent relations." The progressives' project, says Rodgers, was "to try to realize the implicit collectivism of the city on conscious and public lines."[10] This is just what I had seen in my own studies of the work of Wilcox and other municipal reformers. They hoped to draw on the forced interdependence of modern urban life to build a genuine mutuality—a public community, as I imagined it—through formal structures and institutions. One of those institutions was the daily newspaper.

Like many activist intellectuals of his generation, Wilcox believed in science as John Winthrop's congregation had believed in God. He believed that scientific inquiry could reveal to humankind an ordered, intelligible, and meaningful cosmos. His special interest was the municipal utility franchise, in all its legal and financial technicality. For Wilcox, what was needed to solve the vexing problems of great cities was information. He aimed not to steal government from the people and turn it over to scientific experts but to make the people expert. He wrote his learned books and popular articles to lay the factual basis for public opinion, to show everyone in a city what they shared, what their stake was in utility regulation. He hoped to "kindle a fire under every sleepy citizen till even the street gamins, the club women, and the great merchants on Broadway know what a franchise signifies."[11] He trusted democracy because he believed in the ultimate political triumph of factual truth. Sure of the power of information, Wilcox hated and loved the press. He denounced the fakes, libels, and sensations of the so-called yellow press of his era, but he idealized the democratic and community-building function of the metropolitan newspaper filled with facts, facts, and more facts. For Wilcox, the essence of science, of public opinion, of democracy, of journalism was the authority of facts.

Wilcox's understanding of the function of journalism—the authority of facts—captures one model of what a newspaper might be and do. It is both a normative model and an actual, though partial, description of what newspapers were becoming a century ago. Part professional ethos and part industrial procedure, this model came to be labeled journalistic "objectivity." "Journalists began to adopt the language of 'objectivity' to describe the ethics of their profession," writes Michael Schudson in his recent history of American citizenship. "Buoyed by ideas of neutrality in science and efficiency in political administration, the very idea of information took on a kind of dazzle."[12] I first observed American journalism history through the window of the progressive era, and I thought I saw there the genesis of the modern newspaper: empirical, professional, bureaucratic, commercial, industrial. Other historians have seen it too. In *Just the Facts,* a study of journalistic method, David Mindich writes, "By the 1890s, especially with the rise of the *New York Times* and other papers that shared the 'objective' paradigm, what we recognize as the traits of 'objectivity' were . . . all in place."[13] One of those traits was the authority of facts.

In this model the newspaper does not build communities; it provides the factual materials for others to do so. Reporters and editors sought to "Get the news! Get the news!" and leave the moralizing and politicking to the readers—or so they said. "This was not difficult for writers of the Progressive era to accept," says Schudson, "for they understood facts to provide moral direction of themselves and prided themselves that their own moral precepts grew naturally out of their association with the real world."[14] Reformers organized associations and committees that in the 1890s were largely devoted to gathering and disseminating information. The facts, they believed, would purify public opinion and energize civic action. Newspapermen agreed. The *St. Louis Post-Dispatch* summarized this faith nicely in 1893: "The influence of a newspaper on public opinion is measured by the information it imparts to men capable of doing their own thinking."[15]

The progressive faith in the authority of facts, held firmly by both journalists and reformers, was part of what David Shi has called a broader "mania for facts" that permeated all of American social science, public policy, art, and literature in the second half of the nineteenth century.[16] But the roots of "facticity," as it is sometimes called, run much deeper than that. They reach back into the inductive, Baconian science of the first half of the century and further still into a Protestant theology that took for granted that the human mind could perceive in nature a true, empirical reality ordained by God.[17] The first American "journalists," the seventeenth-century Puritan ministers and almanac writers whose stories I tell in chapter 1, had no doubt that facts could speak, for they spoke for the God who made them. In secular journalism the straightforward reporting of facts was paramount from the beginning. The prospectus for America's first newspaper, *Publick Occurrences,* was mainly a publisher's promise to get the facts right. Even in the ideologically charged atmosphere of the Revolution, political arguments in newspapers were routinely framed and conducted as matters of fact.[18]

The authority of facts, however, is not the only element of journalistic objectivity, and the information model is not the only model of the function of a newspaper. And for community building it may not be the most important one. In 1990 the social critic and historian Christopher Lasch decried the progressive-era embrace of information and the abandonment of what he called the "public forum" function of the press. He attacked objectivity and praised dialogue, discussion, and conversation. "What democracy requires is public debate, not information," he wrote. "Information, usually seen as the precondition of debate, is better understood as its by-product."[19] Lasch used the famous controversy between Walter Lippmann and John Dewey in the 1920s to elaborate that distinction, with Lippmann celebrating the independent authority of science and expertise in public life and Dewey insisting on participation and conversation, not information, as the essence of democracy and community. For Lippmann, democracy was a kind of court of appeals to ratify or reject the work of experts, insiders, and institutions; for Dewey, democracy was a way of life, a habit of the heart. For each, public communication was important, but the function was different. James Carey, our most thoughtful commentator on the history of American journalism, sets up a similar distinction between two journalisms: one based on the "model of information," the other on the "model of conversation." Like Lasch, he believes that the information model displaced the forum model in the progressive era. And that was a mistake, for facticity is a chimera. "All journalism can do," he says, "is preside over and within the conversation of our culture."[20]

The conversation, or public forum, model also is an old one; we can trace it to the early history of journalism in America and abroad. The general idea of religious and political tolerance in Europe and America grew not from a belief that the truth is relative but from the conviction that the truth will emerge and prevail in debate, in dialogue. This belief drove not only a faith in fact but also a faith in argumentation in the public forum. In England the classic statement of the positive value of truth grappling with error, good with evil, is John Milton's *Areopagitica* (1644). America's Benjamin Franklin offered a similar, though more lighthearted, defense of the forum function of the press in his *Apology for Printers* (1731): "Printers are educated in the belief, that when men differ in opinion, both sides ought equally to have the advantage of being heard by the public; and that when truth and error have fair play, the former is always an overmatch for the latter. Hence they cheerfully serve all contending writers that pay them well, without regarding on which side they are of the question in dispute."[21] Franklin was talking about job printing, but a similar notion seeped into the management of newspapers as well. Especially when they faced little or no competition, colonial printers had an economic incentive to operate their newspapers as common carriers, open to all, or at least to all who had some social, political, or economic clout. As Franklin suggested, pay comes into play. The marketplace of ideas is a literal as well as metaphorical concept.[22]

In recent years scholars have associated the early modern culture of printed communication with the terms *public sphere* and *civil society,* which name the realm of social life that lies between the state and the individual. That is the realm in which public communities can be found. Alexis de Tocqueville was an early and perceptive commentator on the function of newspapers in that realm, and the function he saw was conversation, connection, and common action, not facts and information. Observing American journalism in the 1830s, Tocqueville linked newspapers with *associations,* a term he used broadly to name government subdivisions as well as voluntary organizations. He wrote:

> Newspapers make associations, and associations make newspapers; and if it were true to say that associations must multiply as quickly as conditions become equal, it is equally certain that the number of papers increases in proportion as associations multiply. . . . Newspapers do not multiply simply because they are cheap, but according to the more or less frequent need felt by a great number of people to communicate with one another and to act together. . . . A newspaper can only survive if it gives publicity to feelings or principles common to a large number of men. A newspaper therefore always represents an association whose members are its regular readers.[23]

Both models of journalism—facts and forum—have been sharply criticized in the decades since the progressive era and for the same reason: Neither accounts very well for the workings of political, economic, and cultural power. In the twentieth century, it became increasingly clear that facts do not speak for themselves; indeed, they do not exist until they are "constructed" by someone as culturally significant. Typically, powerful interests are in the best position to collect, name, and interpret "the facts" of our common lives. For our skeptical age, the phrase "the authority of facts" seems less apt than something like "the facts of authority." As an element of journalistic objectivity, faith in facts came to be labeled as "naive empiricism," not science.[24]

At the same time the forum model of journalism, seemingly more suited to an age of relativism, pluralism, and postmodernism, also gathered critics. Far from a wide open marketplace of ideas or a neutral common carrier, the forum of journalism is clearly more open to some interests than to others. The voices that speak in the news, the people who inhabit the news beats of reporters, usually speak for the most powerful, well-organized interests, especially government officials. News media bias in favor of powerful and official sources has been a main theme of mass media research for many years. Recently, one scholar has argued that journalism's enthrallment with official sources is so intimate, so symbiotic, that the news media should properly be considered an integral part of government.[25]

Criticism of the press derives in part from doubt about the neutrality of science, inspired by the sociology of science and the postmodern turn in philosophy.[26] But mainly it has grown from the broad critique of American pluralism that emerged in the 1960s and '70s. According to pluralist theory, the direct relationship between the individual citizen and government, which is assumed by classical democratic theory, is impossible in a modern society. Instead, the work of the polity takes place among groups. Groups mediate between the individual and the state, and group competition serves as a rough approximation of democratic action.[27] Critics of pluralism, however, found the group system anything but a fair and democratic marketplace of ideas. They saw it as overwhelmingly biased in favor of well-heeled, well-organized, well-defined interests. The system excludes interests that are weak, diffuse, or difficult to organize. Tolerance—the apparent virtue of pluralism—masked systematic bias and inequality. In this critique journalism, with its dependence on groups as sources for both fact and commentary, faithfully reflects the appalling inequities of American pluralism.[28]

But critics exaggerate the case when they charge that journalism is simply the stenography of power.[29] If it were, the powerful would complain less about it. The methodologies of journalism—facts and forum—have long provided opportunities for the weak and the marginalized as well as for the rich and strong. Indeed, weak interests have routinely gained influence by expanding the "scope of conflict," to borrow a phrase from E. E. Schattschneider, by socializing what might have remained narrowly controlled private interests.[30] And they have done it through the press. The weak, like the strong, can provide the press with what it needs, including facts. Furthermore, making a claim to access in the name of balance, fairness, and diversity is a play upon the forum function of the press, and such a claim has the force of professional and historical tradition. For the truly powerless, who are excluded completely from the pluralist realm of legitimate controversy, the fact function of the press provides another opening. For journalists, a newsworthy event is a fact, and the people and groups that are not insiders can gain access to the media by causing events to happen. Such pseudoevents may range from press conferences to demonstrations to terrorist bombings, but the effect is the same: The press shows up and reports the facts. This is not to say that either American pluralism or the press is open to all. It is to say that an exclusive focus on the bias of the system obscures how the system actually works and how a variety of interests can exploit the structures and traditions of the press.

Pressure groups, talking heads, public relations, spin, stunts, pseudoevents, bogus surveys, sit-ins, fertilizer bombs. These forms of communication are surely not what Delos Wilcox or Alexis de Tocqueville had in mind when they spoke idealistically of the fact and forum functions of the press. But this is the press we have. Critics often decry the press of today and mourn a lost golden age. Liberals and communitarians lament the loss of the forum function of the press; conservatives lament the loss of the authority of facts. Declension is a powerful cultural theme and an easy one. I've played that tune myself. But truth to tell, American journalism has never had a golden age. Americans have always exploited the press, have always used both the information and forum functions of the press to build groups and communities in their own interest and image—and to tear others down. Schattschneider's description of political organization as "the mobilization of bias" applies to the press as well as to politics.[31] Bias does not just exist; it is organized and mobilized. Mobilization of bias creates and maintains groups and communities. And some of that political and cultural work has been done through newspapers.

* * *

> I think a newspaper's fundamental job is not reporting or
> editorializing, it's bringing people together.
> —Mike Phillips, editor, the *Sun,* Bremerton, Wash., 1991[32]

As a historian, I try to understand things, not change them. But in the spring of 1991 I stepped out of character and wrote an argumentative essay for the *ASNE Bulletin,* the trade magazine of the American Society of Newspaper Editors. At the time I was fascinated by how computer bulletin boards had made it possible for people who were spread out across the globe to talk, share information, and argue about the Persian Gulf War. These bulletin boards, which were fairly new at the time, reminded me of early nineteenth-century associational newspapers, which had depended heavily on reader participation. And I believed that was a good thing. It seemed to me that the gap be-

tween professional information and reader participation—between the fact
and forum functions of the press—has hurt modern newspapers, and I urged
editors to close it. (That article is chapter 12 in this book.)

Since 1991 great changes have roiled American journalism, and some touch
directly on the nature of American community and on the relationship between the information and forum functions of the press. Most striking has
been the fragmentation of media and media audiences. This began for broadcast journalism in the 1980s, as rapid growth in the number of cable channels gave rise to CNN and to a variety of news and "reality-based" programs
and channels beyond the three traditional networks. For newspapers, the rise
of the Internet and the World Wide Web in the 1990s has been the fragmenting force. Most newspapers still get out the paper in the usual way, but they
all see profound and disruptive change looming on the horizon. At the beginning of the new century, cable and the Internet have blurred all traditional
distinctions in journalism, including the distinctions between information
and forum, between journalist and reader.[33] Internet true believers see a radically and wonderfully transformed media world, with everyone a journalist. Critics worry that in such a fragmented media world, there will be no
common public sphere, only many special interest sphericules, to borrow
Todd Gitlin's term. But it is not just technology buffs and critics who are
impressed. The characteristics of the new technology—the ability to reach
specialized, niche audiences and interact with readers—pose fascinating
challenges and opportunities to anyone interested in the community-building power of the press.[34]

Newspaper publishers, reluctant to write their own obituaries, are scrambling to meet the challenge, with Web sites, new commercial partnerships,
mergers, and all manner of synergistic schemes. Newspapers have always been
commercial ventures, but the catch phrase "market-driven journalism" seems
especially apt for our time.[35] Newspapers are willing to do almost anything
to hang on to readers and advertisers. Many of their schemes explicitly seek
to give readers whatever they want, especially in their individual, private lives
of family, lifestyle, and consumption. This is "news you can use." But one
idea, which has captured the interest of some newspapers and many academics, is not a pitch for individual readers or readers as consumers. It is a plea
for community and the newspaper's place in it. It is about readers as citizens.
This idea—a movement, really—has a name: civic journalism.

Civic journalism (or public journalism, as it is often called) embraces many
ideas and practices but at its core is an effort to build community through
the forum function of the press. Civic journalism was born in the late 1980s
and early '90s in an atmosphere of despair over the declining vitality of civ-

ic life in America. Participation in political and community activities seemed on the decline and public cynicism on the rise.[36] A handful of editors and journalism scholars began to argue that journalism had an obligation to help civic life go well. Self-interest was also at stake, for the fiscal health of newspapers depended upon the public health of the communities they served. In the words of one of the founders of the movement, Davis "Buzz" Merritt, "Telling the news is not enough." Newspapers needed to help people get involved in community affairs by providing a forum for deliberation and for discovery of shared values.[37] Jay Rosen, the movement's chief academic enthusiast, writes that civic journalism is about "civic participation, deliberative dialogue, cooperative problem solving, taking responsibility for the place where you live, making democracy work."[38]

Civic journalism has attracted much interest and also much criticism. The criticism usually takes two forms. One line of critique comes from within the professional ranks of journalism. Some reporters and editors have defended the traditional fact function of the press, arguing that civic journalism crosses the line that should separate information and analysis from actual involvement in community action. The job of journalism is to inform, they say, not to engage in politics or community organization. Defenders of civic journalism are unimpressed by this critique, and properly so, for newspapers have always crossed that line; they have always been thoroughly enmeshed in the political and cultural lives of their communities.[39]

The second line of critique seems more apt, and both journalists and academics have raised it. This critique sees civic journalism as naively idealistic, as resting on a simplistic notion of community and the common good. The problem with standard journalism, say the promoters of civic journalism, is its divisiveness and cynicism. Practitioners of civic journalism hope to discover shared values and to bring people together. Rosen speaks of "finding common ground," of "getting the connections right," of seeking the ties that hold people "together as a community of the whole."[40] To many skeptical newspaper professionals this sounds like old-fashioned boosterism. It glosses over real divisions in a community. It's a feel-good thing. It's market-driven journalism of the most cloying and hypocritical sort.[41]

The academic version of this critique also questions civic journalism's obsession with the common good. Civic journalism calls for direct citizen participation in the community-building process. The hero is the individual citizen. The community is the community of the whole, a single public sphere, the town or city the newspaper serves. The goal is civility, consensus, and commonality. Liberal critics such as Michael Schudson and Theodore Glasser are skeptical of this unitary vision of community life. They argue that civic journalism does not take seriously political and cultural difference and political and cultural power. In this critique civic journalism reflects the traditional American tendency to seek community values, inappropriately, in the public sphere.[42] It is part of what James Morone has called "the democratic wish," a fantasy that has beguiled the American people since John Winthrop landed at Boston. "The democratic wish," Morone writes, "imagines a single, united people, bound together by a consensus over the public good which is discerned through direct citizen participation in community settings. It is a utopian image."[43]

Though civic journalism idealizes the individual citizen in the community of the whole, not all groups are alien to the ideal of civic journalism. Local voluntary organizations such as churches, service clubs, and civic associations are acceptable because they look beyond self-interest to the commonweal. Like nearly everyone these days, civic journalists are neo-Tocquevillians; they laud the American genius for association. Civic journalists also favor what they sometimes call, in anthropological jargon, "third places," informal sites where people gather to chat without structure or leadership.[44] But true interest groups are anathema. To civic journalism, interest groups are part of the problem that needs to be fixed. Such groups seek private payoffs, not community welfare. Operating as news sources, interest groups are part of what makes ordinary journalism adversarial, cynical, and oblivious to the common good and, in turn, what makes individual citizens feel excluded and apathetic. Rosen poses the problem of interest groups in a series of questions that he traces (through James Carey) to John Dewey's plea for genuine participatory democracy: "If politics is organized interests battling it out, how can people arrive at a sense of the common interest? And what about public challenges that aren't represented well in the capital—or at city hall? How do citizens come to engage each other in reciprocal fashion, so that the rising din of interests being defended doesn't drown out the interests we share, the problems we need to solve together?"[45]

Civic journalism's aversion to interest groups may sound like the standard critique of pluralism, that is, the system is inequitable. But in the critics' view, civic journalism poses no serious challenge to political and cultural power as it is embodied in the pluralist system. Civic journalists seem not even to notice that the newspaper itself, as a business corporation, is a special interest. To the critics civic journalism is as naively communal as old-fashioned journalism is naively empirical. Civic journalism hopes to finesse the unpleasantries of power by invoking the democratic wish.[46]

I think the academic critics are largely right. Civic journalism longs for the city on a hill, the single community, the unified people that eluded Winthrop and the Puritan settlers so long ago. Like it or not, ours is an interest group society. That is how power works, and that is how it has always worked, in one form or another. If civic journalists are serious about the goal of making public life go well—and I believe they are—they should try to make pluralism go well. In addition to creating space for individual citizens to speak, they should help groups to form and then teach the leaders of those groups how to write for the newspaper. They should take journalism as it is, which is mainly source reporting with groups as sources, and make that journalism work better. That is one of the strategies I urged on editors in 1992. Dissent, conflict, ideological passion, and "unintermitted agitation," as Wendell Phillips put it, are fine traditions in American journalism. They too are associated with community building, as I argue in this book. Shared values are not the only important ones. Indeed, they often turn out to be the least important ones.

Yet I am deeply sympathetic to the civic journalism ideal, to the utopian democratic wish. I believe that real community can be found in the public sphere, that people sometimes can come together as a unified community, and that this can happen in the press. That is another story that I try to tell in the pages of this book. Sometimes a city or an entire nation can become a community of communities.

As I write this introduction, the residents of my own city, Bloomington, Indiana, are grieving together over the abduction and disappearance of a young woman. Everyday our newspaper carries stories about the case, even though the police have found no clues. There is no news in the sense of new facts or information. Instead, the stories are about people, churches, groups, and organizations from all parts of the community that are coming together to offer support and solace to the parents—and to each other. For some Bloomingtonians, this growing community of concern has emerged in face-to-face encounters in organizations and "third places." But for most of us, the newspaper is the place we go for this community experience; indeed, it is the only place where this community exists.

In a letter to the editor in today's newspaper, one Bloomington woman described this community:

> I am writing to express my support and love to the Behrman family during this time, and to express my appreciation to this wonderfully supportive community we live in.
>
> First, to the Behrman family, I want you to know that I have kept you and Jill in my prayers since day one. I have never met you, nor may ever, but that doesn't matter. We are part of the same "family"—God's family—and I share in your sorrow. . . . I'm sorry if I've invaded your personal space through the

media coverage, but in all sincerity, I've welcomed the intrusion into your life because I care about you and your daughter.

To the community of Bloomington, I want to express my gratitude and admiration for your outpouring of support and love toward the Behrman family. Your corporate response epitomizes the principle of love in the Bible: weeping with those that weep, carrying one another's burdens and loving your neighbor as yourself. I am blessed by your love toward them. The English poet John Donne once wrote, "Ask not for whom the bell tolls, it tolls for thee." He was expressing the corporateness of the human race, that when one suffers or hurts, all are affected by it because "no man is an island."[47]

This letter writer's community experience is authentic, I believe, and it is an experience of public community. It flows not from face-to-face associations but from the printed word—from the Bible, from John Donne, and, not least, from the Bloomington *Herald-Times*.

*　*　*

The chapters in this book approach the history of American journalism from two angles. Part 1 focuses on the producers, the institutions, and the content of journalism. In those chapters I explore journalism in a variety of community settings, going back to the beginnings of English settlement in America. Coming into the study of journalism history through the portal of the progressive era, I was fascinated by reformers and journalists who believed in both expertise and democracy, in both facts and public opinion, in both the information function and the forum function of the press. I wanted to learn how the public role of journalism had taken shape in earlier eras. From the 1890s I worked my way back to 1630, when the Puritans landed at Boston harbor. Part 2 focuses on the readers of journalism. My studies of producers, institutions, and content led me to wonder: What about the readers? How did readers understand the functions of journalism? Did they take in the information? Did they join in the conversation? Inspired by reader-response criticism in literary studies and by audience research in mass media studies, I began in the 1980s to search for evidence of how journalism was actually used in community life in the past. I wanted to know how readers read.

Chapter 1, "Teleology and News," is about links between religion and journalism. I explore the fascination in Puritan New England with providential occurrences, and I link that fascination to an emergent style for reporting and publishing what we would call the news. In the community life of seventeenth-century Massachusetts, events possessed public meaning because in events people could see the designing hand of God. Colonial elites hoped to marshal the power of print to control the communal interpretation of events, but they also believed that plain description of providential occurrences—the authority of facts—would automatically reveal an inherent and orthodox meaning. They gradually and unhappily discovered, however, that heresy could lurk in the reading of news as in the reading of the Bible. My thinking about religion in early America and the religious roots of journalistic style was aided by the work of many historians of colonial America, especially David D. Hall, Harry S. Stout, Jon Butler, and Sacvan Bercovitch.[48] In the decade since "Teleology and News" was published in article form, much good work has appeared on print culture in early America, including Michael Warner's *Letters of the Republic* (1990) and Richard Brown's *The Strength of a People* (1996). Charles Clark's *The Public Prints* (1994) is the best recent study of the colonial newspaper; it emphasizes much more than I do the English roots of American journalism. The most comprehensive overview of print culture before the Revolution is Hugh Amory and David D. Hall's *The Colonial Book in the Atlantic World* (2000), the first volume of *A History of the Book in America*.[49]

Chapter 2, "The Authority of Truth," sets the famous seditious libel case of the newspaper printer John Peter Zenger into the context of religious dissent and religious individualism in the era of the Great Awakening. The nature of truth lay at the heart of the case, and the key claim by Zenger's defense was that the jury, as individuals and as members of a local community, possessed the right and the competence to determine what truth was. Drawing on the arguments and contexts of the case, I speculate on how the belief that truth is revealed to the individual conscience may have migrated from the realm of religion to the realm of juries, politics, and political expression. My thinking about the origins of religious and civil liberties in America was first stimulated by my mentor at the University of Wisconsin, Harold L. Nelson, as he argued with Leonard Levy's 1960 classic *Legacy of Suppression*. Since "Authority of Truth" was first published in 1985, that debate has been carried on with passion by Levy himself and by David Anderson, Jeffery A. Smith, and others.[50] Paul Finkelman's introduction to a 1997 edition of *A Brief Narrative of the Case and Tryal of John Peter Zenger* offers an excellent overview of the Zenger case and the literature on it.[51]

Chapter 3, "Newspapers and American Nationhood, 1776–1826," began life as a lecture at the American Antiquarian Society in a 1990 series commemorating three hundred years of the newspaper in America. I talked about the decades after the Revolution, when American newspapers, along with the politics they served, were as pugnacious, quarrelsome, and fractious as they have ever been. Many of those who suffered newspaper attacks believed, with some justification, that newspapers were genuinely seditious. Yet these angry debates about the nature of the new American state, I argue, cultivated a shared nationalism grounded in a common political language. To argue about the state was to be a member of the nation, to be an American. My broad inspiration for this chapter was Benedict Anderson's *Imagined Communities* (1983).[52] My favorite historical sketch of the press in the Revolution is Thomas C. Leonard's "News for a Revolution." I also have learned much from the splendid recent historiography of the Revolution and its aftermath, especially the work of Gordon Wood, Edward Countryman, Alfred Young, Robert Shalhope, Isaac Kramnick, Joyce Appleby, James Roger Sharp, Stanley Elkins, and Eric McKitrick.[53] Recent studies by David Waldstreicher, Richard D. Brown, and Richard John have extended my understanding of political language, popular political participation, and communication policy in the early Republic. Since the original publication of "Newspapers and American Nationhood," several case studies of newspapers in this era have appeared, including books by Michael Durey, James Tagg, Jeffery Smith, and Richard N. Rosenfeld.[54]

Chapter 4, "Tocqueville, Garrison, and the Perfection of Journalism," argues that voluntary associationism in the early nineteenth century was fundamentally journalistic. Alexis de Tocqueville wrote that a newspaper "represents an association whose members are its regular readers." How so? I wondered. Using William Lloyd Garrison's *Liberator* as a case study, I explore the forum function of the press in building scattered communities. Though Garrison's idiosyncrasies shaped the *Liberator,* one of his consistent values was free discussion. He preferred the freedom of journalism to the coercion of government. And through the *Liberator* he allowed his readers to fashion the kind of voluntary, noncoercive community that he idealized. This chapter was inspired by the press criticism of James Carey and by my own dissatisfaction with the celebration in standard journalism histories of the hegemony of the commercial penny press. I was assisted in this project by the many splendid histories of reform and voluntary associations in the early nineteenth century, including works on abolitionism by Ronald G. Walters, Merton Dillon, Lawrence Friedman, Leonard L. Richards, and Thomas Haskell.[55] Recent ambitious books on abolition include Paul Goodman's *Of One Blood* (1998) and Henry Mayer's biography of Garrison, *All on Fire* (1998). A good overview of the age of reform is Steven Mintz's *Moralists and Modernizers* (1995).[56] Helpful studies of the associational press include works by Richard John, John Nerone, Jane Rhodes, Frankie Hutton, Martha Solomon, and Linda Steiner.[57]

Chapter 5, "The Public Community," focuses on Chicago in the 1870s, a period of rapid population growth and industrialization. In the maelstrom of modern urban life the boundary between public and private was blurred in new ways. I argue that newspapers played a role in building a new kind of collective life—a hybrid of public and private—in the new urban metropolis of late nineteenth-century America. In writing this chapter, I tried to wrestle directly with the idea and the definition of *community*. To help me think about cities and communities I drew on the work of Thomas Bender, Richard Sennett, Gunther Barth, Alan Trachtenberg, and Michael Frisch.[58] Good studies of newspapers and cities that appeared after this chapter was written include Janet Steele on the *New York Sun* (1993), Sally F. Griffith on the *Emporia Gazette* (1989), Gerald Baldasty on the E. W. Scripps chain (1999), and David Henkin on the press of antebellum New York (1998).[59]

Chapter 6, "The Business Values of American Newspapers," is a companion piece to chapter 5. It is another exploration of urban community and communication, in which I continue to pursue the idea that a new, ad hoc collectivism grew from the circumstances of modern city life. But in this study of Chicago journalism in the late nineteenth century, I pay more attention to the business side of the newspaper. I argue that newspapers, in their effort to sell a product to everyone in the city, backed into support for protoprogressive values, including public interest consumerism and organizational modes of conflict resolution. In other words, the nature of the newspaper business itself had much to do with the role a newspaper played in public and community life. My interest in the relationship between business and the origins of progressivism goes back to my reading of William Appleman Williams, Gabriel Kolko, and Robert Wiebe while I was in grad school.[60] Good work in recent years on the business of journalism in the late nineteenth century has been done by Gerald Baldasty, David Nasaw, and others.[61]

Chapter 7, "The Paradox of Municipal Reform in the Late Nineteenth Century," is the oldest essay in the book, and it reflects my earliest interest in the role of newspapers in municipal reform in late nineteenth-century cities. The ideal of newspapers as suppliers of facts and information is vividly on display in this chapter. Reformers and newspaper publishers believed in democracy because they believed in the power of information. They believed, paradoxically, in government by expertise *and* by the people. In this article and in the book from which it was derived, *Newspapers and New Politics* (1981), I first began to work through the idea of public community. I was influenced by a generation of historians in the 1960s and '70s who wrote about bosses, reformers, and cities, but most of all I was influenced by David P. Thelen's *The New Citizenship* (1972), which helped me think about the role of information and communication in progressive politics.[62] Recently, two very different books on progressivism have suggested to me that Thelen and I were on the right track more than twenty years ago. They are Kevin

Mattson's brief and elegant *Creating a Democratic Public* (1998) and Daniel Rodgers's magisterial *Atlantic Crossings* (1998).[63]

Chapter 8, "A Republican Literature," is a study of readers and reading in the 1790s. I tracked down the readers of the *New-York Magazine* in the hope of understanding the uses a magazine might have had for its readers in an era when people professed to believe in a republic of knowledge. I determined that many readers were artisans and middling shopkeepers, even though the content of the magazine would have suggested a more elite audience. I argue that the magazine was an arena in which different economic classes could participate in a common culture, that reading was an entry into the new social order of post-Revolutionary America. This was one of my first attempts to do a historical study of readership, and I was drawn into that work by Cathy Davidson, David D. Hall, Richard D. Brown, Robert Darnton, Carl Kaestle, and William Gilmore-Lehne.[64] Since the article was first published, the cultural history of reading in America has mushroomed. Representative overviews have been collected by Cathy Davidson, James Machor, and James Danky and Wayne Wiegand.[65]

Chapter 9, "Readership as Citizenship in Late Eighteenth-Century Philadelphia," explores how readers used different forms of written and printed communication, especially the newspaper, to maintain the bonds of community life during an urban crisis, the Philadelphia yellow fever epidemic of 1793. The authorities and the elites of the city tried to capture the newspaper and use it to authenticate and control information. Ordinary readers, on the other hand, had a more expansive and communal view of the function of the newspaper. For them, it was not just a source of information but a forum for participation, a place to carry on, in James Carey's words, the conversation of their community. My chief guide to the history of eighteenth-century cities has long been Gary Nash.[66]

Chapter 10, "Working-Class Readers," draws on cost-of-living statistics gathered by the U.S. commissioner of labor in the 1880s. I try to reconstruct the relationship between reading and community structure in different geographic regions of the United States. These government surveys collected data on a wide variety of family expenditures, including spending on newspapers and books. I used these data to explore correlations between reading and ethnic, demographic, regional, and community variables. This was my first foray into the empirical study of readers in the past. I came to the study of reading through the social history of literacy, especially the work of Kenneth Lockridge and Harvey Graff.[67] Since I wrote this article, the study of readers and reading has been a lively field of cultural history, though the quantitative study of literacy has faded. One of the few histories of reading to draw on the commissioner of labor data is by Lawrence C. Stedman, Katherine Tinsley, and Carl F. Kaestle and appears in *Literacy in the United States* (1991), edited by Kaestle and colleagues.[68]

Chapter 11, "Reading the Newspaper," examines readers' response to urban newspapers in the early twentieth century. Drawing on manuscript letters sent to a Chicago newspaper editor, I explore the strategies that readers used to make sense of what they read. I argue that reader response was often not idiosyncratic; it was linked to reading conventions and to what reader response critics call "interpretive communities." And organized political interest groups sometimes influenced these conventions and communities. My thinking about how readers read has been influenced most by the work of literary scholars, including Stanley Fish, Norman Holland, and Janice Radway.[69] The historical study of readers of newspapers is difficult to do because newspapers are so ephemeral and reading them so unremarkable. But a few researchers have tried to do it, including Thomas Leonard, David Henkin, Isabelle Lehuu, Ronald Zboray, and Mary Zboray.[70]

Chapter 12, "Readers Love to Argue about the News—But Not in Newspapers," is not a research article but a polemic and a plea. Drawing on some of the history recounted in this book, I urge newspaper editors to close the gap between the information and forum functions of the press, to promote more genuine argumentation and debate among the sources who contribute the news of the day, and to invite their readers to help them write the newspaper.

The afterword, "Newspapers, Readers, and Communities Today," looks at how American newspapers have treated their readers and communities in the era of the Internet.

Notes

1. John Winthrop, "The Model of Christian Charity," in *American Visions and Revisions, 1607–1865,* ed. David Grimsted (Acton, Mass.: Copley, 1999), 25.

2. This was the rejoinder of a New England man when urged by a minister to remember the religious motives for settlement. The story is told in Cotton Mather, *Magnalia Christi Americana* (1702), quoted in David D. Hall, *Worlds of Wonder, Days of Judgment: Popular Religious Belief in Early New England* (New York: Knopf, 1989), 16.

3. Darrett B. Rutman, *Winthrop's Boston: A Portrait of a Puritan Town, 1630–1649* (New York: W. W. Norton, 1972), 21–22.

4. James A. Morone, *The Democratic Wish: Popular Participation and the Limits of American Government,* rev. ed. (New Haven, Conn.: Yale University Press, 1998), 337–38; Thomas Bender, *Community and Social Change in America* (New Brunswick, N.J.: Rutgers University Press, 1978), 6–7, 148–50; Richard Sennett, *The Fall of Public Man* (New York: Vintage, 1976), 4–5; Robert Booth Fowler, *The Dance with Community: The Con-*

temporary Debate in American Political Thought (Lawrence: University Press of Kansas, 1991), 1–4. A new communitarianism has emerged in recent years that is more sympathetic to the idea of community values in public life. See, for example, Amitai Etzioni, *The New Golden Rule: Community and Morality in a Democratic Society* (New York: Basic, 1996); and Michael J. Sandel, *Democracy's Discontent: American in Search of a Public Philosophy* (Cambridge, Mass.: Belknap, 1996).

5. Hugh Amory, "Printing and Bookselling in New England, 1638–1713," in *A History of the Book in America*, vol. 1: *The Colonial Book in the Atlantic World*, ed. Hugh Amory and David D. Hall (Cambridge: Cambridge University Press, 2000). See also George Parker Winship, *The Cambridge Press, 1638–1692: A Reexamination of the Evidence Concerning the Bay Psalm Book and the Eliot Indian Bible as Well as Other Contemporary Books and People* (Philadelphia: University of Pennsylvania Press, 1945).

6. Centralization *and* growing diversity in print culture in early America is a running theme in Amory and Hall's *Colonial Book in the Atlantic World*.

7. See chapter 1 in this book. See also Hall, *Worlds of Wonder*, 19–20, 69–70; and Richard D. Brown, *Knowledge Is Power: The Diffusion of Information in Early America, 1700–1865* (New York: Oxford University Press, 1989), 41.

8. Delos F. Wilcox, "The American Newspaper: A Study in Social Psychology," *Annals* 16 (July 1900): 56.

9. Christopher Lasch, "Journalism, Publicity, and the Lost Art of Argument," *Gannett Center Journal* 4 (Spring 1990): 1. A version of this article also appears in Christopher Lasch, *The Revolt of the Elites and the Betrayal of Democracy* (New York: W. W. Norton, 1995).

10. Daniel T. Rodgers, *Atlantic Crossings: Social Politics in a Progressive Age* (Cambridge, Mass.: Belknap, 1998), 114–17. See also David Paul Nord, "The Experts versus the Experts: Conflicting Philosophies of Municipal Utility Regulation in the Progressive Era," *Wisconsin Magazine of History* 58 (Spring 1975): 219–36.

11. Delos F. Wilcox, *Municipal Franchises*, vol. 2 (New York: Engineering News, 1911), 809. I write about Wilcox in chapter 7.

12. Michael Schudson, *The Good Citizen: A History of American Civic Life* (Cambridge, Mass.: Harvard University Press, 1998), 196–97.

13. David T. Z. Mindich, *Just the Facts: How "Objectivity" Came to Define American Journalism* (New York: New York University Press, 1998), 11. In Mindich's formulation the five elements of objectivity in journalism are detachment, nonpartisanship, facticity, balance, and the inverted pyramid form of news-story construction.

14. Michael Schudson, *Discovering the News: A Social History of American Newspapers* (New York: Basic, 1978), 87. See also Dan Schiller, *Objectivity and the News: The Public and the Rise of Commercial Journalism* (Philadelphia: University of Pennsylvania Press, 1981).

15. *St. Louis Post-Dispatch*, Apr. 8, 1893.

16. David E. Shi, *Facing Facts: Realism in American Thought and Culture, 1850–1920* (New York: Oxford University Press, 1995), 67–72. See also Theodore M. Porter, *Trust in Numbers: The Pursuit of Objectivity in Science and Public Life* (Princeton, N.J.: Princeton University Press, 1995); and Dorothy Ross, *The Origins of American Social Science* (Cambridge: Cambridge University Press, 1991).

17. George H. Daniels, *American Science in the Age of Jackson* (Tuscaloosa: University of Alabama Press, 1968), chap. 3. See also Lorraine Daston, "Baconian Facts, Academic

Civility, and the Prehistory of Objectivity," in *Rethinking Objectivity,* ed. Allan Megill
(Durham, N.C.: Duke University Press, 1994); Theodore Dwight Bozeman, *Protestants in
an Age of Science: The Baconian Ideal and Ante-Bellum American Religious Thought* (Chapel
Hill: University of North Carolina Press, 1977); and Herbert Hovencamp, *Science and
Religion in America, 1800–1860* (Philadelphia: University of Pennsylvania Press, 1978).

18. *Publick Occurrences, Both Forreign and Domestick,* Sept. 25, 1690, reproduced in
America's Front Page News, 1690–1970, ed. Michael C. Emery, R. Smith Schuneman, and
Edwin Emery (Minneapolis: Vis-Com, 1970). See also Charles E. Clark, *The Public Prints:
The Newspaper in Anglo-American Culture* (New York: Oxford University Press, 1994). On
the role of facts in Revolutionary journalism, see Thomas C. Leonard, *The Power of the
Press: The Birth of American Political Reporting* (New York: Oxford University Press, 1986),
chap. 2.

19. Lasch, "Journalism, Publicity, and the Lost Art of Argument," 1–3.

20. James W. Carey, "The Press and the Public Discourse," *Center Magazine* 20 (Mar.–
Apr. 1987): 14. Carey's best essays are collected in James W. Carey, *Communication as
Culture: Essays on Media and Society* (Boston: Unwin Hyman, 1989); and in Eve Stryker
Munson and Catherine A. Warren, eds., *James Carey: A Critical Reader* (Minneapolis:
University of Minnesota Press, 1997).

21. Benjamin Franklin, *An Apology for Printers,* ed. Randolph Goodman (Washington,
D.C.: Acropolis, 1965), 5–6. See also Schudson, *Good Citizen,* 38–40.

22. James N. Green, "English Books and Printing in the Age of Franklin," in *Colonial Book
in the Atlantic World,* ed. Amory and Hall, 255–57; Charles E. Clark, "Early American Jour-
nalism: News and Opinion in the Popular Press," in *Colonial Book in the Atlantic World,* ed.
Amory and Hall, 357. See also Stephen Botein, "'Meer Mechanics' and an Open Press: The
Business and Political Strategies of Colonial American Printers," *Perspectives in American
History* 9 (1975): 127–225; and Jeffery A. Smith, *Printers and Press Freedom: The Ideology of
Early American Journalism* (New York: Oxford University Press, 1988).

23. Alexis de Tocqueville, *Democracy in America,* ed. J. P. Mayer (New York: Doubleday
Anchor, 1969), 518–20. On civil society in America see John Ehrenberg, *Civil Society: The
Critical History of an Idea* (New York: New York University Press, 1999), chap. 8. On pub-
lic communication and the historical public sphere in America, see Michael Warner, *The
Letters of the Republic: Publication and the Public Sphere in Eighteenth-Century America*
(Cambridge, Mass.: Harvard University Press, 1990). See also the essays in Craig Calhoun,
ed., *Habermas and the Public Sphere* (Cambridge, Mass.: MIT Press, 1992), pt. 3.

24. Schudson, *Discovering the News,* 122. On the social construction of facts see Doni-
leen R. Loseke, *Thinking about Social Problems: An Introduction to Constructionist Perspectives* (New York: Aldine de Gruyter, 1999), chap. 1; and Malcolm Spector and John I. Kit-
suse, *Constructing Social Problems,* 2d ed. (Hawthorne, N.Y.: Aldine de Gruyter, 1987).

25. Timothy E. Cook, *Governing with the News: The News Media as a Political Institution* (Chicago: University of Chicago Press, 1998), 3. Classic studies of source reporting
in journalism are Leon V. Sigal, *Reporters and Officials* (Lexington, Mass.: Heath, 1973);
Herbert J. Gans, *Deciding What's News: A Study of CBS Evening News, NBC Nightly News,
Newsweek, and Time* (New York: Vintage, 1980); Gaye Tuchman, *Making News: A Study
in the Construction of Reality* (New York: Free Press, 1978); and Mark Fishman, *Manufacturing the News* (Austin: University of Texas Press, 1980).

26. Key American texts are Thomas S. Kuhn, *The Structure of Scientific Revolutions,* 2d ed. (Chicago: University of Chicago Press, 1970); and Richard Rorty, *Philosophy and the Mirror of Nature* (Princeton, N.J.: Princeton University Press, 1979).

27. Robert A. Dahl, *Who Governs? Democracy and Power in an American City* (New Haven, Conn.: Yale University Press, 1961); Nelson W. Polsby, *Community Power and Political Theory* (New Haven, Conn.: Yale University Press, 1963). Dahl's recent work includes *On Democracy* (New Haven, Conn.: Yale University Press, 1998); and *Democracy and Its Critics* (New Haven, Conn.: Yale University Press, 1989).

28. Robert Paul Wolff, Barrington Moore Jr., and Herbert Marcuse, *A Critique of Pure Tolerance* (Boston: Beacon, 1965), vi; Grant McConnell, *Private Power and American Democracy* (New York: Vintage, 1970), 5–6. See also Peter Bachrach, *The Theory of Democratic Elitism: A Critique* (Boston: Little, Brown, 1967); Steven Lukes, *Power: A Radical View* (New York: Macmillan, 1974); and Jeffrey C. Isaac, *Power and Marxist Theory: A Realist View* (Ithaca, N.Y.: Cornell University Press, 1987).

29. See, for example, Edward S. Herman and Noam Chomsky, *Manufacturing Consent: The Political Economy of the Mass Media* (New York: Pantheon, 1988); and Norman Solomon and Jeff Cohen, *Wizards of Media Oz: Behind the Curtain of Mainstream News* (Monroe, Maine: Common Courage Press, 1997).

30. E. E. Schattschneider, *The Semisovereign People: A Realist's View of Democracy in America,* 2d ed. (Hinsdale, Ill.: Dryden, 1975), 40; Roger W. Cobb and Charles D. Elder, *Participation in American Politics: The Dynamics of Agenda-Building,* 2d ed. (Baltimore: Johns Hopkins University Press, 1983), chap. 7.

31. Schattschneider, *Semisovereign People,* 69.

32. *Sun,* Oct. 6, 1991, Bremerton, Wash. Barbara Zang explores the *Sun*'s early venture into civic journalism in "A Possible Press: Participatory Journalism and the Case of the Sun" (Ph.D. diss., Indiana University, 1997).

33. Recent critical overviews of the new media world include Robert W. McChesney, *Rich Media, Poor Democracy: Communication Politics in Dubious Times* (Urbana: University of Illinois Press, 1999); Dan Schiller, *Digital Capitalism: Networking the Global Market System* (Cambridge, Mass.: MIT Press, 1999); and Ben H. Bagdikian, *The Media Monopoly,* 6th ed. (Boston: Beacon, 2000).

34. Todd Gitlin, "Public Sphere or Public Sphericules?" in *Media, Ritual, and Identity,* ed. Tamar Liebes and James Curran (New York: Routledge, 1998), 172–73. Scholars have given much thought to using the Internet for community building. See, for example, Jeffrey Abramson, "The Internet and Community," *Annual Review of the Institute for Information Studies* (1998): 59–80; Lewis A. Friedland, "Electronic Democracy and the New Citizenship," *Media, Culture, and Society* 18 (Apr. 1996): 185–212; Kevin A. Hill and John E. Hughes, *Cyberpolitics: Citizen Activism in the Age of the Internet* (Lanham, Md.: Rowman and Littlefield, 1998); and Roza Tsagarousianou, Damian Tambini, and Cathy Bryan, eds., *Cyberdemocracy: Technology, Cities, and Civic Networks* (New York: Routledge, 1998).

35. Neil Hickey, "Money Lust: How Pressure for Profit Is Perverting Journalism," *Columbia Journalism Review* (July–Aug. 1998): 28–36; John McManus, *Market-Driven Journalism: Let the Citizen Beware?* (Thousand Oaks, Calif.: Sage, 1994).

36. Robert D. Putnam, "Bowling Alone: America's Declining Social Capital," *Journal*

of Democracy 6 (Jan. 1995): 65–78. See also Robert D. Putnam, *Bowling Alone: The Collapse and Revival of American Community* (New York: Simon and Schuster, 2000); Theda Skocpol and Morris P. Fiorina, eds., *Civic Engagement in American Democracy* (Washington, D.C.: Brookings Institution, 1999); Robert Wuthnow, *Loose Connections: Joining Together in America's Fragmented Communities* (Cambridge, Mass.: Harvard University Press, 1998); Todd Gitlin, *The Twilight of Common Dreams: Why America Is Wracked by Culture Wars* (New York: Metropolitan/Holt, 1995); Joseph N. Cappella and Kathleen Hall Jamieson, *Spiral of Cynicism: The Press and the Public Good* (New York: Oxford University Press, 1997).

37. Davis Merritt, *Public Journalism and Public Life: Why Telling the News Is Not Enough* (Hillsdale, N.J.: Lawrence Erlbaum, 1995), 7. Early overviews of civic journalism include Jay Rosen and Davis Merritt, *Public Journalism: Theory and Practice* (Dayton, Ohio: Kettering Foundation, 1994); and Arthur Charity, *Doing Public Journalism* (New York: Guilford, 1995).

38. Jay Rosen, Davis Merritt, and Lisa Austin, *Public Journalism: Theory and Practice, Lessons from Experience* (Dayton, Ohio: Kettering Foundation, 1997), 7.

39. Rosen summarizes and answers the professional critics in Jay Rosen, *What Are Journalists For?* (New Haven, Conn.: Yale University Press, 1999), chaps. 6–7.

40. Jay Rosen, *Getting the Connections Right: Public Journalism and the Troubles in the Press* (New York: Twentieth Century Fund, 1996), 7; Rosen, *What Are Journalists For?* 5.

41. David Remnick, "Scoop," *New Yorker,* Jan. 29, 1996, p. 42; Michael Gartner, "Public Journalism—Seeing through the Gimmicks," *Media Studies Journal* 11 (Winter 1997): 69–75.

42. Michael Schudson, "What Public Journalism Knows about Journalism but Doesn't Know about 'Public,'" in *The Idea of Public Journalism,* ed. Theodore L. Glasser (New York: Guilford, 1999), 128–31; Theodore L. Glasser, "The Idea of Public Journalism," in *Idea of Public Journalism,* 10; John J. Pauly, "Journalism and the Sociology of Public Life," in *Idea of Public Journalism,* ed. Glasser, 145.

43. Morone, *Democratic Wish,* 7.

44. Richard C. Harwood and Jeff McCrehan, *Tapping Civic Life: How to Report First, and Best, What's Happening in Your Community,* 2d ed. (Washington, D.C.: Pew Center for Civic Journalism, 2000), 10. See also David Mathews, *Politics for People* (Urbana: University of Illinois Press, 1994); and Brian O'Connell, *Civil Society: The Underpinnings of American Democracy* (Hanover, N.H.: University Press of New England, 1999).

45. Rosen, *What Are Journalists For?* 68; James W. Carey, "The Press, Public Opinion, and Public Discourse," in *Public Opinion and the Communication of Consent,* ed. Theodore L. Glasser and Charles T. Salmon (New York: Guilford, 1995).

46. Glasser, "Idea of Public Journalism," 11–12; Theodore L. Glasser and Stephanie Craft, "Public Journalism and the Search for Democratic Ideals," in *Media, Ritual, and Identity,* ed. Liebes and Curran, 214–15.

47. Andrea R. Maldari, letter to the editor, *(Bloomington, Ind.) Herald-Times,* June 1, 2000.

48. Hall, *Worlds of Wonder;* Harry S. Stout, *The New England Soul: Preaching and Religious Culture in Colonial New England* (New York: Oxford University Press, 1986); Jon Butler, *Awash in a Sea of Faith: Christianizing the American People* (Cambridge, Mass.:

Harvard University Press, 1990); Jon Butler, *Becoming America: The Revolution before 1776* (Cambridge, Mass.: Harvard University Press, 2000); and Sacvan Bercovitch, *The American Jeremiad* (Madison: University of Wisconsin Press, 1978).

49. Warner, *Letters of the Republic;* Richard D. Brown, *The Strength of a People: The Idea of an Informed Citizenry in America, 1650–1870* (Chapel Hill: University of North Carolina Press, 1996); Clark, *Public Prints; Colonial Book in the Atlantic World,* ed. Amory and Hall. Other recent histories of the colonial press include William David Sloan and Julie Hedgepeth Williams, *The Early American Press, 1690–1783* (Westport, Conn.: Greenwood, 1994); and David A. Copeland, *Colonial American Newspapers: Character and Content* (Newark: University of Delaware Press, 1997).

50. Leonard W. Levy, *Legacy of Suppression: Freedom of Speech and Press in Early American History* (Cambridge, Mass.: Harvard University Press, 1960); Leonard W. Levy, *Emergence of a Free Press* (New York: Oxford University Press, 1985); Leonard W. Levy, *Origins of the Bill of Rights* (New Haven, Conn.: Yale University Press, 1999), chap. 5; Harold L. Nelson, "Seditious Libel in Colonial America," *American Journal of Legal History* 3 (Apr. 1959): 160–72; David A. Anderson, "The Origins of the Press Clause," *UCLA Law Review* 30 (Feb. 1983): 455–541; Smith, *Printers and Press Freedom;* Larry D. Eldridge, *A Distant Heritage: The Growth of Free Speech in Early America* (New York: New York University Press, 1991).

51. *A Brief Narrative of the Case and Tryal of John Peter Zenger,* ed. Paul Finkelman (St. James, N.Y.: Brandywine, 1997).

52. Benedict Anderson, *Imagined Communities: Reflections on the Origins and Spread of Nationalism* (London: Verso, 1983).

53. Leonard, "News for a Revolution," in *Power of the Press;* Gordon S. Wood, *The Radicalism of the American Revolution* (New York: Knopf, 1992); Gordon S. Wood, *The Creation of the American Republic, 1776–1787* (Chapel Hill: University of North Carolina Press, 1969); Edward Countryman, *The American Revolution* (New York: Hill and Wang, 1985); Alfred F. Young, ed., *Beyond the American Revolution: Explorations in the History of American Radicalism* (DeKalb: Northern Illinois University Press, 1993); Robert E. Shalhope, *The Roots of America: American Thought and Culture, 1760–1800* (Boston: Twayne, 1990); Isaac Kramnick, *Republicanism and Bourgeois Radicalism: Political Ideology in Late Eighteenth-Century England and America* (Ithaca, N.Y.: Cornell University Press, 1990); Joyce Appleby, *Capitalism and a New Social Order: The Republican Vision of the 1790s* (New York: New York University Press, 1984); James Roger Sharp, *American Politics in the Early Republic: The New Nation in Crisis* (New Haven, Conn.: Yale University Press, 1993); and Stanley Elkins and Eric McKitrick, *The Age of Federalism: The Early American Republic, 1788–1800* (New York: Oxford University Press, 1993).

54. David Waldstreicher, *In the Midst of Perpetual Fetes: The Making of American Nationalism, 1776–1820* (Chapel Hill: University of North Carolina Press, 1997); R. Brown, *Strength of a People;* Richard R. John, *Spreading the News: The American Postal System from Franklin to Morse* (Cambridge, Mass.: Harvard University Press, 1995); Michael Durey, *"With the Hammer of Truth": James Thomson Callender and America's Early National Heroes* (Charlottesville: University Press of Virginia, 1990); James Tagg, *Benjamin Franklin Bache and the Philadelphia "Aurora"* (Philadelphia: University of Pennsylvania Press, 1991); Jeffery A. Smith, *Franklin and Bache: Envisioning the Enlightened Republic* (New York:

Oxford University Press, 1990); Richard N. Rosenfeld, *American Aurora: A Democratic-Republican Returns* (New York: St. Martin's, 1997). See also Carol Sue Humphrey, *The Press of the Young Republic, 1783–1833* (Westport, Conn.: Greenwood, 1996).

55. Ronald G. Walters, *The Antislavery Appeal: American Abolitionism after 1830* (Baltimore: Johns Hopkins University Press, 1976); Merton L. Dillon, *The Abolitionists: The Growth of a Dissenting Minority* (New York: W. W. Norton, 1979); Lawrence J. Friedman, *Gregarious Saints: Self and Community in American Abolitionism, 1830–1870* (New York: Cambridge University Press, 1982); Leonard L. Richards, *"Gentlemen of Property and Standing": Anti-Abolition Mobs in Jacksonian America* (New York: Oxford University Press, 1970); Thomas L. Haskell, "Capitalism and the Origins of the Humanitarian Sensibility," in *The Antislavery Debate: Capitalism and Abolitionism as a Problem in Historical Interpretation,* ed. Thomas Bender (Berkeley: University of California Press, 1992).

56. Paul Goodman, *Of One Blood: Abolitionism and the Origins of Racial Equality* (Berkeley: University of California Press, 1998); Henry Mayer, *All on Fire: William Lloyd Garrison and the Abolition of Slavery* (New York: St. Martin's, 1998); Steven Mintz, *Moralists and Modernizers: America's Pre–Civil War Reformers* (Baltimore: Johns Hopkins University Press, 1995). See also David Paul Nord, "Systematic Benevolence: Religious Publishing and the Marketplace in Early Nineteenth-Century America," in *Communication and Change in American Religious History,* ed. Leonard I. Sweet (Grand Rapids, Mich.: Eerdmans, 1993); and Nathan O. Hatch, *The Democratization of American Christianity* (New Haven, Conn.: Yale University Press, 1989).

57. John, *Spreading the News;* John C. Nerone, *Violence against the Press: Policing the Public Sphere in U.S. History* (New York: Oxford University Press, 1994), chap. 4; Jane Rhodes, *Mary Ann Shadd Cary: The Black Press and Protest in the Nineteenth Century* (Bloomington: Indiana University Press, 1998); Frankie Hutton, *The Early Black Press in America, 1820s to 1860s* (New York: Greenwood, 1992); Martha M. Solomon, ed., *A Voice of Their Own: The Woman Suffrage Press, 1840–1910* (Tuscaloosa: University of Alabama Press, 1991); Linda Steiner, "Nineteenth-Century Suffrage Periodicals: Conceptions of Womanhood and the Press," in *Ruthless Criticism: New Perspectives in U.S. Communication History,* ed. William S. Solomon and Robert W. McChesney (Minneapolis: University of Minnesota Press, 1993).

58. Bender, *Community and Social Change;* Sennett, *Fall of Public Man;* Gunther Barth, *City People: The Rise of Modern City Culture in Nineteenth-Century America* (New York: Oxford University Press, 1980); Alan Trachtenberg, *The Incorporation of America: Culture and Society in the Gilded Age* (New York: Hill and Wang, 1982); Michael H. Frisch, *Town into City: Springfield, Massachusetts, and the Meaning of Community, 1840–1880* (Cambridge, Mass.: Harvard University Press, 1972).

59. Janet E. Steele, *The Sun Shines for All: Journalism and Ideology in the Life of Charles A. Dana* (Syracuse, N.Y.: Syracuse University Press, 1993); Sally F. Griffith, *Home-Town News: William Allen White and the "Emporia Gazette"* (New York: Oxford University Press, 1989); Gerald J. Baldasty, *E. W. Scripps and the Business of Newspapers* (Urbana: University of Illinois Press, 1999); David Henkin, *City Reading: Written Words and Public Spaces in Antebellum New York* (New York: Columbia University Press, 1998).

60. William Appleman Williams, *The Contours of American History* (Chicago: Quadrangle, 1966); Gabriel Kolko, *The Triumph of Conservatism: A Re-Interpretation of Amer-*

ican History, 1900–1916 (New York: Free Press of Glencoe, 1963); Robert H. Wiebe, *The Search for Order, 1877–1920* (New York: Hill and Wang, 1967).

61. Gerald J. Baldasty, *The Commercialization of News in the Nineteenth Century* (Madison: University of Wisconsin Press, 1992); David Nasaw, *The Chief: The Life of William Randolph Hearst* (Boston: Houghton Mifflin, 2000); Barbara Cloud, *The Business of Newspapers on the Western Frontier* (Reno: University of Nevada Press, 1992); Richard Kaplan, "The Economics of Popular Journalism in the Gilded Age: The Detroit *Evening News* in 1873 and 1888," *Journalism History* 21 (Summer 1995): 65–78.

62. David P. Thelen, *The New Citizenship: Origins of Progressivism in Wisconsin, 1885–1900* (Columbia: University of Missouri Press, 1972); David Paul Nord, *Newspapers and New Politics: Midwestern Municipal Reform, 1890–1900* (Ann Arbor, Mich.: UMI Research Press, 1981).

63. Kevin Mattson, *Creating a Democratic Public: The Struggle for Urban Participatory Democracy during the Progressive Era* (University Park: Pennsylvania State University Press, 1998); Rodgers, *Atlantic Crossings.*

64. Cathy N. Davidson, *Revolution and the Word: The Rise of the Novel in America* (New York: Oxford University Press, 1986); David D. Hall, *Cultures of Print: Essays in the History of the Book* (Amherst: University of Massachusetts Press, 1996); R. Brown, *Knowledge Is Power;* Robert Darnton, *The Great Cat Massacre and Other Episodes in French Cultural History* (New York: Basic, 1984); Robert Darnton, *The Kiss of Lamourette: Reflections in Cultural History* (New York: W. W. Norton, 1990); Carl F. Kaestle et al., *Literacy in the United States: Readers and Reading since 1880* (New Haven, Conn.: Yale University Press, 1991); William J. Gilmore, *Reading Becomes a Necessity of Life: Material and Cultural Life in Rural New England* (Knoxville: University of Tennessee Press, 1989).

65. Cathy N. Davidson, ed., *Reading in America: Literature and Social History* (Baltimore: Johns Hopkins University Press, 1989); James L. Machor, ed., *Readers in History: Nineteenth-Century American Literature and the Contexts of Response* (Baltimore: Johns Hopkins University Press, 1993); James P. Danky and Wayne A. Wiegand, eds., *Print Culture in a Diverse America* (Urbana: University of Illinois Press, 1998).

66. Gary B. Nash, *The Urban Crucible: Social Change, Political Consciousness, and the Origins of the American Revolution* (Cambridge, Mass.: Harvard University Press, 1979); Gary B. Nash, *Forging Freedom: The Formation of Philadelphia's Black Community, 1720–1840* (Cambridge, Mass.: Harvard University Press, 1988); Gary B. Nash, "The Social Evolution of Preindustrial American Cities, 1700–1820: Reflections and New Directions," *Journal of Urban History* 13 (Feb. 1987): 115–45.

67. Kenneth A. Lockridge, *Literacy in Colonial New England: An Enquiry into the Social Context of Literacy in the Early Modern West* (New York: W. W. Norton, 1974); Harvey J. Graff, *The Literacy Myth: Literacy and Social Structure in the Nineteenth-Century City* (New York: Academic, 1979). The history of libraries also influenced my thinking about research on readers. See, for example, Robert A. Gross, *Books and Libraries in Thoreau's Concord* (Worcester, Mass.: American Antiquarian Society, 1988); Donald G. Davis Jr., ed., *Libraries, Books, and Culture* (Austin: Graduate School of Library and Information Science, University of Texas, 1986); Ronald J. Zboray, *A Fictive People: Antebellum Economic Development and the American Reading Public* (New York: Oxford University Press, 1993), chap. 11.

68. Lawrence C. Stedman, Katherine Tinsley, and Carl F. Kaestle, "Literacy as a Consumer Activity," in Kaestle et al., *Literacy in the United States*. On the role of statistics in public policy see Porter, *Trust in Numbers*.

69. Stanley Fish, *Is There a Text in This Class? The Authority of Interpretive Communities* (Cambridge, Mass.: Harvard University Press, 1980); Norman N. Holland, *The Critical I* (New York: Columbia University Press, 1992); Janice Radway, "Interpretive Communities and Variable Literacies: The Functions of Romance Reading," *Daedalus* 113 (Summer 1984): 49–73.

70. Thomas C. Leonard, "How Americans Learned to Read the News," in *News for All: America's Coming of Age with the Press* (New York: Oxford University Press, 1995), chap. 1; Henkin, "Print in Public, Public in Print: The Rise of the Daily Newspaper," in *City Reading*, chap. 5; Isabelle Lehuu, *Carnival on the Page: Popular Print Media in Antebellum America* (Chapel Hill: University of North Carolina Press, 2000); Ronald J. Zboray and Mary Saracino Zboray, "Political News and Female Readership in Antebellum Boston and Its Region," *Journalism History* 22 (Spring 1996): 2–14.

PART 1

Communities of Production

1. Teleology and News: The Religious Roots of American Journalism, 1630–1730

ON OCTOBER 17, 1637, Mary Dyer, a supporter of Anne Hutchinson's in the religious controversy then swirling through Boston, delivered a hideously deformed stillborn child. The women attending the birth decided to keep the miscarriage quiet, but rumors began to spread through the town. Eventually, Gov. John Winthrop heard of it, investigated, and ordered the body exhumed. The exhumation was something of a sensation; a crowd of more than one hundred people gathered to gape at the grotesque little corpse.[1]

Mary Dyer's "monstrous birth" was *news*. Winthrop wrote about it in his journal, suggesting that it was the talk of the town by the spring of 1638. The story was published in a news sheet in London in 1642, one of the first publications of a "strange occurrence" to come out of New England. It was featured in the first account of the Hutchinson controversy, published in 1644. And it appeared in the "Chronological Table of some few memorable occurrences" in one of the earliest New England almanacs. Along with Indian wars, deep snows, earthquakes, shipwrecks, droughts, epidemics, and strange lights in the southern sky, there it was: "Mrs. Dier brought forth her horned-fouretalented [taloned]-monster."[2]

Why was this sad miscarriage news in New England in the 1630s? More generally, what was news for these people and why was it news? What was the nature and function of news in the public life of seventeenth-century New England? And what legacy did this conception of news leave for the development of American newspaper journalism in the eighteenth century? These are the questions this chapter will address. Specifically, I will argue that the characteristics of American news—its subject matter and its method of reporting—are deeply rooted in the religious culture of seventeenth-century New England.

Both subject matter *and* method of reporting are important to any definition of news; they are crucial to my argument about news in New England.
Put simply, news is the reporting of current public occurrences. But this
definition is less simple than it seems, for the meaning of each term—*occurrence, current, public,* and *reporting*—is contingent upon the social contexts
of time and place. For example, news is always associated with *occurrences,*
but not all occurrences are news. Which are and which are not is a social
decision, always being redefined and renegotiated. News is about *current*
events but not in any simple sense. Though particular news events may be
new and unique, they are rarely novel or unconventional. Indeed, news is
usually current in the sense of recurrent. Thus the distinction between news
and history is a subtle one, closely related to a people's understanding of the
patterning of their past and its intermingling with the present and future.
News is always *public.* But the definition of what has public meaning and what
does not is highly variable, a product of the exercise of political, economic,
and social power. And, last, news is *reported,* usually in plain and empirical
simplicity. But the simplicity is always deceptive. Though presented as na-
ked empiricism, uninterpreted and self-evident, news is actually a highly
complex social construction, forged in the fires of cultural convention, interpretation, and power. The meanings of these four elements define the
nature of news and the function of journalism in a particular time and place.

In seventeenth-century New England all four of these defining elements
of news—occurrence, current, public, and reporting—were shaped by the
belief that everything happened according to God's perfect plan. News was,
in a word, teleological. The teleological order was not only divine; it was
patterned, recurrent, meaningful, and intelligible. It was not only meaningful; the meaning was social and public. And that meaning was not only intelligible; it was also self-evident. Thus New England generated a kind of news
that was oriented to current events yet conventional, patterned, and recurrent in subject matter. It was religious and public in importance and purpose
yet directly accessible to individual people. It was controlled and reported by
public authority yet was simple, plain, and empirical in form.

Toward the end of the century the teleological meaning of news faded. The
combination of public importance (yet individual accessibility) and of what
I will call authoritative interpretation (yet reportorial empiricism) proved as
unstable in news as in religion. And by the eighteenth century heresy was
rampant in both. American newspapers began to distinguish between news
that is *important* (stories of official public action) and news that is merely
interesting (stories of unusual private occurrences). This distinction still lies
at the heart of conventional practice in journalism.[3] Yet the fundamental

characteristics of news and the methods of news reporting laid down in the seventeenth century persisted. In other words, after the seventeenth century the meaning and purpose of much of the news was lost; only the news itself remained.

This is not to say that American news was invented in New England. Journalism, like all early American literature, was part of "the extension of British culture into the new world."[4] The Mary Dyer story was typical of popular English street literature of the era. Ballads and broadsides describing "monsters"—both animal and human—and other "strange occurrences" were standard fare in Britain and Europe. And, of course, sensational printed news derived from oral folklore, with roots in time immemorial. Clearly, readers then as now were fascinated by sensational stories.[5]

But Mary Dyer's miscarriage was more than a simple scrap of sensationalism. It was authoritative public news. The Dyer story did not become part of the official public news system in New England because it was sensational or popular or even because it contained a religious meaning. It was made news by the civil authorities because it contained important public information. The governor himself conducted the investigation and wrote much of the major report of the episode. He did so because he saw in this strange birth the designing hand of God and a message for the commonwealth of Massachusetts. The Dyers were followers of the heretical Anne Hutchinson, and the birth of their "monster" was interpreted as a clear sign of God's opposition to their "monstrous opinions," which were undermining the religious and civil authority of the colony.[6] In other words, Mary Dyer's "monstrous birth" was not a private affair; it was a "public occurrence" of public importance. It was a "divine providence" laden with public meaning.

Historians have often found in the doctrine of divine providence a clue to Puritan theology and sociology. Some have stressed the Puritan enthrallment with history. Both Perry Miller and Sacvan Bercovitch, for example, though disagreeing on much, do agree that the teleology of Puritan thought prompted an obsession with history. History was nothing less than the unfolding of God's plan for mankind and New England's special place in it. David Scobey and Michael G. Hall have shown how history was used as a political tool by the second-generation Puritan elite to make sense of the present and to legitimate their own management of it. Thus, in the Puritan view of history, the present and the past were part of a single patterned tapestry.[7] Other historians (including Miller, of course) have stressed the Puritan interest in nature and cosmology. As in human history, God spoke through the natural order of the cosmos. The interest of Puritan intellectuals in the new science was an effort to read God's meaning out of the book of nature.[8] Still other historians have emphasized the Puritan fascination with divine prodigies, strange and wondrous occurrences, ranging from fires and shipwrecks to Mary Dyer's baby.[9]

None of these characteristics placed New England belief outside the tradition of English Protestantism or even the more general traditions of European Christianity and folk culture. Protestants and Catholics, astrologers and assorted supernaturalists, all shared an encompassing sense of divine immanence, of the reality of God's intervening presence in nature and in human affairs. In other words, the doctrine of divine providence emigrated to America with the Puritans from early modern Europe.[10]

But more than their cousins in England or in other parts of British America, the New Englanders made the doctrine central to public life, to civic affairs. Certainly, the idea of divine providence pervaded the popular press of seventeenth-century England—the ballads, the chapbooks, the almanacs. But this literature was strikingly diverse and even contradictory in meaning; it was produced by an enormous variety of commercial printers; and it was usually associated with individual moral exhortation. Even the early English newspapers of the Puritan Revolution used the doctrine more as a political slogan than as a political creed.[11] Similarly, the descriptive literature out of Virginia and other southern American colonies was touched by the doctrine of divine providence but not controlled by it. John Smith and later writers used the term frequently, but it did not guide their interpretations of public life and civic action.[12] In New England, more than anywhere else in Britain or British America, the doctrine of divine providence directed the official, authoritative representation and interpretation of the public life of the community.

Historians have long been fond of the doctrine of divine providence, for it has seemed to explain the Puritan sense of mission and errand and perhaps ultimately the American dream of destiny and progress.[13] Such a vision of American exceptionalism and homogeneity now seems wrongheaded, and it is not my purpose to chase after it in this chapter.[14] My purpose is more modest. It is to look at New England's institutions of public communication, not because the New England way was or is a metaphor for America but simply because New England was the place where printing, printed news, and the newspaper first flowered in America. I propose to explore the practical relationship between the doctrine of divine providence and the official public news system of seventeenth-century New England. This chapter should contribute to a growing literature on "public communication" in early New England. Richard D. Brown has described, at the individual level and for a somewhat later period, how information in general moved through early American society. Ian Steele and David Cressy have surveyed the trans-

Atlantic communication system. Harry Stout and David Hall have explored the system of popular religious communication.[15] My focus is on another aspect of public communication: reporting the news.

* * *

The nature of the teleological news system of seventeenth-century New England is suggested by the career of Samuel Danforth. Danforth was not the most famous of the early ministers of Massachusetts or the most profound. But the range of his career as Harvard tutor, astronomer, preacher, and publicist and the nature of his writing nicely illustrate the interplay among religion, public affairs, and the news in seventeenth-century New England.[16]

For six years following his graduation in 1643, Danforth served as a reader and fellow at Harvard College. In addition to his major responsibility as tutor to the undergraduates, Danforth studied for the master's degree and became involved with one of the adjunct enterprises of the college, the printing press. The printing press was a small and tenuous operation at Cambridge in the 1640s, but it was an important one for the mission of the colony. It is a commonplace of Reformation history that the doctrines of *sola scriptura* (scripture alone) and the priesthood of all believers helped to make Protestants a race of Bible readers.[17] But for New Englanders Bible reading was only part of their obligation to literacy and learning. The special nature of their covenanted society and its place in history required informed participation in public affairs. Given the need of the people to understand God's plan, to interpret his history, and to build his kingdom, it is not surprising that from the beginning New Englanders were people of the word—and of printing.[18]

The early products of the Cambridge press reflected the public mission of print in the Puritan community. The first imprint was the "Freeman's Oath" (1639), the formal contract or covenant required of members of the civil government of the colony. The first major work of the press was the so-called *Bay Psalm Book* (1640), a new translation of the psalms. Soon the press was turning out catechisms, school books, legal documents, and sermons. None of these works was meant for the private consumption of disconnected individuals. All were conceived and executed as part of the official *public* life of the community.[19]

Another product of the Cambridge press was the almanac, and the compiler of the earliest surviving almanacs was Samuel Danforth. The almanacs were basically simple books of nature, reference guides to the cycles of the sun and moon, the tides and seasons. They were clearly intended for a popular audience. The title pages declared that the astronomical data "may generally serve for the most part of New-England." In addition to astronomy,

Danforth's almanacs also carried bits of verse, usually associated with the changing seasons of the year.[20]

But nature was not the only subject of these almanacs. History—especially recent history—was another. A standard feature was a "Chronological Table of some few memorable occurrences," beginning with the arrival of Winthrop's fleet in 1630. These "memorable occurrences," all keyed to specific dates, were a mixture of historical and natural events. The first type of event included the arrival of the fleet, the first session of the General Court, the Pequot War, and the beginning of printing in the colony. The second included droughts, epidemics, earthquakes, storms, untimely deaths, strange plagues of pigeons and caterpillars, and, of course, the monstrous birth of Mary Dyer's baby.[21] The two types of occurrences were mingled, and they were presented in the same plain, uninterpreted, matter-of-fact style as the movements of the tides and eclipses of the sun. Astronomy, meteorology, history, and prodigy—all blended together because their meaning was the same. All told parts of the same grand story: God's work in New England.

Danforth's almanacs followed English models rather closely, including the use of the chronological table. There were differences, however. The early American almanacs avoided astrology, especially prognostication. Events recorded were all past occurrences, not predictions. Furthermore, the events in the chronologies were recent; they carried information of current public importance. In England the chronologies tended to more distant history. Perhaps most important, English almanacs were diverse, specialized, commercial, and often highly partisan.[22] The Cambridge almanac was the only American almanac; it was published under the supervision of the religious and civil authorities of the colony. Like the weekly sermon, the town meeting, and the other imprints of the Cambridge press, the almanac was part of the *official* public communication system of New England.

In 1650 Danforth left Harvard and the almanacs to begin a pastorate in Roxbury. But he never lost his interest in astronomy, public occurrences, and providence—and the relationship among them. In 1665 he published a pamphlet titled *An Astronomical Description Of The Late Comet, Or Blazing Star, As it appeared in New-England in the 9th, 10th 11th, and in the beginning of the 12th Moneth, 1644, Together With a brief Theological Application thereof.* As the title indicates, the pamphlet is divided into two parts: a description of the comet of 1664 and an interpretation of its meaning. The first section is highly empirical. In a plain, straightforward presentation, Danforth discussed the comet's size, its composition, its movement in a highly "eccentric orb," and the illumination of its tail by the sun. This is factual reporting. Then comes the "theological application." This section is also empirical, in its way: it is historical. Danforth argued that "the Histories of former Ages, do absolutely testifie that Comets have been many times Heralds of wrath to a secure and impenitent World." He listed many such events, beginning with a comet described by the Roman author Seneca and ending with one seen in 1652. Next he turned to New England, listing other signs (an earthquake in 1663, deaths of eminent people, a drought, early frosts). Danforth's history is drawn up to the present, historical events entwined with current public occurrences, to make the point that the Lord right now "calls upon New-England to awake and to repent."[23]

Danforth saw the hand of God in more local occurrences as well. In 1674, for example, a young man named Benjamin Goad was hanged for the crime of bestiality. Danforth preached a sermon at the execution, and that sermon became the first American imprint of another popular type of event-oriented publication, the execution sermon. Like the comet's flight, the case of Benjamin Goad was a specific event but an event filled with public meaning. "Gods End in inflicting remarkable Judgements upon some, is for Caution and Warning to all others," Danforth declared. Thus the sad end of this one sad boy became for Puritan New England a story worth preaching and publishing.[24]

Hangings had long been news in England, and the execution ballad and broadside were staples of English street literature.[25] But the American Puritans changed the genre. In the English world only the New Englanders made the public sermon central to execution literature. In England the form was more narrative, with a simple moral exhortation directed to the individual criminal or reader. In New England the execution and its attendant literature was much more communal than individual.[26] Once again, God's providence and the news it generated were seen as public, not private, affairs.

Danforth's most famous work was an early contribution to yet another type of current affairs publication, the election sermon. Election sermons were preached to the representatives of the various towns who gathered in Boston each spring to elect the governor's council and to take part in the work of the General Court. The themes of the sermons changed over time, of course, but in the late seventeenth century many of them focused on the special place of New England in God's plan for human history. One of these was Samuel Danforth's election sermon of 1670, the title of which contributed a classic phrase to the vocabulary of American historiography. He called his talk *A Brief Recognition of New-Englands Errand into the Wilderness.*[27]

Danforth's theme in this famous sermon was declension—that is, the decline in commitment of the people to what Danforth and his contemporaries took to be the founding mission of the colony. This loss of commitment angered God, and the evidence of his anger could be found in current events. "Why hath the Lord smitten us with Blasting and Mildew now seven years together, superadding sometimes severe Drought, sometimes great Tempests, Floods, and sweeping Rains, that leave no food behinde them? Is it not because the Lords House lyeth waste? Temple-work in our Hearts, Families, Churches is shamefully neglected?"[28]

The three types of sermons preached by Samuel Danforth—the election sermon, the execution sermon, and the natural event sermon—exemplify the structure and the range of what has come to be called the Puritan jeremiad. Another type that usually followed the jeremiad style was the "humiliation sermon." Those sermons were preached on days officially set aside for fasting and humiliation, when the people humbled themselves before God and prayed for a return of his favor. Like the other types, the humiliation sermon was almost always a report of, and a meditation on, current public occurrences.[29]

It is not surprising that all of Danforth's publications were event oriented. Most publications in New England in the seventeenth century were. My own rough survey of the seventeenth-century New England titles listed in Charles Evans's *American Bibliography* shows that 55 percent were clearly and principally linked to actions and events, mostly current events. Even within the category that I have labeled "narratives and histories," 80 percent were primarily narratives of *current* public occurrences. That is, they were news. (See table 1.1; see also table 1.2 on p. 42.)[30]

For most New England publicists, the great movements of celestial and human history, unfolding before them, were the prime considerations. But little things carried meaning as well. In what might be the first flu story in the history of American news reporting, Michael Wigglesworth wrote these stanzas in 1662 in his poem "God's Controversy with New England":

> Our healthfull dayes are at an end
>   And sicknesses come on
> From yeer to yeer, becaus oʳ hearts
>   Away from God are gone.
>
> * * *
>
> Now colds and coughs, Rhewms, and sore-throats,
>   Do more & more abound:
> Now Agues sore & Fevers strong
>   In every place are found.[31]

In sum, reporting on events and making sense of them were important tasks for ministers, for public officials, and for the printing press. Harry Stout, though writing about sermons only, makes this point quite well: "Through-

Table 1.1. Event-Oriented Imprints Published in New England
during and after the Restriction of Printing to Cambridge

	1639–1674	1675–1700	1639–1700
Event imprints	94 (48%)	332 (57%)	426 (55%)
All imprints	197 (100%)	580 (100%)	777 (100%)

Source: Charles Evans, *American Bibliography,* vol. 1 (Chicago, 1903). See note 30.

out the 1670s and 1680s, more fast day sermons (fourteen) were printed at
Cambridge than any other type of sermon except election sermons. To understand this publishing pattern, one must recognize that in New England
print functioned primarily as a historical tool rather than evangelistic tool.
It was not intended to represent regular preaching but to chart the children's
location in providential history."[32]

My only quibble with Stout is over his use of the term *historical tool.* Perhaps *journalistic tool* would be the more appropriate phrase, for it was *current* events ("the children's location"), not remote historical occurrences, that
energized and dominated the teleological literature of seventeenth-century
New England.

* * *

Samuel Danforth died in 1674, the year the General Court of Massachusetts
lifted its ban on printing outside Cambridge.[33] This easing of official control
over the printing process would have profound consequences. Quickly, Boston would eclipse Cambridge as the printing capital of New England; more
slowly, the commercial milieu of Boston would transform printing from a
purely public enterprise to a nearly private one. The privatization of printing would proceed gradually over many decades. But from the beginning the
Boston printers were more attuned to market demand, including their audiences' interest in current public occurrences.[34] In their earliest publications
they tried to meet this demand in their choice of material while staying within
the official traditions of authoritative interpretation laid down in Cambridge
in Danforth's day. In other words, they continued to print teleological news.

The first two imprints struck off the first Boston press, set up by John
Foster in 1675, were typical teleological news pieces. Both were keyed to local current events; both were efforts to explicate and to control the official
meaning of those events for public life. The full titles nicely summarize the
subject matter and the purpose of these two sermons:

*The Wicked mans Portion. Or A Sermon (Preached at the Lecture in Boston in
New-England the 18th day of the 1 Moneth 1674, when two Men were executed,*

*who had Murthered their Master.) Wherein is shewed That excesse in wickedness
doth bring untimely Death.*

*The Times of men are in the hands of God. Or A Sermon Occasioned by that awfull
Providence which hapned in Boston in New England, the 4th Day of the 3d Moneth
1675 (when part of a Vessel was blown up in the Harbour, and nine men hurt, and
three mortally wounded) wherein is shewed how we should sanctifie the dreadfull
Name of God under such awfull Dispensations.*

The author of both sermons was Increase Mather, soon to be the chief
patron of the new Boston press. No prominent Puritan leader was more
enthralled than Mather by events and their meaning for public life. His personal theology, his political prominence, and his penchant for publication
all combined with the crush of occurrences after 1675 to call forth an outpouring of teleological news in Boston. Indeed, given his obsession with the
reporting of current public occurrences, it may fairly be said that Increase
Mather's publication record in the last quarter of the seventeenth century
represents the first major flowering of an indigenous American journalism.[35]

The wellspring of Increase Mather's journalism was his ardent devotion
to the doctrine of divine providence. In 1675, when New England suffered the
worst calamity in its history, Mather was convinced that he had seen it coming the year before, in his jeremiad *The Day of Trouble Is Near.* "It was much
in my thoughts that God would visit with the sword for the reason mentioned
in my sermons," he wrote later in his autobiography. "Afterwards I saw that
those thoughts were from God. For in the year 1675 the warr with the Indians (which lasted for several years) began."[36]

This was King Philip's War. New Englanders had fought Indians before,
but never had the Indians been so well armed or so relentless as they now
were under King Philip, the chief sachem of the Wampanoag. At war's end—
with Philip dead and thousands of his followers slaughtered or sold into slavery—the colonists were victorious. But it was a melancholy victory. In a little more than one year in 1675–76, one of every sixteen New England men
had been killed. Half the towns were damaged; at least twelve were completely
destroyed.[37]

For Increase Mather, the war was a providence of terrifying import. Long
before the war ended, he began the process of reporting and interpretation,
of reading out of the events of the war God's message for the people of New
England. In 1676 he published the most substantial piece of American journalism up to that time, *A Brief History of the Warr with the Indians in New-
England.* Mather's theme was simple: This war was a judgment laid down upon
a sinful people, a people "which hath not so pursued, as ought to have been,
the blessed design of their Fathers, in following the Lord into this wilderness."[38]

Increase Mather's style was as simple as his theme. In *A Brief History* he said his purpose was simply to provide an impartial narrative of events. At the end he wrote: "Thus have we a brief, plain, and true Story of the war with the Indians in New England, how it began, and how it hath made its progress; and what present hopes there are of a comfortable closure and conclusion of this trouble; which hath been continued for a whole year and more. Designing only a Breviary of the History of this war; I have not enlarged upon the circumstances of things, but shall leave that to others, who have advantages and leisure to go on with such an undertaking."[39]

Certainly his method was plain, empirical, and narrative. *A Brief History* reads unmistakably as a piece of journalism, an instant book dashed off while the fires of the war were still smoldering. But Mather's statement that he did not enlarge upon the circumstances of things is disingenuous, as such statements usually are. The story is built of rough-cut occurrences, but the teleological themes, or circumstances, are always clear. Indeed, God speaks as clearly through Mather's war as he had through Danforth's comet.[40]

For Increase Mather, as for New England in general, King Philip's War was only the beginning of a flood tide of momentous events. And many of Mather's publications, from 1676 until his death in 1723 at age eighty-four, were devoted to the reporting and interpretation of teleological news. Mather's most famous work of this type (something of a best-seller for its time) was *An Essay for the Recording of Illustrious Providences,* published in Boston in 1684. This book grew from a proposal adopted by the ministers of the colony in 1681 to collect, organize, and publish accounts of "illustrious providences" and "remarkable occurrences," such as "Divine Judgements, Tempests, Floods, Earth-quakes, Thunders as are unusual, strange Apparitions, or what ever else shall happen that is Prodigious."[41] The book lived up to the proposal. It is a thick compilation of wonder stories of all sorts, ranging from witchcrafts to harrowing shipwrecks to medical oddities. *Essay for the Recording of Illustrious Providences* is enormously detailed and eclectic. It demonstrates some appreciation for the new science, yet it is equally dependent upon the older genres of the supernatural that were still popular in the folklore and the popular literature of England and Europe.[42]

Throughout his long life Increase Mather remained fascinated by current events in New England, especially strange occurrences, and he continued to write about them. He published works on comets in the 1680s, on witchcrafts in the 1690s, on storms, earthquakes, and fires in the early eighteenth century. His theme remained as steady as his fascination. In 1711, with much of Boston in charred ruins, Mather explained the meaning of this most prodigious event of the new century: "When there is a Fire kindled among a People, it is the Lord that hath kindled it. . . . All things whatsoever, are ordered by the Providence of God."[43]

Increase Mather's interest in current events, however, was not limited to "wonders." He also participated in, reported on, and interpreted the major political events of his time. And political events broke rapidly after 1676. With King Philip's war barely ended, Massachusetts entered upon nearly two decades of imperial turmoil. The major events are well known: the tightening of English imperial control in the 1670s; the revocation of the Massachusetts charter and the creation of the Dominion of New England in 1683–84; the Glorious Revolution of 1688–89 in England and America; the restoration of the charter (much altered) in 1691.[44] These events were news in New England. As table 1.2 suggests, a good deal of the increase in "event-oriented publication" in New England after 1674 came in the form of nonsermon narratives. Many of these were political tracts and news sheets concerning these great events of empire.

Increase Mather was a chief contributor to this new political journalism. While serving as agent for Massachusetts Bay in London from 1688 to 1691, Mather wrote several political pieces. The most notable was *A Narrative of the Miseries of New-England, by Reason of an Arbitrary Government Erected There under Sir Edmund Andros* (London, 1688). This pamphlet was directed mainly toward English readers, though it circulated in America as well. For the home audience, he wrote several letters that were published as the broadside *The Present State of the New-English Affairs* (Boston, 1689).[45] Neither of these news tracts is overtly teleological, except for conventional phrases such as "it has pleased God to succeed Endeavours and Sollicitations here so far." For the most part, Increase Mather builds his arguments with a purely political vocabulary, including the rights of property and due process

Table 1.2. Event-Oriented Imprints Published in New England during and after the Restriction of Printing to Cambridge, by Type of Publication

Publication	1639–1674		1675–1700	
	Number	Percentage	Number	Percentage
1. Proclamations, orders, and laws	30	32%	132	40%
2. Sermons on official public occasions	25	27	56	17
3. Sermons and reports on natural occurrences	3	3	20	6
4. Histories and narratives	2	2	53	16
5. Almanacs	27	29	43	13
6. Obituaries	7	7	28	8
Total event-oriented imprints	94	100	332	100

Source: Charles Evans, *American Bibliography,* vol. 1 (Chicago, 1903). See note 30.

of law. But underlying Mather's political argumentation lay the bedrock of the covenant and of New England's special place in history. When the Crown first proposed to alter the beloved charter, Mather insisted that the issue was more than political. To submit would be sin, for the charter, like New England itself, was ordained of God.[46]

Though Increase Mather was the leading proponent of the teleological news system in New England in the late seventeenth century, he certainly was not alone. As the tables show, a large proportion of all publications were devoted to current events. For example, teleological news routinely figured into the work of Cotton Mather, Increase's son and the leading Boston publicist of his generation. Cotton's first published sermon was an execution sermon. In 1686 the twenty-three-year-old minister preached to a large crowd gathered for the hanging of the murderer James Morgan. Like Danforth, Mather drew general meaning from the specific event, portraying Morgan as merely the ripened fruit of the sin that infected all New England. His performance was apparently a strong one, for people throughout the region "very greedily desired the Publication" of it, Cotton Mather noted in his diary; and it subsequently "sold exceedingly."[47] At the end of his life Cotton Mather was still reporting and interpreting the events of the day. His last sermons, preached in the late fall of 1727, dwelled upon the meaning of an earthquake that had shaken New England. Cotton Mather's sermons and their technical appendixes provided an empirical account of the earthquake, much as Danforth had described the comet of 1664. And like Danforth, Cotton Mather had no doubt that this event carried profound public meaning. His first sentence, preached the morning after the quake, makes this vividly clear: "The Glorious God has Roared out of Zion."[48]

Cotton Mather did not always preach or write on current events, of course, but the doctrine of God's providence was never far from his mind. Once, during a church service, a thunderstorm swept through Boston. While the storm raged, Mather preached an impromptu sermon on the meaning of thunderstorms—and later published it.[49]

Cotton Mather's great work, *Magnalia Christi Americana* (London, 1702), represents a culmination of seventeenth-century teleological publication. This massive work is a virtual encyclopedia of events in the history of New England. He explained in his introduction that his interest was "the *Actions* of a more Eminent Importance, that have signalized those Colonies," as well as the "Memorable Occurrences, and amazing Judgments and Mercies befalling many particular persons among the People of New-England."[50] But *Magnalia Christi Americana* was journalism as well as history, for its subject matter was the present as well as the past. Like his father, Cotton Mather

believed that he was called by God to be a news reporter: "To *Regard* the illustrious Displays of that Providence, wherewith our Lord Christ governs the
world, is a Work, than which there is none more Needful, or Useful, for a
Christian: To *Record* them is a Work, than which, none more proper for a
Minister."[51]

* * *

Current events loomed large in the Puritan imagination. This has been the
theme so far. Belief in the role of divine providence in the public life of New
England clothed all occurrences—from major political events to odd changes
in the weather—with meaning and importance. It is little wonder, then, that
the reporting of current events held such a central place in seventeenth-century New England publication, from Samuel Danforth's almanacs to Cotton Mather's *Magnalia.* Simple event orientation, however, was not the only
common characteristic of this literature. There were similarities as well in
how events were selected and reported and in how they were interpreted. I
will call these characteristic styles *reportorial empiricism* and *authoritative
interpretation.* The fact that these characteristics—reporting and interpretation—can be considered separately is important for understanding both
their harmony in the seventeenth century and their frequent disharmony
thereafter.

By reportorial empiricism I mean that the teleological news literature of
seventeenth-century New England was highly empirical, but the style was
eclectic and reportorial, not systematic and scientific. The methodology was
essentially what we today call news reporting: the routine collation and ci-
tation of the statements of sources.[52] The sources ranged widely, from the best
scientists of the age to folklore to the average person with a story to tell. The
role of the writer was not to conduct systematic empirical research but rather
to report the empirical statements of others. Such a methodology was empiricism without science. It was, in a word, journalism.

The earliest almanacs provide the model, in skeletal form, for this kind of
eclectic, reportorial empiricism. On the one hand, they were handbooks of
astronomy, based on the most dependable scientific sources. On the other
hand, they were lists of scattered occurrences, based on official record, local
legend, and word of mouth. Danforth elaborated this method in his teleological sermons. His comet sermon of 1665, for example, combined scientific
observation with long lists of occurrences, chosen to show that comets were
heralds of calamity. Some of these occurrences were well-known recent
events: earthquakes, droughts, early frosts. Others were borrowed from a
variety of sources, named and unnamed, from Roman times onward. Events

were selected and included because they fit a conventional pattern. For Danforth, the recent comet was a remarkable event but not a mysterious one. Its meaning was conventional and clear, for it was merely the latest manifestation of a type of event that had occurred and recurred throughout history.[53]

Increase Mather's method was also relentlessly empirical but in this same reportorial fashion. Mather was intensely curious about the natural world and deeply impressed by the scientific method. In fact, his early twentieth-century biographer portrays him as something of a genuine scientist.[54] More recently, Increase Mather's method in such works as *An Essay for the Recording of Illustrious Providences* has been described as "pseudo-science." Throughout *An Essay* Mather endeavored to tell stories that were accurate and true. He assured the reader that this information came from reliable sources.[55] But for the most part, Mather did not systematically evaluate the quality of this information. He merely reported it. His sources ranged from scientific treatises to folklore to rumor. Most of the stories he simply heard from people around New England, who were as interested in current events as he was. And he permitted all to have their say.[56] Though Robert Middlekauff has argued that such a style "is not genuinely empirical," it is empirical in its way. The empirical data are the statements of the sources. Increase Mather's method is the empiricism not of the scientist but of the news reporter.[57]

Cotton Mather was more of a scientist than his father was. More than any other American of his age, Cotton studied the new sciences then blossoming in England and Europe. But Cotton Mather was mainly "a disseminator and popularizer of new scientific knowledge," according to biographer Kenneth Silverman. Cotton Mather engaged in careful observations of nature, but he was not a true experimentalist. Moreover, he was an indiscriminate collector of curiosa, which he regularly sent to the Royal Society of London. They included stories of prehistoric bones, medical oddities and cures, dreams, apparitions, and "rainbows as prognostics." Some of his curiosa were supported with references to René Descartes, Edmund Halley, and Isaac Newton; others seem based more in local folklore and current gossip. Like his father, Cotton Mather rarely evaluated the quality of such information. He simply reported it as given by his sources. His method, as Silverman has said, was often "an amassment of illustrations and quotations." Silverman resists charging Mather with "credulity," as his nineteenth-century critics were prone to do, because Mather's method was a common one of the time.[58] Indeed, it was—especially among those for whom religion was more compelling than science.

The eclectic, reportorial method of inquiry illustrated by Danforth and the Mathers was especially congenial to an empiricism that was "always a handmaid to religion."[59] The purpose of these writers was not to build or to test theory. Their theory was given. The doctrine of divine providence specified the "first cause" of historical, natural, and seemingly unnatural occurrences. These occurrences, despite their surface strangeness, were intelligible because they represented types of events that had occurred before in an intelligible pattern, a pattern drawn by God. Like the scientific method, the method of Danforth and the Mathers was profoundly empirical, for the Lord spoke through the concrete reality of the material world. But unlike the scientific method, their method was not truly experimental, for its object was the documentation of the already known. Precisely for this reason the Puritan publicists freely urged believers to study events themselves, to read God's word in the book of nature, history, and current events, just as they urged the common folk to search the Scriptures. They had no doubts that anyone could see what God himself had placed there to be seen.

Because they believed that the meaning of an event was embedded within the event itself, the Puritan leaders of seventeenth-century New England talked more about reporting providences than interpreting them. Collecting, recording, and publishing simple factual accounts of occurrences was a valuable and meaningful project in itself. The almanacs offered no interpretation, just lists of occurrences. Similarly, the great histories and collections of providences, such as *An Essay for the Recording of Illustrious Providences* and *Magnalia Christi Americana,* were more narrative reports than interpretations. Even sermons, though laden with a good deal more interpretative baggage, were self-professedly plain and simple in style because the word of the minister was not supposed to mediate the word of God—whether revealed in Scripture, nature, or current events. Not uncommonly, published sermons carried purely "factual" sections, such as accounts of fires, transcripts of criminals' last words, or descriptions of astronomical phenomena.[60]

But these writers had no doubts about the true meaning, the one proper interpretation, of these empirical reports. The reporting was simple and plain only because new events struck the reporters as so obviously part of a recurrent pattern of occurrences. If interpretation was simple or even neglected entirely, it was only because the proper interpretation seemed self-evident. Behind the bare-bones recording of occurrences lay an unmistakable commitment to interpretation by authority.

Mary Dyer's monstrous birth, for instance, was at first concealed, with the consent of the Reverend John Cotton, who thought the divine message contained in it might have been intended for the private instruction of the parents alone. Governor Winthrop listened to this argument courteously, then brushed it aside. The interpretation of such an occurrence must be a public, not a private, matter. As the official leaders of the community, he and the other magistrates would decide what it meant.[61] This pattern persisted. In all the teleological literature the people were urged to open their eyes to the events of the age, but they must see what the authorities wanted them to see.

Authoritative control of interpretation took several forms. Most important, perhaps, was simply the conventional nature of teleological news. Because events were considered part of a recurrent pattern, some events were more likely to be reported than others. They were standard genres, and everyone knew what they meant. The chapters of Increase Mather's *An Essay for the Recording of Illustrious Providences,* for example, nicely suggest the conventional topics of seventeenth-century teleological news: shipwrecks, preservations, thunder and lightning, tempests, witches and demons, deformities, and so on. No matter how strange or new, such events were meaningful, for they were merely the latest recurrences of types of events that fit into the larger pattern of God's work in history.

Other forms of authoritative control over interpretation were more direct. One was the designation by the government of official days of humiliation and thanksgiving keyed to current public occurrences. Although New Englanders were encouraged to examine their own lives in private and to meditate upon their private sins, the interpretation of current events was made explicitly public through specific governmental proclamation. Another form of authoritative control lay in the system of public preaching. The simple regularity of community worship and the centrality of the sermon in the New England church placed each local minister in a unique position to interpret events, as they happened, week by week.[62]

Control by authority was most strict and centralized when publication was involved. In 1662 the General Court set up an official board of censorship "for prevention of irregularities & abuse to the authority of this country by the printing presse." This system of supervising and licensing publication continued, on and off, until it gradually faded away in the early eighteenth century. One of the members of the licensing board in the 1670s, when printing was first permitted in Boston, was none other than the chief customer of the press, Increase Mather.[63] There were nongovernmental controls on publication as well. For example, though the ministers encouraged widespread collecting of providential stories, they sought only centralized, authorized publication. The 1681 proposal for "the Recording of Illustrious Providences," passed by a general meeting of the ministers of the colony, was explicit: "When any thing of this Nature shall be ready for the Presse, it appears on sundry Grounds very expedient, that it should be read, and approved of at some Meeting of the Elders, before Publication."[64]

In times of troubles, when divine providences seemed to multiply, the centralized control over the interpretation and publication of current events tended at first to strengthen the authority of the elite. This was true, for example, during King Philip's War. This catastrophe produced a flood of publications: proclamations, news sheets, narratives, and instant histories.[65] The worse the calamity, the stronger the claim to authority of those prophets who had seen it coming. Increase Mather exalted in that rejuvenated authority during King Philip's War: "Hearken to the voice of God in the Ministry of his Word, mind what the Messengers of God speak in his name, for surely the Lord will do nothing, but he revealeth his secrets to his Servants the Prophets."[66]

King Philip's War was the first great news story for the Boston press, and nearly all of the first local publications on the war rested squarely within the authoritative teleological news tradition. This includes, of course, Increase Mather's *A Brief History,* the sole purpose of which was to teach New England to obey the Lord. Other instant accounts include Benjamin Tompson's *New Englands Crisis* and Thomas Wheeler's *A Thankefull Remembrance,* both highly empirical and providential narratives. Utilitarian proclamations issued by the magistrates during the war were also sometimes steeped in an overtly teleological understanding of events: "The Lord hath been, and is still debating with us, we having greatly incensed him to stir up many Adversaries against us."[67] Even William Hubbard's largely secular narrative of the conflict, published in 1677, took for granted that the war was a meaningful and intelligible episode in the history of God's work in New England.[68]

But despite a shared conviction that the events of the war were teleological news, and despite a shared commitment to reportorial empiricism and authoritative interpretation, Increase Mather and William Hubbard produced narratives that were quite different. Mather's account portrayed the events of the war as showing God's displeasure with specific public sins, and his *Brief History,* therefore, reflected rather badly on the civil authorities' management of public morality in the colony. Hubbard's account was much more general and distant in its reading of divine providence, and his *Narrative* showed the colonial administration in a much more favorable light. Both Mather and Hubbard had no doubt that the events of the war pointed toward a single authoritative interpretation. But in this crisis the authorities of the colony were split; and as authority itself wavered, so did the authoritative meaning of God's handiwork.[69]

The disagreement between Mather and Hubbard was only the beginning of trouble for the authoritative interpretation of news. King Philip's War also stirred up an entirely new sort of journalism that was unconcerned with interpretation by authority. Most of this material wasn't published immediately, but the fact that it was published at all suggests even more strongly than the Mather-Hubbard controversy what could happen in a system that emphasized the eclectic reporting of events: Reporting had the potential to drift beyond the control of authoritative interpretation.[70]

An early example of this alternative journalism was Mary Rowlandson's account of her captivity by the Indians, *The Soveraignty and Goodness of God*, published in 1682. This was the first of what would become a very popular genre of American literature, the captivity narrative. Like the instant histories, Rowlandson's story seemed to be a simple chronological report of occurrences. Yet thematically, it was a much more subtle and personal work. As its title suggests, its theme was God's providence. But the perspective was much more individual than public. Mrs. Rowlandson's story was not antithetical to a public, teleological interpretation, just different. Another example of alternative journalism, written at the time of the war, was Peter Folger's *A Looking Glass for the Times*, a political tract in verse. In subject and style Folger's piece was conventional teleological news; its purpose was to read the providential meaning of current events. But the meaning Folger saw in events was unconventional and unorthodox. He viewed the war as God's punishment upon the Puritan authorities for their persecution of Quakers and Baptists. Folger's tract probably circulated in manuscript form in the 1670s. Benjamin Church's *Entertaining Passages Relating to Philip's War* was antithetical not only to the authoritative interpretation of the war but to the very idea of teleological news. Church was a frontiersman and leader of troops in battle, and his narrative was a story of self-reliant individualism. Divine providence entered into his story not at all. Significantly, Church's narrative did not appear in print in Boston until 1716 and Folger's not until 1725.[71]

In the seventeenth century there was little disharmony in print between the reporting and the authoritative interpretation of occurrences. But as the Mather-Hubbard controversy and the Folger, Rowlandson, and Church narratives suggest, an eclectic, decentralized method for reporting events has the potential to undermine the centralized, authoritative interpretation of them. Events have lives of their own, and people will read out of them what they will. Witchcraft, for example, provides another illustration of how New Englanders read public meaning from current events. The history of witchcraft accusations as well as slander charges that involved witchcraft suggests how the widespread observation, reporting, and interpretation of occurrences by common folk could take turns quite different from what the authorities had in mind.[72] Even the simple crime narrative suggests this tension. The purpose of execution sermons and criminal conversion narratives in New England was clear: to affirm public authority and divine order. Yet it was also possible to read out of these narratives (even those published by authorities such as Cotton Mather) an individualistic defiance of authority and order, and that defiance gradually came to dominate the genre in the eighteenth century.[73]

The potential for heresy lurks in journalism as well as in religion. The situation is perfectly analogous to doctrinal conflict in Bible-based Protestantism. When believers are urged to search the Scriptures, they sometimes see things that the authorities do not see. *Sola scriptura* and the priesthood of all believers are the formulas for schism. So it is in journalism—that is, in reading God's book of occurrences. Thus the characteristics of news and news reporting that emerged in seventeenth-century New England—current-event orientation, supported by reportorial empiricism and authoritative interpretation—left a wonderfully ambiguous legacy, a legacy for *both* orthodoxy and heresy in modern American journalism.[74]

* * *

By the time the newspaper arrived in New England in the early eighteenth century, the news system was in place. Of course, the newspaper itself was nothing new. New Englanders had long read newspapers from England, and to a large extent the first American newspapers simply copied the London newspaper press of the time.[75] Still, though derivative of the London model, the style of newspaper journalism that emerged in eighteenth-century America was also remarkably consistent with the teleological news system of seventeenth-century New England. Though increasingly secular, the news would remain event oriented, devoted to unusual (but conventional) occurrences, and dependent upon the method of reportorial empiricism. Newspapers would also tend to remain within the fold of authority, but journalistic heresy would grow endemic in the system as well.

The first successful American newspaper, the *Boston News-Letter,* founded in 1704, is a case in point. Though the paper sometimes carried pamphlet reprints, political speeches, and opinion pieces, it was essentially a weekly journal of occurrences. This reflected the London model, much beloved of the *News-Letter* proprietor John Campbell. Campbell was the postmaster of Boston, closely associated with the governor's circle in Massachusetts, and closely linked with other New England authorities through a handwritten newsletter service that he had conducted before he turned to print. During his years as editor of the *Boston News-Letter,* Campbell's main concern was to build an ongoing public record of events. He made this purpose clear in a self-congratulatory summary statement at the end of his first year in business: "And if any will consult the Publick Prints of England in that time, considering that they Print 2 or 3 times a week, & that we did Print here but once in a week; they will find no one piece of material News that is in them, omitted in ours: As also in our Prints you have the publick Occurrences from the West-Indies and other parts: and likewise those from our Neighbouring Provinces, besides those of this and the Province of New-Hampshire . . . and a great many Providences now Recorded, that would otherwise be lost."[76]

In other words, Campbell's purpose was to imitate the London newspaper press while also continuing the tradition of the "recording of providences." The first year of publication set the pattern. The lead news was usually European chronology—court politics, battle action, official pronouncements— reported as sequentially as possible. Political news from Boston and the other American colonies was spottier but also wedded, as much as Campbell could make it, to a chronological record of official events. Then there were the "providences." Reports of storms, fires, executions, and other such familiar fare appeared in the first year's run of the *Boston News-Letter*. How these occurrences were handled suggests something about the new role for the newspaper in the teleological news system of New England.

Most of Campbell's providential items were factual and terse. He mentions in a brief story about a fire in the Anchor Tavern that the blaze was quickly put out "by God's good and signal Providence." But usually only the facts, no interpretations, were presented. For example: "On Friday last, There was a great Thunder Shower of Rain, together with great Hail stones." That is the complete story and a fairly typical one.[77] Several major events drew more extended coverage in the *News-Letter* in 1704. For several issues, the paper carried accounts of a great storm that had swept through England and Europe. On the local level Campbell published a series of stories on the capture, trial, and execution of several pirates in Boston. Like the reports of the storm in Europe, the piracy news was highly empirical, with very few interpretive statements included.[78]

The interpretation of these occurrences was supplied outside the newspaper by the ministerial and political elite. The very afternoon of the Anchor Tavern fire, both Increase Mather and Samuel Willard prayed and preached on the subject. Cotton Mather delivered a sermon on the execution of the pirates and published it shortly thereafter. Increase Mather preached at least twice on the great storm in Europe. He reviewed the details of the news and then moved on to the standard teleological theme: Storms were "public judgments" sent by God to punish sin and to presage other calamities.[79]

Interpretation in the newspaper itself came almost exclusively in the form of official political statements. Punctuating the terse chronologies were the texts of proclamations and speeches by the governor, the queen, and the Parliament.[80] Governmental authority was the only voice of interpretation in the *Boston News-Letter*. For reporting the facts of occurrences, however, Campbell relied on whatever information happened to come to him. In his third issue, for example, he related an exciting story about a young girl kidnapped briefly by Indians. It turned out to be a hoax, concocted and reported by the girl herself. This was probably the first, though certainly not the last, time Campbell was hoodwinked by an unreliable source.[81] But, then, he never saw the systematic verification of information as his duty. Following in the tradition of reportorial empiricism, he simply recorded information supplied to him by his sources.

In this way the *Boston News-Letter* continued the news selection and reporting style that had characterized the teleological news system of seventeenth-century New England. When overtly interpretative material was included, it was official and authoritative. But for the most part, Campbell's method was plain, reportorial empiricism. Usually, there was no interpretation at all, especially of the "providential" occurrences. Perhaps, like his seventeenth-century Puritan predecessors, Campbell assumed that the meaning of these occurrences was self-evident. Or perhaps, like a more secular citizen of the new century, he assumed that readers could, would, even should make of these occurrences what they chose. Whatever the case, Campbell was pleased to leave the interpretation out of the newspaper, to report teleological news but without the teleology.

Not all early eighteenth-century newspapers were as deferential to authority as the *Boston News-Letter,* and not all were as concerned about recording the official "thread of occurrences" in European politics. Some remained overtly religious and providential in tone. Many carried a good deal of interpretation, in the form of political essays and commentary. Yet, despite enormous differences, all were devoted to the recording of current events and to reportorial empiricism. Even James Franklin's *New-England Courant,* the first overtly heretical newspaper in America, fit the emerging pattern. Indeed, Franklin, an ambitious political outsider, cunningly used the tradition of reportorial empiricism to justify his assault upon the authority of Boston's ministerial elite. For example, during the controversy that raged in Boston in 1721–22 over smallpox inoculation, Franklin declared his newspaper "impartial." "The *Courant* was never design'd for a Party Paper," he wrote. "I have once and again given out, that both Inoculators and Anti-Inoculators are welcome to speak their Minds in it. . . . What my own Sentiments of things are, is of no Consequence, nor any matter to any Body."[82]

Franklin claimed impartiality because he simply reported the statements of his sources. He did not investigate anything himself; he merely reported. Of course, nearly all of his sources happened to be opposed to inoculation as well as highly critical of local ministerial authority. To the old guard, such as Increase Mather, then in his eighties, Franklin's newspaper was reckless, impudent, and outrageous—a libelous assault upon traditional authority. Indeed, it was. But it was also couched in the style of reportorial empiricism that Mather himself had helped to establish nearly half a century before. As Thomas Leonard has put it: "The journalist had taken over the role of Jeremiah." He had taken over the methodology of Jeremiah as well. Like James Franklin, Increase Mather had assured his readers in his account of King Philip's War that he simply reported the facts: "I hope that in one thing, (though it may be in little else) I have performed the part of an Historian, viz. in endeavouring to relate things truly and impartially."[83]

Few American newspapers of the eighteenth century were as blandly orthodox as Campbell's *News-Letter* or as stridently heretical as Franklin's *Courant*. Most fell somewhere in between, including the classic American newspaper of the age, the *Pennsylvania Gazette*. Published after 1729 by James Franklin's brother Benjamin, the *Pennsylvania Gazette* bore a resemblance to both the *New-England Courant* and the *Boston News-Letter*. Like the *Courant*, the *Gazette* was not merely the voice of authority; and like James, Ben relied on the tradition of eclectic reporting to explain the (usually mild) heterodoxy of the paper. As a printer and journalist (if not as a scientist), Benjamin Franklin followed the style of reportorial empiricism, collecting and recording information from whatever sources he could tap. In words reminiscent of the *Courant*'s, he idealized the method in his famous *Apology for Printers:* "Printers are educated in the Belief, that when Men differ in Opinion, both Sides ought equally to have the Advantage of being heard by the Publick." When people complained about something in the paper, he simply invited them to become sources themselves.[84]

In the matter of news the *Pennsylvania Gazette* bore a strong resemblance to the *Boston News-Letter*. The first issue under Franklin's editorship carried a speech by the governor and brief items on foreign occurrences, local elections, local court rulings, and ship sailings.[85] For Franklin, like Campbell, news meant the orderly, factual record of official public occurrences—but not only that. Shortly after he took charge of the *Gazette*, Franklin asked his readers to become sources. He asked them to send in reports of "every remarkable Accident, Occurrence, &c. fit for publick Notice." Apparently, they did, for over the next few weeks the paper carried some remarkable (though not unfamiliar) items: some drownings, a large panther shot, two men hanged, a one-hundred-year-old woman dead, a murder trial, a snake active in winter, and so on. Some were written in the newspaper style that would later be termed *bright*. For example: "And sometime last Week, we are informed, that one Piles, a Fidler, with his Wife, were overset in a Canoo near Newtown Creek. The good Man, 'tis said, prudently secur'd his Fiddle, and let his Wife go to the Bottom."[86]

All of these stories would still be familiar newspaper fare today. And they would have been familiar as well one hundred years earlier in Franklin's native New England. The reporting of current public occurrences mattered to Benjamin Franklin, just as it had mattered to Increase Mather and Samuel Danforth and John Winthrop—but with a difference. What had been divine providence had become, by 1729, simply the news.

* * *

It could be said that in seventeenth-century New England news was anything that might cause the reader or listener to say, "Oh, my God." In the late nineteenth century the same definition was used by the purveyors of popular "yellow" journalism.[87] But by then the news, like the exclamation, had been drained of religious meaning. Just as the phrase "Oh, my God" lived on long after it had lost its force as prayer, so the news lived on after it had lost its role in religion. News that had once been important had become merely interesting.

The method of reporting the news remained familiar as well. The great metropolitan newspapers of the late nineteenth century developed, for the first time, professional reporting staffs. But the enormous eclecticism of news reporting continued, even increased, as newspapers harnessed modern communications technology to the gathering and printing of "all the news," everything that could be gleaned from every varied source imaginable. Some newspapers preferred sensational events: murders, sex scandals, monstrous births. But sensationalism was only part of it, a small part. All newspapers, whether sensational or not, gathered news items simply because they fit the usual pattern of unusual occurrences. The Chicago *Times* of the 1870s and '80s, for example, every day carried long columns of news briefs, thousands of little occurrences reported from all over the world. Here are just the first few items from one such column of news from the Midwest:

> They have a chain gang in Fort Wayne.
> Terre Haute is going to have a soup house.
> An Indiana man has 17,000 cat skins for sale.
> Here comes Greencastle, Ind., with the small pox.[88]

And so on and on and on. What was the meaning of this strange litany? There was no meaning. It was just the news.

The pattern persists in our own day. The astonishing eclecticism of the late nineteenth-century papers such as the *Times* has subsided; newspapers are now more selective and tightly edited. But the reporting of interesting—if no longer important—news items continues in the familiar way.[89] Ordinarily, the news is not very sensational: an auto accident nearby, a hail storm in Texas, a chicken egg shaped like a bowling pin. Major disasters and wonders warrant more elaborate reporting. Even strange births still make the news, especially in the supermarket tabloids:

> 78-Year-Old Granny Is Expecting Twins.
>
> Electric Shock Makes 5-Year-Old Girl Pregnant.
>
> Great Grandma, 66, Has 11-Ounce Baby.[90]

The ring of the news is familiar. Though the stories are singular, they are not surprising. They are part of a conventional pattern. As in the seventeenth century, the remarkable occurrence still seems more an archetypal recurrence than something genuinely new. Only now no one knows what the stories mean.

My purpose in this chapter is not to argue that modern American journalism is nothing more than secular Puritanism or that the modern journalist is merely a fallen saint. Journalism is more complex than that, and Puritanism was far from the only force acting upon American journalism in its formative years. My purpose is more limited. It is simply to suggest that Puritanism in New England—especially the stridently public and communal understanding of the doctrine of divine providence—provided an enormously rich environment for the growth of news and for the growth of a particular methodology for identifying, gathering, reporting, and publishing news stories.

Notes

1. John Winthrop, *Winthrop's Journal: "History of New England,"* ed. James Kendall Hosmer, 2 vols. (New York, 1908), 1:266–68.

2. *Newes from New-England of a Most Strange and Prodigious Birth* [London, 1642]; [John Winthrop], *A Short Story of the Rise, Reign, and Ruin of the Antinomians, Familists and Libertines, That Infected the Churches of New-England* (London, 1644); [Samuel Danforth], *An Almanack for the Year of Our Lord 1648* (Cambridge, Mass., 1648). The Dyer story and the publications connected with it are discussed in David D. Hall, *Worlds of Wonder, Days of Judgment: Popular Religious Belief in Early New England* (New York, 1989), 100–102. In dates throughout this chapter I have begun the new year on January 1.

3. See, for example, Everette E. Dennis and Arnold H. Ismach, *Reporting Processes and Practices: Newswriting for Today's Reporters* (Belmont, Calif., 1981), 30–31; Brian S. Brooks et al., *News Reporting and Writing* (New York, 1985), 4–5; Julian Harriss, Kelly Leiter, and

Stanley Johnson, *The Complete Reporter: Fundamentals of News Gathering, Writing, and Editing, Complete with Exercises* (New York, 1985), 33–37.

4. Quote from William C. Spengemann, "Discovering the Literature of British America," *Early American Literature* 18 (Spring 1983): 7; see also Philip F. Gura, "The Study of Colonial American Literature, 1966–1987: A Vade Mecum," *William and Mary Quarterly* 45 (Apr. 1988): 316.

5. Matthias A. Shaaber, *Some Forerunners of the Newspaper in England, 1476–1622* (Philadelphia, 1929), 151–56; Robert Collison, *The Story of Street Literature: Forerunner of the Popular Press* (Santa Barbara, Calif., 1973), 144–49; Katherine Park and Lorraine F. Daston, "Unnatural Conceptions: The Study of Monsters in Sixteenth- and Seventeenth-Century France and England," *Past and Present* 92 (Aug. 1981): 20–54. On the role of sensational news in folklore see Mitchell Stephens, *A History of News: From the Drum to the Satellite* (New York, 1988); and Harold Schechter, *The Bosom Serpent: Folklore and Popular Art* (Iowa City, 1988).

6. [Winthrop], *A Short Story*, 43–45.

7. Perry Miller, *The New England Mind: The Seventeenth Century* (New York, 1939), 463–65; Sacvan Bercovitch, *The Puritan Origins of the American Self* (New Haven, Conn., 1975), 54–55; David M. Scobey, "Revising the Errand: New England's Ways and the Puritan Sense of the Past," *William and Mary Quarterly* 41 (Jan. 1984): 30–31; Michael G. Hall, *The Last American Puritan: The Life of Increase Mather, 1639–1723* (Middletown, Conn., 1988), 85–87.

8. Miller, *New England Mind*, 216, 228–29; M. Hall, *Last American Puritan*, 167–74; Keith Thomas, *Man and the Natural World: Changing Attitudes in England, 1500–1800* (London, 1983); Keith Thomas, *Religion and the Decline of Magic: Studies in Popular Beliefs in Sixteenth- and Seventeenth-Century England* (London, 1971).

9. David D. Hall, "A World of Wonders: The Mentality of the Supernatural in Seventeenth-Century New England," in *Seventeenth-Century New England*, ed. David D. Hall and David Grayson Allen (Boston, 1984); Richard Weisman, *Witchcraft, Magic, and Religion in Seventeenth-Century Massachusetts* (Amherst, Mass., 1983), 31–34.

10. D. Hall, *Worlds of Wonder*, 72–74; Park and Daston, "Unnatural Conceptions," 20–23; Patrick Curry, *Prophesy and Power: Astrology in Early Modern England* (Princeton, N.J., 1989).

11. Shaaber, *Some Forerunners*, 141–56; Collison, *Story of Street Literature*, 3; Bernard Capp, *English Almanacs, 1500–1800: Astrology and the Popular Press* (Ithaca, N.Y., 1979), 149; Joseph Frank, *The Beginnings of the English Newspaper, 1620–1660* (Cambridge, Mass., 1961), 272.

12. Richard Beale Davis, *Intellectual Life in the Colonial South, 1585–1763*, 3 vols. (Knoxville, Tenn., 1978), 1:67; Lewis P. Simpson, "The Act of Thought in Virginia," *Early American Literature* 14 (Winter 1979–80): 253–54; Gura, "Study of Colonial American Literature," 319. See, for example, John Smith, *A True Relation* (London, 1608), reprinted in *The Complete Works of Captain John Smith (1580–1631)*, ed. Philip L. Barbour, 3 vols. (Chapel Hill, N.C., 1986), 1:31, 33, 41.

13. Sacvan Bercovitch, *The American Jeremiad* (Madison, Wisc., 1978), 176–79; John F. Berens, *Providence and Patriotism in Early America, 1640–1815* (Charlottesville, Va., 1978), 165–70; Paul K. Conkin, *Puritans and Pragmatists: Eight Eminent American Thinkers* (Bloomington, Ind., 1968), 1–3, 34–35.

14. Theodore Dwight Bozeman, "The Puritans' 'Errand into the Wilderness' Reconsidered," *New England Quarterly* 59 (June 1986): 231–51. An excellent overview of American Puritan studies, including a critique of the exceptionalism thesis, is David D. Hall, "On Common Ground: The Coherence of American Puritan Studies," *William and Mary Quarterly* 44 (Apr. 1987): 193–229. For a rebuttal of the idea that New England Puritanism is the source of American culture, see Jack P. Greene, *Pursuits of Happiness: The Social Development of Early Modern British Colonies and the Formation of American Culture* (Chapel Hill, N.C., 1988).

15. Richard D. Brown, *Knowledge Is Power: The Diffusion of Information in Early America, 1700–1865* (New York, 1989); Ian K. Steele, *The English Atlantic, 1675–1740: An Exploration of Communication and Community* (New York, 1986); David Cressy, *Coming Over: Migration and Communication between England and New England in the Seventeenth Century* (Cambridge, U.K., 1987); Hall, *Worlds of Wonder;* Harry S. Stout, *The New England Soul: Preaching and Religious Culture in Colonial New England* (New York, 1986).

16. For biographical sketches of Danforth, see Cotton Mather, *Magnalia Christi Americana; or, The Ecclesiastical History of New-England* (London, 1702), bk. 4, 153–57; and John Langdon Sibley, *Biographical Sketches of Graduates of Harvard University,* 3 vols. (Cambridge, Mass., 1873), 1:88–92.

17. Elizabeth L. Eisenstein, *The Printing Revolution in Early Modern Europe* (Cambridge, Eng., 1983), 147–51.

18. D. Hall, *Worlds of Wonder,* 18–19, 38–39; David D. Hall, "The World of Print and Collective Mentality in Seventeenth-Century New England," in *New Directions in American Intellectual History,* ed. John Higham and Paul K. Conkin (Baltimore, 1979); Kenneth A. Lockridge, *Literacy in Colonial New England: An Enquiry into the Social Context of Literacy in the Early Modern West* (New York, 1974), 69–71. By contrast, the world of print was a much less important one in the American South in the first century of settlement. See Davis, *Intellectual Life,* 2:595–609. Reading has virtually no role in the Rutmans' detailed social history of Middlesex County, Virginia. See Darrett B. Rutman and Anita H. Rutman, *A Place in Time: Middlesex County, Virginia, 1650–1750* (New York, 1984).

19. On the Cambridge press see George Parker Winship, *The Cambridge Press, 1638–1692: A Reexamination of the Evidence Concerning the Bay Psalm Book and the Eliot Indian Bible as Well as Other Contemporary Books and People* (Philadelphia, 1945); Samuel Eliot Morison, *Founding of Harvard College* (Cambridge, Mass., 1935).

20. [Danforth], *An Almanack for the Year of Our Lord 1647* (Cambridge, Mass., 1647) and subsequent editions for 1648 and 1649. See also Winship, *Cambridge Press,* 74–80; and Marion Barber Stowell, *Early American Almanacs: The Colonial Weekday Bible* (New York, 1977).

21. Danforth, *An Almanack . . . for 1647; An Almanack . . . for 1648.*

22. Capp, *English Almanacs,* 271–76.

23. Samuel Danforth, *An Astronomical Description Of The Late Comet, Or Blazing Star, as It Appeared in New-England* (Cambridge, Mass., 1665), 15–17, 21.

24. Samuel Danforth, *The Cry of Sodom Enquired into, upon Occasion of the Arraignment and Condemnation of Benjamin Goad, for His Prodigious Villany* (Cambridge, Mass., 1674), 12–13; Ronald A. Bosco, introduction to *Sermons for Days of Fast, Prayer, and Humiliation and Execution Sermons* (facsimile reproductions; Delmar, N.Y., 1978), lxxiii–lxxxiv.

25. Shaaber, *Some Forerunners*, 141–44; Collison, *Story of Street Literature*, 31–32; Stephens, *History of News*, 100–131.

26. Ronald A. Bosco, "Lectures at the Pillory: The Early American Execution Sermon," *American Quarterly* 30 (Summer 1978): 159, 162, 174; Daniel E. Williams, "'Behold a Tragic Scene Strangely Changed into a Theater of Mercy': The Structure and Significance of Criminal Conversion Narratives in Early New England," *American Quarterly* 38 (Winter 1986): 830; D. Hall, *Worlds of Wonder*, 178–85.

27. Samuel Danforth, *A Brief Recognition of New-Englands Errand into the Wilderness* (Cambridge, Mass., 1671). Danforth was not the first preacher to use the phrase "errand into the wilderness," but his sermon was the first published use of it. On the interpretative uses of this title and the concept of "errand," see Perry Miller, *Errand into the Wilderness* (Cambridge, Mass., 1956); Sacvan Bercovitch, "New England's Errand Reappraised," in *New Directions*, ed. Higham and Conkin; and Bozeman, "The Puritans' 'Errand.'"

28. Danforth, *Brief Recognition*, 19. On the "declension" theme, see D. Hall, "On Common Ground," 221.

29. Sacvan Bercovitch uses *A Brief Recognition* as an exemplar of the jeremiad style. See Bercovitch, *American Jeremiad*, 16; Bosco, introduction, xxi–lxxiii; and George Harrison Orians, introduction to Cotton Mather, *Days of Humiliation, Times of Affliction and Disaster: Nine Sermons for Restoring Favor with an Angry God (1696–1727)*, ed. George Harrison Orians (Gainesville, Fla., 1970).

30. I derived the data reported in the tables through a classification of all the titles printed in New England before 1701 as listed in Charles Evans, *American Bibliography*, vol. 1 (Chicago, 1903). I simply followed the manifest content of the title to make the classifications that appear in table 1.2. (Table 1.1 is a summary of table 1.2.) If the proper classification was not clearly indicated by the title, I did not include that title. I made no effort to purge Evans's "ghost" publications, of which there are many, including some very early almanacs. On the other hand, Evans is short on proclamations and orders, as is clear from a glance at Roger P. Bristol, *Supplement to Charles Evans' American Bibliography* (Charlottesville, Va., 1970). On the whole, I suspect that my count is a somewhat conservative estimate of event orientation.

31. Michael Wigglesworth, "God's Controversy with New-England," in *Proceedings of the Massachusetts Historical Society* 12 (May 1871): 91. This poem was written in 1662.

32. Stout, *New England Soul*, 74–75. Southern ministers preached "occasional" sermons as well, but very few were published. See Davis, *Intellectual Life*, 2:705–22.

33. On the General Court's regulation of printing see Clyde Augustus Duniway, *The Development of Freedom of the Press in Massachusetts* (New York, 1906), 41–82. On the move of printing to Boston see Winship, *Cambridge Press*, 267–69; and Lawrence C. Wroth, *The Colonial Printer* (Portland, Maine, 1938), 18.

34. D. Hall, *Worlds of Wonder*, 182–85; M. Hall, *Last American Puritan*, 136 and 160. See table 1.1.

35. The standard biography of Increase Mather is M. Hall, *Last American Puritan*. Other biographical studies include Kenneth Ballard Murdock, *Increase Mather: The Foremost American Puritan* (Cambridge, Mass., 1925); Robert Middlekauff, *The Mathers: Three*

Generations of Puritan Intellectuals, 1596–1728 (New York, 1971); and Mason I. Lowance Jr., *Increase Mather* (New York, 1974).

36. Increase Mather, *The Day of Trouble Is Near. Two Sermons Wherein Is Shewed, What Are the Signs of a Day of Trouble Being Near* (Cambridge, Mass., 1674); Increase Mather, "The Autobiography of Increase Mather," ed. Michael G. Hall, *Proceedings of the American Antiquarian Society* 71 (Oct. 1961): 302. See also Middlekauff, *The Mathers*, 106–7; and Lowance, *Increase Mather*, 31–32, 60–75.

37. Stephen Saunders Webb, *1676: The End of American Independence* (Cambridge, Mass., 1985), 243. The standard history of King Philip's war is Douglas Edward Leach, *Flintlock and Tomahawk: New England in King Philip's War* (New York, 1958).

38. Increase Mather, *A Brief History of the Warr with the Indians in New-England* (Boston, 1676), 2. Mather's history and several other narratives have been reprinted, with annotations and helpful introductions, in *So Dreadfull a Judgment: Puritan Responses to King Philip's War, 1676–1677*, ed. Richard Slotkin and James K. Folsom (Middletown, Conn., 1978).

39. Increase Mather, *Brief History*, 48.

40. The accounts of an important contemporaneous news event in Virginia, Bacon's Rebellion, 1675–77, make reference to divine providence as the cause of the turmoil, but teleological themes do not shape the narratives in this way. And the Bacon's Rebellion literature was not published in America at the time. See Davis, *Intellectual Life*, 1:74–80; Charles M. Andrews, ed., *Narratives of the Insurrections, 1675–1690* (New York, 1915); and Webb, *1676*.

41. Increase Mather, "Some Proposals Concerning the Recording of Illustrious Providences," in *An Essay for the Recording of Illustrious Providences, Wherein an Account Is Given of Many Remarkable and Very Memorable Events, Which Have Happened in This Last Age; Especially in New-England* (Boston, 1684), xi–xiv. See also Increase Mather, *The Doctrine of Divine Providences, Opened and Applyed* (Boston, 1684).

42. D. Hall, *Worlds of Wonder*, 82–85; Lowance, *Increase Mather*, 89–90; M. Hall, *Last American Puritan*, 72–73.

43. Increase Mather, *Heavens Alarm to the World; or, A Sermon Wherein Is Shewed, That Fearful Sights and Signs in Heaven Are the Presages of Great Calamities at Hand* (Boston, 1681); *Kometographia; or, A Discourse Concerning Comets* (Boston, 1683); *Cases of Conscience Concerning Evil Spirits Personating Men, Witchcrafts, Infallible Proofs of Guilt in Such as Are Accused with That Crime* (Boston, 1693); *The Voice of God, in Stormy Winds. Considered, in Two Sermons, Occasioned by the Dreadfull and Unparallel'd Storm, in the European Nations. Novemb. 27th. 1703* (Boston, 1704); *A Discourse Concerning Earthquakes* (Boston, 1706); *Burnings Bewailed. In a Sermon, Occasioned by the Lamentable Fire Which Was in Boston, Octob. 2. 1711. In Which the Sins Which Provoke the Lord to Kindle Fires, Are Enquired into* (Boston, 1711), 4.

44. For example, see Webb, *1676*; Richard R. Johnson, *Adjustments to Empire: The New England Colonies, 1676–1715* (New Brunswick, N.J., 1981); and David S. Lovejoy, *The Glorious Revolution in America* (New York, 1972). See also Robert E. Moody and Richard C. Simmons, eds., *The Glorious Revolution in Massachusetts: Selected Documents, 1689–1692* (Charlottesville, Va., 1989).

45. Both of these tracts and other Increase Mather pieces are reprinted in *Publications of the Prince Society,* vol. 6: *The Andros Tracts* (Boston, 1869).

46. Quote from Increase Mather, *A Narrative of the Miseries of New-England, by Reason of an Arbitrary Government Erected There under Sir Edmund Andros* (London, 1688), 6–7; see also Increase Mather, "Autobiography," 308. For discussions of Mather's political writing, see M. Hall, *Last American Puritan,* 205, 265; and Lovejoy, *Glorious Revolution,* 154.

47. Cotton Mather, *The Diary of Cotton Mather,* ed. Worthington C. Ford, 2 vols. (New York, 1957), 1:122–23; Cotton Mather, *Call of the Gospel, Applyed unto All Men in General, and unto a Condemned Malefactor in Particular* (Boston, 1686). See also Kenneth Silverman, *The Life and Times of Cotton Mather* (New York, 1985), 47–48; and D. Hall, *Worlds of Wonder,* 182.

48. Quote from Cotton Mather, *The Terror of the Lord. Some Account of the Earthquake That Shook New-England, in the Night, between the 29 and 30 of October, 1727* (Boston, 1727), 5; see also *Boanerges. A Short Essay to Preserve and Strengthen Good Impressions Produced by Earthquakes on the Minds of People That Have Been Awakened with Them* (Boston, 1727). These and other current event sermons by Cotton Mather are reproduced in *Days of Humiliation,* ed. Orians.

49. Cotton Mather, *Brontologia Sacra: The Voice of the Glorious God in the Thunder* (London, 1795), also in Mather, *Magnalia,* bk. 6, 15–20; Silverman, *Life and Times of Cotton Mather,* 195, 197. For a man who published some 388 separate titles in his career, such spontaneity may suggest an attention to efficiency and vanity as much as to teleology. On Cotton Mather's publishing record see George Selement, "Publication and the Puritan Minister," *William and Mary Quarterly* 37 (Apr. 1980): 223–24.

50. Cotton Mather, general introduction to *Magnalia.* The doctrine of divine providence also shaped the first published general history of New England, Edward Johnson's *Wonder-working Providence of Sions Saviour in New-England* (London, 1654).

51. Cotton Mather, *Magnalia,* bk. 6, 1. Another major work of American history appeared almost simultaneously with Mather's *Magnalia:* Robert Beverley's *The History and Present State of Virginia, in Four Parts* (London, 1705). Beverley's history, however, is not at all providential in the New England style but "secular and realistic and environmental." See Davis, *Intellectual Life,* 1:86.

52. Leon V. Sigal, "Sources Make the News," in *Reading the News,* ed. Robert Karl Manoff and Michael Schudson (New York, 1986); Gaye Tuchman, "Objectivity as Strategic Ritual: An Examination of Newsmen's Notions of Objectivity," *American Journal of Sociology* 77 (Jan. 1972): 660–77.

53. Danforth, *An Almanack . . . for 1647,* and for 1648 and 1649; Danforth, *Astronomical Description,* 16–20. This is how most news stories are still reported today. See S. Elizabeth Bird and Robert W. Dardenne, "Myth, Chronicle, and Story: Exploring the Narrative Qualities of News," in *Media, Myths, and Narratives: Television and the Press,* ed. James W. Carey (Newbury Park, Calif., 1988); Robert Darnton, "Writing News and Telling Stories," *Daedalus* 104 (Spring 1975): 175–94; and Paul Rock, "News as Eternal Recurrence," in *The Manufacture of News: A Reader,* ed. Stanley Cohen and Jock Young (Beverly Hills, Calif., 1973).

54. Murdock, *Increase Mather,* 146–47, 167–71.

55. Increase Mather, preface to *An Essay;* Lowance, *Increase Mather,* 89–90; M. Hall, *Last American Puritan,* 170–73. See also Mather's reference to his historical method ("to relate things truly and impartially") in *Brief History,* ii.

56. David Hall describes the common practice of recording providential occurrences in diaries, notebooks, and the margins of almanacs, which, he says, "reveals a wide curiosity about events in New England." See Hall, *Worlds of Wonder,* 82–85.

57. Middlekauff, *The Mathers,* 145. This is precisely the conventional method of modern journalism. See Sigal, "Sources Make the News," 15–16; Tuchman, "Objectivity as Strategic Ritual," 660–77.

58. Silverman, *Life and Times of Cotton Mather,* 247–53; David Levin, "Giants in the Earth: Science and the Occult in Cotton Mather's Letters to the Royal Society," *William and Mary Quarterly* 45 (Oct. 1988): 751–70; George Lyman Kittredge, "Cotton Mather's Scientific Communications to the Royal Society," *Proceedings of the American Antiquarian Society* 26 (Apr. 1916): 18–57. This style is common in Cotton Mather's work. See, for example, Mather, *Magnalia;* and Cotton Mather, *The Wonders of the Invisible World: Being an Account of the Tryals of Several Witches, Lately Excuted in New-England: And of Several Remarkable Curiosities Therein Occurring* (Boston, 1693).

59. Quoted in Silverman, *Life and Times of Cotton Mather,* 252; see also M. Hall, *Last American Puritan,* 170.

60. D. Hall, *Worlds of Wonder,* 26–27, 182; Stout, *New England Soul,* 19, 69. For examples of this organization in sermons over time, see Danforth, *Astronomical Description;* Increase Mather, *Sermon Occasioned by the Execution of a Man Found Guilty of Murder* (Boston, 1686); and Cotton Mather, *Advice from Taberah. A Sermon Preached after the Terrible Fire, Which (Attended with Some Very Lamentable and Memorable Circumstances, on Oct. 2, 3. 1711.) Laid a Considerable Part of Boston in Ashes* (Boston, 1711).

61. Winthrop, *Winthrop's Journal,* 1:267–68.

62. D. Hall, *Worlds of Wonder,* 169; Stout, *New England Soul,* 3–4. Stout writes: "For all intents and purposes, the sermon was the only regular voice of authority."

63. Duniway, *Development of Freedom of the Press,* 41–42, 56, 102–3.

64. Increase Mather, "Some Proposals Concerning the Recording of Illustrious Providences," xi–xiv. See also the concern for authoritative control of publication in a similar proposal of 1694: "Proposals Made by the President and Fellows of Harvard College . . . to Observe and Record Illustrious Discoveries of the Divine Providence" [written 1694], in Mather, *Magnalia,* bk. 6, 1–2. An early official effort to record and control the interpretation of events was made by the General Court, which voted in 1672 to collect and report providences as a way to encourage citizens to obey the Lord. See Nathaniel B. Shurtleff, ed., *Records of the Governor and Company of the Massachusetts Bay,* 5 vols. (Boston, 1854), 4:515.

65. Evans, *American Bibliography,* 1:37–44; Bristol, *Supplement to Charles Evans,* 4–5. For King Philip's War publications, see *So Dreadfull a Judgment,* ed. Slotkin and Folsom; *Narratives of the Indian Wars, 1675–1699,* ed. Charles H. Lincoln (New York, 1913); *King Philip's War Narratives* (Ann Arbor, Mich., 1966).

66. Increase Mather, *An Earnest Exhortation to the Inhabitants of New-England, to Hearken to the Voice of God in His Late and Present Dispensations* (Boston, 1676), 4. See also Stout, *New England Soul,* 78–82.

67. Increase Mather, *Brief History;* [Benjamin Thompson], *New Englands Crisis; or, A Brief Narrative of New-Englands Lamentable Estate at Present, Compar'd with the Former (but Few) Years of Prosperity* (Boston, 1676); Thomas Wheeler, *A Thankefull Remembrance of Gods Mercy to Several Persons at Quabaug or Brookfield: Partly in a Collection of Providences about Them, and Gracious Appearances for Them* (Boston, 1676); *At a Council Held at Boston, Sept. 17. 1675* (Boston, 1675). These accounts are reprinted in *So Dreadfull a Judgment,* ed. Slotkin and Folsom.

68. William Hubbard, *A Narrative of the Troubles with the Indians In New-England, from the First Planting Thereof in the Year 1607. to This Present Year 1677. but Chiefly of the Late Troubles in the Two Last Years, 1675 and 1676* (Boston, 1677). Although Hubbard believed in divine providence and had no doubt that the war was God's doing, his narrative dealt mainly with the secular story of the war and the natural secondary causes of events. See Kenneth B. Murdock, "William Hubbard and the Providential Interpretation of History," *Proceedings of the American Antiquarian Society* 52 (Apr. 1942): 15–37.

69. Anne Kusener Nelson, "King Philip's War and the Hubbard-Mather Rivalry," *William and Mary Quarterly* 27 (Oct. 1970): 615–29; M. Hall, *Last American Puritan,* 118–26. Hubbard's pro-administration stance is especially clear in his election sermon for 1676. See William Hubbard, *The Happiness of a People in the Wisdome of Their Rulers Directing and in the Obedience of Their Brethern Attending unto What Israel Ougho* [sic] *To Do* (Boston, 1676).

70. The war news published in London during the war was outside the authoritative Puritan teleological style. Indeed, the London newspapers and news sheets tended to credit the war to Puritan incompetence and maladministration rather than to divine providence. See Webb, *1676,* 221–22. For a critical narrative written from the Quaker point of view, see [Edward Wharton], *New-Englands Present Sufferings, under Their Cruel Neighbouring Indians* (London, 1675).

71. Mary Rowlandson, *The Soveraignty and Goodness of God, Together, with the Faithfulness of His Promises Displayed; Being a Narrative of the Captivity and Restauration of Mrs. Mary Rowlandson* (Boston, 1682); Peter Folger, *A Looking Glass for the Times; Or, The Former Spirit of New-England Revived in This Generation* (Boston, 1725); T.C. [Thomas Church], *Entertaining Passages Relating to Philip's War Which Began in the Month of June, 1675* (Boston, 1716). Thomas Church, Benjamin Church's son, compiled the book from his father's diaries and correspondence. The Rowlandson and Church narratives are reprinted in *So Dreadfull a Judgment,* ed. Slotkin and Folsom. See also Kathryn Zabelle Derounian, "Puritan Orthodoxy and the 'Survivor Syndrome' in Mary Rowlandson's Indian Captivity Narrative," *Early American Literature* 22 (Spring 1987): 82–93.

72. John Demos, *Entertaining Satan: Witchcraft and the Culture of Early New England* (New York, 1982).

73. Daniel E. Williams, "Rogues, Rascals, and Scoundrels: The Underworld Literature of Early America," *American Studies* 24 (Fall 1983): 5–6; Daniel E. Williams, "Puritans and Pirates: A Confrontation between Cotton Mather and William Fly in 1726," *Early American Literature* 22 (Winter 1987): 233–51.

74. The similarity between journalism and Protestantism is rooted in the shared belief that the meaning of a "text" (a literary text or a sequence of events) lies in the text itself and not in the eye of the beholder. It is precisely this steadfast teleological faith that puts

both Protestantism and journalism at constant risk of heresy. For a perceptive discussion of how the doctrine of *sola scriptura* and the system of religious literacy and printing bred interpretive diversity in popular New England religion, see D. Hall, *Worlds of Wonder,* 242–45. See also Philip F. Gura, *A Glimpse of Sion's Glory: Puritan Radicalism in New England, 1620–1660* (Middletown, Conn., 1984), 3–15; and Brown, *Knowledge Is Power,* 41.

75. The first newspaper to be printed in America was a copy, pure and simple. In 1685 Samuel Green reprinted in Boston the February 9, 1685, issue of the *London Gazette,* announcing the death of King Charles. It is reprinted in *Proceedings of the Massachusetts Historical Society* 13 (Nov. 1873): 105–8. Later American newspapers continued to model themselves on the *London Gazette.* See Charles E. Clark and Charles Wetherell, "The Measure of Maturity: The *Pennsylvania Gazette,* 1728–1765," *William and Mary Quarterly* 46 (Apr. 1989): 279–303; and Willard G. Bleyer, *Main Currents in the History of American Journalism* (Boston, 1927), 1–28.

76. *Boston News-Letter,* Apr. 30, 1705. The best study of Campbell and his relationship to London journalism is Charles E. Clark, *The Public Prints: The Newspaper in Anglo-American Culture* (New York, 1994).

77. *Boston News-Letter,* July 17 and Aug. 28, 1704.

78. *Boston News-Letter,* May 29, June 5, June 12, June 19, June 26, July 3, 1704.

79. Samuel Sewall, *The Diary of Samuel Sewall, 1674–1729,* ed. M. Halsey Thomas, 2 vols. (New York, 1973), 1:512; Cotton Mather, *Faithful Warnings to Prevent Fearful Judgments. Uttered in a Brief Discourse, Occasioned, by a Tragical Spectacle, in a Number of Miserables under a Sentence of Death for Piracy* (Boston, 1704); Increase Mather, *Voice of God.*

80. See, for example, *Boston News-Letter,* Apr. 24, May 8, May 15, June 19, 1704.

81. *Boston News-Letter,* May 8, 1704. A contemporary handwritten note on the American Antiquarian Society copy explains the deception. For another source-based hoax, see *Boston News-Letter,* Nov. 5 and 12, 1705. Charles Clark points out that Campbell never apologized for misleading his readers but rather congratulated himself in a later issue for exposing the hoax. See Clark, *Public Prints.*

82. *New-England Courant,* Dec. 4, 1721. See also Jeffery A. Smith, *Printers and Press Freedom: The Ideology of Early American Journalism* (New York, 1988), 99–100; and C. Edward Wilson, "The Boston Inoculation Controversy: A Revisionist Interpretation," *Journalism History* 7 (Spring 1980): 16–19, 40.

83. *New-England Courant,* Feb. 5, 1722; Thomas C. Leonard, *The Power of the Press: The Birth of American Political Reporting* (New York, 1986), 22; Increase Mather, *Brief History,* ii.

84. *Pennsylvania Gazette,* June 10, 1731, reprinted in Leonard W. Labaree, ed., *The Papers of Benjamin Franklin,* vol. 1 (New Haven, Conn., 1959), 195; *Pennsylvania Gazette,* July 30, 1730. See also J. A. Smith, *Printers and Press Freedom,* 117; and Stephen Botein, "'Meer Mechanics' and an Open Press: The Business and Political Strategies of Colonial American Printers," *Perspectives in American History* 9 (1975): 127–225.

85. *Pennsylvania Gazette,* Oct. 2, 1729. Franklin's prospectus appears as "The Printer to the Reader" in Labaree, *Papers of Benjamin Franklin,* 1:157–59. For a quantitative content analysis of the *Gazette,* see Clark and Wetherell, "Measure of Maturity," 291–300.

86. *Pennsylvania Gazette,* Oct. 16, Oct. 27, and Dec. 1, 1729, and Jan. 6, 13, and 27, 1730. Some of these items are reprinted in Labaree, *Papers of Benjamin Franklin,* 1:164–68, 184–

89. Between 1728 and 1765 stories of accidents, fires, crimes, natural phenomena, and so on—items once called "providences"—made up nearly 15 percent of the *Gazette*'s news space. See Clark and Wetherell, "Measure of Maturity," 293.

87. Another catchphrase in turn-of-the-century American journalism was the "gee-whiz emotion." As William Randolph Hearst's great editor Arthur McEwen put it, "We run our paper so that when the reader opens it he says: 'Gee-whiz!'" Quoted in Will Irwin, "The American Newspaper: III—The Fourth Current," *Collier's* 46 (Feb. 18, 1911): 15. A current expression still carries the religious echo: "Reporters call it a 'Holy shit!' story, the kind that freezes the reader's cup of coffee—or at least the arm holding it—in mid-air." See Carlin Romano, "The Grisly Truth about Bare Facts," in *Reading the News*, ed. Manoff and Schudson, 44–45.

88. *Times*, Jan. 24, 1876, Chicago. See also David Paul Nord, "The Public Community: The Urbanization of Journalism in Chicago," *Journal of Urban History* 11 (Aug. 1985): 411–41 (chap. 5 in this book).

89. Romano, "The Grisly Truth." See also Gaye Tuchman, *Making News: A Study in the Construction of Reality* (New York, 1978); and Herbert Gans, *Deciding What's News: A Study of CBS Evening News, NBC Nightly News, Newsweek, and Time* (New York, 1980).

90. These were the lead stories in three different papers *in the same week: Weekly World News*, Feb. 10, 1987; *Sun*, Feb. 10, 1987; *National Examiner*, Feb. 10, 1987. On the links between folklore and mass media, with special reference to supermarket tabloids and strange birth stories, see Schechter, *Bosom Serpent*, 109–11.

2. The Authority of Truth: Religion and the John Peter Zenger Case

In New York a man may make very free with his god, but he must take special care what he says of his governor.
—Andrew Hamilton, 1735[1]

THIS CHAPTER is about religion in the John Peter Zenger case of 1735. I argue that an appreciation of the religious milieu of the case can help to explain the nature of Zenger's defense, the meaning of the jury's verdict, and the ambiguous legacy of the trial for freedom of expression in America. In essence, the Zenger case was a disputation on *truth* and on how truth is revealed to man. Because this issue lay at the heart of Protestant religion as well as colonial politics in the 1730s, the Zenger case can be seen as an interesting intersection of the two. Throughout their history Americans have been strangely intolerant libertarians, often suppressing individual liberties in the name of a more transcendent freedom. I believe that America's heritage of freedom of expression is ambiguous, at least in part, because of its religious roots. And some of those roots are revealed in the Zenger affair.

* * *

Though religion lay beneath the surface and between the lines of the Zenger case, the overt issues were political and legal. John Peter Zenger's *New York Weekly Journal,* which commenced publication in 1733, has been described as the "first political independent" newspaper in America.[2] This is not quite true. It would be more accurate to call it the first political party paper. The *Journal* was launched by a group of New York politicians, led by Lewis Morris, one of the province's most wealthy and powerful men. The aim of the Morrisite party was to undermine the administration of Gov. William Cosby, who had arrived in New York in 1732. The purpose of the paper was to stir up public opinion in order to turn a narrow political struggle into a popular crusade.[3] Although Zenger was the printer and proprietor of the

Journal, the true editor seems to have been James Alexander, a well-known lawyer, a member of the Morrisite circle, and later mastermind of Zenger's defense.[4]

The content of the *Journal* clearly reflected its unabashed political purpose. The heart of each issue was usually a political essay, either an excerpt from "Cato's Letters" or a pseudonymous letter written by Alexander or one of the other Morrisite leaders. Most of these essays were abstract attacks on tyranny and official abuse of power, but the connection to the Cosby administration was always unmistakable. Like other American newspapers of the time, the *Journal* also carried the usual foreign news briefs, shipping notices, and local advertisements. But even some of the ads were thinly disguised satiric attacks on the governor and his supporters.[5] Not surprisingly, Governor Cosby immediately began to plot his revenge. Throughout 1734 Cosby sought, unsuccessfully, the help of the New York Grand Jury and the colonial assembly in suppressing the paper. Finally, in November 1734 Zenger was arrested and charged with publishing seditious libels. After much legal wrangling and more than seven months in jail, Zenger came to trial in August 1735.[6]

The story of the trial itself is well known, largely because of the perennial popularity of James Alexander's pamphlet *A Brief Narrative of the Case and Trial of John Peter Zenger,* which was first published in 1736 and frequently reprinted thereafter.[7] In the trial, attorney Andrew Hamilton, then the most celebrated of American courtroom lawyers, made his famous plea that truth should be admitted as a defense and that the jury should decide not only the facts of publication but also how the law should be applied. These two principles were good politics in New York but bad law in an English court, and the presiding judge rejected them both. Hamilton ignored the rulings from the bench, however, and appealed directly to the jury. He admitted that Zenger published the statements in question, but he argued that they were true statements and therefore not libelous. And he told the jurors that they had the right to so decide. Hamilton's plea on both principles was persuasive, and the jury brought in a verdict of "not guilty." When the verdict was read, three "huzzas" rang out in the courtroom. And later that night the Morrisites gathered at the Black Horse Tavern to drink toasts to Hamilton and to celebrate the vindication of liberty in America.[8]

The legal and political significance of the Zenger case seemed simple enough to the celebrants that night at the Black Horse. But the meaning of the case has been warmly debated by historians, lawyers, and journalists ever since. In the nineteenth century the trial was generally viewed as a landmark in the growth of political freedom and resistance to tyranny in America—something like the first shot fired in the American Revolution.[9] In the early twentieth century the case came to be celebrated more as a legal landmark in the development of the law of libel. Vincent Buranelli's laudatory account of the trial was probably the apotheosis of this view. He declared in 1957 that Zenger's acquittal "was not just a personal thing, or the wresting of a momentary privilege from an indolent or interested official. It was a legal precedent."[10] After 1960, prompted chiefly by the work of Leonard Levy, historians moved away from this view, generally agreeing that the Zenger verdict had no direct impact on the law of libel and little indirect legal impact of any sort.[11] The standard view today seems to be that the case was neither a political nor a legal landmark but that it did become an important symbolic event for eighteenth-century politics in America—a kind of "guiding light for those who were gradually developing an ideology of freedom of expression."[12]

But what was this developing ideology of free expression? It was not, certainly, an unqualified libertarian commitment to individualism and individual freedom. It was, rather, a belief that people should have the right to speak the truth. This was Andrew Hamilton's plea to the twelve jurymen. He asked them to affirm not the sanctity of Zenger's individual rights but the sanctity of the truth. "*Truth* ought to govern the whole affair of libels," Hamilton told the jury. "For as it is truth alone which can excuse or justify any man for complaining of a bad administration, I as frankly agree that nothing ought to excuse a man who raises a false charge or accusation." Time and time again, Hamilton made it clear that he was pleading only for Zenger's right to speak the truth.[13] Leonard Levy, writing from the perspective of a twentieth-century libertarian, has criticized this doctrine as an exceedingly weak foundation for freedom of expression. According to Levy, "Hamilton did not appreciate that truth is a mischievous, often an illusory, standard that often defies knowledge or understanding and cannot always be established by the rules of evidence." It is "shallow soil" in which to plant the seeds of liberty.[14]

Levy, of course, is probably right. But his perspective is too present-minded, and he misses the point. Truth could not have been avoided as the standard in the Zenger trial, because the nature of truth was what the trial was all about. Hamilton did not, he could not, ask the jury to decide the nature and extent of individualism and free thought. He asked them instead to decide the question, "What is truth?" In our age of relativism and skepticism this would seem to be the more troubling question. But in 1735 the jury was prepared to take it on. It is my contention that the audacity displayed by the Zenger jury in accepting the burden of this great question is understandable only when viewed in the context of religion—religion as displayed in the trial itself, in the pages of the *New York Weekly Journal,* and in the wider society of colonial New York in 1735.

* * *

First, it is clear from the text of the trial that Hamilton meant to associate politics and political liberty with religion and religious dissent. Several of the cases he cited as precedents, such as the famous libel trial of the seven bishops in England in 1688, involved religious disputes rather than purely political matters.[15] In his discussion of the evils that arise when judges and other authorities have too much power, Hamilton used images of religious repression and "popery." He told the jury:

> There is heresy in law as well as in religion, and both have changed very much; and we well know that it is not two centuries ago that a man would have been burnt as an heretic for owning such opinions in matters of religion as are publicly wrote and printed at this day. They were fallible men, it seems, and we take the liberty not only to differ from them in religious opinions, but to condemn them and their opinions too; and I must presume that in taking these freedoms in thinking and speaking about matters of faith or religion, we are in the right.[16]

The phrase "we are in the right" is an important one, for it suggests the centrality of truth. Hamilton did not argue, in this passage or anywhere in the trial, that men should be freed from the obligation of truth, whether in religion or government. He argued only that the history of religion and politics showed that great men, including kings and judges, popes and bishops, could be wrong. The people of England, he said, had learned during the reigns of the Catholic Stuart kings that it was dangerous to trust even "the greatest men in the kingdom" with the power to judge what was true and what was false. So who should judge what is true or false? In a trial, Hamilton said, it must be the jury.[17] And he went to some trouble in the Zenger trial to demonstrate that the question of truth was peculiarly the jury's domain.

Hamilton's argument was twofold. First, he pointed out that the jurymen brought special knowledge to the case from their experience outside the courtroom. "The law supposes you to be summoned out of the neighborhood where the fact is alleged to be committed," he said, "and the reason of your being taken out of the neighborhood is because you are supposed to have the best knowledge of the fact that is to be tried."[18] Actually, this was a rather shaky legal position. By 1735 the practice had already been long established that juries were to consider only evidence presented in the trial itself.[19] The special knowledge of jurors, however, was not the main thrust of Hamilton's argument. His second and main point was that libel exists in the eye of the beholder. For a statement to be libel, it must be "understood" to be libelous. This perceptual quality of libel confounds the issues of fact with issues of law, for in Hamilton's scheme the truth or falsity of the statements must affect how they are "understood." Thus the decision on both fact and law becomes the province of the jury. "Then it follows," Hamilton declared, "that those twelve men must *understand* the words in the information to be scandalous, that is to say false."[20]

Hamilton admonished the jurors that they did not have to defer to any authority on matters of truth. "A man cannot see with another's eye, nor hear with another's ear; no more can a man conclude or infer the thing by another's understanding or reasoning," he told them. Thus "jurymen are to see with their own eyes, to hear with their own ears, and to make use of their own consciences and understandings in judging of the lives, liberties, or estates of their fellow subjects."[21] Hamilton made it clear to the jurors that authority lay within themselves: "A proper confidence in a court is commendable; but as the verdict (whatever it is) will be yours, you ought to refer no part of your duty to the direction of other persons."[22]

To make the point that libel exists in the eye of the beholder, Hamilton talked about the interpretation of Bible passages. He cited passages that speak of corrupt leaders, of blind watchmen, and of "greedy dogs that can never have enough." He suggested that any of these passages could, with the help of innuendoes connecting them to the Cosby administration, be denounced as libels.[23] Like Zenger's paper or any other publication, even the Bible might be interpreted differently by different people. Thus it behooved the jury not to abandon their right of interpretation to an ostensibly higher authority. In matters of interpretation of truth, no man possessed more authority than another.

Hamilton's biblical allusions puzzled and infuriated the first great critic of the Zenger case, a West Indian lawyer who published a detailed rebuttal of Hamilton's arguments in the *Barbados Gazette* in 1737 under the pseudonym "Anglo-Americanus."[24] Though critical of Hamilton on every point, Anglo-Americanus seemed especially annoyed that "the Holy Scriptures [were] brought in to season his jokes." But, he added sarcastically, because this misuse of the Bible seemed "designed only for a sally of wit and humor, I shall not offer to detract from its merit; considering too it had so happy an effect as to set the good people alaughing when they heard the word of God most ingeniously burlesqued in a Christian court."[25]

In fact, Hamilton's exercise in biblical exegesis apparently evoked not derision but "applause" and "approbation" from the spectators in the courtroom.[26] Considering the verdict as well as the applause, it appears that these New Yorkers did not view Hamilton's little homily as a burlesque upon religion. Quite the contrary. They seemed to understand his point very well—

perhaps because it grew naturally from the arguments that had been pro-
pounded both in the pages of the *New York Weekly Journal* and in the sermons of popular preachers of the time.

* * *

In several ways, including religious sentiment, Hamilton's courtroom plea
reflected the principles that John Peter Zenger's newspaper had professed
during the two years before his trial. The themes developed in the *Journal*
were chiefly legal and political, just as they were in the trial. But the association of political liberty with religious dissent was the underlying foundation
upon which many of the key arguments were built. As in the trial, the fundamental question was: What is truth, and how is it revealed to humankind?

The *New York Weekly Journal* is sometimes remembered today as a virtual
anthology of "Cato's Letters." This is an exaggeration, but it is true that those
famous radical Whig essays were frequently and prominently featured. "Cato's Letters," written by John Trenchard and Thomas Gordon, were first
published in London newspapers beginning in 1720.[27] Many American newspapers, in addition to the *Journal,* quickly became devoted admirers of Cato,
and the essays were regularly reprinted and quoted throughout America
during the fifty years before the Revolution. In "Cato's Letters" Trenchard
and Gordon developed a philosophy of liberty that had at its core the concept of freedom of expression.[28] Central to Cato's philosophy was the principle that governmental authority must be limited and that it could be limited only if individuals were free to speak truth to power.

The Cato essays reprinted in the *Journal* always made truth the chief bulwark against the tyranny of power. Like Hamilton in the Zenger trial, Cato
did not advocate "that men should have an uncontrolled liberty to calum-
niate their superiors, or one another. . . . We have very good laws to punish
any abuses of this kind already, and I will approve them, whilst they are prudently and honest executed, which I really believe they have for the most part
been since the Revolution."[29] It was the abuse of these laws to suppress truth
that Cato opposed. So long as men were free to speak the truth, Cato believed,
a wicked and tyrannical government could not stand.[30]

To an extent not often appreciated, Cato's understanding of truth was
rooted in religion. All human authority and power were divinely limited, in
Cato's view. "Power without control appertains to God alone," he wrote, "and
no man ought to be trusted with what no man is equal to."[31] Throughout
the essays Cato associated political liberty with religious dissent. While supporting "right religion" and the "present Protestant establishment," Cato
argued that each individual had the right and the duty to seek truth in his
own way, for the simple reason that no one else could be trusted to do it for

him. "Every man's religion is his own," Cato declared, "nor can the religion of any man, of what nature or figure soever, be the religion of another man, unless he also chooses it; which action utterly excludes all force, power, or government."[32] Truth will triumph in both religion and politics, Cato believed; but it must triumph through its own strength, never through the exercise of human power.[33]

Though truth possessed a life of its own in Cato's philosophy, it necessarily fell to each individual to seek truth for himself: "Every man is, in nature and reason, the judge and disposer of his own domestic affairs; and, according to the rules of religion and equity, every man must carry his own conscience."[34] If individual reason and conscience were the way to divine truth, then the authority of human law, whether ecclesiastical or secular, could never be absolute. For Cato, "the violation, therefore, of law does not constitute a crime where the law is bad; but the violation of what ought to be law, is a crime even where there is now law."[35] Cato never developed the specific argument that juries should decide the law as well as the fact in libel cases. But from the Cato essays published in the *Journal* this notion would have been only a modest extrapolation.

"Cato's Letters" were not the only political essays in the *New York Weekly Journal* that reflected a fundamentally religious understanding of truth and authority. Many of the writers in the *Journal* discussed political liberty and religious dissent in similar terms. In both religion and politics, tyranny was attributed to a false authority based upon power rather than truth. An anonymous essay at the end of 1733 declared: "If we reverence men for their power alone, why do we not reverence the Devil, who has so much more power than men? But if reverence is due only to virtuous qualities and useful actions, it is as ridiculous and superstitious to adore great mischievous men as it is to worship a false god or Satan in the stead of God. . . . A right honorable or a right reverend rogue is the most dangerous rogue, and consequently the most detestable."[36] Another writer described the link between religion and politics in more direct and more general terms: "We often pray for the propagation of Christianity; and yet of how little use would that be to a people who are not yet free? Let us join to it our wishes, that those two invaluable blessings may go together, and that with a religion which is itself freedom, the whole race of mankind may be restored to that liberty which is their undoubted natural right."[37]

Like Cato, the anonymous writers for the *Journal* usually placed the burden of judging truth upon the reason and conscience of the individual. The history of religious tyranny demonstrated the danger of leaving the interpretation of truth in the hands of power. Using a religious example, one writer explained that he agreed that "the abuse, and not the use of the press, is blamable. But the difficulty lies [in] who shall be the judges of this abuse. . . . In Spain and Portugal to write against transubstantiation is a horrible abuse; in England as great a one (though not so fatal) to write for it."[38] Significantly, several *Journal* writers explicitly developed this general notion into a theory of the role of juries.

Much of the discussion of the jury system in the *Journal* was mainly political and legal. Several articles praised the jury system as the most valuable of English political privileges: "this great jewel of liberty, . . . the only security between the king and his subjects."[39] Some of the essays, however, went beyond politics to place the jury system squarely within the realm of religious practice. The key link in this association was the juror's oath. In several discussions of the role of juries, *Journal* writers argued that jurymen were divinely bound by their oaths to be "true" and to do what was right, regardless of human law. "There is none of this story of *matter of fact*, distinguished from *law* in your oath," said one article.[40] Another writer argued that because of their oaths jurors were not required to follow a judge's direction any more than they were required to believe a witness's testimony. They were bound only by God and only to the truth. He wrote that "anything any jury does ought to be *quoadem evangelium,* to be what they laid their hands on taking their oath; when they write *billa vera* on an indictment, they undeniably compare the truth of the contents therein to the truth of the Gospel, and this upon oath."[41]

In sum, though the *New York Weekly Journal* was essentially a political newspaper, it professed a politics with deep religious roots. The easy interplay between politics and religion in the pages of the *Journal* suggests that for many New Yorkers the two were actually one. For example, in an article in early 1734 on the importance of freedom of the press, the author made it clear that freedom of thought and expression played the same role in both politics and religion—that is, the discovery of truth. He added: "Such points of religion and politics do stand upon a very weak foundation, if the maintainers of them can be afraid of having their doctrines and measures fairly examined and brought to the test of REASON and DIVINE REVELATION. Those that deny these maxims sap the foundation of our Reformation and Revolution, upon which our religious and civil rights are now established, and therefore they are justly to be esteemed enemies to them, and friends to popery and arbitrary power."[42]

* * *

Such blasts against popery and arbitrary power in the *Journal* were the standard invocations of Protestantism. But there was more than just the usual dissent in American Protestantism in 1735. In New England and in the Middle Colonies, religious revivals were brewing, revivals that expressed in purely religious terms the same themes of truth and individual conscience that pervaded the Zenger trial and the Zenger press. A close look at the wider religious milieu of the 1730s suggests that the trial of John Peter Zenger may, in some revealing ways, be viewed as part of the early stages of the Great Awakening.

At least since the work of Alan Heimert in the 1960s, the Great Awakening has been made to explain much about American politics as well as religion—perhaps too much. Historians such as Gary B. Nash, Rhys Isaac, and Kenneth Lockridge have found in the religious enthusiasm that swept the colonies in the 1730s and '40s some of the roots of a crisis of authority that eventually expressed itself politically in the Revolution. William G. McLoughlin has even gone so far as to describe "the Great Awakening as the key to the Revolution."[43] More recently, however, Jon Butler has argued that the Great Awakening is largely an "interpretive fiction" concocted by historians. In fact, he says, the revivals were "erratic, heterogeneous, and politically benign"; and historians have been "'over-run with Enthusiasm,'" much like the revivalists they have studied.[44] Yet despite his own perhaps overly strident revisionist "enthusiasm," Butler does demonstrate persuasively the need to look more closely and narrowly at specific aspects of specific revivals in specific places.

For example, the Great Awakening has always been portrayed as a rather modest affair in New York compared to New England. Neither the New York pastors nor their parishioners are well remembered by historians for their theology or their enthusiasm.[45] But New Yorkers were involved directly in the early 1730s in several revival-related controversies, including controversies in the rapidly growing Presbyterian churches. As in the revivals of New England, the great issue for the Presbyterians was, at heart, the fundamental question of Protestant Christianity: How are individuals to know God and God's truth? The answers proposed by the leaders of the revival in the Middle Colonies bear a resemblance to Andrew Hamilton's arguments in the Zenger case about truth and men's apprehension of it. And several of the first and most important revival sermons on this question were published in 1735 in the print shop of John Peter Zenger.[46]

Zenger was an early printer and promoter of the works of Gilbert Tennent, for instance. Tennent, a graduate of the famous Log College founded by his father in New Jersey, was the most important of the revivalist preachers in the Middle Colonies. He began his ministry in New Brunswick in 1726, and soon his several congregations between New Brunswick and Staten Island were stirring with religious life. As in all revivals, Tennent's aim was to break up the "presumptuous security" of nominal Christians. He preached "conviction" and "assurance"—that is, the notion that an individual must feel convicted of sin and must pass through the terror of realizing he was not a true Christian before he could at last feel the genuine assurance of salvation.[47] Tennent's sermons were often filled with hellfire and damnation. But, like Jonathan Edwards, who was then orchestrating a similar revival in Massachusetts, Tennent believed in using the harsh conviction of God's law only to make way for the sweet assurance of the Gospel.[48]

Central to Tennent's revivalist theology was the notion that each individual must experience a direct and very personal conversion. Understandably, his opponents charged that such a view of purely personal conviction and especially assurance undermined the doctrine and authority of the church.[49] But despite the emotional quality of the conversion experience, Tennent never sought to take reason out of religion. On the contrary, He argued in one of his popular New York sermons, printed by Zenger in 1735, that God deals with people "in a way best suited to their rational natures."[50] People have the duty to use their reason to ponder and to choose that which is good—a duty that he called "consideration." "Consideration" was an eminently rational activity, in Tennent's view; but it was also very personal. "This day of *consideration* imports serious and solemn deliberation, when the mind of God is not only understood and known, but seriously pondered and laid to heart," he said. This can happen only "when a person *communes with his own heart* about it."[51]

The belief that conversion was a direct and personal experience, rather than a purely intellectual process of understanding, made the revivalists skeptical of creeds and formal statements of doctrine. This skepticism led to a serious controversy in American Presbyterianism in the 1720s and '30s over the issue of "subscription." Conservatives hoped to protect the church from heretical ministers by requiring them to "subscribe" to the Westminster Confession. Many New York and New Jersey Presbyterians, however, opposed enforced subscription to any creedal interpretation of Scripture. They did not hold that ministers should not be examined. They merely believed that no manmade creed could be infallible, no matter how learned the authorities who devised it. They urged instead subscription to the Bible alone.[52]

The leader of the antisubscriptionist party in the Middle Colonies was Jonathan Dickinson, another minister whose works were published by John Peter Zenger in New York in the 1730s. In an important sermon, "The Vanity of Human Institutions," Dickinson proclaimed that "the Bible is our only directory."[53] Like Tennent, Dickinson urged that each individual must experience the communion of God for himself, without compulsion. In words reminiscent of Cato and the anonymous writers for the *New York Weekly Journal,* Dickinson declared:

> Imposing any terms of communion by any penal sanctions is eminently teaching for doctrines the commandments of men. Every person in the world has an equal right to judge for themselves, in the affairs of conscience and eternal salvation. And all have the same natural right to all the benefits and comforts of life. By what pretense therefore may they be deprived of any natural right; because they don't subject their consciences to other men's decision? What dreadful work has been made in the world by using methods of force in matters of opinion and conscience.[54]

Dickinson went so far as to call religion based on coercion a kind of idolatry. He said:

> If they without conviction submit to our opinions, they subject their consciences to human, and not to divine authority; and our requiring this of any is demanding a subjection to us, and not to Christ. We have indeed a right to give the reasons of our opinion; and to endeavor to convince others, of what we esteem to be truth: But we have no right to claim their assent with conviction; nor to be offended with them, for not thinking as we do; any more than they have to be offended with us for not thinking as they do. For every one have the same claim as we have, to judge for themselves.[55]

Neither Tennent nor Dickinson—nor any of the preachers of the Great Awakening—sought to undermine the authority of religion or of the churches. Their aim was merely to return the churches to the truth; and they believed that God's truth could be discerned by man. But their very belief in the divinity of truth had led them—as it did Hamilton and Cato and the Zenger jury—to the principle that individuals must judge for themselves.

* * *

The Zenger case, then, was as much a religious as a political or legal phenomenon. Like the religious awakenings, the Zenger trial reflected the skepticism for human authority felt by ordinary people who possessed a deep faith in the existence of God and of truth. Like the ministers of "awakened" congregations, who were willing to reject the authority of creeds and hierarchies, the Zenger jurors were willing to reject the instructions of the chief justice of New York. Like the revival converts who asserted their right to interpret the law of God, the Zenger jury asserted the right of ordinary people to interpret the law of man. In both cases the operative principle was not freedom but truth. Andrew Hamilton, like a revival preacher, told the jurors that authority lay not in them but in truth. He did not ask them to condone individualism or to approve individual diversity of expression—only truth. The subtle twist, of course, was that it fell to individuals to decide what truth was. And the authority of God and truth and the authority of the individual turned out to be the same.

Thus did America back into freedom of expression in politics and journalism, as it backed into tolerance and diversity in religion. At its origin freedom of speech and press had little to do with the sanctity of the individual mind. The individual had the right only to serve the truth, as men were free to serve God. Gradually, in the two centuries after Zenger, a genuine philosophy of liberalism and individualism emerged in the realm of freedom of expression. But the recurrent episodes of repression in American history since 1735 surely suggest that the "truth" standard, whether in religion or in politics, still lies just beneath the surface of American liberty.

Notes

1. Andrew Hamilton, quoted in [James Alexander], *A Brief Narrative of the Case and Trial of John Peter Zenger,* ed. by Stanley Nider Katz, 2d ed. (Cambridge, Mass.: Belknap, 1972), 87. The narrative of the Zenger trial was first printed by Zenger himself in 1736.

2. Vincent Buranelli, introduction to *The Trial of Peter Zenger,* ed. Vincent Buranelli (New York: New York University Press, 1957), 24.

3. Gary B. Nash, *The Urban Crucible: Social Change, Political Consciousness, and the Origins of the American Revolution* (Cambridge, Mass.: Harvard University Press, 1979), 140–46. See also Patricia U. Bonomi, *A Factious People: Politics and Society in Colonial New York* (New York: Columbia University Press, 1971), pt. 4; and William Smith Jr., *The History of the Province of New York,* ed. Michael Kammen, 2 vols. (Cambridge, Mass.: Belknap, 1972), 2:3–23. The first edition of Smith's work appeared in 1757.

4. Stanley Nider Katz, introduction to *A Brief Narrative,* ed. Katz, 8. See also Vincent Buranelli, "Peter Zenger's Editor," *American Quarterly* 7 (Summer 1955): 174–81; and Cathy Covert, "'Passion Is Ye Prevailing Motive': The Feud behind the Zenger Case," *Journalism Quarterly* 50 (Spring 1973): 3–10.

5. *New York Weekly Journal,* 1733–34, passim. A few selections from the *Journal* are reprinted in the Katz edition of *A Brief Narrative of the Case and Trial of John Peter Zenger,* app. A; and in Leonard W. Levy, ed., *Freedom of the Press from Zenger to Jefferson: Early American Libertarian Theories* (Indianapolis: Bobbs-Merrill, 1966), pt. 1.

6. *A Brief Narrative,* ed. Katz, 20–23. Katz also includes reprints of pretrial materials, in appendixes B and D.

7. I refer to the text of the Katz edition of the trial throughout this chapter. The standard literal version of the trial narrative is contained in Livingston Rutherfurd, *John Peter Zenger: His Press, His Trial and a Bibliography of Zenger Imprints* (New York: Dodd, Mead, 1904).

8. *A Brief Narrative,* ed. Katz, 101 and passim; Rutherfurd, *John Peter Zenger,* 126.

9. For example, see George Bancroft, *History of the United States from the Discovery of the American Continent,* 10 vols. (Boston: Little, Brown, 1859), 3:393–94; and Richard Hildreth, *The History of the United States of America,* 6 vols. (New York: Harper and Brothers, 1882), 2:360.

10. Buranelli, *Trial of Peter Zenger,* 57. See also John Fiske, *The Dutch and Quaker Colonies in America,* 2 vols. (Boston: Houghton Mifflin, 1900), 2:296; and Rutherfurd, *John Peter Zenger,* 131.

11. Levy, *Freedom of the Press,* xxxi–xxxiii. See also Levy, *Legacy of Suppression: Freedom of Speech and Press in Early American History* (Cambridge, Mass.: Harvard University Press, 1960), 133; Katz, introduction to *A Brief Narrative,* 1–2; and Warren C. Price, "Reflections on the Trial of John Peter Zenger," *Journalism Quarterly* 32 (Spring 1955): 161–68. *Legacy of Suppression* was revised and reissued as Leonard W. Levy, *Emergence of a Free Press* (New York: Oxford University Press, 1985).

12. Paul Finkelman, "The Zenger Case: Prototype of a Political Trial," in *American Political Trials,* ed. Michal R. Belknap (Westport, Conn.: Greenwood, 1981), 40. See also Clark Rivera, "Ideals, Interests, and Civil Liberty: The Colonial Press and Freedom," *Journalism Quarterly* 55 (Spring 1978): 47–53; and Edwin Emery and Michael Emery, *The Press and America,* 4th ed. (Englewood Cliffs, N.J.: Prentice-Hall, 1978), 43–47.

13. *A Brief Narrative,* ed. Katz, 62, 69, 75, 84, and 99.

14. Levy, *Freedom of the Press,* xxxii; Levy, *Legacy of Suppression,* 133.

15. *A Brief Narrative,* ed. Katz, 72. See also Hamilton's discussion of the case of Edward Hales, pp. 85–86, and the London Quakers, pp. 92–93, in the Katz edition. On the trial of the seven bishops see Thomas Macaulay, *History of England from the Accession of James II,* 6 vols. (London: Longman, 1849–1861), 2:990–1039.

16. *A Brief Narrative,* ed. Katz, 87.

17. Ibid., 90–91.

18. Ibid., 75 and 92.

19. Ibid., 227n.

20. Ibid., 69 and 78.

21. Ibid., 92–93.

22. Ibid., 96.

23. Ibid., 95–96.

24. *Barbados Gazette,* July 20, 1737. This letter was reprinted in a pamphlet titled *Remarks on Zenger's Trial, Taken Out of the Barbados Gazette for the Benefit of the Students in Law, and Others in North America* (New York: William Bradford, 1737). It is also reprinted in *A Brief Narrative,* ed. Katz, app. C.

25. *Barbados Gazette,* July 20, 1737, in *A Brief Narrative,* ed. Katz, 180.

26. Cadwallader Colden, "History of Gov. William Cosby's Administration and of Lt.-Gov. George Clarke's Administration through 1737," *Collections of the New York Historical Society* 68 (1935): 337.

27. "Cato" (John Trenchard and Thomas Gordon), *Cato's Letters; or, Essays on Liberty, Civil and Religious, and Other Important Subjects,* 4 vols. (London: T. Woodward, 1733–55). This four-volume compilation was reprinted (1971) in two volumes by Da Capo Press.

28. Levy, *Freedom of the Press,* xxiv; Bernard Bailyn, *The Ideological Origins of the American Revolution* (Cambridge, Mass.: Harvard University Press, 1967), chap. 2.

29. *New York Weekly Journal,* Dec. 9, 1734.

30. Ibid. See also *New York Weekly Journal,* Nov. 11, 1734, and Mar. 4, 1734.

31. *New York Weekly Journal,* Mar. 11, 1734. See also Bailyn, *Ideological Origins,* chap. 3.

32. *New York Weekly Journal,* Aug. 25, 1735.

33. *New York Weekly Journal,* Dec. 9, 1734.

34. *New York Weekly Journal,* Sept. 8, 1735.

35. *New York Weekly Journal,* July 7, 1735.

36. *New York Weekly Journal,* Dec. 31, 1733.

37. *New York Weekly Journal,* Jan. 13, 1735.

38. *New York Weekly Journal,* Feb. 18, 1734.

39. *New York Weekly Journal,* Dec. 3, 1733. See also *New York Weekly Journal,* Jan. 7, Jan. 14, and Feb. 11, 1734, and Jan. 20 and July 28, 1735.

40. *New York Weekly Journal,* Aug. 2, 1735.

41. *New York Weekly Journal,* Jan. 13, 1735.

42. *New York Weekly Journal,* Jan. 14, 1734.

43. Alan Heimert, *Religion and the American Mind from the Great Awakening to the Revolution* (Cambridge, Mass.: Harvard University Press, 1966), viii; Nash, *Urban Crucible,* chap. 8; Rhys Isaac, *The Transformation of Virginia, 1740–1790* (Chapel Hill: University of North Carolina Press, 1982), chaps. 8–9; Kenneth A. Lockridge, *Settlement and Unsettlement in Early America: The Crisis of Political Legitimacy before the Revolution* (Cambridge: Cambridge University Press, 1981), 43–48; William G. McLoughlin, "'Enthusiasm for Liberty': The Great Awakening as the Key to the Revolution," in *Preachers and Politicians: Two Essays on the Origins of the American Revolution,* ed. Jack P. Greene and William G. McLoughlin (Worcester, Mass.: American Antiquarian Society, 1977). See also Richard L. Bushman, introduction to *The Great Awakening: Documents on the Revival of Religion, 1740–1745,* ed. Richard L. Bushman (New York: Atheneum, 1970), xiv.

44. Jon Butler, "Enthusiasm Described and Decried: The Great Awakening as Interpretive Fiction," *Journal of American History* 69 (Sept. 1982): 325.

45. A classic account is Charles Hartshorn Maxson, *The Great Awakening in the Middle Colonies* (Chicago: University of Chicago Press, 1920). See also Michael Kammen, *Colonial New York: A History* (New York: Scribner's, 1975), chap. 9; and Martin E. Lodge, "The Crisis of the Churches in the Middle Colonies, 1720–1750," *Pennsylvania Magazine of History and Biography* 95 (Apr. 1971): 195–220.

46. For a list of the sermons printed by Zenger, see "Bibliography of the Issues of the Zenger Press, 1725–1751," in Rutherfurd, *John Peter Zenger.* See also Charles Evans, *American Bibliography* (New York: Peter Smith, 1941), 2:1730–50. This is a reprint of the original 1904 edition.

47. Leonard J. Trinterud, *The Forming of an American Tradition: A Re-examination of Colonial Presbyterianism* (Philadelphia: Westminster, 1949), 58–59. See also Maxson, *Great Awakening,* chap. 3.

48. Heimert, *Religion and the American Mind,* 39–40. See, for example, Gilbert Tennent, *A Solemn Warning to the Secure World from the God of Terrible Majesty; or, The Presumptuous Sinner Detected, His Please Considered, and His Doom Displayed* (Boston: S. Kneeland and T. Green, 1735). This was the only Tennent sermon published outside New York in 1735.

49. Trinterud, *Forming of an American Tradition,* 60. See also Heimert, *Religion and the American Mind,* chap. 4. While it is certainly true, as Jon Butler argues, that Tennent never attacked the authority of the ministry itself, it is also true that Tennent's attacks on *illegitimate* authority did have an unsettling effect on church hierarchy. Just as in politics, crises of authority in religion invariably begin as attacks upon illegitimacy, not upon authority itself. See Butler, "Enthusiasm Described and Decried," 314. See also Gilbert Tennent, *The Danger of an Unconverted Ministry* (1742), reprinted in *The Great Awakening,* ed. Bushman, 87–93.

50. Gilbert Tennent, *The Danger of Forgetting God, and the Duty of Considering Our Ways Explained* (New York: John Peter Zenger, 1735), 11, 26.

51. Ibid., 5. See also Gilbert Tennent, *The Espousals; or, A Passionate Persuasive to a Marriage with the Lamb of God, Wherein the Sinner's Misery and the Redeemer's Glory Is Unveiled* (New York: John Peter Zenger, 1735), 33, 61.

52. Trinterud, *Forming of an American Tradition,* 43–52; Maxson, *Great Awakening,* 23–25.

53. Jonathan Dickinson, *The Vanity of Human Institutions in the Worship of God* (New York: John Peter Zenger, 1736), 15–16. This was also a recurrent theme of Ebenezer Pemberton, a New York minister and another supporter of the Presbyterian revival whose sermons were published by Zenger in the mid-1730s. See Ebenezer Pemberton, *A Sermon Preached before the Commission of the Synod at Philadelphia* (New York: John Peter Zenger, 1735), 19–20.

54. Dickinson, *Vanity of Human Institutions,* 11.

55. Ibid., 31. Zenger was also the printer and seller for a number of sermons by the famous revivalist George Whitefield in the late 1730s and early 1740s.

3. Newspapers and American Nationhood, 1776–1826

HISTORIANS LOOK BACK for origins; journalists look ahead for outcomes. The conventional style of history is the chronology; the conventional style of journalism is the inverted pyramid. Thus historians tend to begin their stories at the beginning; journalists begin theirs at the end. So where does that leave me, a journalism historian? In an effort to comply simultaneously with the conventions of *both* of my professions—history and journalism— I will begin my story precisely in the middle. The period of American history that I am talking about this evening is the first half-century of independence, 1776 to 1826. As the application of quantitative methodology quickly tells us, the middle is 1801. So, let's begin in 1801.

The year 1801 has sometimes been celebrated as the end of the American Revolution. The story is a familiar one. In that year Thomas Jefferson assumed the presidency, following an election that Jefferson liked to call the "Revolution of 1800." Though bitterly contested, the election was lawful, and the transfer of power peaceful. The Federalists' acceptance of defeat and of Jefferson's inauguration as president signaled the end of the constitutional crisis that had loomed since 1789. For the first time in history, a political party relinquished power because a constitution told it to do so. The Constitution worked. The Republic was secure. And the bright and manifest destiny of an American continent and an American century lay ahead.

But this account of 1801 is a myth—a national myth of our day distilled from a Jeffersonian myth of that day. At the time the losers—the Federalists— saw the scene in quite a different light. They had no intention of fading into a Jeffersonian edition of American history. They believed the country had been betrayed and debauched. Though their party was now splintered and demoralized, the Federalists in 1801 planned their revival and their revenge. They plotted to build a great weapon to carry on the battle to save the country. And what was that weapon? A newspaper—the *New York Evening Post.* The *Post* was launched in November 1801 by Alexander Hamilton's faction of the Federalist Party and placed under the editorship of William Coleman. The purpose of the *Post* was to boost the Federalist cause and to destroy Jefferson. If that purpose required the editor to vilify his party's opponents as liars and traitors, to attack the president as a moral degenerate with a slave harem, or to shoot a Republican dead in the street in a duel, so be it.[1] That was what newspaper work was all about in 1801.

And not just in 1801. Throughout the fifty years after 1776 newspapers were usually outrageously partisan, and factional in other ways as well. Newspapers represented and exacerbated *all* the lines of cleavage in the early Republic. In every case of alleged sedition or treason the newspapers were there: the treason of loyalism, the treason of Republican Jacobinism, the treason of Federalist monarchism, of the Jay Treaty, of the Sedition Law of 1798, of the Virginia and Kentucky Resolutions, of the New England secessionist conspiracies of 1804 and 1814, and of the Missouri crisis of 1819. And on and on. To hear the newspapers tell it, traitors and seditionists lurked everywhere. Even beyond the government, newspapers cultivated faction and dissension. In religion, for example, newspapers in the early nineteenth century were often the carriers of radical evangelical doctrines that undermined the standing order of religious orthodoxy. In other words, when Americans in the early Republic saw treason, sedition, fragmentation, dissension, disintegration, degeneration, disunion, anarchy, and chaos, they usually saw it first in the newspaper.

At this point you may be wondering how treason, sedition, fragmentation, dissension, disintegration, degeneration, disunion, anarchy, and chaos figure into a lecture with the very solemn title "Newspapers and American Nationhood, 1776–1826." That's a fair question. Indeed, it is the question I would like to pursue this evening. Let me rephrase it slightly: Can an instigator of treason be an agency of nationhood? Can an organ of faction be an instrument of nationality? My title, I suppose, gives me away: My answer is yes— but not a simple yes. There is a paradox involved here that begs explanation. The relationship between faction and nation is a subtle one in the American experience. An exploration of how newspapers could have been builders of both is my subject this evening.

The quest must begin with the key concepts: state, nation, and nationalism. In our day the concepts of "nation" and "state" are often fused into a single term: *nation-state.* But the breakup of the Soviet Union and the perpetual crisis in the Middle East should remind us that a "state" is not always the political expression of a "nation." There are multinational states and stateless nations, and there always have been. So distinctions are crucial.[2] By *state* I mean the formal structures of political sovereignty. By *nation* I mean a people, a people who share a culture, the institutions of culture, and a history. By *nationalism* I mean the organized political voice of a nation.

The conventional historical model of the origins of modern nations and nationalism grows from the experience of Central and Eastern Europe in the nineteenth century, where language-based national political movements (such as Polish, Czech, Slovak, and Magyar) rose in opposition to the state (the dynastic realm of Habsburg). The myths of nationalism always locate the origin of the nation in time immemorial, for the legitimacy of the nation derives from its claim on tradition. This is why nationalism is often linked with language and religion, two institutions with appropriately deep historical roots.

The power of nationalism always rests upon its claim to be the spontaneous political expression of a legitimate nation. Yet despite this universal tenet of nationalism, the opposite is often true. Often—perhaps even most of the time—it is not the nation that makes nationalism; it is the nationalists who make the nation. Nations are *modern* entities—invented, shaped, and directed by political will. They are, in the words of Benedict Anderson, "imagined communities." A nation can exist only when people can imagine it, can imagine that they are part of "a people," nearly all of whom they will never know or see. Only in the age of modern political organization (modern state building) and modern communication has such imagination been possible for the vast majority of humankind.[3]

The characteristics of the nation have a great deal to do with the nature of the state into which it is born. American nationhood, for example, is more like that of Latin America than Europe. European nations grew in the wreckage of feudal states and dynastic empires. In the nineteenth century these emergent nations struggled to achieve a new form of statehood: a state contiguous with a nation. In Latin America and the United States it was otherwise. All the American states—in North and South America—were "creole states." They were founded by Europeans born in America. These people shared language and culture with the metropole, England or Spain. In South America every one of the newly independent states of the early nineteenth century had been an administrative unit of a European colonial empire. These states were not created by indigenous peoples but by creoles, often former colonial functionaries. Only the accident of American birth had set them apart from (and made them subordinate to) the Spanish and Portuguese "peninsulars." In other words, these American creoles seized colonial provinces, made them states, and *then* began the tedious task of shaping them into nations.[4]

The story in our part of North American is roughly similar. As in South America, the colonial administrative units became "states," and the erstwhile creole functionaries became nationalists. The difference in North America was that thirteen of these administrative units joined together in a federal union, itself also a state. This was possible partly because the English colonies were so small. (All thirteen comprised an area smaller than Venezuela and one-third the size of Argentina.) Proximity permitted the emergence of an intercolonial creole elite with a shared "American" ethos. But within this ethos vast differences existed that carried enormous implications for both state making and nation making. The idea of union was strong among the elites of the thirteen English colonies. But what sort of union? Where was the sovereign state in these United States? Disagreement over that question was endemic throughout the early national period, before becoming epidemic in 1861, leaving 600,000 dead.

The American case, then, is not an example of a nation becoming a state *or* of a state becoming a nation. Rather it is the case of a nation emerging within the controversies and crises of state building. In the ordeal of the state the nation was forged. And here is where we come back to treason, chaos, and the newspaper. In the first fifty years of independence, in every effort to undermine the government or disrupt the state, the newspaper was implicated. Newspapers were the organizers of faction and sedition. Yet in their efforts to subvert the state, they helped to build the nation. American nationhood coalesced in the constitutional crises of the state. Though organizers of faction, newspapers helped to standardize a political language of state, which came in turn to serve as the mythic language of the nation.

This is not quite what the North American creoles—our founding fathers—had in mind. They were appalled by the ordeal of their state and the role that the newspapers played in it. The federalists and antifederalists of the era of constitutional ratification and the Federalists and Republicans of the era of the first party system argued about the nature of the union, but they believed in the idea of union.[5] Even the most strident states' rights antifederalists (such as Luther Martin of Maryland) saw a role for an American union (though not the role of "state" or perhaps even "nation"). Most federalists of 1787, including those who later became Jeffersonian Republicans, were genuine American nationalists. Jefferson and Madison, for example, struggled vigorously with their adversaries over affairs of state, but both were ardent believers in and promoters of an American nation.

In short, the founders were nationalists. They disputed the nature of the state, but they agreed on the need for institutions of national communication and culture. Some proposed national ceremonies and rituals. Some wrote poetry—national epic poetry—such as Philip Freneau's *A Poem on the Rising Glory of America* or Joel Barlow's *The Vision of Columbus*. Federalist and Republican literati clashed over issues of state and cultural politics, but they shared a vision of an American national literature.[6] Others promoted education for American citizenship. Men such as Benjamin Rush and Noah Webster disagreed on politics yet spoke a similar language of education. Education would fashion model Americans, model republican citizens.[7]

But perhaps the nationalists' favorite institution of national culture was the newspaper. From the Revolutionary War onward, American leaders of all political stripes talked incessantly about the need for a general "diffusion of information," and newspapers were always part of the plan.[8] In 1791 James Madison explained (in a newspaper article) the relationship between public communication and republican government. "Whatever facilitates a general intercourse of sentiments," he said, "as good roads, domestic commerce, a free press, and particularly a circulation of newspapers through the entire body of the people, . . . is equivalent to a contraction of territorial limits, and is favorable to liberty."[9] The next year Congress passed a postal act that clearly established the newspaper as a favored instrument of national communication policy. This act set postage for newspapers so low that newspaper circulation would be heavily subsidized. In the debates over this 1792 act no one proposed setting newspaper rates equal to letter rates; everyone took the subsidy of newspaper circulation to be a proper function of federal policy making.[10] Throughout the period the arguments changed little. In 1817 John C. Calhoun seemed almost to be quoting Madison's essay of 1791. He urged Congress to "bind the republic together with a perfect system of roads and canals. Let us conquer space. . . . It is thus that a citizen of the West will read the news of Boston still moist from the press. The mail and the press are the nerves of the body politic."[11]

Support for the diffusion of newspapers was nearly universal among the national elites, regardless of party. In the 1780s and '90s the Federalists controlled the government, the mails, and most of the newspapers. For them, the newspaper was the bulwark of social order; increased newspaper circulation meant the dissemination of "correct principles" from the nationalist gentry to the masses.[12] The Republicans were somewhat more egalitarian, but they too viewed the newspaper chiefly as a instrument of education and mobilization from the top down. Jefferson's efforts to create a national party newspaper in the early 1790s were quite frankly based on notions of a national center and a provincial periphery. He asked Benjamin Franklin Bache to make his *General Advertiser* "a paper of general circulation, thro' the states, . . . a purely republican vehicle of news established between the seat of government and all its parts."[13] In 1799 Jefferson urged his lieutenants to use the newspapers to propagate the Republican message throughout the land. After the election of 1800 one Jeffersonian editor, sounding much like a good Federalist, attributed the rising tide of Republicanism to "the diffusion of correct information, among those who are uninformed, by means of Newspapers devoted to the cause of morality and freedom." Years later Jefferson himself remembered the Republican press of 1800 for "its unquestionable effect in the revolution produced on the public mind."[14]

This was a kind of administrative nationalism, a nationalism first "imagined" by an elite of creole colonial functionaries who then took the idea to the people. Elites usually play a key role in national movements, as Tom Nairn has so nicely put it: "The new middle-class intelligentsia of nationalism had to invite the masses into history; and the invitation-card had to be written in a language they understood."[15] The American nationalists used the languages of ceremony, of poetry, of art, of education. And, especially, of the newspaper.

But the masses, once invited into history, have a way of doing there what they will—much to the annoyance and sometimes horror of the elites. And elites themselves have a way of fragmenting into factions. So it was in American society, which by 1800 was bubbling with "cultural ferment," in the words of Robert Shalhope.[16] Jefferson's election did not end the Revolution; it broadened it, deepened it, and reinvigorated it. People everywhere—common people, peripheral people—increasingly sought their own place in the new republican society of America. Urban mechanics and artisans developed a brand of radical class-based politics that Sean Wilentz has labeled "artisan republicanism." Western farmers and traders actively resisted the domination of the eastern metropole. And religious people everywhere, especially in rural areas, began to shake off the dust of Calvinism. In 1801 America stood at the threshold of an age, not of national unity but of unprecedented geographical, economic, political, religious, and cultural pluralism.[17]

In the 1790s the press had gradually come to reflect this pluralism. Of course, the elites struggled to maintain their control of the press from the center, to guide the "diffusion of information" from the top down. The orderly distribution through the newspapers of the Declaration of Independence in 1776 and the *Federalist* papers in 1787–88 was what the founders had in mind. When common people rebelled against the nationalist center, their causes at first fared badly in the press. This was true of the backcountry rebellions in Massachusetts and Virginia in the 1780s. It was true as late as 1794 of the Whiskey Rebellion in western Pennsylvania. The Federalists were still able to guide much of the interpretation of that event in the newspapers and the early histories. Federalist editors everywhere condemned the whiskey rebels as Jacobins and traitors, and they portrayed the crushing of the rebellion as a brilliant exercise of national authority and as the apotheosis of General Washington.[18]

If there ever had been a centralized newspaper voice in America, however, this was its last gasp. The press of the Democratic-Republican movement that proliferated in the 1790s was strikingly diverse and decentralized, despite Jefferson's efforts to support a center of national journalism in Philadelphia. Benjamin Franklin Bache's *General Advertiser* (later *Aurora*) emerged as the leading Republican paper after 1793, but it was only one strong voice in an increasingly discordant choir.[19] In 1793 and after, Democratic-Republican clubs sprang up all across the country to support revolution abroad and republicanism at home. These clubs brought common people into the political process and into journalism as well. The newspapers in the 1790s swelled with invective against the government, from readers as well as from editors and politicians. When the Federalists denounced these people as rabble, they responded with newspaper essays proudly signed "one of the swinish multitude" or "only a mechanic and one of the rabble." And they mocked the Federalists as men who "despise mechanics because they have not snored through four years at Princeton."[20]

President Washington hated the Democratic-Republican clubs and denounced them as "the most diabolical attempts to destroy the best fabric of human government and happiness, that has ever been presented for the acceptance of mankind." He hated them as much for their independence as for their ideology. They were "self created," decentralized, anarchic.[21] The same charges were levied against the Republican newspapers, by Washington and others. Jefferson defended them. "It is wonderful indeed," he said, "that the President should have permitted himself to be the organ of such an attack on the freedom of discussion, the freedom of writing, printing and publishing."[22]

This was just the beginning. The Republican movement grew steadily more diverse and more hostile to the central government. The papers brimmed with charges of bribery, thievery, and treachery of every sort. By 1798 the government had had enough; Congress passed the Sedition Law, an act to punish "any false, scandalous, and malicious writing or writings against the government of the United States."[23] Under the Sedition Law twenty-five persons were arrested, ten tried, and ten convicted—mostly Republican printers. Nearly every opposition newspaper suffered under the "reign of terror," as Jefferson called it. The Republicans responded with the Virginia and Kentucky Resolutions, which declared the law unconstitutional and which came perilously close to the states' rights doctrine of "nullification." The century ended in violent controversy over the nature of the state, and the newspapers were at the center of it.

The election of Jefferson did not end the controversy; it merely turned the tables. Now the Republicans were in, the Federalists out. And the Federalist press—newspapers such as William Coleman's *New York Evening Post*—carried the opposition from the periphery (now New England and New York) to the center (now Washington). The Federalist press during the early years of the nineteenth century was just as diverse and seditious as the Republican press of the 1790s. New England newspapers did all they could to undermine Jefferson's diplomacy, subvert the embargo of 1807, and obstruct the war effort that followed. If Republicans of the South and West had embraced nullification in 1798, the Federalists of the Northeast courted secession in 1804 and 1814.[24] And the newspapers again were in the thick of it. Stung by the constant abuse, even Jefferson, a true friend of press freedom, suggested that "a few prosecutions of the most prominent offenders would have a wholesome effect in restoring the integrity of the presses."[25]

Though the Federalist Party collapsed with the end of the war in 1815, this did not exactly herald an "Era of Good Feelings," as this period once was called. The feelings seemed good only because they were so weak in Washington. Power and controversy retreated to the states after 1815, and the national parties disappeared along with their relevance. The westward movement had long fed sectional differences and animosities (North/South, East/West), and these were now multiplied a hundredfold by the Louisiana Purchase. A better name for this period might be, in the words of Robert Wiebe, "The Era of State Power." With the threat of foreign war ended, people turned their attention to private enterprise and to the states, which were positioned to promote and subsidize it. Washington withered. From Congress, Henry Clay reported that "the topic of disunion is frequently discussed with as little emotion as an ordinary affair of legislation." Silas Wright, a New York politician, had a maxim: "Love the state and let the nation save itself."[26]

When the crisis over the extension of slavery into Missouri erupted in 1819, the aging Jefferson heard it as "a fire-bell in the night." The fragmentation of the country into geographical factions, which Washington had warned against in his Farewell Address, now seemed at hand. But few heard the alarm. The compromise—the papering over of the crisis—was faint comfort to Jefferson, but it seemed to satisfy most Americans, who were anxious to get on with the business of business. The end of a half-century of colonial and international war had changed everything. States now rushed ahead with plans for "internal improvements"—harbors, roads, and canals. People rushed westward. And the federal government languished. In the words of Robert Wiebe: "Now the national government mattered so little that irrelevance threatened to dissolve the union."[27]

Some national men in the tradition of the founders still carried on in the Washington of the 1820s. Daniel Webster, Henry Clay, and John C. Calhoun come to mind, although Calhoun was soon to drift stateward as well. But many nationalists seemed to despair of government. Rather than smashing up in political warfare, the country now seemed more likely simply to fade away, following the sun over the western horizon. Many nationalizers turned to private institutions: colleges, home missionary societies, Bible and tract societies, reform associations. They hoped to use private enterprise to battle the centrifugal forces of privatism.[28] Lyman Beecher said it well in 1820 in an address to the Charitable Society for the Education of Indigent Pious Young Men for the Ministry of the Gospel:

> The integrity of the Union demands special exertions to produce in the nation a more homogeneous character and bind us together with firmer bonds. . . . The prevalence of pious, intelligent, enterprising ministers through the nation, at the ratio of one of a thousand, would establish schools, and academies, and colleges, and habits, and institutions of homogeneous influence. These would produce a sameness of views, and feelings, and interests, which would lay the foundation of our empire upon a rock. Religion is the central attraction which must supply the deficiency of political affinity and interest.[29]

Most newspapers reflected the turn outward to the West and inward to the states. The number of newspapers grew remarkably in the fifteen years after 1810—from fewer than four hundred to more than eight hundred. This number made the United States by far the greatest newspaper country in the world. In second place was Great Britain, with about half that number.[30] Most of these newspapers were small weeklies scattered across the land. They carried large amounts of foreign and national news, and they spoke the same language of liberty and republicanism. But their political and cultural orientations were to their states. They represented state parties and state economic interests. More than ever before, newspapers became boosters of private business and the politics of economic development. Once again, newspapers reflected the political disaggregation and decentralization of the country.

From time to time in the 1820s Americans (and their newspapers) were briefly able to raise themselves high enough to see the country as a whole, to see the *nation*. On July 4, 1826—fifty years to the day after the Declaration of

Independence—John Adams and Thomas Jefferson died. This "double apotheosis" of "twin sons of liberty," this "setting of two suns" on the same historic day, was an astonishingly providential and national event. As the news slowly spread from Quincy and Monticello throughout the land, Americans were awakened by their own past. They seemed to realize with some surprise, as Merrill Peterson put it, that they "had a past, a golden age, a glorious heritage."[31] Adams and Jefferson had been bitter foes in the political wars of the '90s. But in the last fourteen years of their lives they had renewed their correspondence and their affection. Their reunion, now consummated in patriotic death on the Fourth of July, seemed laden with symbolic meaning for the nation. Everywhere orators and newspapers drew from it lessons of harmony, unity, and nationality.[32]

Most of the orators and newspaper writers seemed to equate reunion and harmony. But, in fact, this was not the case for Adams and Jefferson. They were reunited but never harmonious. Early in their renewed correspondence, Adams had written to Jefferson: "You and I ought not to die, before we have explained ourselves to each other."[33] They tried but failed. On the most fundamental issues of political philosophy and statecraft, neither fully appreciated what the other was saying. Yet despite their enduring and passionate disagreement, their affections grew as their correspondence continued. *Despite* may be the wrong word here. Perhaps *because* of their passionate disagreement their affections grew. Perhaps their love (Adams's word) lived in that endless controversy.

And perhaps the same might be said of the nation. In political matters Americans have never succeeded in explaining themselves to each other— certainly not in the period 1776–1826. In the early years of the Republic the state was fragile and its future uncertain. Disputes over the key terms of political philosophy and practice were incessant, passionate, and sometimes violent. Americans used the same words, but the meanings were different. Yet the conversation went on, and in that conversation grew the symbolic language of the nation: republicanism, liberty, independence, representation, separation of powers, popular sovereignty, the people. In the controversy of the *state*—the ordeal of the union—the *nation* was born. In other words, to be an American was to participate in the "revolutionary dialogue" that Adams and Jefferson had begun.

In the early Republic newspapers did not soften or diffuse the hostilities generated by this dialogue. On the contrary. They amplified the hostilities and intensified the crises of the state. But they made the dialogue possible. And that is the link between newspapers and American nationhood, 1776– 1826.

Notes

1. Allan Nevins, *The Evening Post: A Century of Journalism* (New York: Boni and Liveright, 1922), 36, 48, and chap. 1 passim.

2. John Breuilly, *Nationalism and the State* (New York: St. Martin's, 1982).

3. Benedict Anderson, *Imagined Communities: Reflections on the Origins and Spread of Nationalism* (London: Verso, 1983), 13–15.

4. Ibid., chap. 4.

5. J. R. Pole, *The Idea of Union* (Alexandria, Va.: Bicentennial Council of the Thirteen Original States Fund, 1977).

6. Robert E. Shalhope, *The Roots of Democracy: American Thought and Culture, 1760–1800* (Boston: Twayne, 1990), chap. 3.

7. Ibid., 116.

8. Jefferson uses the phrase "diffusion of information" in his first inaugural address.

9. Quoted in Robert A Gross, "Printing, Politics, and the People," *Proceedings of the American Antiquarian Society* 90 (Oct. 1989): 389.

10. Richard B. Kielbowicz, *News in the Mail: The Press, Post Office, and Public Information, 1700–1860s* (Westport, Conn.: Greenwood, 1989), 32–34.

11. Quoted in Richard Kielbowicz, "The Press, Post Office, and Flow of News in the Early Republic," *Journal of the Early Republic* 3 (Fall 1983): 280.

12. Robert H. Wiebe, *The Opening of American Society: From the Adoption of the Constitution to the Eve of Disunion* (New York: Knopf, 1984), 38–41; Gross, "Printing, Politics, and the People," 388–89.

13. Quoted in Jeffery A. Smith, *Franklin and Bache: Envisioning the Enlightened Republic* (New York: Oxford University Press, 1990), 107.

14. Both quotations are in Donald H. Stewart, *The Opposition Press of the Federalist Period* (Albany: State University of New York Press, 1969), 633–34.

15. Tom Nairn, *The Break-up of Britain* (London: New Left Books, 1977), 340.

16. Shalhope, *Roots of Democracy,* chap. 6.

17. Ibid., 165. See also Sean Wilentz, *Chants Democratic: New York City and the Rise of the American Working Class, 1788–1850* (New York: Oxford University Press, 1984); and Nathan O. Hatch, *The Democratization of American Christianity* (New Haven, Conn.: Yale University Press, 1989).

18. Mary K. Bonsteel Tachau, "A New Look at the Whiskey Rebellion," in *The Whiskey Rebellion: Past and Present Perspectives,* ed. Steven R. Boyd (Westport, Conn.: Greenwood, 1985).

19. On Bache and his journalism see Smith, *Franklin and Bache,* chap. 7.

20. Quoted in Shalhope, *Roots of Democracy,* 156.

21. Wiebe, *Opening of American Society,* 73–74.

22. Quoted in Merrill D. Peterson, *Adams and Jefferson: A Revolutionary Dialogue* (Athens: University of Georgia Press, 1976), 80.

23. Text of the law reprinted in James Morton Smith, *Freedom's Fetters: The Alien and Sedition Laws and American Civil Liberties* (Ithaca, N.Y.: Cornell University Press, 1956), 441–42.

24. Richard Buel Jr., *Securing the Revolution: Ideology in American Politics, 1789–1815*

(Ithaca, N.Y.: Cornell University Press, 1972), chap. 12. In his chapter on the New England secessionist "conspiracy" of 1804, Henry Adams put it rather nicely: "The Federalists in Congress wrought themselves into a dangerous state of excitement." See Henry Adams, *History of the United States of America during the Administrations of Thomas Jefferson* (New York: Library of America, 1986), 409. Adams's nine-volume history of the Jefferson and Madison administrations was originally published by Scribner's in 1889–91.

25. Quoted in Buel, *Securing the Revolution,* 267. See also Leonard Levy, *Jefferson and Civil Liberties: The Darker Side* (Cambridge, Mass.: Harvard University Press, 1963).

26. Quoted in Wiebe, *Opening of American Society,* 202–3, 206.

27. Ibid., 203.

28. Ronald G. Walters, *American Reformers, 1815–1860* (New York: Hill and Wang, 1978), 4–5; David Paul Nord, "The Evangelical Origins of Mass Media in America, 1815–1835," *Journalism Monographs* 88 (May 1984): 3–4. See also Peter Dobkin Hall, *The Organization of American Culture, 1700–1900: Private Institutions, Elites, and the Origins of American Nationality* (New York: New York University Press, 1982).

29. Quoted in Hall, *Organization of American Culture,* 88.

30. Edwin Emery, *The Press and America: An Interpretative History of Journalism,* 2d ed. (Englewood Cliffs, N.J.: Prentice-Hall, 1962), 193; Allan R. Pred, *Urban Growth and the Circulation of Information: The United States System of Cities, 1790–1840* (Cambridge, Mass.: Harvard University Press, 1973), 21; *Statistical View of the United States . . . A Compendium of the Seventh Census,* comp. J. D. B. De Bow (Washington, D.C.: Beverley Tucker, Senate Printer, 1854), 154–58.

31. John Murray Allison, *Adams and Jefferson: The Story of a Friendship* (Norman: University of Oklahoma Press, 1966), 324, 330; Peterson, *Adams and Jefferson,* 128–29.

32. Peterson, *Adams and Jefferson,* 129.

33. Quoted in Peterson, *Adams and Jefferson,* 111.

4. Tocqueville, Garrison, and the Perfection of Journalism

WHAT IS THE PURPOSE of the newspaper in a democratic society? Alexis de Tocqueville thought he knew, and he thought he saw emerging in the United States in the 1830s a newspaper system that would serve democracy well. Tocqueville's vision, however, usually so prescient and sure, was uncharacteristically shortsighted when focused upon the press. Within two years of Tocqueville's visit to the United States in 1831–32, a democratic revolution of sorts in the American newspaper press had indeed begun, with the arrival of the first penny paper in New York City. The first volume of Tocqueville's *Democracy in America* appeared the same year (1835) as the greatest of the early penny papers, James Gordon Bennett's *New York Herald*. But democratization via commercialization, the hallmark of the penny press, was not at all what Tocqueville thought he saw at hand in 1831–32. Tocqueville was misled because he had visited the United States during what was perhaps the most critical turning point in American press history. Tocqueville observed the American press through a kind of democratic, pluralist window that seemed to have opened in America with the rise of voluntary associationism and that would close again with the onslaught of journalistic commercialism. It was a fleeting glimpse of what democratic journalism might have been in America—but never was.

This chapter is about Tocqueville's vision and how that vision was embodied in one American newspaper in the 1830s, William Lloyd Garrison's abolitionist newspaper, the *Liberator*. I will argue that the 1830s marked a lush first flowering of democratic journalism in America—associational, participatory journalism of the sort that Tocqueville heralded. But this flush of democracy in journalism had nothing to do with the rise of the penny press, as standard journalism histories take for granted; in fact, the penny press was inherently inimical to it.

Because the *Liberator* was such a relentlessly personal organ for its editor, it may seem a poor example of associational or participatory journalism. I believe, however, that it is a good example and a useful one, precisely because it suggests that personal, even fanatical, editorship was not inconsistent with the democratic function of journalism. In fact, I will argue that William Lloyd Garrison's vision of participatory journalism was as central to his understanding of human society as was his vision of abolition and universal emancipation.

Certainly, Garrison did not share Tocqueville's rather benign view of democratic pluralism; Garrison had no trouble determining which interests were right and which were wrong. But despite fundamental differences in political philosophy, the two men seemed to share an understanding of the democratic function of journalism. Indeed, it might be said that for both Garrison and Tocqueville the perfection of democratic society and the perfection of journalism were one.

* * *

For Tocqueville, one of the most remarkable traits of Americans was their penchant for organizing voluntary associations. He wrote:

> There are not only commercial and industrial associations in which all take part, but others of a thousand different types—religious, moral, serious, futile, very general and very limited, immensely large and very minute. Americans combine to give fetes, found seminaries, build churches, distribute books, and send missionaries to the antipodes. Hospitals, prisons, and schools take shape in that way. Finally, if they want to proclaim a truth or propagate some feeling by the encouragement of a great example, they form an association.[1]

Tocqueville explained the Americans' lust to organize according to his central theme about American society: equality. "Among democratic peoples," he said, "associations must take the place of the powerful private persons whom equality of conditions has eliminated."[2]

Newspapers, Tocqueville believed, were crucial instruments for democratic association building: "Newspapers make associations, and associations make newspapers; and if it were true to say that associations must multiply as quickly as conditions become equal, it is equally certain that the number of papers increases in proportion as associations multiply."[3] In a democratic society such as the United States, the newspaper emerges as one of the few bulwarks against the menace of individualism. In other words, for Tocqueville newspapers played an important role in easing the central tension of democracy, the tension between individual and community. Thus Tocqueville was extravagant in his hopes for newspapers. "We should underrate their importance," he wrote, "if we thought they just guaranteed liberty; they maintain civilization."[4]

Newspapers maintain civilization in a democracy, Tocqueville believed, by making collective thought and action possible. They permit many people to think the same thoughts and to feel the same feelings simultaneously. A newspaper will live only if it serves this communitarian function. "A newspaper therefore always represents an association whose members are its regular readers. This association may be more or less strictly defined, more or less closed, more or less numerous, but there must at least be the seed of it in men's minds, for otherwise the paper would not survive." Newspapers thrive in a democracy not because they are cheap but because people need them "to communicate with one another and to act together."[5]

Tocqueville's assertion that America was the greatest newspaper country in the world was almost an understatement. At the time of Tocqueville's visit in the early 1830s, the United States had some nine hundred newspapers, about twice as many as Great Britain, its nearest rival. Aggregate newspaper circulation in America was significantly higher as well. Moreover, the newspaper business was growing rapidly. By 1840 the census counted 1,631 papers; by 1850 the figure reached 2,526, with a total annual circulation of nearly half a billion copies. The decades from 1820 to 1850 might be called the take-off stage for *daily* newspapers. From a handful of 24 dailies in 1820 the daily newspaper industry grew to 138 papers in 1840 and to 254 in 1850. By 1850 dailies accounted for more than half of the annual circulation of all periodicals in America. Yet the rise of the daily notwithstanding, the weekly newspaper was then and would remain for some time to come the most common and ubiquitous form of newspaper journalism in America.[6]

The plethora of newspapers reflected the pluralism of America, in Tocqueville's view. Partly this was due to the federal principle in government, which was in turn the product of an intense localism in American public life. Each county, township, and village held its sacred portion of governmental authority, and thus each developed a local political culture and a local political press. This was the era of the frontier newspaper and the local booster press. But pluralism was not an aspect of geographical localism only, for much of the association building that Tocqueville observed was beginning to be statewide, regional, even national. Many of the hundreds of new weekly journals that emerged in this era were translocal and specialized by content and audience.[7] If this was the era of the urban daily and the frontier weekly, it was also the era of another new kind of journalism that impressed Tocqueville very much: the national associational press.

The 1830s and '40s have been called the Age of Reform, and perhaps no other period in American history has displayed such intensity, diversity, and optimism in reform ideology or in the organization of reform work. The nation's founding fathers were now dead, and to their children had fallen the duty to preserve and perfect the American experiment. Many viewed this as a heavy burden indeed, for America was rapidly changing in challenging and often disturbing ways. Manufacturing, urbanization, immigration, changes in political, social, and family life—all seemed to require some kind of intervention, some kind of reformation. The result was the temperance movement, prison reform, utopian communitarianism, religious missions and Sunday schools, public school reform, insane asylums, feminism, labor unionism, pacifism, and more. This was, as activists then termed it, a great "Sisterhood of Reforms."[8]

A unifying spirit of this age of reform was perfectionism. Narrowly construed, perfectionism was an evangelical religious doctrine that rejected the pessimistic Calvinist view of human nature, declaring instead that individual sinners could themselves repudiate sin and become sanctified on earth.[9] But the spirit of perfectionism flowed far beyond evangelical Protestant Christianity. The notion that men and women could do something to save themselves meant also that they could act to save their world. In any age the great impetus to reform is not the realization that man is sinful and the world flawed; people have always known that. Reform grows from the belief that individuals can do something about it. In the 1830s and '40s religious doctrines of perfectionism merged nicely with democratic, romantic, and progressive impulses in the secular world to produce a great flood tide of reform.[10]

The growth of national reform associations, however, depended also upon things more mundane than religious spirit. To organize on a national or regional scale, a reform group needed an effective communication network. The infrastructure for such networks was beginning to be built in the 1830s, as America gradually moved into an industrial revolution. Most important was the so-called transportation revolution, including post roads and turnpikes, river and ocean steamers, interior canals, and, finally, railroads. These improvements in transportation permitted the faster and cheaper movement not only of manufactured goods and agricultural produce but of preachers, lecturers, and organization agents as well.[11]

Meanwhile, improvements in printing and paper-making technologies reduced the cost of producing books, pamphlets, newspapers, and other associational literature. By the 1830s, perhaps for the first time in American history, a man could actually make a living as a reform lecturer or organizational journalist.[12] This communication revolution seemed to hold great promise for the perfection of both journalism and democracy in America.

One relatively minor reform movement of the early 1830s eventually grew to touch, in one way or another, nearly every aspect of reform thought and action by the 1850s. This was the movement for the abolition of slavery. Though abolitionists were strikingly diverse in the doctrines they professed and in the methods they practiced, they shared the perfectionist faith that the nation could be saved from sin by the works of individual people.[13] They also shared a shrewd understanding of the new technological possibilities for mass communication.

Between its founding in 1833 and its factional split in 1840, the American Anti-Slavery Society displayed vividly how an organization could exploit the transportation-communication revolution. From the beginning the society saw its chief purpose as agitation and propaganda: the moral suasion of American public opinion. They society's Declaration of Sentiments, adopted at the founding convention in December 1833, makes this intent clear:

> We shall organize Anti-Slavery Societies, if possible, in every city, town and village in our land.
> We shall send forth agents to lift up the voice of remonstrance, of warning, of entreaty, and of rebuke.
> We shall circulate, unsparingly and extensively, anti-slavery tracts and periodicals.
> We shall enlist the pulpit and the press in the cause of the suffering and the dumb.[14]

The abolitionists found most pulpits closed to them, but the printing press proved to be a ready and powerful ally. After quickly founding a weekly newspaper, the *Emancipator,* the society next launched what was up to that time the greatest printed propaganda campaign in American history. In 1835 the society flooded the mails with more than a million pieces of antislavery literature, which were sent free to people all over the country, especially in the South. The materials ranged from several new monthly journals and a children's newspaper to woodcuts, handkerchiefs, and even chocolate wrappers.[15]

Public reaction to this onslaught of abolition propaganda was close to hysterical, especially in the South. Southern newspapers denounced the "incendiary literature"; mobs burned the mail sacks; postmasters stopped delivery, with the blessing of Postmaster General Amos Kendall; and, finally, Southern state legislatures prohibited the importation of "inflammatory" publications.[16]

For Southerners, the mammoth scale of the 1835 propaganda campaign seemed clear evidence that abolitionism was an enormously rich and powerful conspiracy, centered in New York, a conspiracy bent on destroying traditional local values and institutions. For them, this nationalization of organization and communication was a threat to the decentralized structure of American republicanism. In reality the American Anti-Slavery Society was neither rich nor powerful. It only seemed so because printing and postage were cheap. Printing rates for the society, in fact, had fallen almost by half in a single year, between 1834 and 1835.[17] What both Southerners and Northerners saw in the great "postal campaign" of 1835 was the birth of a new kind of journalism, which was intimately wedded to a new participant in American pluralism: the national voluntary association.

The printing press was an instrument not solely for propaganda and agitation. Perhaps more important, it was also a builder of community among the already converted, the role that Tocqueville was most interested in. The abolitionist movement became a kind of religious congregation in the 1830s, with its members scattered across the land, linked together through letters, traveling agents and lecturers, pamphlets, and, perhaps especially, newspapers. In addition, the transportation revolution permitted more people to travel to annual conventions, abolitionists' fairs and bazaars, and even to antislavery conclaves abroad. At least a few leaders could dedicate their lives to the cause and make a living at it.[18] This was something new to American democracy and to American journalism as well.

* * *

One man who made his living in the reform movement was William Lloyd Garrison, a journalist by training and temperament and for thirty-five years the editor of the most notorious abolitionist newspaper of them all. Garrison has regularly been glorified and vilified, in a kind of cyclical fashion, since his death in 1879. Historical opinion has at times portrayed him as the moral conscience of the nation; at other times it has dismissed him as a nettlesome, egotistical fanatic.[19] Nearly everyone, however, including his most ardent debunkers, has paid tribute to his skills as a journalist. The most relentless of Garrison's twentieth-century detractors, Gilbert H. Barnes, wrote: "He was equipped by taste and temperament for free-lance journalism and for nothing else. As a journalist, he was brilliant and provocative; as a leader for the anti-slavery host he was a name, an embodied motto, a figurehead of fanaticism."[20]

But despite agreement that he was a talented journalist and despite his looming presence in the standard histories of American journalism, surpris-

ingly little attention has been paid to Garrison's philosophy of journalism.
This is surprising, not because journalism is so important in itself but because journalism was central to Garrison's understanding of emancipation
and of the nature of a good society.

Above all else, Garrison believed in God; and because he believed in God
he believed in truth. Truth—God's truth—was what he proposed to tell in
the pages of the *Liberator,* the little abolitionist paper that he launched in 1831.
"I desire to thank God," he wrote in his famous opening statement, "that he
enables me to disregard 'the fear of man which bringeth a snare,' and to speak
his truth in its simplicity and power." In the second issue he reaffirmed his
"unshaken reliance in the omnipotence of truth." This would continue to be
the *Liberator*'s clarion call for thirty-five years.[21] During the turbulent postal campaign of 1835, when the whole country seemed bent upon silencing the
abolitionists, Garrison consistently and serenely held up God's truth as the
one sure defense. "Ours is that fanaticism which listens to the voice of God,"
he wrote. "Ours is the incendiary spirit of truth, that burns up error."[22]

People who declare God's truth to hard-hearted sinners are usually called
prophets, and this is indeed what Garrison thought he was. His language was
harsh, he often said, because truth was harsh—and people did not want to
hear it. But truth would eventually have its way.[23] After the Nat Turner insurrection in August 1831 Garrison wrote with biblical sureness: "Read the
account of the insurrection in Virginia, and say whether our prophesy be not
fulfilled." On another occasion he said of his "hard language": "Like the
hand-writing upon the wall of the palace, it has caused the knees of the
American Belshazzar to smite together in terror, and filled with dismay all
who follow in his train."[24] What Garrison called prophesy others called agitation. We today might call it agenda setting. By whatever name it is called,
the abolitionists' aim was to keep their unpopular message constantly before
the public until the consciences of the people were finally touched. This incessant "truth telling" was central to the abolitionists' mission, as Garrison
and many others defined it.[25]

Garrison's reputation as a self-righteous, egocentric, intolerant fanatic
stems from strident pronouncements such as these about God and truth and
prophesy. Certainly, Garrison was not modest about his opinions, nor was
he reluctant to argue them vigorously. He attacked opponents like a bird of
prey, with beak and talons flashing. Indeed, Garrison *was* a self-righteous,
egocentric fanatic.[26] But it would be wrong to call him intolerant. Despite his
own certainty that he knew the truth, Garrison was a believer throughout
his career in free discussion and untrammeled inquiry. Despite his own deep

religiosity, he always defended reason and free thought—and on several rather different grounds.

First, Garrison argued that free inquiry would lead to truth. This was essentially the standard Anglo-American faith in free discussion that dated at least to John Milton's *Areopagitica.* In what is perhaps his fullest statement of his philosophy of free expression, Garrison clearly had Milton in mind: "My conviction of the weakness and mutability of error is such, that the free utterance of any opinion, however contrary to my own, has long since ceased to give me any uneasiness as to the final triumph of Right. My confidence in the unconquerable energy of Truth is absolute; and therefore I ask for it, what only it requires, 'a fair field and no quarter.'"[27] Applying this doctrine to abolitionism, Garrison believed simply that slavery could not stand up to free discussion. The violent reaction of the South to the 1835 propaganda campaign was ample proof of that. Censorship was the South's only possible defense, for "the slave-system cannot bear investigation." After 1835 free expression became a cause closely associated with abolitionism. Garrison made the connection simply and confidently in his prospectus for 1836: "Slavery and freedom of the press cannot exist together."[28]

Garrison's devotion to free inquiry, however, extended beyond its tactical utility in the pursuit of truth. Increasingly, as he moved from a narrow antislavery stance to advocacy of "universal emancipation," free expression and free exercise of reason became for Garrison not merely the way to truth but truth itself. Individual freedom of thought and conscience for everyone, along with physical independence for slaves, was what universal emancipation was all about. "The emancipation of our whole race from the domination of man"—this was the goal. By the 1840s Garrison had rejected all forms of coercion, religious hierarchy, and human government as incompatible with individual conscience and the government of God. Only when the individual is perfectly free could he be free to serve God perfectly.[29] As early as 1832, Garrison dedicated the *Liberator* to a long list of individual rights and freedoms, in addition to the abolition of slavery; and he summarized all of these goals as freedom of thought and speech, freedom of choice and action.[30]

But Garrison had yet another reason for favoring open discussion and free inquiry, a reason that was at heart journalistic and organizational. For Garrison, discussion was the essence of journalism. Though the *Liberator* is usually remembered for the vividness of its invective, perhaps a more striking characteristic was its devotion to reader participation through correspondence and to the interchange of information and opinions on abolition and all the other reform questions that the paper pursued. From its founding in

1831 to its termination in 1865, the *Liberator* was never merely a propaganda sheet for Garrison's favorite causes. It was a forum open to the scattered individuals who viewed themselves as a community of reformers. It was a gathering together of the faithful. It was, as Garrison said in his valedictory editorial, the group's "weekly method of communicating with each other."[31]

The *Liberator* was not, however, an official organ of any association, though it was supported by the Garrison-dominated Massachusetts Anti-Slavery Society. Garrison was much too self-centered and self-righteous to accept editorial direction from anyone. Yet the *Liberator* was an associational newspaper, nonetheless, in that it helped to build, in Tocqueville's words, "an association whose members are its regular readers." And this is precisely what Garrison had in mind. He regularly argued that the *Liberator*'s independence was necessary to secure its role as an open forum for discussion. This was its purpose and the secret of its success, Garrison said, though friends and foes alike did not always understand or agree. Both sides often attacked the eccentricities of the *Liberator,* because they believed the paper reflected or should reflect the principles of the abolitionist movement in general. Not so, Garrison declared. It reflected only his personal views and the views of his readers and correspondents, as he frequently reminded his critics:

> For the hundredth time I repeat it,—the Liberator is an independent journal. . . . Hence it is not only unjust, but extremely base, to make any anti-slavery society responsible for what appears in its columns, and equally absurd and unreasonable to complain that it is open to the discussion of other questions besides that of chattel slavery; and most unjust is it to hold me responsible for the views of my correspondents, any further than they are approved by me. Those who do not want, or cannot tolerate such a paper, have a very simple remedy at hand, so far as they are concerned—either not to subscribe to it, or, if they are subscribers, to discontinue it whenever they think it proper. I mean that the Liberator shall be a FREE PRESS, in a comprehensive and manly sense; and I advise those who cannot endure free discussion to beware how they give it any countenance.[32]

The *Liberator,* in other words, is a good example of associational journalism because of its participatory character, not because it was the official news medium of a formal organization. Certainly, other reform newspapers that *were* official organs played similar roles. But official organizational status was not central to either Tocqueville's or Garrison's understanding of the associational character of journalism. In fact, Garrison thought that such formal ties were detrimental to the freedom of the press. For if to tell the truth was the virtue of the reformer, as Garrison believed, to be free was the virtue of the press.

In the course of his life Garrison was an editor first and a reformer later, and he never changed the philosophy of journalism and editorship that he developed in the 1820s on the *Free Press* in Newburyport, Massachusetts, and the *Journal of the Times* in Bennington, Vermont.[33] As the new twenty-year-old editor of the *Free Press*, Garrison promised his readers that his columns would be open to everyone, but he would never seek their approval or solicit their patronage. They could subscribe or cancel, as they saw fit. He said the same to his readers two years later in Vermont. He would accept advice on every subject accept one: how he should run the paper. In other words, as editor he expected to have complete freedom to speak the truth as he saw it. But he offered the same right to those who chose to participate in the community that the newspaper gathered around itself.[34]

Garrison conducted the *Liberator* on these same editorial principles. From the beginning the forum function was central to its mission:

> Before the Liberator was established, I doubt whether, on either side of the Atlantic, there existed a newspaper or periodical that admitted its opponents to be freely and impartially heard through its columns—as freely as its friends. Without boasting, I claim to have set an example of fairness and magnanimity, in this respect, such as had never been set before; cheerfully conceding to those who were hostile to my views, on any subject discussed in the Liberator, not only as much space as I, or as others agreeing with me, might occupy, but even more, if they desired it.[35]

At his retirement in 1865 Garrison reaffirmed his belief in his early editorial principles. "I have never consulted either the subscription list of the paper or public sentiment in printing, or omitting to print, any article touching any matter whatever," he said. "No journal . . . has granted such freedom in its columns to its opponents; none has so scrupulously and uniformly presented all sides of every question discussed in its pages."[36]

Of course, no mortal could have been as just, fair, and magnanimous as Garrison liked to remember that he was. And yet the pages of the *Liberator*, week after week and year after year, do bear witness to the general accuracy of Garrison's memory. Certainly, Garrison never held back his own views. In his famous opening statement in 1831, he promised: "I will not equivocate—I will not excuse—I will not retreat a single inch."[37] Historians generally agree that this is one editorial promise that the editor kept. But Garrison also fulfilled his promise to keep the *Liberator*'s columns open for free discussion. The "Communications" department was always a centerpiece of the paper, often taking all of the first page and more of the four-page sheet. Indeed, in the paper's first year Garrison sometimes complained that "to accommodate our numerous correspondents we are again necessitated to exclude our own communications to the public."[38] When philosophical or tactical debates arose among abolitionists, such as the conflict over political action at the end of the 1830s, Garrison fought aggressively for his point of view. But he gave space to all. At such times the *Liberator* was practically given over to publication of letters, articles, speeches, statements, and rebuttals from all sides of the controversy.[39]

The *Liberator* also carried materials from true enemies as well as from factional opponents within the movement. Garrison seemed almost to delight in reprinting the abuse that the mainstream newspapers, from North and South, heaped upon him and the antislavery movement. Newspapers were not his only enemies. In a private letter in 1831 he wrote, "I am constantly receiving anonymous letters, filled with abominable and bloody sentiments. These trouble me less than the wind." In 1834 Garrison even started a new department of the paper called "Refuge of Oppression" to highlight these attacks and denunciations. Sometimes he offered editorial replies; sometimes he did not.[40]

Not all the material in the *Liberator* was controversial. From the first, the paper performed the more mundane organizational function of publicizing meetings and activities and publishing minutes and convention proceedings. The *Liberator* also carried informational, inspirational, and purely entertaining news and features. Its regular departments included children's stories, poetry, ladies' features, marriage and death notices, foreign and domestic news briefs, miscellaneous "brights," and a few advertisements for books, medicines, and boardinghouses. Despite his reputation for dour earnestness, Garrison even included jokes in the *Liberator*—and some were actually funny. Though the content of the paper fluctuated with the flux of events, this diversity was never missing. Even on the day that Garrison printed his famous account of how he was nearly killed by the Boston mob of 1835, the paper included the usual brights and anecdotes, including an account of a "shocking homicide" in Grafton and an item about a man who trained his hogs to work in harness.[41]

Garrison's editorial philosophy led him into a kind of love-hate relationship with public opinion. One of his favorite quotes was a line from Cicero, which he had used as the motto of the *Journal of the Times:* "Reason shall prevail with us more than Popular Opinion." And throughout his long career on the *Liberator* he seemed to glory in public odium. When he retired, he counted the paper's short subscription list as a badge of honor. Yet he also believed that reason and popular opinion could be brought together through moral suasion and the power of the press. "We expect to conquer through the majesty of public opinion," he wrote in 1831. "Appalling as is the evil of slavery, the press is able to cope with it; and without the agency of the press, no impression can be made, no plan perfected, no victory achieved."[42] Like other abolitionists, Garrison believed that the American people, North and South, could be converted to the antislavery cause through the dissemination of information and sound argument. "Let information be circulated among them as prodigally as the light of heaven, and they cannot long act and reason as they now do," he said. To this end one of the chief functions of an antislavery society must be "to scatter tracts, like raindrops, over the land" and to help start a hundred new periodicals devoted to the cause of emancipation.[43]

In short, Garrison idealized journalism. To him journalism was the animator of social life, for it served the two great functions of social reform: agitation and discussion. Agitation is the function most often associated with the abolitionist press. But certainly agitation (or prophesy) was not all that Garrison had in mind for the journalism of reform. Not agitation but discussion—free inquiry among the members of a community of readers—seems to have been the chief work of the *Liberator*. Indeed, it might be argued that for Garrison, free discussion was a substitute for government—a kind of democracy without coercion. From the late 1830s onward, Garrison rejected government in any form, including democracy, because all human governments rested upon coercion and power. But Garrison did believe in public sentiment, moral suasion, and voluntary reform organization as legitimate methods for change in society. And he believed that the press—as agitator and, even more important, as forum for free discussion—could and should lead the way. For Garrison, if discussion was the essence of journalism, journalism was the essence of a perfect democracy.

* * *

William Lloyd Garrison's *Liberator* was just one rather obscure point of light in the pluralist universe that Tocqueville observed in American journalism. A thousand other American newspapers were also at work, gathering communities of readers about them. Together they shaped the enormously complex system of American social life and American democracy. Tocqueville was more interested than Garrison in the workings of journalism at this systemic level. Tocqueville was a philosopher of democratic pluralism; Garrison was an opponent of pluralism, though an energetic participant in it. On the political role of newspapers, however, they were not far apart. Both believed that the purpose of newspapers lay with the collective thought and action of the groups, the associations, the communities that grew up with them. If group

politics was what made American democracy special, discussion and agitation were the necessary contributions of journalism. For both Tocqueville and
Garrison, then, participation in journalism was one phase—an increasingly
important phase—of participation in democracy.

A participatory, associational, group-based press may have been a good
thing for American democracy, as Tocqueville thought, but this was not the
direction of the revolution in American journalism in the 1830s. Newspapers
were indeed democratized but not in the way that Tocqueville foresaw. Instead, they were commercialized; that is, they were turned into cheap consumer products to be sold for profit in the marketplace along with the other
new products of the industrial revolution. The participatory and associational
nature of the newspaper was increasingly subdued in this new world of the
commercial popular press.

Neither agitation nor discussion played a central role for these new "penny papers." They continued both functions to some extent, especially in the
discussion of politics and in the promotion of local business. Some editors,
such as Horace Greeley of the *New York Tribune,* made valiant and partially
successful efforts to carry some of the spirit of associational journalism into
the commercial press. But, in general, the commercial papers were more interested in expanding circulations than in organizing communities of readers for political or social action. And agitation (unpopular "truth telling")
and discussion (open access to a paper's columns) did not necessarily serve
the circulation-building function. In place of agitation and discussion the
penny papers and their descendants preferred to report "the news"—that is,
to tell interesting stories of occurrences.[44] In place of an active group of readers who participated directly in the journalism process, the readers of the
commercial popular press became an audience of passive spectators, watch-
ing a splendid show of which they were not a part.[45]

The associational press would continue to develop in America in the late
nineteenth century but largely as a separate form of journalism, increasingly far removed from the mainstream. The mainstream, flowing from the
penny paper experiments of the 1830s and '40s, would have its virtues, including some democratic, political virtues. But reader participation—association building—would not be one of them.

Notes

1. Alexis de Tocqueville, *Democracy in America,* ed. J. P. Mayer (New York: Doubleday,
1969), 513.
2. Ibid., 516.
3. Ibid., 518.

4. Ibid., 517.

5. Ibid., 519–20.

6. *Statistical View of the United States . . . A Compendium of the Seventh Census,* comp. J. D. B. De Bow (Washington, D.C.: Beverley Tucker, Senate Printer, 1854), 154–58. See also Clarence S. Brigham, *History and Bibliography of American Newspapers, 1690–1820,* 2 vols. (Worcester, Mass.: American Antiquarian Society, 1947).

7. *Statistical View,* 154–58; Tocqueville, *Democracy in America,* 519.

8. Ronald G. Walters, *American Reformers, 1815–1860* (New York: Hill and Wang, 1978), ix–xiv; Richard D. Brown, *Modernization: The Transformation of American Life, 1600–1865* (New York: Hill and Wang, 1976), chaps. 5–6. The classic study of antebellum reform is Alice F. Tyler, *Freedom's Ferment* (Minneapolis: University of Minnesota Press, 1944).

9. The term *perfectionism* derives from Jesus' Sermon on the Mount: "Be ye therefore perfect, even as your Father which is in heaven is perfect" (Matthew 5:48).

10. Walters, *American Reformers,* 28–29. See also Thomas L. Haskell, "Capitalism and the Origins of the Humanitarian Sensibility," pts. 1 and 2, *American Historical Review* 90 (Apr. 1985): 339–61, and *American Historical Review* 90 (June 1985): 547–66; and Laurence Veysey, ed., *The Perfectionists: Radical Social Thought in the North, 1815–1860* (New York: John Wiley and Sons, 1973).

11. David Paul Nord, "The Evangelical Origins of Mass Media in America, 1815–1835," *Journalism Monographs* 88 (May 1984): 1–30. See also Allan R. Pred, *Urban Growth and the Circulation of Information: The United States System of Cities, 1790–1840* (Cambridge, Mass.: Harvard University Press, 1973), chap. 5. See also George Rogers Taylor, *The Transportation Revolution, 1815–1860* (New York: Rinehart, 1951).

12. Walters, *American Reformers,* 5–6; Nord, "Evangelical Origins," 7–13. See also Robert Hoe, *Short History of the Printing Press* (New York: R. Hoe, 1902); Dard Hunter, *Papermaking: The History and Technique of an Ancient Craft,* 2d ed. (New York: Knopf, 1947), 340ff.; Alfred McClung Lee, *The Daily Newspaper in America* (New York: Macmillan, 1947), chap. 5.

13. The literature on abolitionism is vast. Two valuable overviews are Ronald G. Walters, *The Antislavery Appeal: American Abolitionism after 1830* (Baltimore: Johns Hopkins University Press, 1976); and Merton L. Dillon, *The Abolitionists: The Growth of a Dissenting Minority* (New York: W. W. Norton, 1979). Standard older histories include Gilbert H. Barnes, *The Antislavery Impulse, 1830–1844* (New York: D. Appleton-Century, 1933); and Louis Filler, *The Crusade against Slavery, 1830–1860* (New York: Harper and Bros., 1960). See also the essays collected in Martin Duberman, ed., *The Antislavery Vanguard: New Essays on the Abolitionists* (Princeton, N.J.: Princeton University Press, 1965); and Lewis Perry and Michael Fellman, eds., *Antislavery Reconsidered: New Perspectives on the Abolitionists* (Baton Rouge: Louisiana State University Press, 1979).

14. *Proceedings of the Anti-Slavery Convention, Assembled at Philadelphia, December 4, 5, and 6, 1833* (New York: Dorr and Butterfield, 1833). The Declaration of Sentiments, which was written by Garrison, is reprinted in Louis Ruchames, ed., *The Abolitionists: A Collection of Their Writings* (New York: G. P. Putnam's Sons, 1863), 78–83.

15. The postal campaign and the reaction to it are described in Leonard L. Richards, *"Gentlemen of Property and Standing": Anti-Abolition Mobs in Jacksonian America* (New York: Oxford University Press, 1970), chap. 3; and Bertram Wyatt-Brown, *Lewis Tappan*

and the Evangelical War against Slavery (Cleveland: Case Western Reserve University Press, 1969), 149–63.

16. Filler, *Crusade against Slavery,* 97–98. See also W. Sherman Savage, *The Controversy over the Distribution of Abolition Literature, 1830–1860* (Washington, D.C.: Association for the Study of Negro Life and History, 1938).

17. Richards, *"Gentlemen of Property,"* 55–62, 71–73.

18. Walters, *Antislavery Appeal,* chap. 2.

19. For example, see the range of historical opinion in George M. Fredrickson, ed., *William Lloyd Garrison* (Englewood Cliffs, N.J.: Prentice-Hall, 1968).

20. Barnes, *Antislavery Impulse,* 58.

21. *Liberator,* Jan. 1 and Jan. 8, 1831. Some of Garrison's articles from the *Liberator* have been reprinted in collections. See Fredrickson, *William Lloyd Garrison;* Truman Nelson, ed., *Documents of Upheaval: Selections from William Lloyd Garrison's* The Liberator, *1831–1865* (New York: Hill and Wang, 1966); and William Lloyd Garrison, *Selections from the Writings and Speeches of William Lloyd Garrison* (Boston: R. F. Wallcut, 1852).

22. *Liberator,* Sept. 12, 1835. See also the edition of Aug. 22, 1835.

23. See, for example, "Harsh Language—Retarding the Cause" and "Vindication of the *Liberator*" in Garrison, *Selections,* 121–22, 178–81. See also *Liberator,* Aug. 22, 1835.

24. *Liberator,* Sept. 3, 1831; Garrison, *Selections,* 122.

25. Historians have long been interested in the agitation function of abolitionism. See especially Aileen S. Kraditor, *Means and Ends in American Abolitionism: Garrison and His Critics on Strategy and Tactics, 1834–1850* (New York: Pantheon, 1969), chap. 2. See also James Stewart Brewer, *Wendell Phillips: Liberty's Hero* (Baton Rouge: Louisiana State University Press, 1986); and Louis Filler, ed., *Wendell Phillips on Civil Rights and Freedom* (New York: Hill and Wang, 1965).

26. Garrison's personal style is explored critically but sympathetically in standard biographies: John L. Thomas, *The Liberator: William Lloyd Garrison, a Biography* (Boston: Little, Brown, 1963); and Walter M. Merrill, *Against Wind and Tide: A Biography of Wm. Lloyd Garrison* (Cambridge, Mass.: Harvard University Press, 1963).

27. *Liberator,* Jan. 30, 1846. See also Kraditor, *Means and Ends,* 93–94, 104–6.

28. *Liberator,* Dec. 22, 1832, and Aug. 29, Sept. 9, Nov. 7, and Dec. 12, 1835. See also Russel B. Nye, *Fettered Freedom* (East Lansing: Michigan State College Press, 1949).

29. *Liberator,* Dec. 15, 1837, and Sept. 28, 1838. See also Lewis Perry, *Radical Abolitionism: Anarchy and the Government of God in Antislavery Thought* (Ithaca, N.Y.: Cornell University Press, 1873), chaps. 2–3.

30. *Liberator,* Jan. 7, 1832.

31. *Liberator,* Dec. 29, 1865. See also James Brewer Stewart, "Garrison Again, and Again, and Again, and Again . . . ," *Reviews in American History* 14 (Dec. 1976): 554–45.

32. Garrison, "Vindication of the *Liberator,*" in *Selections,* 185–86. This is one of the clearest statements of Garrison's views of the role of the organizational press. See also the *Liberator*'s 1840 prospectus and a mock dialogue on factionalism within the American Anti-Slavery Society, both in *Liberator,* Dec. 27, 1839.

33. A full account of Garrison's preabolition journalism is Francis Jackson Garrison and Wendell Phillips Garrison, *William Lloyd Garrison, 1805–1879: The Story of His Life,*

vol. 1 (New York: Century, 1885), chaps. 3–5. This is the first volume of a four-volume biography by Garrison's sons.

34. *Free Press*, Mar. 22, 1826, and Sept. 21, 1826, Newburyport, Mass.; *Journal of the Times*, Oct. 3, 1828, and Mar. 27, 1829, Bennington, Vt. Parts of these statements are reprinted in Garrison and Garrison, *William Lloyd Garrison*, 61–62, 70–71, 102–4, and 121–22.

35. Garrison, *Selections*, 184–85.

36. *Liberator*, Dec. 29, 1865.

37. *Liberator*, Jan. 1, 1831.

38. *Liberator*, Feb. 19, 1831.

39. See, for example, *Liberator*, Dec. 1839, every issue.

40. William Lloyd Garrison to Henry E. Benson, Oct. 19, 1831, in *The Letters of William Lloyd Garrison*, vol. 1, ed. Walter M. Merrill (Cambridge, Mass.: Belknap, 1971), 139. For examples of *Liberator* reprints of this sort, see *Liberator*, June 6, June 13, and Aug. 15, 1835, and Jan. 28, 1837. See also Thomas, *The Liberator*, 131–33.

41. *Liberator*, Nov. 7, 1835. Examples of this kind of material can be found in every issue in the 1830s, usually on the third and fourth pages.

42. *Liberator*, June 18, 1831, and Dec. 22, 1832.

43. *Liberator*, Mar. 26 and July 30, 1831.

44. Michael Schudson, *Discovering the News: A Social History of American Newspapers* (New York: Basic, 1978), 21–23; Alexander Saxton, "Problems of Class and Race in the Origins of the Mass Circulation Press," *American Quarterly* 36 (Summer 1984): 211–34. On the "forum function" of Greeley's *New York Tribune*, see Warren G. Bovee, "Horace Greeley and Social Responsibility," *Journalism Quarterly* 63 (Summer 1986): 251–59.

45. Gunther Barth, *City People: The Rise of Modern City Culture in Nineteenth-Century America* (New York: Oxford University Press, 1980), 64–65; Alan Trachtenberg, *The Incorporation of America: Culture and Society in the Gilded Age* (New York: Hill and Wang, 1982), chap. 4. See also Dan Schiller, *Objectivity and the News: The Public and the Rise of Commercial Journalism* (Philadelphia: University of Pennsylvania Press, 1981), chap. 2. My argument in this paragraph has to do with participation. The late nineteenth-century metropolitan press certainly had a role in building a public community in the sense of a common frame of reference for diverse peoples. But this was different from the active associational journalism that Tocqueville lauded and Garrison practiced. See chapter 5 in this book.

5. The Public Community: The Urbanization of Journalism in Chicago

THOUGH NEWSPAPERS have always resided in cities, they have not always lived in them—lived in the sense of understanding, embracing, and building an ethos of urbanism. The urbanization of the American newspaper was a late nineteenth-century phenomenon, and a prototype of the new "urbanized" popular press was the *Chicago Daily News,* founded in 1875.

The *Chicago Daily News,* and newspapers like it, represent a kind of second stage in the development of the modern, urban newspaper in America. Earlier big-city newspapers of midcentury were more modern than urban. They were modern not merely in their business and journalistic practices but in their ready acceptance of the formal, contractual society and their enthusiastic promotion of capitalism, industrialism, and the justice and discipline of the marketplace. Their very modern economic and political views, however, were rooted in notions of private property rights, individualism, and laissez-faire that were being challenged in the late nineteenth century by the imperatives and growing complexities of urban life. Like many city institutions built by individual entrepreneurs, big-city newspapers, even self-consciously popular ones, did not necessarily grasp what was happening to the collective life in the metropolis. Publishers were rather like Jeffersonian yeomen transplanted unthinkingly into capitalism. Their newspapers were the products of the "private city," and they remained private in outlook, thoroughly individualistic in editorial policy and news philosophy.[1]

Newspapers such as the *Chicago Daily News,* on the other hand, began in the 1870s and 1880s to develop a new vision of community life for a new kind of city—the modern metropolis. Theirs was a vision of community that was inspired less by a nostalgic longing for the communal seventeenth century than by a fear of the very tangible social problems of the capitalistic, individualistic nineteenth. This was community forced by urban life and, it was hoped, suited to the inherent impersonality of large-scale urban existence. It was *public community*—that is, a kind of association founded upon communitarian notions of interdependence and identity, of sentiment and sympathy, yet powered by formal organizations and activist government and guided by the new agencies of mass communication.

The important differences between the urban press of the late nineteenth century, such as the *Chicago Daily News,* and the big-city press of earlier decades were not what they sometimes are thought to have been. The *Daily News* was not the first sensational paper, the first politically independent paper, the first departmentalized paper, the first telegraph newspaper, the first multiclass paper, or the first screaming headline paper in Chicago. In short, it was neither the first popular nor the first modern newspaper in the city. But it was the first thoroughly urban one—that is, the first to articulate a vision of public community. What that vision was and how it differed from the philosophy and practice of the older-style popular press is the subject of this chapter.

* * *

The transformation of community life in American cities is a subject of intense and increasing interest in historical studies. The idea of community, of course, has always been central to both urban sociology and urban history. Until recently, however, both have tended to treat the concept rather ahistorically. Community traditionally has been discussed as an idea type—sometimes lost, sometimes hoped for, but seldom explored in the intricacies of historical context. A long tradition of urban sociology developed around the dichotomous typologies of Ferdinand Tönnies (*Gemeinschaft* vs. *Gesellschaft*), Emile Durkheim (organic vs. mechanical solidarity), and Max Weber (communal vs. associative relationships). The essence of modernization was thought to have been the eclipse of community and the rise of impersonal, contractual, and mechanistic modes of association.[2] The parts of the dichotomies were usually seen as temporally sequential and thus historical. The many empirical "community studies" of the 1920s and later, however, did not really test these theories in history so much as assume a history to fit the theory. "Community" became what the town had had sometime before the investigator arrived to find it gone. Oddly, historians often have been equally ahistorical. Steeped in the sociological tradition, they have assumed a priori that the march from traditional past to modern present meant the breakdown of community. And different historians have found that time of breakdown in just about every decade from the 1650s to the 1920s.[3]

These traditions of ahistorical urban sociology and urban history, like the idealized vision of community they created, are now in decline. Increasingly, students of America's urban past and present have rejected the dichotomous and sequential nature of *Gemeinschaft* and *Gesellschaft,* community and society. The materials of the past have reaffirmed what historians have always professed to believe, that the meaning of human life is complex and the direction of historical change ambiguous. Studies of nineteenth-century town and city growth and other aspects of modernization now more typically stress the persistence of traditional values and community structures. Some historians, such as Samuel Hays and Richard Jensen, have continued to use dichotomous idea types (e.g., modern vs. traditional, cosmopolitan vs. local), but they tend to link them with competing classes or groups within the same society at the same time.[4] Other historians, such as Thomas Bender, suggest that each individual person experiences *both Gemeinschaft* and *Gesellschaft,* both community and formal organization, in the complexity of modern life.[5]

Though reaffirming the complexities and ambiguities of the history of community life, scholars still tend to insist upon the distinction between public and private in their definitions of community. Community is seen as a private affair of family, kin, and face-to-face relationships. "Community," in the words of Robert Nisbet, "is founded on man conceived in his wholeness rather than in one or another of the roles, taken separately, that he may hold in a social order. It draws its psychological strength from levels of motivation deeper than those of mere volition or interest."[6] The public culture, on the other hand, is the sphere of roles, interests, organizations, contracts, and politics. In fact, the careless confusion of the public and private realms in the nineteenth century has caused many of our most serious modern problems, according to Richard Sennett, whose brilliant book *The Fall of Public Man* is largely an extended effort to distinguish between the two.

Sennett argues that public life was eroded in the eighteenth and nineteenth centuries as people began to project private, psychological values and modes of thought into the public realm. "As a result, confusion has arisen between public and intimate life; people are working out in terms of personal feelings such matters which properly can be dealt with only through codes of impersonal meaning." Because people ceased to deal with each other in impersonal, formal, public ways, "community" became merely "shared personality" based upon a common psychological fantasy of imagined but unachievable intimacy.[7] Thomas Bender makes a similar distinction. Though he argues that community need not involve geographical proximity, he does insist that community is a private affair that should be separate from the public sphere.[8]

If the malaise of the twentieth-century American is a product of the confusion of the public and private realms of life, then newspapers such as the
Chicago Daily News surely contributed to it, for these papers directly challenged traditional ideas of private property and public action in the nineteenth-century city.[9] With great fervor and optimism they urged a community spirit in what Sennett would define as the public realm. Furthermore,
they provided their audience with a limited, organized, common frame of
reference, so that diverse city dwellers could communicate with each other—
communicate in the sense that they could think about the same things at the
same time and thus share a vision of social reality. These newspapers saw in
the fragmenting forces of urbanization the germ of public community.

* * *

The *Chicago Daily News* was born into a city that was becoming a giant
metropolis. By the time of the great fire of 1871, nearly 300,000 Chicagoans
crowded along the shores of Lake Michigan. The fire scarcely slowed the pace
of growth. By 1880 Chicago was a city of 500,000; by 1890 more than one
million.[10] Such rapid growth undermined traditional community life in
Chicago. These many thousands of newcomers were a diverse lot, arriving
from all parts of America and the world and bringing with them their peculiar institutions, habits, and prejudices. By the 1870s neighborhoods, churches,
social clubs, immigrant newspapers, mutual aid societies, patriotic associations, and political organizations were fragmented and isolated from one
another along class, ethnic, and linguistic lines. And the pot was slow to melt
these disparate, wary, fearful peoples.[11]

Public institutions in Chicago in the 1870s were also fragmented and were
increasingly unable to cope with the growing problems of collective life in a
large, modern city. The rapid concentration of industry and population created enormous environmental and social problems that defied solution by
traditional means. Problems of sewerage, water supply, transportation, smoke
abatement, crime and fire control, housing, unemployment, and scores of
other matters of health, sanitation, and public welfare all grew more intense
as the city grew more complex and congested. But neither public nor private
institutions were well equipped to confront these crises of urbanization. After
a brief spurt of public spirit and concerted action after the fire of 1871, Chicago's city government seemed to decline in power and effectiveness during
the 1870s. Though population continued to rise, taxes and revenues fell, and
public works and services remained undone.[12] The depression of 1873–77 was
the chief culprit but not the only one. The public philosophy of Chicago was
as fragmented as the material life of the city. Chicago remained a private city,

with no consensus on what should be the public response to urbanization, no consensus on the place of public action in economics and social life, no consensus on the meaning of community in the modern metropolis.

In the early 1870s, before the *Daily News* entered this new urban world, the largest and most popular newspaper in Chicago was the *Times*, perhaps the apotheosis of modern big-city journalism in midnineteenth-century America. Like the popular press of other large cities, the *Times* was sensational, irreverent, diverse in content, and quick in news coverage. Its very modern production practices influenced papers all over the country.[13] Yet, while the *Times* was a paper that would sell *in* the city, it was never a part *of* the city. Despite its popularity, the *Times* never developed a particularly urban outlook. Despite its cosmopolitan veneer, the *Times* remained committed to conventional values of individualism, private property, and small-scale, face-to-face community.

The *Times* was the creature of Wilbur F. Storey, a kind of nineteenth-century entrepreneur run amok. Storey's most striking personality trait was his ferocious, idiosyncratic, absolutely rock-hard independence. He is remembered today, if he is remembered at all, as the journalistic nemesis of Abraham Lincoln, as the vitriolic Copperhead editor whose paper was shut down by Gen. Ambrose Burnside for two days in 1863.[14] Yet, despite his unwavering devotion to the Democratic Party during the Civil War, Storey broke with the party after the war because it failed to follow him. He was guided and he guided his paper by his own lights. The *Times* masthead declared simply: "The *Times* . . . by W. F. Storey."

Storey was notorious in Chicago in the 1860s and 1870s for what his longtime associate Franc Wilkie called the *Times*'s "glaring indecency . . . which reeked, seethed like a hell's broth in the *Times* cauldrons."[15] In the idiom of the era the *Times* was salacious, licentious, scurrilous, vituperative, blasphemous, obscene, debased, debauched, depraved, and generally deplored. No American newspaper before the Hearst papers of the 1890s or perhaps even the jazzy New York tabloids of the 1920s was as dedicated as the *Times* to sensationalism. Sexual violence was probably the *Times*'s favorite form of sensation, though either sex or violence separately served almost as well. Rapists, lechers, sadists, polygamists, arsenic fiends, and spouse roasters—all clamored for coverage in the *Times*, and all found room in the daily roundups of "Heathenish Horrors," "Sin and Sorrow," "The Age's Abominations," and "The Prevailing Putridity."[16] Executions were always hot news for the *Times*, and Storey's most famous headline was one that stood at the top of an account in 1875 of four murderers who had repented of their sins at the gallows: "Jerked to Jesus."[17]

By the time he died, Storey was heartily despised by the "better element" of Chicago, but he was also a millionaire. His genius lay in mingling sensation and scandal with solid news reporting. In its golden age in the 1860s and 1870s no other newspaper west of New York carried so much news. Storey knew how to produce a paper with murder, suicide, and divorce on one page and the most extensive and complete market reports in town on another. By all accounts, the *Times*'s readership was wide, cutting across class lines and neighborhood boundaries, both within Chicago and throughout the Midwest.[18]

In its fascination with the sordid underworld of city life on the one hand and its devotion to the city's business world on the other, the *Times* would seem a decidedly urban institution. In a sense it was. But the *Times* had no vision of the collective life of Chicago. The city was merely a complex of marketplaces where individuals conducted their private affairs. Like its editor and many of its readers, the *Times* remained a wary stranger in the city, an outsider, an uneasy spectator. Its values remained private, individualistic values, and these values shaped both the editorials and the news content of the paper.

For the *Times,* the city of Chicago meant the individual people and the private property in it. In editorials Storey spoke explicitly for the "owners of Chicago," that is, the people who actually held title to the lots, the buildings, and the businesses. During the first half of 1876, when the new *Daily News* was just getting started in Chicago, the *Times* was tremendously agitated and outraged by what it saw as the depredations of local government "tax-eaters" upon these owners of the city.[19] The *Times* insisted that the "city" was merely individual people, and people must take care of themselves. Government must be small and weak, and only property owners should be allowed to vote and participate in it. Voluntary associations must be small and local and built upon neighborhood relationships.[20]

Lower taxes, government retrenchment, and protection for property owners from corrupt office holders—these were Storey's chief local concerns in the 1870s. In the first six months of 1876 the *Times* carried sixty major editorials calling for drastic cutbacks in local government and taxes, and another seventy denouncing local government officials, editorials in which "tax-eating" was the common theme. This was fully half of all editorials on local subjects. In Storey's view, government was an "irresponsible, corrupt devourer of property and industry" that had to be stopped. The *Times* urged individuals to take matters into their own hands, to resist taxes; and the paper heartily applauded those "patriots" who simply declined to pay.[21] "There is no way to compel the devouring monster called government to surrender and submit to the economic law, but to cut off the supplies."[22]

The *Times* did not shrink from the obvious logic that to cut off taxes meant to cut off government. The dismantling of government, except for the barest of necessities, was precisely what the paper proposed. At least two-thirds of the city government should be abolished, the *Times* declared—maybe all of it. The board of health, the fire department, the building inspector's office, the library, and other examples of "useless officialdom" should be killed outright. Other agencies, such as the police department and the public schools, should be saved but greatly reduced. On occasion the *Times* argued that even these should go.[23]

In place of an increasingly complex and, in the view of the *Times,* increasingly corrupt and paternalistic city government, the paper urged upon the citizens of Chicago the traditional virtues of self-help, self-sufficiency, and free enterprise. Abolish the fire department, and the insurance underwriters would quickly organize private brigades. Abolish the police department, and within forty-eight hours its place would be filled by an extension of the private night watch services. Abolish the public works department, and property owners would hire their own private contractors for sewer and street improvements. Abolish the public schools, and people would be forced to spend their own money instead of someone else's on their own education.[24] The *Times* proposed to fragment the municipality into hundreds of small neighborhood subdivisions, each with its own "New England town meeting." These many meetings of neighbors could contract for their own police, fire, and community services. Only a skeleton central city government should be retained. Such a decentralized system would make government directly responsible to the individual taxpayers, the owners of Chicago.[25] It would allow each citizen to live his own private life, in but not of the metropolis.

Permeating the *Times*'s editorial philosophy was a firm belief in the morality and the efficacy of free markets, private enterprise, and competition. Monopoly, where it existed in railroads, public utilities, or other businesses, was the result of unnatural government regulation, the product of the "statute spawners." In scores of editorials in 1876 the *Times* railed against the tariff and currency policies of the federal government and against any kind of "special legislation."[26] Moreover, in arguments that echoed the social Darwinist philosophy of the day, the *Times* carried its belief in laissez-faire beyond the business world to denounce charity and social reform and to embrace personal liberty for individuals in matters such as temperance and observance of the Sabbath.[27] The paper followed what Storey took to be the philosophy of Jefferson and Jackson, insisting that in this world individuals must make their own way. The rise of the city made no difference. Storey's image of Chicago was a marketplace, where individuals struck the best deal they could. If lighting gas prices were too high, switch to kerosene; if there were no jobs, move to the country.[28] Neither government nor charity could contravene the iron laws of the market and of individual responsibility.

The popularity of the *Times* undoubtedly did not rest upon its editorials. After its demise, the paper was remembered for its editorials, but it was celebrated for its news.[29] Like most American newspapers from that era to our own, the *Times* emphasized the news of government, politics, and business. Major national government stories could dominate front-page coverage for months. But the most striking characteristic of the *Tribune*'s news coverage, taken as a whole, was its astonishing diversity.

In 1876 the *Times* was a daily extravaganza of information. Major stories, such as the Whiskey Ring trials and the Hays-Tilden election, were covered in stupefyingly fine detail, frequently with long verbatim transcripts of legal proceedings, legislative debates, speeches, letters, and interviews. But more striking than the depth of the *Times*'s news coverage was its breadth. The paper was filled with column after column of tiny stories from everywhere on every conceivable subject. Many of these were unrelated, one- or two-sentence items grouped together under headings such as "Slices of News," "News Nebulae," or "Local Skimmings." Counting all of these little unconnected items along with the scores of longer stories, it was not uncommon for an eight-page paper to contain more than a thousand separate bits of news.

The "News Nebulae" column suggests the nature of this approach to news. One of these columns begins:

> They have a chain gang in Fort Wayne.
> Terre Haute is going to have a soup house.
> An Indiana man has 17,000 cat skins for sale.
> Here comes Greencastle, Ind., with the smallpox.
> The crusaders of Keokuk will soon commence street work.[30]

Some of the news bits were departmentalized, as in "The Religious World." An example:

> There are 77 Protestant Episcopal churches in New York.
> The death is announced of Rev. A. H. De Mora, a Protestant Episcopal minister, at Lisbon, Portugal.
> The report that Mr. Moody received a purse of $1,500 at Augusta, Ga., is denied on the best authority.[31]

These examples are merely the first few items; each of these columns goes on and on. And columns such as these appeared daily throughout the paper.

This strange randomness of news was not confined to the special columns of miscellany. Though the longer stories were usually grouped and classified in a more orderly fashion, the tendency of the whole paper was toward the miscellaneous. Government news ranged from the doings of President Grant to the exact amount of fees collected yesterday at the Water Department; court news ranged from Supreme Court decisions to minor bankruptcies in distant cities; religious news, from the health of the pope to the number of Quakers in Iowa (there were 8,865); foreign news, from the crisis in Turkey to an ice-skating accident in France. In short, virtually any event from any-where in the world could make the paper.

Storey's goal was to provide something for everyone, individual items for individuals. This approach to news did not develop accidentally at the *Times;* it complemented the editorial philosophy of the paper. In the 1870s the *Times* was a marketplace of the sort that Storey favored, filled with infinite choice. The news content of the *Times* was as diverse, fragmented, disorganized, and bewildering as the life of the city it served. The modern city scene portrayed in the news columns was an enormously complicated spectacle, spread out in disarray before the reader like the city itself.[32]

In the 1870s the chief competitor of the *Times* was the *Chicago Tribune.* Unlike the *Times,* the *Tribune* did not aspire to be a general circulation news-paper, nor did it pretend to appeal to the masses. It was, by its own declara-tion, "the businessman's newspaper," and it scoffed at the *Times*'s efforts to entice readers from the "slums and back alleys" of Chicago.[33] The *Tribune* prided itself on being part of the modern metropolis that Chicago had grown to be by the 1870s. The paper chided the *Times* for its lingering small-town ways. To the *Tribune* the *Times*'s endless, miscellaneous gossip from the lo-cal churches and neighborhoods "belongs to the worst class of newspaper enterprise of small towns, where everybody knows everyone else." The *Tri-bune* reminded Storey that "the mingled town and village aspects are gone. . . . The tendency is to the metropolitan in everything—buildings and their uses, stores and their occupants. And village notions are passing away with them. . . . We are getting to be a community of strangers. No one expects to know and nod to half the audience at church or theatre, and, as to knowing one's neighbors, that has become a lost art."[34] Yet, despite the *Tribune*'s mock-ery of the *Times*'s outmoded vision of city life in Chicago, the two papers were not strikingly different in their understanding of either urban community or urban journalism.

After 1874, when he gained controlling interest, Joseph Medill was the ed-itor and guiding light of the *Tribune* in much the same autocratic way as the *Times* was "by W. F. Storey." Storey hated Medill, and Medill hated Storey. They were antagonistic in almost every way—in politics, in business, in social circles, and in personal style. Yet beneath surface contrasts lay similar commitments to private property and individualism and similar notions of what news should be in a big-city newspaper. Medill was closer than Storey to the political and social elites of Chicago, but the values reflected in the editorials and in the news content of the *Tribune* remained, like the *Times*'s values, private and individualistic.[35]

Because Medill was a political as well as a business and social insider, the *Tribune* harbored less suspicion than Storey and the *Times* of government per se. Medill was an organizer of the Republican Party, a drafter of the Illinois state constitution of 1871, and mayor of Chicago from 1871 to 1873 in the aftermath of the great fire.[36] Through the *Tribune* Medill affirmed the necessity of urban government and branded the *Times*'s call for complete tax resistance in 1876 as "an infamous incendiary appeal." The *Tribune* argued simply that life would not be endurable in Chicago without tax-supported government to handle essential services such as water supply, sewerage, police, and fire protection.[37]

Medill believed that the range of proper government authority was broader than the *Times* perceived it to be, but that range was still quite limited. Though a party regular, Medill was in other ways a part of the philosophical tradition of the liberal Republican and Mugwump movements of the 1870s and 1880s.[38] He believed that the purpose of government was the preservation of private property and free business enterprise. Like Storey, Medill viewed Chicago as essentially a marketplace. The *Tribune* fought taxes because taxes encumbered property and hurt business. Private property and business, however, required a minimal level of public collective action. Commerce depended upon paved streets, well-maintained bridges, and even schools and libraries.[39] As a former mayor elected on the "Union-Fireproof" ticket, Medill was especially concerned about fire protection. Fires were bad for business, and fire insurance rates were sky high in Chicago after 1871.[40] For the *Tribune*, fire control was a clear case of an appropriate collective function; the protection of life and (as the editorials more typically suggested) property.

Government activities not directed toward those ends were inappropriate, in the opinion of the *Tribune*. The paper was especially opposed to the notion that government should serve a welfare function, except for orphans and the disabled who were without family. On that subject the *Tribune* saw no difference between the industrial, metropolitan Chicago of 1876 and the village of Chicago forty years before. People must take care of themselves. The government should be out of the charity business almost altogether, and even private philanthropy should be curtailed in order to preserve the character of the individual and the vitality of individualism in society.[41]

Even the appropriate functions of local government must be strictly limited to achieve salutary ends. The *Tribune* argued in 1876, for example, that
the great public works of the city were largely done. The street grade had been
raised to improve drainage, the main streets were paved, the water supply was
supposedly pure and ample, the river was a bit less horrible. Now property
owners could take care of their own street and sewer extensions and repairs
without the intrusion of government. The collective work of the city could
now be limited to routine maintenance of the infrastructure that had already
been built. Thus, the paper argued, government could be reduced significantly and taxes cut dramatically, all of which would increase the value of property and enhance the true business of Chicago, which was business.[42]

Though it chastised the *Times* for rejecting government altogether, the
Tribune was nearly as hostile as the *Times* to the continuing expansion of local
government and to what it perceived to be the corrupt domination of government by loafers, bummers, and tax-eaters.[43] In the first six months of 1876
the *Tribune* carried 115 major editorials pleading for retrenchment and lower taxes in local government and another 119 attacking local government
officials, usually for extravagance and corruption. This adds up to nearly two-
thirds of all editorials on local subjects. Like the *Times,* the *Tribune* brooded
and fulminated over the "spendthrift, reckless demagogues who think that
Governments are instituted for no other purpose than to confiscate private
property."[44]

The *Tribune* preferred that local government be run as an adjunct to the
business culture of the city. The paper professed a belief in democracy, while
at the same time it insisted that government should be the province of the
"better classes"—"men of brains, wealth, and standing in the community."[45]
Medill could openly favor aristocracy because he believed it was merely
meritocracy, rule by a natural, free-market-generated elite. So convinced was
the *Tribune* of the righteousness and efficiency of private enterprise and the
free market in urban life that it saw no need, as the *Times* did, to limit democracy. Surely, all rational people could be persuaded to support a busi-
ness-oriented government, because what was good for business was good for
Chicago.[46]

At the same time that it professed an abiding faith in democracy and
American public institutions, the *Tribune* warned in 1876 that the country
was rapidly sliding into a deep and general moral decline. The corruption
of government, ranging from the Grant administration to the ward machines
of Chicago, the *Tribune* traced to individual immorality. To solve the problem the paper continually urged a return to old-fashioned honesty, frugali-
ty, simplicity, work, church, and family. Society was simply the gathering

together of individual people and very small-scale communal institutions, and "individual integrity and purity of life must be again recognized as among the highest requisites of social life."[47]

In 1876 Wilbur Storey bragged that the *Times* spent twice as much as the *Tribune* on news gathering and that the *Tribune* was a decadent and decaying news medium.[48] The content of the two papers suggests otherwise. The *Tribune* was the rival of the *Times* in all departments of news and information. Medill's paper was less scandalous and sensational than Storey's, but the variety of subjects covered and the amount of space devoted to broad categories of subjects were virtually identical in the two papers, despite their differences in ideology, politics, and target audiences. Like the *Times*, the *Tribune* favored news of government, politics, and business. Moreover, the *Tribune* handled the news much as the *Times* did. Every day the paper contained hundreds of items of the most amazing diversity. Like the *Times*, the *Tribune* was a teeming marketplace of miscellaneous information.

The organization of this mass of information was not altogether random. Typically, it was well classified under headings such as "Foreign," "Washington," "The City," "The Court," "Criminal News," "Fires," and "Finance and Trade." Under any one of these broad categorical headings, the scores of items usually varied enormously and included much the same kind of trivia that filled the pages of the *Times*. For example, the *Tribune*'s "Washington" column was filled daily with stories, reports, statements, speeches, and the verbatim proceedings of Congress. The "City Hall" column listed virtually every official happening in city government, many in single-sentence briefs, from the day's water rent receipts to the number of buildings inspected. "The City" included personal gossip, real estate transfers, anything that could be written in the form of a brief statement of fact.[49] Like Storey, Medill proposed to print all the news of the day.

The *Tribune* in the 1870s called itself the businessman's newspaper, and so it was. But as a circulation leader it was not unlike an aggressively popular newspaper such as the *Times*. On the editorial page it stood for conventional values—individualism, private property, and free enterprise. In the news pages it conducted a marketplace of information with something for everyone—a spectacular bazaar that reflected more than interpreted the complexity and diversity, the individualism and privatism of the modern metropolitan city.

It was into this urban and journalistic milieu that the *Chicago Daily News* was born in December 1875. The *Daily News* succeeded almost from the start. By the early weeks of 1876 the paper claimed a larger circulation than any other evening paper in Chicago, about ten thousand daily. This was probably an exaggeration. But by June of its second year the *Daily News* averaged about twenty thousand per day, a figure surpassed in Chicago only by the two giants, the *Times* and the *Tribune*.[50] By the 1880s the *Daily News* itself was the giant, with a circulation of more than 150,000. Although no other Chicago paper (except the *Record*, the morning edition from the *Daily News* shop) achieved a steady circulation of 100,000 before the twentieth century, the *Daily News* hit 200,000 by 1895. Publisher Victor Lawson boasted matter-of-factly in 1886 that nearly everyone who read English in Chicago read the *Daily News*.[51] This was exaggeration, to be sure, but not by much. The *Daily News* was the only approximation to a modern medium of mass communication in Chicago in the nineteenth century.

The *Daily News* was a newspaper quite unlike the *Times* or the *Tribune* or any other paper in Chicago. It was a "penny paper," a small-format, four-page sheet, selling for one cent instead of the usual four or five cents. In appearance alone it was strikingly different. Everything was on a smaller scale— smaller format, fewer stories, and fewer departments; everything tightly edited and drastically condensed. But, in a more subtle sense, its philosophy was as different as its look. Of course, the *Daily News* was a business enterprise, and its enterprising founders shared many of the business values of men like Wilbur Storey and Joseph Medill. The *Daily News* also reflected many of the social values of the dominant, Protestant, native-born elites of Chicago. Yet, when it turned to concrete issues in the city of Chicago, the *Daily News* seemed to recognize certain imperatives of collective life in the modern metropolis. Despite its general commitment to private enterprise, the paper promoted from the beginning a kind of community life much less dominated by rigid notions of private property and individualism. In both editorial philosophy and journalistic technique the *Daily News* was an *urban* newspaper, an activist portrayer and promoter of the public community.

The founder of the *Daily News* was Melville E. Stone, a classic example of the self-made man, the son of a poor itinerant Methodist minister and destined to become one of the most prominent journalists of his time. Throughout his life Stone celebrated the homely virtues of his childhood on the Illinois frontier—family, honesty, hard work, equality.[52] As a young, energetic citizen of post–Civil War Chicago, Stone became an active participant in the associational life of the city, serving on the boards of a variety of government agencies and private organizations. In politics he was a Lincoln admirer and a Mugwump, or, as he liked to say, "a Republican with a conscience." He professed to believe that a newspaper should be independent of party politics, devoted to the presentation of "facts" rather than the manipulation of public opinion.[53] Stone's partner almost from the beginning of the *Daily News* was

Victor Lawson, a man much like Stone in personal background, political philosophy, and social vision. Lawson took over sole control of the *Daily News*
in 1888 and continued Stone's editorial tradition while contributing his own
special talent for the promotion of advertising and circulation.[54]

Although Stone and Lawson were probably more involved in voluntary
organizations than most businessmen, they were in most respects not excep-
tional men in nineteenth-century America. Their biographies read much like
those of other self-made businessmen, including newspaper publishers such
as Storey and Medill. Their professed values were conventional. But the nature of their newspaper led Stone and Lawson, almost in spite of themselves,
down a different path, away from an unexamined devotion to private property and individualism and toward a vision of collective life and community in the fragmented "private city" of the late nineteenth century. Stone's aim
was not to publish a smorgasbord paper, with some different thing for everyone, in the style of the *Times* and the *Tribune* and other popular papers.
His aim was to print a small newspaper, edited so that a majority of the content would appeal to a majority of the readers. Like the *Times*, the *Daily News*
was to be a mass-audience paper, aimed at all the citizens of Chicago. But
rather than serve the individual tastes of individual readers, Stone sought out
the common tastes of a community of readers.[55]

The image of Chicago evoked in *Daily News* editorials was one of community and family rather than of individualism and marketplace. From the beginning the editorial philosophy of the paper was much more attuned to interdependence than to individualism in the great metropolises of the late
nineteenth century. The social obligations of Chicago to its people were frequent editorial themes. In a remarkable editorial during its first month of life,
the *Daily News* argued that the city should provide public relief and employment for all in times of need, because hard times were much more difficult
for the unemployed in a modern city than in the countryside or a small town.
Moreover, to care for the poor was to care for the whole community. Such a
plan, of course, would cost money, the paper admitted; but in a larger sense
"nothing would be lost, but simply capital would be removed from one pocket
to another, to be circulated for the good of the community." And, anyway,
community spirit, not cost, should be the sole concern: "Are we, citizens of
the boasted Queen of the West, the first in every enterprise, to pause to consider a question of dollars and cents when a great end is to be accomplished?"[56]
The argument was based less on Christian charity and more on the practical
requirements of life in a large city. "No class in society can afford to ignore
another," the paper declared; "we are far too interdependent."[57]

To some extent Melville Stone's editorial philosophy grew out of his own personal sense of place in Chicago. On the one hand, Stone was part of the business and social elite of the city, relishing his membership and leadership in upper-class clubs and societies. On the other hand, Stone loved the "other half" of Chicago just as well. He seemed to attract and to support with great good humor a long line of drunks and vagabond reporters and editors on the staff of the *Daily News*. He proudly numbered among his friends drifters and burglars as well as business magnates and presidents. Fifty years later he recalled how he had loved it all, from top to bottom. "As Dean Swift would have said," he wrote, "we lived all the days of our life."[58]

More specifically, the Chicago fire of 1871 became an enormously important event and symbol for Melville Stone's understanding of Chicago and of urban life in general. During the unhappy winter of 1871–72, Stone was one of the chief directors of relief efforts in the city, and he came away from the experience much impressed by the commonality of interests among residents of a large city, regardless of their class or occupation. "There was no shelter for the rich, none for the poor; for the time being the millionaire was no better off in worldly goods than the pauper," Stone wrote on the fifth anniversary of the fire. In that fall of 1876, with the city in economic depression, Stone reminded Chicagoans that the whole community must rise together as it had five years before. "The poor shall not suffer, the sick shall not be neglected," he wrote, "and all must look forward to better times that are coming."[59] In effect, Stone had accepted the idea that private property in a large city has social roots and community obligations—a view not fashioned through study and reflection but forged in the fire of 1871.

Because of its belief in the interdependent nature of urban society, the *Daily News* was much less inclined than the *Times* or the *Tribune* to place the blame for social problems upon the heads of individuals. Stone argued that the poor were poor because of hard times; prostitutes were prostitutes because they could find no honest work; bad boys were bad because of poor nurture in the schools and churches.[60] With such a view of the power of environment and community over the individual, it is not surprising that the *Daily News* was a strong advocate of charity and an early proponent of what would soon be called the Social Gospel. The paper urged the creation of all sorts of philanthropic organizations, including shelters for prostitutes and homeless waifs, public baths, soup kitchens, mutual aid building societies, and especially unemployment relief agencies.[61] Almost always, interdependence and sympathy were the key ideas, the organic city the key image. In calling for large-scale, organized charity for the approaching winter of 1876–77, the *Daily News* rejected the idea that a person should have to be a property owner to be a part of the city. "It is enough for charitable people, for

Christian people, for humane people, to know that a man is in need, whether he comes from Maine or California, from Illinois or Kentucky, from Germany, Ireland, or the Cape of Good Hope, he is still a man." But, as usual, Stone's reasoning was based as much on the *practical* interdependence of city life as on the *moral* obligations of Christian charity. Recalling again the aftermath of the fire, Stone reminded Chicagoans that "the man who would refuse to aid his fellow man this hard winter will, in all probability, find use for a soup house himself before he dies."[62]

While promoting voluntary association as a way to strengthen community life in the city, the *Daily News* also urged formal public action through government. In this respect the *Daily News* early drifted from the individualistic and voluntaristic reform ideology of conventional Mugwump organizations such as the Chicago Citizens' Association, founded in 1874 as the city's first permanent municipal reform group.[63] Melville Stone was certainly no socialist in the ideological sense. Like Medill and Storey, he complained about high taxes and governmental waste and corruption. He even sometimes spoke in the abstract of immutable laws of political economy.[64] But on most concrete cases the *Daily News* found itself advocating increased governmental intervention in business and urban life and even arguing from time to time that taxes were not too high, considering the social tasks at hand. In the first six months of 1876 the paper carried more than three times as many editorials calling for expansion of government activities as for retrenchment.[65] While the *Times* was calling for the dismantling of city government and the *Tribune* was carefully drawing the boundaries between the proper realms of public and private action, the *Daily News* was urging more government enterprise and more government regulation as the only way to make life livable in a modern city.

The *Daily News* promoted government enterprise for two reasons. First, the paper argued that large-scale urban centers such as Chicago demanded large-scale public works. For simple reasons of health and safety, streets must be repaired and extended, sewers and waterworks maintained, trash collected, schools and parks operated, public baths built, air pollution controlled, and hospitals improved.[66] In this the *Daily News* was not unlike the *Tribune*. But in its advocacy of public works the *Daily News* went far beyond the *Tribune* and the business-dominated reform tradition in Chicago. The *Daily News* urged government enterprise not only because it was necessary to provide an economic infrastructure for private enterprise but also as a way to provide work for the unemployed. In early 1876 the *Daily News* called upon the city to provide a job to every man who needed one. The paper believed that the community owed its most unfortunate members help in time of need, for their misfortune was no fault of their own and was the community's misfortune as well. While the *Times* was counseling the unemployed to get out of town, the *Daily News* was urging the town to take them in. In a traditional community this might have been accomplished by the private action of kin or clan. In the modern urban world such community building would require the formal, organized effort of government. It would require the public community.[67]

The *Daily News* promoted an expanded role for government in regulation as well as enterprise. The paper proposed that city and state governments take more responsibility for ensuring the health and safety of citizens, through the control of railroad and wagon traffic, the regulation of food and drug quality, the enforcement of fire codes, the inspection of buildings, the abatement of smoke and foul odors, and the regulation and municipal ownership of public utilities.[68] The *Daily News* was much less doctrinaire about the rights of private property than were the *Times* or the *Tribune*. In the social scheme of Stone and the *Daily News*, business was meant to serve people, property to serve community. If business and property failed in this service, the people should intervene.

As a penny paper, the *Daily News* gathered an audience that was heavily working class, and the paper sought to affirm its sympathies with the laborers of Chicago.[69] The *Daily News*, however, was not in any sense a socialist or labor paper. Its aim was to promote community across class lines and to appeal to common interests of all classes. While its calls for public works and government regulation of business may have been in the interest of the lower classes, the paper also favored social regulations, such as antigambling laws, liquor control, immigration restrictions, compulsory school and Sunday school attendance, and compulsory English language instruction.[70] This insistence of the *Daily News* upon social control and conformity, along with extensive economic regulation, suggests that the paper's ideology was a transformation of older ideals of an ordered, organic community rather than an incipient class-based socialism. Though the *Daily News*'s program might be labeled socialistic, its goal was not radical social change; rather, it was social and community preservation against the storms of urbanization.[71]

If its editorial philosophy set the *Daily News* apart from the other leading newspapers of Chicago, its news policy was just as different. In a prospectus the first day of publication, Stone promised potential readers a compact newspaper that would cover a variety of news but without the "never-ending miscellany" of other popular Chicago papers. He said the paper would carry the latest telegraph news, plus the criminal, legal, social, religious, political, and trade news of Chicago. He also promised more of what might be

called "urban consumer news"—housekeeping tips and advice on insurance
and other consumer purchases. And Stone promised more sporting news and
a daily short story of "intense dramatic interest"—"instructive as well as
entertaining."[72]

Stone's philosophy of editing was to edit, rather than to print, "all the
news" in the custom of popular newspapers of the day. This, more than the
content of the information, is the key to the paper's news policy. Stone believed that busy readers preferred the condensed format and preferred to
focus their attention on one big, continuing story at a time. Stone criticized
newspapers such as the *Chicago Tribune,* which he said "was conducted upon
the theory that it was justified in publishing whatever it believed the public
would enjoy reading." Perhaps thinking of the *Times,* Stone said, "It is easy
to edit a newspaper if one does no thinking. . . . He then labels all murders
and suicides and hangings and prize fights and chicken fights as news, and
his task is a simple one." Stone did not disapprove of sensationalism and
human interest news. He merely felt that both good business and good morality required editors to be highly selective in shaping their product. Rather than cater to the myriad interests of a complex city, he would seek the
common interest—assuming, of course, that there was such a thing.[73]

In its first year the *Daily News* only partly lived up to its prospectus and
to Stone's notions of good popular journalism. In general, the paper carried
a smaller proportion of government news than the *Times* and the *Tribune*
and somewhat more consumer news and fiction. Stone regularly included
household tips, medical advice, and scientific news, along with a few tersely
written editorials. This material was what Stone had in mind when he talked
of news of interest to the majority of readers. The *Daily News* carried crime
and disaster stories as well as other human interest news, but the paper carried very few purely private items, such as society gossip, church news, and
other such "tittle-tattle," as Stone called it.[74]

The *Daily News* was so condensed in 1876, however, that its only real news
page—page one—read almost like the miscellaneous shorts that Stone had
renounced in his prospectus. Major stories were usually only one or two
column inches long, and many items were single sentences. Neither Stone nor
his staff favored the extreme condensation of the *Daily News* in its very early years; it was forced by the financial needs to keep the paper small while
accepting as much advertising as possible.[75]

Gradually, as the *Daily News* grew in size, it settled upon investigative reporting and crusading as its chief strength. From the beginning Stone was
fond of what he called "detective journalism," especially the "investigation
of public wrongs." In 1877, for example, the *Daily News* began a crusade for

state inspection and regulation of savings banks, as part of its interest in consumer protection. In the course of the investigation Stone exposed a crooked bank president, who fled to Canada and then to Europe. Stone personally gave chase and finally tracked him down in Germany. This was the first of many such investigative stories, and all of them provided just the sort of news that Stone liked: stories of wide interest among *all* readers; stories that continued day after day, focusing the attention of the whole audience; stories that served the "betterment of readers"; and stories laced with drama and inherent sensation.[76]

The old popular city press, such as the *Times* and the *Chicago Tribune,* and the new metropolitan press, such as the *Chicago Daily News,* both had to confront the problems of the growing complexity and diversity in modern cities and the breakdown of traditional community life. To some extent all recognized and celebrated diversity; they had to in order to be broadly popular.[77] And all recognized that much of modern city life had become formal and impersonal. But in a more fundamental sense their confrontations with complexity took quite different turns. The *Times* and *Tribune* conceived their function as serving essentially private interests. As proponents of laissez-faire, they drew a sharp distinction between public and private. Certainly, they covered in great detail the chief public institution, government. But the public realm was strictly limited. The rest of the life of the city was simply the aggregation of private lives, and the task of the newspaper was to serve these private interests—diverse, discrete, and individual. The *Daily News,* on the other hand, conceived of a public of a few broadly shared interests. The *Daily News* understood that the denizens of the modern city did not share many strictly private interests, as did the members of traditional face-to-face communities. The populations of cities were, in fact, becoming increasingly heterogeneous, isolated, and private. Yet, paradoxically, the growing interdependence of life in the modern city made some private interests public, in the sense of being widely and deeply shared. For the *Chicago Daily News,* the task was to locate and to serve those interests, to promote a new kind of public community.

The *Chicago Daily News* was not alone, and Chicago was not unique. In New York City, for example, the popular press was similarly transformed in ethos and ideology in the late nineteenth century. The penny press of the 1830s and 1840s began the modernization process, expanding the definition of *news* and developing a commercial product that would appeal to a wide audience. The successful penny papers of New York, however, were kin to the *Times.* They followed the smorgasbord model of something for everyone, and they generally remained committed to a traditional understanding of private property, free enterprise, and individualism.[78] It was the *New York World*, after Joseph Pulitzer took it over in 1883, that urbanized popular newspaper journalism in New York in the manner of the *Chicago Daily News*. It was the *World* that developed both an editorial and as news policy that played upon and promoted common interests and a pragmatic, collectivist urban vision.[79] The pattern was repeated in other cities as well.[80]

* * *

The history of Chicago and other large American cities suggests that the confusion between public and private was in some ways forced by the urbanization process in the late nineteenth century. Richard Sennett, Thomas Bender, and others have demonstrated that problems arose when public life came to be dominated by private values and individual psychology. True enough. But the forces of the city worked in the opposite direction as well— making private lives matters of public concern. Modern urban life, by its nature, blurred the distinction between private and public. Urbanization perforce created the paradox of people who were increasingly strangers but who were also increasingly dependent upon one another and increasingly affected by one another's private behavior. Private issues became public issues and then private again. City dwellers breathed the same sooty air, drank the same poisoned water, slogged the same muddy streets, shared the same crowded streetcars and the same fatal diseases.[81] The peculiar terror of modern urban life was that it rewarded individualism while making individualism untenable; it undermined traditional community while making community ever more necessary for survival; it sharpened the distinction between public and private in some ways while blurring it in other ways. The *Daily News* and its editors did not set out to sell a program for a collectivist urban utopia. But in their efforts to sell a newspaper that would appeal to some part of everyone in the city, they found such a program thrust upon them by the city itself.

Michael Frisch has suggested that community life in nineteenth-century cities was not eclipsed or necessarily perverted but was transformed. He found that in Springfield, Massachusetts, "the growing public functions of government and the accumulating results of rapid social and physical change were giving to the community a new meaning: it was becoming more important and comprehensive as a symbolic expression of interdependence. Community, in other words, was changing from an informal, direct sensation to a formal, perceived abstraction."[82] This new notion of community grew gradually and pragmatically, shaped by the historical forces of urbanization. Like all abstractions and symbols, it grew in communication. Of course, some traditional forms of communication were lost in the urbanization process. In his effort to show how community became a matter of individual personality in the nineteenth century, Richard Sennett asks rhetorically: "If people are not speaking to one another on the street, how are they to know who they are as a group?"[83] In Springfield, Massachusetts, they found new ways to communicate, including the medium of the *Springfield Republican*.

The broad thesis of this chapter has been that newspapers were a part of the transformation of community life in nineteenth-century American cities. More specifically, I have argued that the major difference between the popular newspaper press of the midnineteenth century and the urban press of the late nineteenth century—*Chicago Daily News*–style—was that the latter believed, whether correctly or not, that modern urbanization had eroded the distinction between public and private. In some ways this was a return to an older tradition of communitarian thought. But it was a belief born not of nostalgia but of practical necessity. While modern life had helped to distinguish the private from the public realm, urban life seemed now to require again a mingling of the two. I have called the urban vision of the *Daily News* a vision of public community—*public* because it was nontraditional, not face to face, nongeographical, built upon government, formal organization, and mass communication; *community* because it was rooted in shared private interests, common experience and sympathy, and a deep sense of interdependence.

Notes

1. The "enduring tradition of privatism" in American cities is described in Sam Bass Warner Jr., *The Private City: Philadelphia in Three Periods of Its Growth* (Philadelphia, 1968). On the transformation of colonial cities from organic communities to impersonal marketplaces, see Gary B. Nash, *The Urban Crucible: Social Change, Political Consciousness, and the Origins of the American Revolution* (Cambridge, Mass., 1979).

2. See, for example, Roland Warren, *The Community in America* (Chicago, 1972); Maurice Stein, *The Eclipse of Community* (Princeton, N.J., 1972).

3. This literature is reviewed in Thomas Bender, *Community and Social Change in America* (New Brunswick, N.J., 1978), chap. 3. See also Richard R. Beeman, "The New Social History and the Search for 'Community' in Colonial America," *American Quarterly* 29 (1977): 422–43; Robert V. Hine, *Community on the American Frontier* (Norman, Okla., 1980); and Park Dixon Goist, *From Main Street to State Street: Town, City and Community in America* (Port Washington, N.Y., 1977).

4. Samuel P. Hays, "A Systematic Social History," in *American History*, ed. George Billias and Gerald N. Grob (New York, 1971), 315–66; Samuel P. Hays, "The Changing Political Structure of the City in Industrial America," *Journal of Urban History* 1 (1974): 6–38; Richard Jensen, *Illinois: A Bicentennial History* (New York, 1978). See also Herbert G. Gutman, *Work, Culture, and Society in Industrializing America: Essays in American Work-*

ing-Class and Social History (New York, 1976); Richard D. Brown, *Modernization: The Transformation of American Life, 1600–1865* (New York, 1976).

5. Bender, *Community and Social Change,* 58–61. See also Don Harrison Doyle, *The Social Order of a Frontier Community* (Urbana, Ill., 1978); Michael H. Frisch, *Town into City: Springfield, Massachusetts, and the Meaning of Community, 1840–1880* (Cambridge, Mass., 1972).

6. Robert Nisbet, *The Sociological Tradition* (New York, 1966), 47–48.

7. Richard Sennett, *The Fall of Public Man* (New York, 1977), 5, 222–23.

8. Bender, *Community and Social Change,* 148.

9. On the changing meaning of private property in American thought, see William B. Scott, *In Pursuit of Happiness: American Conceptions of Property from the Seventeenth to the Twentieth Century* (Bloomington, Ind., 1977).

10. U.S. Census Office, *Report on the Population of the United States at the Eleventh Census: 1890,* pt. 1, lxvii, 580–83, 670–73.

11. Bessie Louise Pierce, *A History of Chicago,* vol. 3: *The Rise of a Modern City, 1871–1893* (New York, 1957), chap. 2. On the growing fear of social disorganization in late nineteenth-century cities, see Paul Boyer, *Urban Masses and Moral Order in America, 1820–1920* (Cambridge, Mass., 1978), 123–31.

12. Pierce, "Municipal Finances," table in *History of Chicago,* 536. Chicago's fiscal problems were like those of other cities of this era. See Morton Keller, *Affairs of the State: Public Life in Late Nineteenth-Century America* (Cambridge, Mass., 1977), 324–26.

13. Willis J. Abbot, "Chicago Newspapers and Their Makers," *Review of Reviews* 11 (1895): 650–51. See also Justin E. Walsh, *To Print the News and Raise Hell! A Biography of Wilbur F. Storey* (Chapel Hill, N.C., 1968), chap. 1.

14. Walsh, *To Print the News,* chap. 7.

15. Franc B. Wilkie, *Personal Reminiscences of Thirty-five Years of Journalism* (Chicago, 1891), 130.

16. These headlines are typical examples from the *Times* in late 1875 and early 1876. Though crime news helped to make the paper's reputation, it was actually not a large proportion of the news content.

17. *Chicago Times,* Nov. 27, 1875.

18. Abbot, "Chicago Newspapers," 651; Walsh, *To Print the News,* 216–17. Determining the size and nature of a nineteenth-century newspaper's circulation is mainly guesswork, though sources seem to agree that the *Times,* along with the *Chicago Tribune,* held circulation leadership in Chicago in the 1870s—both in the thirty to thirty-five thousand range. See George P. Rowell and Company, *American Newspaper Rate Book and Directory, 1870* (New York, 1870); and George P. Rowell and Company, *American Newspaper Directory, 1879* (New York, 1879). For a typical 1870s newspaper donnybrook over rival circulation claims, see *Times,* Apr. 29 and May 2, 1876; *Tribune,* May 1, 1876.

19. The next few paragraphs are based upon a reading of all major (headlined) editorials in the *Times,* January through June 1876. This amounted to 935 editorials, an average of about five per day.

20. *Times,* Jan. 2, 8, 10, 18, and 23, Feb. 26, and May 11, 1876.

21. *Times,* Jan. 11, Feb. 19, Mar. 7, July 23, and July 25, 1876.

22. *Times,* Jan. 4, 1876. See also the editions of Jan. 7, Feb. 2, and Mar. 25, 1876.

23. *Times*, Feb. 2, Feb. 8, Mar. 8, Mar. 14, July 5, and July 25, 1876.

24. *Times*, Feb. 8, May 20, and July 25, 1876.

25. *Times*, July 5, 1876.

26. See, for example, the *Times*, Jan. 18, Jan. 20, and Feb. 19, 1876.

27. *Times*, Jan. 18, Jan. 23, Feb. 22, May 11, and Oct. 22, 1876.

28. *Times*, Jan. 2, Jan. 23, Mar. 30, and May 23, 1876.

29. Abbot, "Chicago Newspapers," 651.

30. *Times*, Jan. 24, 1876.

31. *Times*, July 23, 1876.

32. One of the few writers on journalism history who has tried to describe the metropolitan press as an urban institution is Gunther Barth. In my view, however, Barth is much too sweeping in his thesis that the metro press helped to make diversity "acceptable" and the city "comprehensible." A paper such as the Chicago *Times*, which Barth celebrates, was as fearful of the city and as bewildered as its readers. Barth makes no clear distinctions among the "metropolitan" newspapers he mentions. See Gunther Barth, *City People: The Rise of Modern City Culture in 19th Century America* (New York, 1980), 97–98, 106–7.

33. *Tribune*, May 1, 1876. The *Tribune* and the *Times* were usually considered the largest circulating newspapers in Chicago in the 1870s. See note 18.

34. *Tribune*, Mar. 30, 1873.

35. Standard accounts of Medill's career are Lloyd Wendt, *Chicago Tribune: The Rise of a Great American Newspaper* (Chicago, 1979); and John Tebbel, *An American Dynasty* (Garden City, N.Y., 1947).

36. Wendt, *Chicago Tribune*, chaps. 10–11; Pierce, *History of Chicago*, vol. 3, chaps. 9–10.

37. *Tribune*, Mar. 19, and July 3, 4, 6, and 7, 1876. The next few paragraphs are based upon a reading of all major (headlined) editorials in the *Tribune*, January through June 1876. There were 851.

38. John B. Sproat, *"The Best Men": Liberal Reformers in the Gilded Age* (New York, 1968), 159–60.

39. *Tribune*, Jan. 24, Mar. 5, May 20, and July 7, 1876.

40. *Tribune*, Apr. 7 and May 7, 1876. The news columns also reflected the *Tribune*'s interest in fire control. Most fire stories were from out of town. When a Chicago fire was reported, the paper often played down the losses. See, for example, *Tribune*, Mar. 8, 1876.

41. *Tribune*, Jan. 30, Mar. 2, and June 25, 1876.

42. *Tribune*, Jan. 9, Mar. 12, and July 2, 1876.

43. *Tribune*, Jan. 4 and 24, 1876.

44. *Tribune*, Mar. 16, 1876.

45. *Tribune*, Jan. 4, Mar. 26, and May 14, 1876.

46. *Tribune*, Mar. 12, Apr. 7, and May 20, 1876.

47. *Tribune*, Jan. 9, Feb. 21, Mar. 6, Mar. 10, and July 4, 1876.

48. *Times*, May 2, 1876.

49. See, for example, *Tribune*, Jan. 1 and 2, and Feb. 2 and 15, 1876.

50. *Chicago Daily News*, Oct. 30, 1876; George P. Rowell and Company, *American Newspaper Directory: 1879*; Charles H. Dennis, *Victor Lawson: His Time and His Work* (Chicago, 1935), 33–34, 38–40.

51. Victor Lawson to Melville Stone, Sept. 11, 1888, Victor Lawson Papers, Newberry Library, Chicago; *Daily News* advertising copy, Apr. 14, 1886, in Lawson Papers; N. W. Ayer and Son, *American Newspaper Annual* (Philadelphia, 1887, 1889, and 1895); Dennis, *Victor Lawson,* 139.

52. Melville E. Stone, *Fifty Years a Journalist* (Garden City, N.Y., 1921), 11–14. Stone left the *Daily News* in 1888. He became general manager of the Associated Press in 1892 and was an architect of the AP's rise to world prominence.

53. Stone, *Fifty Years,* 35–36, 53–54, 76, 152–53. See also Gerald W. McFarland, *Mugwumps, Morals, and Politics* (Amherst, Mass., 1975).

54. The best study of Lawson's stewardship of the *Daily News* is Donald J. Abramoske, "The Chicago *Daily News:* A Business History, 1875–1901" (Ph.D. diss., University of Chicago, 1963). See also Dennis, *Victor Lawson,* chaps. 9–10.

55. Prospectus, *Daily News,* Dec. 20, 1875; Stone, *Fifty Years,* 53–54, 56–57, 109–10. See also Donald J. Abramoske, "The Founding of the *Chicago Daily News,*" *Journal of the Illinois Historical Society* 59 (Winter 1966): 341–53.

56. *Daily News,* Jan. 18, 1876.

57. *Daily News,* Apr. 1 and 17, and May 10, 1876. Comments on the *Daily News*'s editorial policy are based largely upon a reading of all major editorials, January through June 1876. There were 340.

58. Stone, *Fifty Years,* 82 and passim.

59. *Daily News,* Oct. 9, 1876. See also Stone, *Fifty Years,* 35–36.

60. *Daily News,* Jan. 11, Feb. 1, Feb. 2, and Dec. 18, 1876.

61. *Daily News,* Jan. 20, Jan. 24, July 15, Oct. 16, Oct. 27, and Nov. 8, 1876. See also Graham Taylor, *Pioneering on Social Frontiers* (Chicago, 1930). Taylor, a vigorous advocate of the Social Gospel, became closely associated with the *Daily News* in the 1890s.

62. *Daily News,* Dec. 18, 1876.

63. On the Citizens' Association and Chicago newspapers, see David Paul Nord, *Newspapers and New Politics: Midwestern Municipal Reform, 1890–1900* (Ann Arbor, Mich., 1981), chap. 4.

64. *Daily News,* Dec. 23, 1875, and Jan. 9, Jan. 10, and July 13, 1876.

65. *Daily News,* Jan. 18 and Feb. 10, 1876.

66. *Daily News,* Feb. 4, Apr. 10, June 24, July 26, July 28, Aug. 23, Aug. 31, and Sept. 11, 1876.

67. *Daily News,* Jan. 18, 1876. On the mingling of formal organization with community-building efforts in nineteenth-century cities, see Thomas Bender, *Toward an Urban Vision* (Lexington, Ky., 1975).

68. *Daily News,* Jan. 7, Jan. 24, Feb. 26, Mar. 30, May 5, May 8, May 12, July 5, Aug. 29, and Sept. 7, 1876.

69. *Daily News,* Apr. 17 and Nov. 2, 1876; Dennis, *Victor Lawson,* 41–42. A good account of the *Daily News*'s views on labor is Royal J. Schmidt, "The *Chicago Daily News* and Illinois Politics, 1876–1920" (Ph.D. diss., University of Chicago, 1957), 150–71.

70. *Daily News,* Jan. 11, Feb. 15, Apr. 21, Sept. 4, and Oct. 9, 1876.

71. The *Daily News* reflected many of the values typical of middle-class reformers. See Boyer, *Urban Masses,* 123–31.

72. *Daily News,* Dec. 20, 1875. The prospectus is in all the early issues.

73. Stone, *Fifty Years,* 52–57, 77, 109–10, 114.

74. Ibid., 11. Statements in this paragraph (and throughout the chapter) about amounts of news content are based upon a simple content analysis of randomly selected, constructed weeks of issues of the three newspapers for the period January–July 1876.

75. Dennis, *Victor Lawson*, 56.

76. Stone, *Fifty Years*, 77–82.

77. This is Gunther Barth's major thesis about the metropolitan press. See Barth, *City People*, 106–9.

78. Dan Schiller, *Objectivity and the News: The Public and the Rise of Commercial Journalism* (Philadelphia, 1981), 71–75. See also Michael Schudson, *Discovering the News: A Social History of American Newspapers* (New York, 1978), chap. 1.

79. George Juergens, *Joseph Pulitzer and the New York World* (Princeton, N.J., 1966), chaps. 1 and 11.

80. For example, St. Louis, Kansas City, and Milwaukee. See Nord, *Newspapers and New Politics*, chap. 7.

81. The importance of shared experiences among city dwellers in the rise of progressivism is a major theme in David P. Thelen, *The New Citizenship: Origins of Progressivism in Wisconsin, 1885–1900* (Columbia, Mo., 1972).

82. Frisch, *Town into City*, 247. See also Bender, *Toward an Urban Vision*, 131–32.

83. Sennett, *Fall of Public Man*, 222.

6. The Business Values of American Newspapers: The Nineteenth-Century Watershed

THE BUSINESS HISTORY of American newspapers has been rather simply told by journalism historians. There are two versions of the story. The first is the Great Forces version; the second is the Great Man version. The Great Forces version is almost pure functionalism, even economic determinism. Newspapers are portrayed as products of the mass media marketplace—that is, they are pulled into existence by the tug of demand. As times changed, new audiences or new advertisers produced new newspapers. Newspapers were business enterprises, and they naturally shared the business values of other businesses of their time. The Great Man version, on the other hand, is almost pure biography. Newspapers are portrayed as the tools, for good or ill, of powerful press lords. They are forced into existence by eccentric geniuses. In this version of the story newspapers embody the business values of their proprietors, which may or may not reflect the values of the business community at large.

These two versions of the business history of American newspapers need not be contradictory. In fact, journalism histories frequently tell both stories. In Emery and Emery's *The Press and America*, for example, Joseph Pulitzer is both the product and the builder of his era, and the *New York World* is both the result of market forces and of individual genius.[1] Of course, both of these things could have been true and probably were. But though not logically inconsistent, such bifurcated theorizing can lead to mushy explanation. The problem is not that the approach is untrue to life but that it is *too* true. It is all encompassing; it explains everything . . . and thus nothing. The uniqueness of the newspaper business is lost in this approach, because every possible behavior of every possible kind of business could be explained by one or the other version of this business history story. Taken together, these two versions are the polar extremes of the whole continuum of business history in general and in all its bewildering complexity.

In this chapter I argue for a middle-range view of newspaper business history that seeks to discover the uniqueness of the newspaper business and to explain how that uniqueness shaped the business values of editors and proprietors. It suggests that newspapers are a peculiar sort of business and that because of their peculiarity they are neither shaped by Great Forces in the same way as other businesses nor are they the mere playthings of Great Men. As a group, newspapers have been interestingly similar regardless of the men at the editorial or managerial helms. In both structure and product, then, newspapers are a special class of business with a special set of business values.

Specifically, this chapter will trace the business values of Chicago newspapers during the formative years of the modern commercial press, the late nineteenth century. I will explore the responses of three leading Chicago newspapers to three great business/labor crises: the 1877 railroad strikes, the 1886 eight-hour-day movement and Haymarket affair, and the 1894 Pullman strike and boycott. My thesis is that despite ideological and idiosyncratic differences the newspapers were curiously similar in their basic values, that this similarity was related to the special nature of the newspaper business and its role in its community, and that these values were protoprogressive in several interesting ways. By protoprogressive I mean that newspapers seem to have been early proponents of progressive-era business values, notably a commitment to public interest consumerism, an obsession with commercial order and social control, and a growing faith in organizational/bureaucratic modes of conflict resolution.

* * *

The nineteenth century was the age of laissez-faire in American business— or at least in American business values. Daniel Webster had set the stage in 1824. "Our age is wholly of a different character," he wrote, "and its legislation takes another turn. Society is full of excitement; competition comes in place of monopoly; and intelligence and industry ask only for fair play and an open field."[2] Private enterprise was to take the place of community tradition and civic virtue, the fading legacies of early modern religion, mercantilism, and classical republicanism. The American ideology of laissez-faire was the legacy of Enlightenment liberalism, refined in the economic thought of Adam Smith and David Ricardo, and rejuvenated in the late nineteenth century by the social Darwinism of Herbert Spencer and William Graham Sumner. Ironically, laissez-faire as an ideology fastened its grip most tightly on the public mind in the late nineteenth century, when the rise of corporate capitalism had begun to make it obsolete as an accurate description of social reality or guide to public policy.[3]

The foundation of laissez-faire was private property, and the growth of laissez-faire in the nineteenth century was essentially an elaboration of long-standing American notions of the rights and prerogatives of property. Since colonial times Americans had associated property ownership with personal independence—or, in the terminology of the time, liberty. The right to property was a fundamental right, a natural right. Classical economic theory turned this personal right into a social virtue. Private ownership of property and its management by independent, self-interested proprietors would produce the most socially beneficial use of property through the magic of the marketplace. The nature of property ownership had changed radically by the late nineteenth century, with large amounts of property in the hands of a few corporations and large numbers of hands with little or no property at all. But the ideology of private property grew ever more vibrant in law and in public sentiment, especially the sentiment of businessmen.[4]

The role of government in the laissez-faire system was to police the stage, not to play a leading role in the drama. Or so held the ideology. In some ways this was the case in the late nineteenth century. Businessmen and business corporations dominated public life. Direct government intervention in economic life was still a small-scale affair compared to what it would later become. Yet the government was hardly inactive or neutral. Often, governments—local, state, national—directly promoted business enterprise. But, more important, the role of government at all levels in America in the nineteenth century was to affirm and legitimate emerging property relations—that is, those property relations generated by private power and by the marketplace. This was the function of courts, which ingeniously justified the growth of corporations and large-scale finance capitalism in terms of individual private property rights.[5]

Conventional business views on labor and labor organization in the age of laissez-faire were also linked to conceptions of private property. On the one hand, the right to work was viewed as a property right and the selling of one's labor as a property transaction. This made labor—a job—an individual-level contract arrangement between the employer and a single employee. Labor unions, especially if they used any sort of forced compliance, were widely denounced as infringements upon the individual's fundamental right to control his own labor, his own property. Furthermore, businessmen frequently argued that strikes or other concerted job actions infringed upon *their* property rights. Strikes were more than men refusing to work; they were conspiracies in restraint of trade. The courts in the late nineteenth century, under the growing sway of laissez-faire philosophy, gradually elaborated these property-based theories of organized labor.[6]

* * *

On the eve of the great business-labor upheavals of 1877–94, the Chicago newspapers generally shared the business values of the age of laissez-faire— but not entirely and not in altogether similar ways. The city's two dominant morning dailies, the *Times* and the *Chicago Tribune*, were quite convention- al in their devotion to individualism, private property, free enterprise, lim- ited government, and the efficacy and sanctity of the marketplace. These were self-conscious champions of the business culture of the city. The leading afternoon daily by 1877 was the upstart *Chicago Daily News*, founded less than two years before as the city's first "penny paper." From the beginning the *Daily News* was much less committed to laissez-faire than its venerable con- temporaries. In the maelstrom of the modern city the *Daily News* saw the need for a softening of the discipline of the marketplace in social relations. As a paper for the lower classes, the *Daily News* was the champion of social rights that moved beyond rigidly defined rights of private property.[7] Yet, despite clear differences in editorial philosophy, these papers shared some fundamental business and social values during the two decades after 1876— values somewhat at variance from the conventional values of the larger busi- ness community. The nature of the newspaper business itself helped to shape their common perspective.

When the great railroad strikes of 1877 began to spread west toward Chi- cago, no one had to guess which side the *Times* would be on. The *Times* was the personal organ of Wilbur F. Storey, a self-made millionaire who believed steadfastly in the virtues of independence and hard work, in the absolute sanctity of private property, and in the morality and efficiency of free mar- kets and private enterprise.[8] In scores of editorials in the mid-1870s Storey praised the "laws of political economy" and railed against government "pa- ternalism," an all-purpose *Times* label for any effort by the government to tinker with the finely tuned mechanisms of the marketplace.[9]

Storey loved the great national railroads, and he blasted the "thugs and lawless mobs" that began to shut them down in July 1877.[10] Even before the labor troubles turned violent, the *Times* denounced the whole idea of trade unionism and strikes as lunatic assaults on the private property of the rail- road companies. "The notion upon which all strikers act," the paper declared, "is that they have a right of employment upon other men's property. . . . Nothing could be more unreasonable."[11] For the *Times*, men would be paid what they were worth, according to the laws of God and economics. "No human contrivance can ever alter the principle that underlies the relation of labor to capital, even as no statute can modify the motions of the planets or control the ocean tides."[12] Once the strikers became unruly and property was damaged, the *Times* raged and thundered with headlines such as "Riot's Rule," "Terror's Reign," and "A Mob's Madness." In editorials the paper now called for the complete suppression of the strikers by armed force. The time for shooting had come.[13]

Even more than the *Times*, the *Chicago Tribune* was self-consciously "the business-men's newspaper." "It is patronized by all those who are in trade and commerce, banking, insurance, navigation, common-carrying, producing and distributing wealth," the paper boasted during a circulation dispute with the *Times* in 1876.[14] The *Tribune* was the handiwork of Joseph Medill, a prominent member of the Republican political and business elite of Chicago.[15] The *Tribune* believed, as ardently as did the *Times*, in private property and free enterprise. As a former mayor, Medill admitted more of a role for government than Storey did, but that role must be strictly limited. The end of government, the *Tribune* argued, was the protection of property.[16]

The *Tribune*'s devotion to individualism led the paper to oppose labor unionism in general and the 1877 railroad strikes in particular. In its first editorial on the strikes the *Tribune*, in its usual pedantic fashion, lectured the strikers on labor economics. Wages were not set by the employers but by the market, and the employee held no lien on the property of the employer. "If these men think that they can't take the wages offered them," the paper said, "they can step out and let others take their place who feel that they can live upon the wages."[17] Like the *Times*, the *Tribune* became highly agitated when violence broke out. The news columns brimmed with sensational accounts of "Bloodshed," "Red War," and "Civil War." The *Tribune* declared that "Mob Violence Must Cease" and law and order must prevail. The whole force of local, state, and national government must be brought to bear. And the orders must be "shoot to kill"—for "a bullet in time saves nine."[18]

The *Chicago Daily News* was a different sort of paper from its morning contemporaries. The *Daily News* was a newcomer to Chicago, a small, cheap paper, designed for the middle and lower classes, and it was already a remarkable success by the summer of 1877.[19] The *Daily News* was founded by Melville E. Stone, a self-made man not unlike Storey and Medill. Despite his basic commitment to the business culture, Stone guided his newspaper down a different ideological path. From the beginning the *Daily News* was much more attuned to the idea of interdependence than to the notion of individualism in the great cities of the late nineteenth century.[20] Unlike the *Times* and the *Tribune*, the *Daily News* promoted public works jobs for the unemployed, economic regulation, and other government intervention and enterprise, including the nationalization of American railroads.[21] In short, the *Daily News* embraced the rudiments of a social understanding of property that was at odds with conventional doctrines of laissez-faire.

In the 1877 railroad strikes the *Daily News* sympathized with the striking workers. Far from preaching at the workers about the immutable law of wages, the *Daily News* denounced the railroads for their "infamous treatment" of their employees and excused the men for replying to this treatment with the only weapon they had: a strike. The *Daily News* blamed the railroads for the strike and declared that the labor problem would not be settled "until the rights of workmen are properly acknowledged."[22] As violence spread to Chicago, the *Daily News* lost some of its sympathy. Like the other Chicago newspapers, it carried scare headlines ("Pandemonium," "The Grave Outlook") and condemned rioting in strong language. After the strike had ended, the *Daily News* denounced the *Times* and the *Tribune* for their bloodthirsty calls to arms, but during the heat of confrontation the *Daily News* also had called for the swift suppression of the mob, through the use of deadly force if necessary.[23]

In some ways, then, these three papers were quite different in their ideologies and sympathies during the 1877 strikes. The *Times* and the *Tribune* were fairly similar in their antiunion stance and their commitment to laissez-faire; the *Daily News* was pro-striker and had begun in general to move, hesitantly, toward a philosophy of activist government and social welfare. In spite of these differences, however, the editorial ruminations in these three newspapers during the 1877 strikes suggest some basic shared values.

The most obvious shared value was the obsession of all three newspapers with the public's role in the strikes. Public opinion and public interest were key terms of the controversy. Notwithstanding their devotion to private property, none of the three editors doubted for a minute that the issue was heavily clothed in the public interest. The newspapers insisted, as the *Daily News* put it, that "the whole question of railroads is a great public one." The *Daily News* reminded its readers that the Supreme Court had declared railroads "quasi-public property." The *Tribune* spoke of railroads as "public corporations within the control of legislation." Even the *Times*, the most doctrinaire laissez-faire enthusiast of the three, declared that "railroad managers must be made to understand distinctly that they as well as other men owe duties to the public—duties which the public cannot safely permit them to evade."[24]

All three papers defined the public interest in the 1877 strikes as a kind of consumers' right. They professed to speak for a community of consumers

of railroad services, whose interests superseded those of the principal participants in the conflict. All three newspapers suggested that the strikers had
early captured the sympathy of the public, but they lost this sympathy as they
precipitated what the *Times* called a "strike against society itself." The *Times*
and the *Tribune* worried most about lost business in industries affected by
the stoppage of rail transport. But all three papers portrayed their concern
as embracing the whole community, the final consumers of food stuffs and
merchandise.[25]

A second basic value shared by the *Times*, the *Tribune*, and the *Daily News*
in 1877 was an absolutely rigid commitment to peace, commercial order, and
social harmony. Each of the papers at one point or another declared that there
were two sides to the question of wages. But the question was irrelevant in
the face of violence. "The first and most important duty is to quell mob rule,"
the *Tribune* said, "to stop violence, pillage, and incendiarism at all hazards."
The other papers agreed completely.[26] The *Times* put it most bluntly: "The
killing of some of the insurgents is not a matter which concerns society at
all. If they stand in the way of society's peaceful order, the sooner they are
killed the better." Even the *Daily News*, the strikers' best newspaper friend
in Chicago, praised the heavy-handed force of the police and militia.[27] All
agreed on law and order at all costs.

A corollary to the papers' commitment to social order was their belief that
most segments of society—including the strikers in fact—*were* orderly. All
the papers believed in a broad community of interest between labor and
capital, with stress on the idea of community.[28] For this reason, the papers
portrayed the rioters as outsiders—not railroad workers at all. The papers
blamed the violence on roughs and rowdies, tramps and vagabonds, com-
munist loafers and vagrants, blackguard boys and guttersnipes. The *Daily
News* was appalled by the "thugs, thieves, and hoodlums that the slums are
now vomiting into our streets."[29] These were outsiders, aliens, violators of
the natural peaceful equilibrium of the consensus community.

This faith in community and insistence upon social harmony was related
to a third basic value that emerged in the newspapers' editorial reaction to
the 1877 strikes: a pragmatic commitment to an organizational/bureaucrat-
ic approach to conflict resolution that flirted with economic regulation. The
Times, the *Tribune*, and the *Daily News* all recognized that the railroad workers had legitimate grievances against some of the railroad companies. All
three papers despised Jay Gould, a railroad tycoon whom they all denounced
for grossly inept, even wicked, management practices. All judged the railroads
as guilty of bringing on the strike as the railroad workers. They tended to view
the strike as an unfortunate and unnecessary result of bad management—

by both corporations and union leadership. They hoped that the turmoil of the strike would have the good result of improving the bureaucratic organization of the industry, to the advantage of both capital and labor—and the public.[30]

Though the *Times* was hazy on how it expected the good to result, both the *Daily News* and the *Tribune* saw the need for some government intervention. In urging the strikers to give up the effort, the *Daily News* assured them that their "demonstration has taught the country a lesson it cannot forget. . . . The most important study of American statesmen for the next five years will be the proper adjustment of the relations between capital and labor." The *Tribune* urged again and again that the proper adjustment should be a national system of arbitration. Both papers believed in negotiation and discussion; they believed in the power of facts and information in the rational settlement of conflict. The *Tribune* also advocated pensions and disability programs funded jointly by employees and employers. Such bureaucratic arrangements would stabilize the industry and would be good for capital, labor, and the public at large.[31] In short, they believed in a natural community of capital and labor, and they sought to strengthen that community through organizational means—assisted, modestly, by government.

The *Times, Chicago Tribune,* and *Chicago Daily News* were all still in business and still circulation leaders in their city in 1886, another critical year in labor and business history in America. The so-called labor problem had continued to perplex the nation during the decade after 1877, and the mid-1880s became, in the words of one classic labor history, "the Great Upheaval."[32] A series of strikes and boycotts and large-scale union organizing efforts in the 1884–86 period came together in the movement for an eight-hour workday, a movement that in turn culminated in nationwide work stoppages on May 1, 1886. In Chicago the eight-hour movement became mixed up with other issues, including socialist and anarchist political agitation. For Chicagoans and for much of the rest of the country, the eight-hour movement was lost in the smoke of the Haymarket bomb, which exploded, with far-reaching repercussions, the night of May 4, 1886.[33]

The *Times,* the *Tribune,* and the *Daily News* interpreted the eight-hour movement and the Haymarket affair much the same as they had the 1877 railroad strikes. As in 1877, the *Times* was the most thoroughly laissez-faire and the most stridently antilabor. Though Wilbur Storey had died in 1884, and the paper had begun to decline in popularity, it still maintained Storey's allegiance to individualism and to the rights of private property. During the eight-hour-day strikes the paper denounced the eight-hour idea and damned all labor organizations, especially the Knights of Labor, led by the "despotic" Terrence Powderly.[34] The *Tribune* was as antistrike as the *Times*, but it was not stridently antiunion. The *Tribune* on several occasions during the heat of crisis in April and May 1886 praised the wisdom and moderation of Powderly. Though opposed on economic principle to the eight-hour idea, the *Tribune* was not hostile to the eight-hour day in practice if it could be worked out through conciliatory means.[35] Once again, as in 1877, the *Daily News* was most sympathetic to labor's cause. Though it too opposed coercive strikes and secondary boycotts, the *Daily News* gave favorable coverage to the eight-hour movement, including the eight-hour strikes.[36]

In spite of fundamental ideological disagreements over the "labor question," the three newspapers again, as in 1877, shared some basic values in their handling of the crisis of 1886. They all agreed that the labor-business confrontation was a great public question of vital interest to the community at large. The *Daily News* declared that public opinion would finally settle the question, once all the opposing facts and information were known and discussed. "Out of all these varying views will come, in time, the fair, unprejudiced, controlling sentiment of general opinion which will set its seal of approval on these perplexing questions. To that decision all interests must in the end yield."[37] All three papers professed concern about the impact of the eight-hour idea on the general business outlook and on the community of consumers. The *Tribune,* for example, argued that the ramifications of the eight-hour day would extend far beyond immediate employer-employee relations. If adopted in a single city, it could undermine the ability of the whole city to compete with other cities. If adopted generally, it could increase the cost of living for all consumers everywhere.[38] All interests in the dispute had great public duties that they must not ignore.

The newspapers' commitment to commercial peace and social order was perhaps even more ardent in 1886 than it had been in 1877. After a mob smashed windows at the McCormick Reaper Works, and especially after the bomb exploded near the Haymarket, all the newspapers called for retribution, swift and sure. The Haymarket bomb provoked the papers to furious cries for law and order. "The community is menaced by a peril the magnitude of which it were folly to underestimate," the *Times* exclaimed. The *Tribune* declared that the whole community must now rise up to stamp out the anarchist menace. Even the *Daily News,* which was sympathetic to the working class, denounced this assault on public order.[39]

Again, as in 1877, the attack on the public peace was seen as coming from outside the legitimate community. For days after Haymarket, the newspapers produced streams of viciously antiforeign editorials. All agreed that it was the Poles, the Bohemians, the Russians, and other un-Americanized eastern

Europeans who caused the trouble, who cause all the trouble in large American cities. All agreed with the *Tribune* that "Chicago has become the rendezvous for the worst elements of the Socialistic, atheistic, alcoholic European classes." In the newspapers' view of public order and community, disorder was artificial, imported from sick, dying civilizations. As in 1877, the papers reasserted their belief in a classless society in which capital and labor recognized their community interest. The dissidents once again were illegitimate, alien outsiders.[40]

All three papers approved of increased social force against industrial violence, including the use of police, militia, and court injunctions. The *Times* did not go much beyond this as a means to conflict resolution. It simply urged that the laws be enforced rigidly and impartially, and the natural peace and order of economic life would be restored.[41] The *Tribune* and the *Daily News*, on the other hand, elaborated, sometimes vaguely and indirectly, an organizational approach to economic conflict resolution. Both newspapers urged that the eight-hour-day issue be worked out in the "spirit of mutual concession." They argued for careful deliberation on the basis of facts, of hard information, negotiation, and compromise. Both supported labor unionism, if the unions eschewed strikes and violence in favor of arbitration. The idea of arbitration still seemed an especially attractive method for settling industrial disputes. If indeed there were no fundamental conflict between capital and labor, as these newspapers believed, arbitration would benefit everyone and hurt no one—including the general public.[42]

Less than a decade after the Haymarket affair, Chicago found itself the storm center of another major nationwide railroad strike—the so-called Pullman strike. The Pullman strike, in its full-blown form in early July 1894, was actually a secondary boycott against railroads that used sleeping cars manufactured by the Pullman Palace Car Company of suburban Chicago. The boycott was mounted in support of striking Pullman workers by the year-old American Railway Union (ARU) under the leadership of Eugene V. Debs. Once in effect, the boycott against Pullman cars quickly developed into a general railroad strike, tying up traffic nationwide and leading to the usual clashes between crowds and police, striking and nonstriking workers, and to the destruction of railroad property. Throughout the turmoil George M. Pullman refused to deal with the ARU or to negotiate with Pullman employees. The strike was broken by federal court injunctions and the intervention of federal troops.[43]

Most of the newspapers of Chicago opposed the boycott, though they were not particularly sympathetic to the stubborn, imperious George M. Pullman.[44] The *Tribune* and the *Daily News* interpreted this new crisis on the basis of now familiar values—values they had developed over two decades of major industrial strife. The *Times,* on the other hand, was an altogether different newspaper from what it had been during the earlier frays. With its flamboyant proprietor dead, the *Times* had fallen on hard times in the late 1880s. The popular Democratic politician Carter Harrison I rescued it in 1891 and turned it into a factional political organ to boost his campaign for mayor in 1893. Under the editorial direction of his son, Carter Harrison II, who later served as mayor himself, the *Times* became an insurgent Democratic organ—the only paper in Chicago in the early 1890s to wholeheartedly support the Pullman strikers.[45]

As in the earlier crises, the *Tribune,* the *Daily News,* and the *Times* in 1894 held different views of the "labor question" and sharply different sympathies. With the *Times* now practically converted to populism, of the three the *Tribune* remained the most attuned to the philosophy of laissez-faire. The *Tribune* still opposed strikes of any sort, and it reacted to the secondary boycott tactic of the ARU with outrage and vigor. After July 1 almost every news story and editorial referred to Debs as "Dictator Debs." For the *Tribune,* Debs became a villain second only to Gov. John Peter Altgeld, who had the year before pardoned the three surviving Haymarket anarchists.[46] The *Daily News* was not hostile to the Pullman strike itself, though it too criticized the secondary railroad boycott. The paper declared that public sympathy lay with the strikers, and it urged the unions to call off the unpopular boycott if they hoped to win the strike at the Pullman works.[47] The *Times,* now shorn of all traces of Storey-style conservatism, thoroughly supported the original Pullman strike, the secondary boycott, and the union leadership of Eugene V. Debs.[48]

Despite these philosophical differences, all three newspapers displayed once again basic, shared values. As in 1877 and 1886, the papers in 1894 agreed that the Pullman strike/boycott was a great public issue in which the general public had a fundamental interest. This was a central editorial theme of all three. The *Tribune* insisted that "the interests of the country are paramount to those involved in any merely personal dispute between the transportation companies and their employees."[49] Both the *Daily News* and the *Times* agreed with the *Tribune* on the deeply public nature of the strike, and they, like the *Tribune,* defined the public's interest as a consumers' right.[50]

The firm commitment to commercial order, social harmony, and social control also ran through the newspapers in 1894. Not surprisingly, the *Tribune* immediately demanded the suppression of the strikers the moment violence broke out. In the *Tribune*'s view, all strikes were violent by nature. The paper applauded the federal courts for issuing injunctions against the strikers, denounced Governor Altgeld for waffling, and congratulated Pres-

ident Cleveland for sending in federal troops. All laws must be rigidly enforced, the paper proclaimed, all mobs suppressed by force.[51] The *Daily News*
also cried "Disperse the Crowds" and supported the federal government's
show of force. "The workingman's best ally is the law," the paper said.[52] Even
the *Times,* which desperately desired that the strike and boycott succeed,
supported almost all official efforts to enforce peace and order. In an editorial titled "Suppress All Riots," the *Times* urged that all disorders be ended
promptly, with "powder and ball and cold steel if necessary."[53]

As in the earlier eras, the papers again attributed the violence and disorder to outsiders. The *Tribune* made Debs the scapegoat. It was Debs and the
anarchistic leaders of the ARU that were bringing the sober, hard-working
wage earners of Chicago to ruin. The *Daily News* blamed "an excited minority" for the rioting—mainly the usual array of un-Americanized immigrants.
In an atmosphere somewhat subdued from the Haymarket days, the *Daily
News* suggested education rather than hanging as the proper remedy. The
Times declared proudly that "no member of the American Railway union
took part in this lawless foray." The outbreaks instead were the work of "sin-
ister influences."[54] Again, the natural state of industrial relations was peace;
violent conflict was a foreign intruder into the community.

By 1894 all three papers had fully committed themselves to organizational schemes for the resolution of business-labor conflict. Despite their opposing sympathies in the strike, all three urged negotiation and compromise.
George Pullman, an ever-faithful son of laissez-faire who refused to negotiate or compromise, was condemned by all three papers because he insisted
on his own selfish private rights in a great public controversy. Pullman became a symbol of a dying age of private, laissez-faire labor relations. The
Times branded Pullman an archaic "slave driver," who now had become a
"conspirator against the peace and good order of the United States." The
Tribune railed against his "absurd stubbornness" and derided him for ignor-
ing the rights and opinions of the general public. The *Daily News* attacked
him for snubbing a labor movement that had offered to negotiate in a "spirit of fairness." The *Daily News* pronounced Pullman a relic of a bygone era,
who "will not bend an inch from his attitude of stubborn self-sufficiency to
avert a great public calamity."[55]

Arbitration was the watchword for all three papers. "This struggle is one
for the principle of arbitration," the *Times* declared, and the *Daily News* and
the *Tribune* agreed. When Pullman refused to arbitrate, he lost the sympathy of the newspapers. The strikers' desire to arbitrate proved to the *Daily
News* that "they are for law and order and against anarchy and violence." The
Tribune had favored arbitration for decades and pressed for the process again

in the Pullman strike.[56] Despite their vastly different sympathies, even the *Tribune* and the *Times* in 1894 shared a basic understanding of industrial government. The *Tribune* advocated paternalistic company pensions and disability programs that would give employees more of a stake in the good fortunes of their companies. The *Times* urged that companies be forced to give labor "a broader field for the exertion of its power."[57] Yet, different as these proposals were, both papers expected the results to be largely the same, for both papers believed in the common interests of labor and capital. And both expected the results to come through negotiation and compromise, through organization and bureaucracy.

Thus it happened that in late nineteenth-century Chicago, newspapers with sharply opposing views on business-labor issues tended to exhibit similar, fundamental business values: a commitment to public interest consumerism, an obsession with commercial order and social harmony, and a growing faith in organizational/bureaucratic modes of conflict resolution. Neither the general business culture's philosophy of laissez-faire at the macro level (Great Forces) nor the idiosyncrasies of individual publishers and editors at the micro level (Great Men) explains this tendency very well. The peculiar nature of the newspaper business explains it better.

* * *

The newspapers' commitment to public interest consumerism in business matters seems to be an obvious reflection of the papers' own thoroughly public nature. Though editors such as Wilbur Storey and Joseph Medill were devoted to the system of private property, private enterprise, and privatism in general, their product and the function of their product were inherently public. The whole business of a newspaper is "publication"—making information, making issues, public. As urban newspapers began to expand their definition of news and to expand their circulations to broader audiences in the midnineteenth century, the realm of public life expanded for them as well.[58] Through the act of publication itself newspapers asserted that a particular issue was no longer a private matter. There is, in fact, no private life for a newspaper. And this structural imperative of news came to dominate values as well and carried with it a subtle assault on the very private world of laissez-faire.

The modern commercial newspaper, as it evolved in the nineteenth century, was a consumer product designed for broad circulation across class, occupational, and neighborhood boundaries. Even a self-proclaimed businessman's paper such as the *Chicago Tribune* served an enormously diverse audience with diverse and often conflicting private interests. To sell the product newspapers sought to understand and to broaden shared public interests. Frequently, the citizens of the new giant metropolises of America shared more as consumers of the outputs of both private business and public government than they did as producers or wageworkers.[59] Thus the consumer orientation was a natural one for newspapers, given the nature of their business and of their product.

As self-proclaimed custodians of the whole public's interest, newspapers not surprisingly abhorred conflict in the community. At one level newspapers did choose sides in social conflict and on occasion secretly blessed the circulation-boosting side-effect of strikes, riots, and other upheavals. At a deeper level, however, conflict subverted the newspapers' social world, and they opposed it. One reason that the newspapers so stridently favored law and order was because they themselves were relatively small, local businesses, members in good standing of the local business community, and vulnerable to business slumps. Their revenues depended upon *local* business conditions, particularly the economic health of local retail merchants, their advertisers. As fundamentally local businesses, newspapers had a pragmatic interest in local order.

Advertising considerations, however, were not the only, or even the primary, contributor to the newspapers' commitment to community order and social control. In their efforts to do business with the whole public, or large segments of it, the newspapers were necessarily thrust into a mediator role. They were gradually becoming mass mediators, mass media. Because they sold their product broadly, they sought broad consensus. Though they often promoted political interest groups and factions, commercial newspapers almost always looked to the broader public. As communication media, they believed in the efficacy of communication, and they had tremendous faith in the power and righteousness of "public opinion." But to be "informed," public opinion must be calm, rational, and deliberate—and this kind of rational public deliberation was impossible in a state of social turmoil. Violent conflict was alien to the newspapers' vision of communication, consensus, and community. If conflict was alien, it is not surprising that aliens were blamed for conflict. They stood outside the rational world of discourse, especially so if they could not even read English, the sine qua non of community membership for English-language metropolitan newspapers.

Devoted to what they conceived to be the general public interest, committed at all costs to public peace and order, newspapers not unexpectedly held the resolution of conflict, by whatever means necessary, a fundamental goal. Laissez-faire individualism, on the one hand, and organized labor strikes, on the other hand, were ideologies of conflict, and they ultimately fell before this goal—despite the nominal editorial sympathies of the newspapers. When order is valued above all else, it is always possible to see room for compromise and negotiation, and newspapers in the late nineteenth century usually did. They viewed the unwavering, public-defying pursuit of principle, whether by a Pullman or a Debs, as reckless, and socially irresponsible. Newspapers in a sense urged the participants in a controversy to follow what really was a newspaper model of conflict resolution: Organize a formal communication system for the exchange of information, and compromise and consensus will follow.

Notwithstanding their widely varying editorial sympathies, Chicago newspapers by the 1890s were great proponents of arbitration in business-labor relations. Perhaps more than anything else, this faith in arbitration reflects the nature of the newspaper enterprise. To champion arbitration as something more than a stopgap last resort, one must believe that business-labor problems are not pure power struggles but are questions that can be resolved fairly through the gathering, analysis, and application of information. This faith in facts and information is a bedrock belief of journalism. It may be a false faith, but it can no more be divorced from journalism than faith in bomb and bullet can be taken from the military. It is the newspaper's raison d'être. Newspapers, in fact, are themselves arbitrators in social relations—or so they conceived themselves. For these Chicago papers, then, industrial arbitration was merely the continuation of newspaper work by other means.

For newspapers such as the *Chicago Daily News,* the government could be trusted to participate more fully in the creation of community order and social welfare. For other papers, such as the *Chicago Tribune,* the lingering tug of laissez-faire greatly slowed the movement toward endorsement of active government involvement in economic and social relations. But by the 1890s the editorial policies of these two newspapers had gradually converged, in business-labor relations and in other areas as well. By 1900 the *Tribune* had joined the *Daily News* in the promotion of government regulation of the public consequences of urban business, including the municipal ownership of public utilities.[60] This convergence of policy was highly pragmatic, forced by the circumstances of modern urban life in the 1890s. But its roots lay deeper in the past. The underlying values that the newspapers shared by 1900 had grown up with the modern newspaper business itself in the latter decades of the nineteenth century.

* * *

The implications of this version of newspaper business history extend beyond journalism history, for the values that these Chicago newspapers shared in the nineteenth century became the values of progressive-era reform and remain the values of contemporary newspaper journalism. Though the so-called progressive era of the late nineteenth and early twentieth centuries was a time much too variegated to characterize by a handful of social values, it is surely not too reckless to suggest that the values of public interest consumerism, economic and social harmony, and organizational conflict resolution were central to the tenor of those times. Certainly, this was the case in business-labor relations, where the essence of progressivism was the gradual working out of organizational and bureaucratic structures and relationships for the peaceful resolution (or suppression) of conflict between organized labor and organized capital. But these values infused the whole spirit of progressivism, as laissez-faire in America gradually gave way to the organizational/bureaucratic society and the regulatory state.[61]

The thesis of this chapter has been simply that urban newspapers were early participants in this great transformation and that their participation grew from the nature of the newspaper business itself and the relationship of the newspaper to its community.

Notes

1. Edwin Emery and Michael Emery, *The Press and America*, 4th ed. (Englewood Cliffs, N.J.: Prentice-Hall, 1978), chap. 16.

2. Quoted in William Appleman Williams, *The Contours of American History* (Chicago: Quadrangle, 1966), 225.

3. Robert H. Wiebe, *The Search for Order, 1877–1920* (New York: Hill and Wang, 1967), 133–36. See also Sidney Fine, *Laissez Faire and the General-Welfare State* (Ann Arbor: University of Michigan Press, 1956); and Sean Wilentz, *Chants Democratic: New York City and the Rise of the American Working Class, 1788–1850* (New York: Oxford University Press, 1984).

4. William B. Scott, *In Pursuit of Happiness: American Conceptions of Property from the Seventeenth to the Twentieth Century* (Bloomington: Indiana University Press, 1977).

5. Williams, *Contours*, 326–30; Fine, *Laissez-Faire*, chap. 5. See also Morton Keller, *Affairs of State: Public Life in Late Nineteenth-Century America* (Cambridge, Mass.: Harvard University Press, 1977), chaps. 9–11.

6. Gerald G. Eggert, *Railroad Labor Disputes: The Beginnings of Federal Strike Policy* (Ann Arbor: University of Michigan Press, 1967); Sidney Lens, *The Labor Wars* (New York: Doubleday, 1973), chap. 1.

7. I discuss the philosophies of these papers in the 1870s in more detail in David Paul Nord, "The Public Community: The Urbanization of Journalism in Chicago," *Journal of Urban History* 11 (Aug. 1985): 411–41. That article is chapter 5 in this book.

8. The standard account of Storey's career is Justin E. Walsh, *To Print the News and Raise Hell! A Biography of Wilbur F. Storey* (Chapel Hill: University of North Carolina Press, 1968).

9. *Chicago Times,* Jan. 18, Jan. 20, Feb. 19, and Mar. 7, 1976, and Aug. 2, 1877.

10. The *Times* devoted most of a special Independence Day issue in 1877 to praising the railroads of America. See *Times,* July 4, 1877. On the railroad strikes of 1877 see Philip S. Foner, *The Great Labor Uprising of 1877* (New York: Monad Press, 1977); and Robert V. Bruce, *1877: Year of Violence* (Indianapolis: Bobbs-Merrill, 1959).

11. *Times,* July 22, July 20, and Aug. 1, 1877.

12. *Times,* July 30, 1877.

13. *Times,* July 25–27 and 31, 1877.

14. *Chicago Tribune,* May 1, 1876.

15. Standard accounts of Medill's career are Lloyd Wendt, *Chicago Tribune: The Rise of a Great American Newspaper* (Chicago: Rand McNally, 1979); and John Tebbel, *An American Dynasty* (Garden City, N.Y.: Doubleday, 1947).

16. *Tribune,* Jan. 24, Mar. 16, May 20, and July 7, 1876.

17. *Tribune,* July 20, 1877. See also Feb. 4 and May 11, 1876.

18. *Tribune,* July 23, 24, 26, and 27, 1877. The outrage of the *Tribune* and the *Times* was typical of other Chicago papers and papers around the nation in 1877. See, for example, Bruce, *1877,* chap. 12. On the reactions of other Chicago papers, see Foner, *Great Labor Uprising,* chap. 8.

19. On the early years of the *Chicago Daily News* see Donald J. Abramoske, "The Founding of the *Chicago Daily News,*" *Journal of the Illinois Historical Society* 59 (Winter 1966): 341–53. See also Melville E. Stone, *Fifty Years a Journalist* (Garden City, N.Y.: Doubleday, 1921); and Charles H. Dennis, *Victor Lawson: His Time and His Work* (Chicago: University of Chicago Press, 1935).

20. *Daily News,* Apr. 1, Apr. 17, May 10, Oct. 9, and Dec. 18, 1876.

21. *Daily News,* Jan. 18, Jan. 25, Feb. 26, Mar. 15, Mar. 30, May 5, May 8, May 12, and July 5, 1876.

22. *Daily News,* July 20, 25, 26, and 28, 1877. See also Dennis, *Victor Lawson,* 41–44. For a general overview of the *Daily News's* approach to labor problems, see Royal J. Schmidt, "The *Chicago Daily News* and Illinois Politics, 1876–1920" (Ph.D. diss., University of Chicago, 1957), chap. 4.

23. *Daily News,* July 23, 27, and 31, and Aug. 7, 1877.

24. *Daily News,* July 25, 1877; *Tribune,* Aug. 4, 1877; *Times,* July 31, 1877.

25. *Times,* July 31 and Aug. 3, 1877; *Tribune,* July 21, 26, and 27, 1877; *Daily News,* July 27, 1877.

26. *Tribune,* July 23, 25, and 27, 1877; *Times,* July 25 and 29, 1877; *Daily News,* July 23 and 25, 1877.

27. *Times,* July 24, 1877; *Daily News,* July 27, 1877; *Tribune,* July 27 and 29, 1877.

28. *Tribune,* Aug. 1 and July 28, 1877; *Times,* July 29 and Aug. 2, 1877; *Daily News,* July 27, 1877.

29. *Tribune,* July 26 and 29, 1877; *Times,* July 29, 1877; *Daily News,* July 25 and Aug. 9, 1877.

30. *Times,* July 24, 1877; *Daily News,* July 20, 26, and 28, 1877; *Tribune,* Aug. 3 and 4, 1877.

31. *Daily News,* July 25, July 27, and Aug. 7, 1877; *Tribune,* Aug. 3, 4, and 8, 1877.

32. John R. Commons et al., *History of Labour in the United States,* vol. 2 (New York: Macmillan, 1918), 356.

33. Henry David, *The History of the Haymarket Affair* (New York: Farrar and Rinehart, 1936); Bessie Louise Pierce, *A History of Chicago*, vol. 3: *The Rise of a Modern City, 1871–1893* (New York: Alfred A. Knopf, 1957), chaps. 7–8.

34. *Times*, Apr. 30, May 1, and May 2, 1886.

35. *Tribune*, Apr. 21, 22, and 24, May 3, and May 10, 1886.

36. *Daily News*, May 1 and 3, 1886.

37. *Daily News*, May 1, 1886; *Tribune*, Apr. 24, 1886; *Times*, May 1, 1886.

38. *Tribune*, May 2, 9, and 12, 1886; *Daily News*, May 1, 1886; *Times*, May 1, 1886.

39. See the three papers' editorials for May 5, 1886, the day after the bombing. See also David, *Haymarket Affair*, chaps. 9–10.

40. See editorials for May 6 and 7, 1886, in all three papers.

41. *Times*, May 8 and 12, 1886.

42. *Tribune*, Apr. 21 and May 3, 10, and 11, 1886; *Daily News*, May 1 and 3, 1886.

43. Almont Lindsey, *The Pullman Strike* (Chicago: University of Chicago Press, 1942). See also Eggert, *Railroad Labor Disputes*, chap. 7; and Stanley Buder, *Pullman: An Experiment in Industrial Order and Community Planning, 1880–1930* (New York: Oxford University Press, 1967), chaps. 12–15.

44. The Chicago (and national) press treatment of the strike is discussed in Lindsey, *Pullman Strike*, chap. 13. See also John R. Finnegan Sr., "The Press and the Pullman Strike: An Analysis of the Coverage of the Railroad Boycott of 1894 by Four Metropolitan Daily Newspapers" (master's thesis, University of Minnesota, 1965).

45. Leroy F. Armstrong, "The Daily Papers of Chicago," *Chautauquan* 27 (Aug. 1898): 541–42. See also Carter H. Harrison II, *Stormy Years: The Autobiography of Carter H. Harrison, Five Times Mayor of Chicago* (Indianapolis: Bobbs-Merrill, 1935).

46. *Tribune*, June 28, June 30, and July 1, 2, and 15, 1894. See also Wendt, *Chicago Tribune*, 311–13.

47. *Daily News*, July 11 and 13, 1894.

48. *Times*, July 3–5, 9, and 15, 1894.

49. *Tribune*, July 6 and 15, 1894.

50. *Tribune*, June 30 and July 2 and 8, 1894; *Daily News*, July 11, 1894; *Times*, July 3, 5, and 14, 1894.

51. *Tribune*, June 30 and July 1, 4, 5, 8, and 11, 1894.

52. *Daily News*, July 7 and 10, 1894.

53. *Times*, July 4–7 and 11, 1894.

54. *Tribune*, July 2, 8, and 11, 1894; *Daily News*, July 10, 1894; *Times*, July 6 and 7, 1894.

55. *Times*, July 4 and 15, 1894; *Tribune*, July 10 and 11, 1894; *Daily News*, July 16 and 21, 1894.

56. *Times*, July 8 and 10, 1894; *Daily News*, July 11, 13, and 14, 1894; *Tribune*, July 8 and 17, 1894.

57. *Tribune*, July 15, 1894; *Times*, July 18, 1894.

58. On the growth of the metropolitan press see Michael Schudson, *Discovering the News: A Social History of American Newspapers* (New York: Basic, 1978), chaps. 1–3; Dan Schiller, *Objectivity and the News: The Public and the Rise of Commercial Journalism* (Philadelphia: University of Pennsylvania Press, 1981), chaps. 1, 2, and 7; Gunther Barth, *City People: The Rise of Modern City Culture in Nineteenth-Century America* (New York: Ox-

ford University Press, 1980), chap. 3; and Alan Trachtenberg, *The Incorporation of America: Culture and Society in the Gilded Age* (New York: Hill and Wang, 1982), chap. 4.

59. On the unifying function of consumerism in the late nineteenth century, see David P. Thelen, *The New Citizenship: Origins of Progressivism in Wisconsin, 1885–1900* (Columbia: University of Missouri Press, 1972). On the newspapers' role in this process see David Paul Nord, *Newspapers and New Politics: Midwestern Municipal Reform, 1890–1900* (Ann Arbor, Mich.: UMI Research Press, 1981).

60. See David Paul Nord, "The Paradox of Municipal Reform in the Nineteenth Century," *Wisconsin Magazine of History* 66 (Winter 1982–83): 128–42. That article is chapter 7 in this book. See also Nord, *Newspapers and New Politics*, chaps. 6–7.

61. Wiebe, *Search for Order*, chaps. 6–7; Martin J. Schiesl, *The Politics of Efficiency* (Berkeley: University of California Press, 1977), chap. 7; Paul Boyer, *Urban Masses and Moral Order in America, 1820–1920* (Cambridge, Mass.: Harvard University Press, 1878), pt. 4; Richard L. McCormick, "The Discovery That Business Corrupts Politics: A Reappraisal of the Origins of Progressivism," *American Historical Review* 86 (Apr. 1981): 247–74.

7. The Paradox of Municipal Reform in the Late Nineteenth Century

IN 1897 JOSEPH MEDILL was seventy-four years old, and he was tired. As owner and editor of the *Chicago Tribune,* he was nearing the end of a long career of fervent battle against what he believed was an infamous pack of "boodlers, bummers, and tax-eaters" who had brought a proud city—his city—to the brink of financial calamity and moral disgrace. These "jackals, cormorants, and incorrigible pap-suckers" were the members of the Chicago City Council and their political attendants—and Medill hated them with all his heart. But what to do? In 1897, in what seemed a rare declaration of editorial uncertainty, Medill threw up his hands in despair, confessed his moral and political exhaustion, and asked *Tribune* readers to send in their own suggestions for ridding the city of corruption.[1]

Medill's readers responded, and the plans poured in. They spanned the range of reform schemes popular at the time, from moral education in the schools to structural reform of city government to increasing the population of public officials in the state penitentiary. Readers were especially fond of structural reforms, such as the initiative and referendum, the direct primary, stronger mayor, and at-large elections.[2]

The *Tribune*'s reply to its readers in this little impromptu contest showed that Medill had only grown frustrated, rather than uncertain, in his old age. When pressed, he still believed that he knew what the problem was and how to solve it. Though the *Tribune* did favor some of the structural reforms urged by the readers, notably civil service and election reforms, the paper and Medill personally were skeptical of such schemes. The *Tribune* was against the initiative and referendum, against at-large aldermanic elections, and against the direct primary. "What is needed is reform of the electorate," the paper declared, "and laws accomplish little in that direction. A change of heart is needed rather than a change in the primary election laws."[3] Throughout his long life as a political journalist, Medill proposed many reform schemes of his own, but always he insisted that real reform could come only through change in the people, not in the laws or the apparatus of government. For his part, he proposed to bring about this change of heart by educating the electorate through the newspaper.

Joseph Medill's thoughts on municipal corruption and municipal reform grew out of an understanding of democracy that was fundamentally paradoxical. On the one hand, Medill was deeply conservative and elitist in his philosophy of local government. In his half-century as editor Medill made the *Tribune* a rock-ribbed Republican organ that stood for sound money, sound business, and sound government by the "best men." It stood against the urban ruffians and riffraff, especially the "un-Americanized aliens," who were "polluting" the great cities of America in the late nineteenth century. Medill blamed runaway democracy for many of the city's ills—democracy that enfranchised an electorate irresponsible and untutored in the solemn obligations of self-government.[4] On the other hand, Medill believed that only democracy could save the city. He believed that reform could come only when the majority of voters willed it. Thus he used his newspaper not so much to promote structural reform schemes to divert power away from the ignorant masses, but rather to educate and arouse the masses, and to bring into the maelstrom of democracy what he thought were the great issues of urban life and urban reform.[5]

Medill's paradoxical aversion yet commitment to democracy was more than just the idiosyncrasy of a cranky old newspaperman and more than just the clash of idle rhetoric with reality. The same paradox lay at the heart of the thinking of many municipal reformers in the 1890s. Reformers frequently were upper-class or middle-class elitists who feared and fought the rabble masses of the metropolis. Yet many held an abiding faith in popular democracy and public opinion and indeed believed that democratic political action was the only hope for genuine municipal reform. Reformers could support class-biased social reforms and undemocratic structural changes in city government while at the same time fervently working and hoping for democracy. This paradox of reform thought helps explain the apparently contradictory aims and actions of municipal reformers in the 1890s, a paradox that shaped reform activities in Milwaukee, Detroit, Cleveland, and other cities throughout the Midwest and indeed throughout America. But Medill's Chicago provides a striking example.

* * *

At the beginning of the 1890s the leading reform group in Chicago was the Citizens' Association, an organization founded in 1874 in the aftermath of the second major downtown fire in three years. In the 1870s and 1880s the Citizens' Association largely succeeded in several of its major campaigns, notably the adoption of reforms to reduce the risk of fire in the city, the creation of a regional sanitary district, and the annexation of large tracts of suburban territory.[6] The Citizens' Association had ambitions beyond these major projects, however. It proposed, in the words of its first president, Franklin MacVeagh, "to look carefully and thoroughly into the whole framework of our city and county system."[7]

The Citizens' Association of Chicago embraced the spirit and philosophy of mugwumpery, in the broad meaning that has been attached to that term by historians of late nineteenth-century reform.[8] Association members believed in individualism and voluntary association, in government by the "better classes," in education and professionalism, in social harmony, order, and morality. In keeping with its mugwump philosophy, the Citizens' Association often took a negative, restrictive stance toward local government and politics. The group generally supported crusades against vice and gambling, limits on taxation and municipal indebtedness, and prosecution of corrupt government officials. In addition, the association worked for the structural reform of local government, including such changes as civil service reform, the secret ballot, and various charter revisions designed to centralize government and taxing authority and to reduce the power of politicians and the multitude of elected officials in Chicago's many overlapping governmental subdivisions.[9]

The tactics of the Citizens' Association reflected its mugwump spirit. As much as possible, the group tried to avoid electoral politics, preferring instead to act as a lobby group, working to collect information on public policy and to pressure governmental bodies to take appropriate action. Though it sometimes engaged in public education crusades, such as in charter, drainage, or annexation elections, the association usually avoided election campaigns and in general had a low opinion of the average voter. In his presidential address of 1874 Franklin MacVeagh said a prime purpose of the association would be to conserve and promote "the good public impulses of this community." But he made it clear that he was talking about the impulses of "the better portion of the community." He saw the Citizens' Association as representing the "good citizens," who were largely disenfranchised by a corrupt political system, and he hoped that the system could be changed structurally, through civil service, election reform, and more centralized authority, to guarantee the hegemony of the "better classes."[10]

The Citizens' Association represented a rather pure and unambiguously upper-class reform tradition. At the other end of the reform spectrum were the socialists and labor politicians, who were growing in influence among the working-class and immigrant populations of Chicago in the 1880s and 1890s. These two extremes, however, were not the only important municipal reform thrusts in Chicago in the early 1890s. The newspapers represented yet another tradition—a tradition that seemed not so much a compromise between extremes as a borrowing of very different elements from both ends of the continuum. This was a tradition that coincided with Citizens' Association mugwumpery on most principles and programs, yet, paradoxically, placed the greater faith, a genuine faith, in the growth of popular democracy in the city.

The publishers of Chicago's large, metropolitan newspapers were themselves members of the city's business and social elite, and from the beginning they were supporters of the Citizens' Association. Joseph Medill of the *Tribune* was an active member of the association in its early years; Victor Lawson of the *Chicago Daily News* was a strong supporter; Herman Kohlsaat, publisher of the *Inter Ocean,* and Melville Stone, general manager of the Associated Press and founder of the *Daily News,* were both on the executive committee in the early 1890s. Despite various partisan loyalties, most of the leading newspaper publishers of Chicago approved of the association's mugwump reform program. They opposed gambling, vice, and governmental corruption. They favored low taxes. They pushed for "business-like" government by the good citizens of the city. But unlike the Citizens' Association, they seemed to believe that the good citizens were the majority—or would be if properly informed and aroused.[11]

The most widely read newspaper in Chicago in the 1890s, the *Daily News,* was also one of the most thoroughly mugwumpish. Its publisher, Victor Lawson, was more a businessman than a newspaperman, but he understood that bright, concise, cheap, nonpartisan news was good business in a large, heterogeneous city like Chicago. He made the *Daily News* a prototype of the new mass-circulation urban newspaper that grew up in all the great cities of late nineteenth-century America.[12] Lawson and the *Daily News* took an interest in the full range of mugwump reform issues. The paper stood for nonpartisan, business-like city government, for the defeat of the party bosses, for civil service, for the enforcement of Sunday closing and antivice laws, and for the election of "able and faithful public servants."[13] In addition to being a political and economic conservative, Lawson was a prominent and somewhat sanctimonious Protestant layman who strongly disapproved of the personal habits of the city's increasingly poor, foreign, and Catholic citizens. He favored restricting immigration to stop "the constant poisoning of the foun-tain-head of justice—American citizenship—by a stream of ignorance, pau-perism, and crime from the old world." In the early 1890s Lawson was a field marshal in the moral war on gambling in Chicago, and the *Daily News* in 1890–91 carried about two stories and an editorial a week exposing or de-nouncing gambling, vice, and Sunday saloons.[14]

These were not, however, the chief troubles of the metropolis, according to the *Daily News*. Even in the early 1890s, the paper argued that the chief problem was the private control of public services, especially the gas, elec-tric, and street railway utilities. Public services were inadequate, inefficient, and corrupted, the *Daily News* declared; but, unlike the Citizens' Association, the paper argued for more public control—for more government, not less: "The root of the evil lies, not in the wrong uses of money, but in the abdica-tion of sovereignty. . . . Cities are badly governed because irresponsibly gov-erned. The people have granted away their social functions to private citi-zens and to corporations which find themselves under the stern necessity of corruption in order to protect themselves. . . . Abolish special privileges, and very soon municipal corruption will in the main disappear."[15]

Such thinking led the *Daily News* as early as 1890 to a reluctant endorse-ment of municipal ownership of public utilities. It was reluctant because the paper, rooted in mugwumpery, believed in private enterprise, feared govern-ment paternalism, and hated the spoils system of the professional politician. But though it opposed paternalism and class legislation, the *Daily News* ar-gued that government itself was not a necessary evil but a positive good, an essential form of social cooperation. When government abdicated its social duties, which in cities logically included the provision of public utilities, the power vacuum was filled by private trusts and monopolies. The *Daily News* disagreed with Franklin MacVeagh and other local mugwump reformers who opposed municipal gas service so long as the city administration was under the spoils system of party politics. While strongly favoring civil service re-form, the paper said the real source of corruption lay outside the government. The council was corrupted by private corporations, not by municipal agen-cies such as the water or street departments. The *Daily News* believed that "municipal gas might give—and, indeed, would give—a new field to the spoilsmen; but it would, at the same time, rid us of a more dangerous foe."[16]

Altogether, in 1890–91 the *Daily News* devoted about one-third of all its local government and public affairs stories to utility matters, many of which were direct vitriolic attacks on the city's leading street railway baron, Charles T. Yerkes. The paper also carried scores of stories and editorials favoring a more active government role in street cleaning and repair, smoke abatement, sewage control, tax assessment reform, and the elimination of railroad grade crossings. Though the *Daily News* recognized and abhorred the corruption in city government, the paper believed that these problems could be solved only through political action, that reform not only must be but *should* be won at the polls. The *Daily News* under Victor Lawson argued that an expansion of municipal democracy would improve the quality of municipal democracy, that responsibility thrust upon the electorate would improve the electorate.[17]

In some ways, then, the *Daily News*'s editorial philosophy and news coverage reflected the mugwumpery of the Citizens' Association. But in other ways, especially in its analysis of utility regulation and the need for an active local government, the paper had begun to move beyond mugwumpery. Perhaps the most telling difference between the reform spirits of the *Daily News* and the Citizens' Association lay in the area of structural reform of local government. Though the paper agreed in principle with the Citizens' Association on civil service reform and centralization of authority, in practice the *Daily News* devoted practically no attention to these matters. Only a handful of items appeared in all of 1890–91. The *Daily News* was much more interested in practical politics, in getting its kind of candidate elected to office. To this end it was committed to increasing citizen participation in government, for it believed that the majority could be led to share its views. Its job as a newspaper was to provide the information that would mold an enlightened public opinion, that would make democracy work.[18]

In the lexicon of Joseph Medill's *Chicago Tribune,* another of the city's leading dailies, "mugwump" was a term of derision, synonymous with "renegade," "apostate," and "moral scratcher," suited to reform groups like the Citizens' Association and newspapers like the *Daily News* that dared attack Republicans in the name of nonpartisanship. But despite its Republican Party loyalty, the *Tribune* espoused most of the reform values of the Citizens' Association. It believed in morality, individualism, low taxes, and business-like government. It differed from the Citizens' Association in the same way the *Daily News* did. The *Tribune* was little interested in structural reform of government but very much in the expansion of city services and public utilities. With an unavoidable growth in public enterprise the need was to get the voters to elect "honest, capable, and prudent men," and the job of the newspaper was to help them do it.[19]

The editorial philosophy and news selection of the *Tribune* in the early 1890s reflected the dilemma of the ideological conservative caught up in the practical problems of making life livable in the modern city. The *Tribune* was much more skeptical than the *Daily News* of municipal enterprise and the

higher taxes needed to support it. While the *Daily News* blamed outside corporate influences for most of the problems of municipal government, the
Tribune blamed Democratic "bummers, loafers, and rounders"—"tax-eaters" who howled for plunder and spoils like "a pack of famished wolves in
quest of prey." In the *Tribune's* opinion the administration of Mayor DeWitt
C. Cregier in the early 1890s was one of unparalleled jobbery, of "shameless,
willful, disgraceful extravagance." Under such circumstances it is not surprising that the *Tribune* opposed municipal ownership and higher taxes. "The
only good feature of this intolerable municipal sloth and shiftlessness is that
it discourages State socialism."[20]

The *Tribune* had a philosophical as well as a practical aversion to socialism and public ownership. In a series of editorials in 1890 the *Tribune* argued
against the cooperative theories of the Bellamy Nationalists and in favor of
acquisitiveness—yes, even of greed. "No greed, no surplus; no surplus, no
railroads," the paper declared with uncharacteristic brevity.[21]

On the municipal level the *Tribune* in the early 1890s supported private
enterprise in public utilities, even street railroads, the great malefactors in the
Daily News's social scheme. The *Tribune* admitted that streetcar service was
sometimes bad and that the city should get a larger share of the monopoly
harvest, "yet it cannot be said that the people have gained nothing or that
their nickels buy them no more today than in 1860. . . . Some men have grown
rich through the street-car system, but the people in general have been largely
the gainers."[22] This ideology was reflected in the *Tribune's* news coverage and
editorial comment. Like the *Daily News*, the *Tribune* devoted a large proportion (about one-fourth) of its local government and political stories to utility matters, but significantly more of these stories were about utility business
and expansion than about regulation or service complaints.

In spite of its homage to private business and its scorn for public enterprise,
the *Tribune* was forced by the circumstances of the city to support, even to fight
for, public works on a grand and sweeping scale. In editorials outlining the
needs of the city in preparation for the world's fair, the paper listed some traditional mugwump concerns about crime and gambling. But more important,
the *Tribune* said, were physical improvements to be done by the city—streets
repaired and cleaned, new water intake tunnels built, the municipal electric
light plant expanded, the river and canal water quality improved, the smoke
nuisance abated.[23] Much of the *Tribune's* local news coverage in 1890–91 dealt
with these issues. Most important of all was "the Great Drainage Channel," a
project the *Tribune* had pushed for and carried detailed information about for
years. This great canal, designed to reverse the flow of the Chicago River, was
one of the largest and most expensive local public works projects anywhere

in the country in the nineteenth century, and the *Tribune* was its champion. Everything connected with drainage and sewerage was prime news for the *Tribune*, including all the financial and engineering details.[24]

Here, then, was the *Tribune*'s dilemma. It opposed positive, paternalistic government, yet it wanted government to act against the problems of the city. It denounced high taxes, yet it listed ways to spend money. It resisted public enterprise, yet it recognized that the public's work must be done. The solution lay with the election of honest men who would administer the city as a business and who would put the welfare of the city above party interests. But this would have to come through the political system as it was. The *Tribune* had little faith in structural reform. It dismissed suggestions to abolish the ward system of aldermanic elections as irrelevant. It denounced the Citizens' Association's city-county consolidation plan as a plot to expand the payrolls.[25] It devoted little attention to structural reform in the news columns. Instead, the *Tribune* advised that "as the political system of managing municipalities has come to stay, the only thing to do is to make the best of it and to see that all possible is done to make the voters intelligent and honest."[26]

To help make the voters intelligent and honest the *Tribune* was filled with information—about twice as many stories on the average as the *Daily News*—covering the range of local government and reform news. Like the *Daily News*, the *Tribune* in 1890–91 worked for the suppression of gambling and vice. It also conducted its own crusade in the early 1890s against smoke pollution.[27] The *Tribune* touched on many other reform issues as well. But perhaps the most interesting feature of the *Tribune* was the depth of coverage, in both news reporting and editorials. The details of water-flow rates in the polluted South Branch of the Chicago River, the fine points of the single tax theory, the specifics of the municipal government of Glasgow, Scotland—*everything* warranted extended description and comment. The aim, and the great difficulty, of municipal reform, the *Tribune* believed, was to wake up and to educate "the great masses of honest voters."[28]

* * *

In 1896 a new reform organization arose in Chicago that embodied the newspapers' tradition of reform and the newspapers' paradoxical commitment to public morality and business-like government on the one hand and to popular democracy on the other. This was the Municipal Voters' League. The Municipal Voters' League began as the political arm of the Chicago Civic Federation, which was born in 1894 in the strange mixture of high hopes and despair bred by the spectacular Chicago world's fair and the disastrous business panic, both of which occurred in 1893.

Though unemployment relief was the Civic Federation's first priority in the winter of 1893–94, the group quickly expanded the scope of its activities to embrace most of the traditional programs of local municipal and social reformers. The work was conducted through six departments: political, municipal, philanthropic, industrial, educational, and moral. Most of the federation's effort was in the mugwump reform tradition. The Municipal Department in 1894, for example, was interested almost exclusively in structural reforms, such as securing from the legislature a new city charter, a civil service system, a primary election law, a corrupt practices act, and changes in the laws regulating revenues and special assessments. Meanwhile, the Moral Department, in perhaps the most visible of the federation's activities, led a vigorous and temporarily successful battle against organized gambling in Chicago.[29] Though the social trauma of the depression had begun to weaken many reformers' traditional faith in individualism, the old mugwump ideals died hard, even for those who worked in the new "scientific" relief efforts. Journalist Ray Stannard Baker nicely captured this lingering mugwump spirit when he wrote in 1895 that "the Philanthropic Department is now engaged in the work of driving beggars from the street."[30]

The Municipal Voters' League, which grew out of the Civic Federation's political activities, shared the federation's roots in traditional mugwump reform. The league was organized from the top down, with power centralized in a president and a nine-member executive committee. The men who served were not Chicago's highest-level businessmen, but they were solid members of the business and professional elite. The league stood for business-like government, civil service reform, fair property assessments, tighter utility regulation, and the election of "aggressively honest and capable men."[31]

Where the Municipal Voters' League stood apart from the mugwump reform tradition was in its belief in public opinion, its commitment to practical politics, and its intense interest in public utilities. The league's main concrete issue in 1896 and after was always the regulation of public utilities, especially street railways.[32] The leaders of the league believed that Chicago street railway magnate Charles T. Yerkes was the chief corrupter of the city council, and the league looked mainly at utility franchise votes in the city council to determine an incumbent alderman's honesty and fitness for office.[33]

The political style of the Municipal Voters' League was a mixture of traditional organization and modern mass communication. The league organized in every ward, and it was happy to cooperate with party machines so long as the party men would endorse the league's brief platform.[34] But the Municipal Voters' League was always primarily a bureau of information. Its work was based on a belief in public opinion, on a belief that the people would vote for the "right men" if they knew "the facts." To this end most of the work of the league involved the investigation and publication of facts about candidates, especially information on the voting records of incumbents. The league did not field its own candidates but merely reported on the candidates of the regular parties.[35]

The newspapers of Chicago, with one minor exception, loved the Municipal Voters' League because it was committed, as they were, to political action as the way to reform and to publicity as the key to politics. In its campaigns the league used a variety of communications media, including form letters, pamphlets, advertisements, and mass meetings. The main channel for league publicity, however, was always the newspaper press. From 1896 on, the League had the full cooperation of nearly all the daily newspapers of Chicago, both English and foreign language.[36] The newspapers were so solid for the league and so filled with league-generated information that Charles Yerkes in 1897 felt he had to buy a newspaper, the *Inter Ocean,* in order to tell his story to the people of Chicago. He used the *Inter Ocean* in 1897 and '98 not only to plead for street railway franchise extensions but to attack the league and the other Chicago papers, which he denounced as a "newspaper trust" determined to ruin him.[37]

By the late 1890s the *Tribune* had joined the *Daily News* in its efforts to mobilize public opinion on the utility issue. In fact, the *Tribune* had become perhaps the most aggressive leader in the fight against Yerkes and his street railway companies.[38] Both papers continued to support traditional mugwump reforms, including antivice crusades and some structural reforms of government. But, as in the early 1890s, they devoted little space to these matters, especially to government reforms, in their news and editorial columns. By far the main interest of both papers was the regulation of street railways. By the end of the decade even the conservative *Tribune* had come to join the *Daily News* in a philosophical approval of municipal ownership.[39] Both papers still struggled with the "bosses and bummers" in city government. But if government were to wield even more power, the voters must make it work, and both papers heartily supported the Municipal Voters' League in its efforts to educate and arouse the voters to work within the political system as it was.[40]

Though the idea of municipal ownership seemed rather heretical to many hard-boiled conservatives and positively outrageous to people who actually owned utility corporations, it was a heresy of widespread and increasing popularity in late nineteenth-century cities. Public ownership of municipal utilities was the common ground, the meeting place, the shared policy goal of a wide variety of city dwellers who shared little else in traditional political or economic realms.[41] For socialists, municipal ownership was the entering wedge of the cooperative commonwealth. For the Municipal Voters' League and the daily newspapers of Chicago, municipal ownership and utility regulation in general were crucial but decidedly less radical goals. Fair compensation to the city for franchises to utility companies was really all the reformers sought. Municipal ownership in the 1890s was more of a long-range pipe dream or merely a threat to frighten the utility barons. More important, neither the league nor most of the newspapers favored lower fares, a reform that would have directly benefited the lower classes. From his perspective as a rich businessman, it seemed logical to Victor Lawson to tell one of his editors in 1899: "Say editorially that the new street car bill is radically defective in proposing a four-cent fare and no compensation to the city. The individual in most cases is but slightly concerned in the matter of a one-cent difference in the fare. The city, on the other hand, is in great need of money with which to repair, clean, and maintain the streets. The compensation should be made as large as possible to the city, but on the basis of a straight five-cent fare."[42]

Despite the upper-class character of its leadership and the mugwumpish, "good government" character of its program, the Municipal Voters' League was remarkably successful in Chicago politics. In elections every year from 1896 until after the turn of the century, substantial numbers of league-supported candidates were elected to the city council. By the turn of the century it was generally conceded that the league held the balance of political power in local Chicago politics.[43] The league was especially successful in generating an aggressive public opinion on the utility issue. By 1899, for example, all the candidates for mayor felt compelled to make street railway regulation the chief issue of their campaigns. They believed the public demanded it.[44] The decade of the 1890s was a ten-year education for the people of Chicago in the subtleties of natural monopoly economics, taxation, franchise regulation, and municipal ownership. And most of this education was conducted by the Municipal Voters' League and the newspapers. By 1899 the *Daily News* could justifiably declare that Chicagoans "used to sit dumb as oysters while their legislative bodies voted away their rights; now they discuss franchises as freely as they once did the weather."[45]

The leaders of the Municipal Voters' League believed that the press was their most faithful and effective ally in the education of public opinion. Every president of the league from 1896 to 1906 gave to the newspapers most of the credit for the league's success, and other observers of the Chicago political scene shared their views.[46] The Municipal Voters' League used the press not only to convey specific information about a particular campaign but also to socialize the citizens of Chicago to the issues of modern urban life, especially issues of public utility regulation. "The long years of education have made our voters what they are," declared the league's second president, William Kent, in 1903.[47]

Kent, who headed the league during several of its most successful campaigns in the late 1890s, is a good example of a reformer in the Chicago newspaper tradition and in the new spirit of the Municipal Voters' League. He was the son of a wealthy meatpacker, a graduate of Yale, and a bona fide member of the business and social elite of Chicago.[48] He supported a variety of mugwump reforms, including civil service reform and antigambling and antivice crusades. But Kent also believed in municipal democracy. He believed that reform depended upon majority rule. He exhibited all the inconsistencies of Joseph Medill, Victor Lawson, and other members of the Municipal Voters' League crowd in Chicago. Kent ridiculed the city council, but he was a member of it. He denounced the aldermen as "good-natured, incompetent dubs" and "polluted freaks," but he admired and worked closely with some of the most venal of them. He supported efforts to end corruption in Chicago elections, but he passed out free beer in his own campaigns. He worked to ban liquor and "blind pigs" from his home community of Hyde Park, but he held his prohibition planning sessions over drinks in the back room of a local drug store. He despaired of the ignorant, ossified masses, yet he felt that he had to turn to them. Like the newspaper publishers and his colleagues in the Municipal Voters' League, Kent hated the people but he loved them too. He believed—hoped—that the majority was good and would rise up to support his efforts. He challenged them: "Reform yourselves and want something better and you will have it."[49]

* * *

The success of a movement such as the Chicago Municipal Voters' League depended upon working-class and lower-class support for an essentially middle-class and upper-class reform program. That such a thing would happen seems unlikely at best. Yet to many reformers it seemed not only possible but almost inevitable, for they believed fervently in democracy as well as in the righteousness of their own reform programs. Might these beliefs be incompatible? That is what seemed unlikely to them, and *that* is the paradox of municipal reform thought in the 1890s.

Ironically, sometimes the two beliefs *were* compatible—at least for a time. In Chicago, for example. The Municipal Voters' League was successful in the late 1890s and early 1900s, and the masses voted for the reformers' reforms. The key to success in Chicago and elsewhere was the development of an issue that would unite people across class, ethnic, and religious differences and across geographical subdivisions of the city.[50] The favorite issue in the 1890s was almost always public utility regulation, especially the control of street railways. This was the issue in Chicago, and so it was in virtually every other city where the mass electorate voted for the work of middle-class and upper-class reformers. In Detroit and Cleveland, for example, charismatic, strong-willed mayors exploited the utility issue to build "reform machines." In Kansas City an extraordinary reform newspaper hammered away at the utility issue to force a rapprochement with powerful local political bosses. In Milwaukee, much as in Chicago, a middle-class reform organization (the Milwaukee Municipal League) joined with a mugwumpish newspaper (the *Sentinel*) and used a street railway franchise battle in the late 1890s to build a cross-class coalition of consumers and taxpayers and, in the process, helped to lay the foundation of La Follette progressivism in Wisconsin.[51]

The utility problem was wonderfully suited to the building of reform coalitions. The issues were better service and more city revenue, and anyone who either rode the cars or owned property had an interest. Even when a lower fare was not an immediate issue, as in Chicago, the possibility was always in the air and the idea of better service for the money was central to the cause. Meanwhile, the companies—frequently monopolies owned by shadowy out-of-town syndicates—were made-to-order political villains. On the utility issue, at least, the common man could understand the reformer' talk about democracy, public interest, and the iniquities of special privilege. In cities where the utility issue was suppressed, diffused, or otherwise missing from the political agenda, reform groups such as the Municipal Voters' League failed.[52]

As the municipal ownership and franchise regulation movements died and utility regulation gradually became a function of independent regulatory commissions in many states after 1907, the utility issue lost its exalted place in local politics. The mass popularity of the more successful municipal reform movements usually lost ground as well. But the reformers' belief in democracy did not always fade as quickly as their success at the polls. Even among the so-called experts and engineers of the progressive era, a remnant remained who believed both in the business-like, scientific regulation of municipal utilities and in the need to keep regulation in the local political arena, subject to direct confrontation with democratic rule. Certainly, this was not the prevailing philosophy in the long run; the independent state commission movement was irresistible.

But utility regulation by democracy was not merely the philosophy of a few sentimental cranks. Some of the leading experts on utility regulation, including Delos Wilcox and others prominent in the National Municipal

League, continued to demand home rule in the regulation of public utilities and continued to oppose the state commission movement precisely because it was undemocratic. Throughout his career Wilcox, who was perhaps the leading authority in America on municipal franchises, argued that "the control of public utilities is a governmental function and must, therefore, in the final analysis, depend for its success upon the approval of the people."[53] Wilcox was not unique. Stiles P. Jones, another utility expert with the National Municipal League, perhaps put it most sharply. He approached the subject, he said, "from the standpoint not of the effect of the establishment of a state commission on administrative efficiency, but rather of its effect on the development of the power of self-government in the people. Efficiency gained at the expense of citizenship is a dear purchase. Efficiency is a fine thing but successful self-government is a better. Democratic government in a free city by an intelligent and disinterested citizenship is the greater ideal to work to. And democracy plus efficiency is not unattainable."[54]

The belief that democracy and efficiency, or democracy and middle-class morality, were compatible or even mutually reinforcing is perhaps paradoxical, but it was a central motif of reform thought in the progressive era, and it was rooted in the cities of the 1890s. In every field of reform some men and women refused to give up either their commitment to "good" government or to popular government, to social control or to democracy. Edwin Burritt Smith, a prominent Chicago lawyer and secretary of the Municipal Voters' League, affirmed this faith in 1900 when he declared, "Self-government is fundamental; good government is incidental." But, of course, he never doubted that the former would produce the latter.[55]

This paradox, as historians have long recognized, is partly the legacy of the reformers' faith in economic progress and the model of the modern business corporation, together with their nostalgic longing for the community and cooperation of an earlier, small-town America. But the paradox is more clearly explained, perhaps, by the reformers' faith in the power of facts and information. This faith allowed them to make the bridge between science and morality, between efficiency and democracy. Progressive-era reformers believed that the truth would set men free. They were elitists in their conviction that truth could be known and that they knew it; but they were democrats in their faith that truth could, should, and would have meaning only through public opinion and majority rule. In short, they fully expected the masses to be as reasonable and right as they.[56]

Many historians have found it difficult to appreciate this paradoxical commitment of reformers to popular democracy on the one hand and to efficiency, business-like administration, structural reforms of government, and social control on the other. Samuel P. Hays concluded many years ago that such talk of democracy was merely rhetoric the reformers used in their political battles with the party bosses. "The expansion of popular involvement in decision-making was frequently a political tactic, not a political system to be established permanently."[57] This view remained the dominant one, as progressive-era historiography in the 1960s and '70s turned from the history of ideas to the history of economic and social classes and movements. Melvin Holli's enduring distinction between "structural reform" and "social reform" also tended to obscure the dimension of democratic sentiment by emphasizing, as Hays did, program and results over philosophy.[58] Holli assumed that social reformers were somehow more democratic than structural reformers. But this was an assumption that glossed over underlying complexities. By focusing his attention on the aims and outcomes of reform programs, Holli missed the interesting paradox that commitment to structural reform or to social reform was not necessarily related to democratic sentiment.

Later work continued to build on the foundation laid by Hays and Holli. The notions of class and social control became central to standard explanations of municipal reform. Structural reform was usually portrayed as an effort to impose the values of one class upon another, and the political battles that surrounded structural reform efforts were shadow plays of class warfare.[59] Yet some upper-class reformers were sometimes genuine democrats, despite their interest in structural reform. On the other hand, social reform, in the style of the charismatic mayors Tom Johnson and "Golden Rule" Jones, was often portrayed as an effort to build in the modern city an organic community that would transcend class and ethnic differences. But social reformers were not always democrats. The abolition of special privilege and the attainment of community, according to Roy Lubove, frequently depended in the social reformers' own schemes "upon the disinterested leadership of experts."[60] Democratic sentiment varied widely among reformers of all stripes, and it varied even within the minds of individual men and women.[61]

Certainly, historians are correct to judge the actions as well as the rhetoric of people in the past. But in human life actions cannot be explained without an understanding of beliefs. And it seems clear that some reformers in the 1890s and after, despite the class bias of their policies and programs, believed in democracy as the final great touchstone of reform.[62]

Perhaps we have been reluctant to conclude that reformers believed what they said they believed because, from our vantage point, we find it unbelievable. The idea that the huddled masses would easily reject their own social habits and institutions and their own political leaders and rise up to support the "better classes" in their efforts to control and purify the modern metropolis seems naive. But such a paradoxical vision is not really naive; it is merely past. It is fixed in a time that is separate from our own. The hope that urban democracy could be mobilized permanently in favor of middle-class and upper-class reform programs, and that this could be done through public information campaigns, was ultimately a futile hope and a lost dream. But in the 1890s, when the great American metropolises were new, such hopes and dreams seemed real and near.

Notes

1. *Chicago Tribune,* June 27, 1897.

2. See the *Tribune's* editorial pages in the early days of July 1897.

3. *Tribune,* Oct. 10, 1897.

4. *Tribune,* July 1 and Oct. 8, 1897, and Oct. 30, 1898.

5. *Tribune,* July 6, July 20, and Oct. 14, 1897.

6. The activities of the Citizens' Association are reviewed in Citizens' Association, *Annual Reports,* 1874–1900. Several unpublished dissertations offer detailed accounts of the work of the Citizens' Association. See Sidney I. Roberts, "Businessmen in Revolt: Chicago, 1874–1900" (Ph.D. diss., Northwestern University, 1960), chap. 1; Michael McCarthy, "Businessmen and Professionals in Municipal Reform: The Chicago Experience, 1877–1920" (Ph.D. diss., Northwestern University, 1970), chap. 1; Donald D. Marks, "Polishing the Gem of the Prairie: The Evolution of Civic Reform Consciousness in Chicago, 1874–1900" (Ph.D. diss., University of Wisconsin, 1974), chap. 3.

7. "Address by Franklin MacVeagh," *Addresses and Reports of the Citizens' Association of Chicago, 1874–1876* (Chicago: Hazlitt and Reed, 1876), 8–9; *Constitution of the Citizens' Association* (Chicago: Citizens' Association, n.d.), in Citizens' Association Papers, Chicago Historical Society. The Citizens' Association Papers at the Chicago Historical Society contain very little material from before 1900.

8. See, for example, David P. Thelen, *The New Citizenship: Origins of Progressivism in Wisconsin, 1885–1900* (Columbia: University of Missouri Press, 1972), 10–11, 139–41; Gerald W. McFarland, *Mugwumps, Morals, and Politics* (Amherst: University of Massachusetts Press, 1975), 173–77.

9. Citizens' Association, *Annual Reports,* 1874–90, passim; William H. Tolman, *Municipal Reform Movements in the United States* (New York: Fleming H. Revell, 1895), 56–57. See also Bessie Louise Pierce, *A History of Chicago,* vol. 3: *The Rise of a Modern City, 1871–1893* (New York: Alfred A. Knopf, 1957).

10. "Address by Franklin MacVeagh," 5–6; Citizens' Association, *Annual Report,* 1889, 3–4.

11. This argument is expanded in David Paul Nord, *Newspapers and New Politics: Midwestern Municipal Reform, 1890–1900* (Ann Arbor, Mich.: UMI Research Press, 1981), chaps. 3–4.

12. David Paul Nord, "The Public Community: The Urbanization of Journalism in Chicago," *Journal of Urban History* 11 (Aug. 1985): 411–41. That article is chapter 5 in this book. See also Charles H. Dennis, *Victor Lawson: His Life and His Work* (Chicago: Uni-

versity of Chicago Press, 1935). Several dissertations review Lawson's career in some detail. See Donald J. Abramoske, "The Chicago *Daily News:* A Business History, 1875–1901" (Ph.D. diss., University of Chicago, 1963); Royal J. Schmidt "The *Chicago Daily News* and Illinois Politics, 1876–1920" (Ph.D. diss., University of Chicago, 1957); Robert L. Tree, "Victor Fremont Lawson and His Newspapers: A Study of the Chicago 'Daily News' and Chicago 'Record'" (Ph.D. diss., Northwestern University, 1959). On the rise of the metropolitan newspaper in this era, see Nord, *Newspapers and New Politics,* chap. 3; Michael Schudson, *Discovering the News: A Social History of American Newspapers* (New York: Basic, 1978), chap. 3; Gunther Barth, *City People: The Rise of Modern City Culture in Nineteenth-Century America* (New York: Oxford University Press, 1980), chap. 3; Alan Trachtenberg, *The Incorporation of America: Culture and Society in the Gilded Age* (New York: Hill and Wang, 1982), chap. 4.

13. A good general statement of the *Chicago Daily News*'s editorial position on municipal reform in the early 1890s is expressed in several editorials in the issue of Jan. 2, 1890.

14. *Daily News,* Apr. 11, 1891. Quantitative statements in this chapter about newspaper coverage are based upon a simple content analysis of the *Daily News* and the *Tribune,* 1890–1900. For a description of the method and details of the results, see Nord, *Newspapers and New Politics,* appendixes 1 and 2.

15. *Daily News,* May 2 and June 25, 1890.

16. *Daily News,* Sept. 17 and June 14, 1890.

17. *Daily News,* Jan. 2, July 16, and Nov. 8, 1890, and Mar. 26 and Apr. 8, 1891. On Lawson's feud with Yerkes see Victor Lawson to Charles H. Dennis, Jan. 12, 1898, Charles H. Dennis Papers, Newberry Library, Chicago; Victor Lawson to Charles M. Faye, Jan. 4, 1898, and to Charles T. Yerkes, Jan. 16, 1897, in Victor Lawson Papers, Newberry Library. Faye was editor of the *Daily News;* Dennis was editor of Lawson's morning paper, the *Chicago Record.* Yerkes's career is summarized in Sidney I. Roberts, "Portrait of a Robber Baron: Charles T. Yerkes," *Business History Review* 35 (Autumn 1961): 344–71.

18. *Daily News,* May 9 and June 10, 1890, and July 2, 1891.

19. *Tribune,* Feb. 26, 1890. A standard history of the *Tribune* is Lloyd Wendt, *Chicago Tribune: The Rise of a Great American Newspaper* (Chicago: Rand McNally, 1979). This is a fairly laudatory account by a former newspaperman with *Tribune* connections.

20. *Tribune,* May 18, June 5, June 8, Aug. 21, and Oct. 1, 1890.

21. *Tribune,* Feb. 9, 1890.

22. *Tribune,* Aug. 3 and July 6, 1890.

23. *Tribune,* Feb. 26 and June 1, 1890.

24. During the first months of 1890 pollution in the South Branch of the Chicago River was practically a daily item, and the coverage was detailed. See, for example, *Tribune,* June 17, 1890. The history of Chicago's drainage problem and the construction of the sanitary canal is told in Louis P. Cain, *Sanitation Strategy for a Lakefront Metropolis: The Case of Chicago* (DeKalb: Northern Illinois University Press, 1978).

25. *Tribune,* Dec. 7, 1890, and Feb. 6 and Mar. 20, 1891.

26. *Tribune,* Dec. 14, 1890.

27. *Tribune,* daily stories, early July 1890.

28. *Tribune,* Oct. 16, 1890.

29. Albion W. Small, "The Civic Federation: A Study in Social Dynamics," *American Journal of Sociology* 1 (July 1895): 82–83, 86–87; *The Civic Federation: What It Has Accom-*

plished Its First Year (Chicago: Civic Federation, 1895); Civic Federation of Chicago, *First Annual Report of the Central Council,* 1895. For regular front-page stories on the gambling fight, see the *Daily News* and the *Tribune,* Sept.–Oct. 1894.

30. Ray Stannard Baker, "The Civic Federation of Chicago," *Outlook* 52 (July 27, 1895): 133.

31. This is the platform the candidates were asked to sign in 1896, and it changed little in the years following. See the 1896 Endorsement Book, Municipal Voters' League Papers, Chicago Historical Society. The pre-1900 material in this collection is contained in four scrapbooks: two books of committee minutes and reports in chronological order; a book of endorsements from 1896; and a book of candidate reports as printed in the newspapers. A good general account of the Municipal Voters' League is Sidney I. Roberts, "Municipal Voters' League and Chicago's Boodlers," *Journal of the Illinois Historical Society* 53 (Summer 1960): 117–48. See also Edwin Burritt Smith, "Council Reform in Chicago: Work of the Municipal Voters' League," *Municipal Affairs* 4 (June 1900): 347–62; Hoyt King, *Citizen Cole of Chicago* (Chicago, Horder's, 1931). Cole was the first president and guiding spirit of the league. Smith was secretary in the early years.

32. Executive Committee Minutes, 1896–1900, Municipal Voters' League Papers. See also George C. Sikes, "How the Chicago City Council Was Regenerated," *Chautuaquan* 36 (Jan. 1903): 400.

33. "Report of the Municipal Voters' League, 1896," and George Cole, circular letter, Dec. 29, 1896, both in Municipal Voters' League Papers. See also King, *Citizen Cole,* 23.

34. Executive Committee Minutes, Feb. 2, 1896, Municipal Voters' League Papers. See also Roberts, "Municipal Voters' League," 147–48.

35. This interest in the "facts" and the power of information is the main theme of virtually all contemporary writing about the league. See, for example, E. Smith, "Council Reform in Chicago," 351; Edwin Burritt Smith, "The Municipal Voters' Leagues of Chicago," *Atlantic Monthly* 85 (June 1900): 836–37; "Municipal Reform in Chicago," *Nation* 70 (May 31, 1900): 412; "The Voters' League of Chicago," *Outlook* 60 (Sept. 10, 1898): 131; Sigmund Zeisler, "The Municipal Voters' League of Chicago," *World Review* 2 (Jan. 25, 1902): 576; Sikes, "How the Chicago City Council Was Regenerated," 399; Frank H. Scott, "The Municipal Situation in Chicago," in *Proceedings of the Detroit Conference for Good City Government* (Philadelphia: National Municipal League, 1903), 151–52; Lincoln Steffens, "Chicago: Half Free and Fighting On," *McClure's* 21 (Oct. 1903): 563–77.

36. Executive Committee Minutes, Feb. and Mar. 1896, Municipal Voters' League Papers. See also E. Smith, "Council Reform in Chicago," 350. Victor Lawson and his newspapers were especially supportive of the league, with editorial and news space and with cash donations. See, for example, Lawson to Edwin Burritt Smith, Mar. 12, 14, and 28, 1896, and Lawson to George E. Cole, Nov. 7, 16, and 21, 1896, all in Lawson Papers.

37. *Daily News,* Oct. 22, 1897; *Inter Ocean,* daily editorials, Nov. 21–Dec. 10, 1897.

38. For some especially vituperative attacks on Yerkes, see *Tribune,* Jan. 11, Jan. 14, May 14, May 20, May 21, and June 10, 1897, and Jan. 13, Dec. 12, and Dec. 14, 1898. On Yerkes's struggles with the press and his general disregard of his public image, see Roberts, "Portrait of a Robber Baron," 351–54.

39. *Tribune,* Jan. 20, Oct. 13, and Nov. 13, 1897, and Jan. 6, Feb. 3, Apr. 3, May 3, and Aug. 24, 1899.

40. On newspaper support in the first league campaign, see *Daily News,* Feb. 24, Mar.

5, Mar. 11, Mar. 13, Mar. 17, Apr. 4, and Apr. 7, 1896; *Tribune,* Jan. 12, Jan. 14, Jan. 27, Mar. 18, Mar. 29, Apr. 5, and Apr. 8, 1896. On newspaper support in the late 1890s, especially in the league's campaign against street railway franchise extensions, see Victor Lawson to Charles H. Dennis, Sept. 24, 1897, Feb. 24, 1898, and Feb. 26, 1898, in Dennis Papers; Lawson to Charles M. Faye, Jan. 14, 1898, and Mar. 10, 1898, in Lawson Papers; *Daily News,* Feb. 5, 25, 26, and 28, and Mar. 8, 10, 14, 19, and 21, 1898; *Tribune,* Feb. 20, Mar. 15, 18, 22, and 29, Apr. 3, and Apr. 4, 1898.

41. David P. Thelen, "Urban Politics: Beyond Bosses and Reformers," *Reviews in American History* 7 (Sept. 1979): 410.

42. Victor Lawson to Charles Faye, Feb. 16, 1899, Lawson Papers. For a full account of the street railway issue in Chicago, see Robert D. Weber, "Rationalizers and Reformers: Chicago Local Transportation in the Nineteenth Century" (Ph.D diss., University of Wisconsin, 1971).

43. Roberts, "Municipal Voters' League," 143; E. Smith, "Council Reform in Chicago," 356–57; Steffens, "Chicago: Half Free and Fighting On," 563–77; Frederic C. Howe, "The Municipal Character and Achievements of Chicago," *World's Work* 5 (Mar. 1903): 3240–46; "Chicago and St. Louis," *Independent* 54 (Apr. 10, 1902): 883–84.

44. *Daily News,* Mar. 16 and 18, 1899; *Tribune,* Mar. 12, Mar. 29, Apr. 3, and Apr. 11, 1899.

45. *Daily News,* Feb. 13, 1899. See also William Ritchie, "The Street Railway Situation in Chicago," in *Proceedings of the Rochester Conference for Good City Government* (Philadelphia: National Municipal League, 1903), 164–78.

46. George E. Cole, "President's Report, 1896," Municipal Voters' League Papers; Walter Fisher, quoted in Elizabeth Kent, "William Kent: Independent" (typescript, July 1950), 133, copy in the library of the University of Chicago.

47. William Kent, quoted in Joel Arthur Tarr, "William Kent to Lincoln Steffens: Origins of Progressivism in Chicago," *Mid-America* (Jan. 1965): 55–57. This is the theme of much of the contemporary writing on the league.

48. Tarr, "William Kent to Lincoln Steffens," 50–51.

49. William Kent, speeches and letters, quoted in Elizabeth Kent, "William Kent," 118, 124–26, 133–34, 136–37, 141–43, 146–47. Kent had a lot of influence on Lincoln Steffens's famous article about the Municipal Voters' League ("Chicago: Half Free and Fighting On"). See Tarr, "William Kent to Lincoln Steffens."

50. David P. Thelen, "Social Tensions and the Origins of Progressivism," *Journal of American History* 56 (Sept. 1969): 323–41; John D. Buenker, John C. Burnham, and Robert M. Crunden, *Progressivism* (Cambridge, Mass.: Schenkman, 1977), chap. 2.

51. Nord, *Newspapers and New Politics,* chap. 7. How the utility issue was used in Milwaukee and Detroit is also described in Thelen, *New Citizenship;* Clay McShane, *Technology and Reform: Street Railways and the Growth of Milwaukee, 1887–1900* (Madison: State Historical Society of Wisconsin, 1974); and Melvin G. Holli, *Reform in Detroit: Hazen S. Pingree and Urban Politics* (New York: Oxford University Press, 1969).

52. St. Louis was such a city. See Nord, *Newspapers and New Politics,* chaps. 5–6.

53. Delos F. Wilcox, "Needed Changes in the Public Service Laws of New York," *Utilities Magazine* 1 (Nov. 1915): 16. See also Wilcox, *The American City: A Problem in Democracy* (New York: Macmillan, 1904). The theme of this paragraph is developed more fully in David Nord, "The Experts versus the Experts: Conflicting Philosophies of Municipal

Utility Regulation in the Progressive Era," *Wisconsin Magazine of History* 58 (Spring 1975): 219–36.

54. Stiles P. Jones, "The Advisability of a State Public Utilities Commission for Minnesota," in Minnesota Academy of Social Sciences, *Papers and Proceedings of the Sixth Annual Meeting* (1913): 66. See also Stiles P. Jones, "State versus Local Regulation," *Annals* 53 (May 1914): 94–107; Stiles P. Jones, "What Certain Cities Have Accomplished without State Regulation," *Annals* 57 (Jan. 1915): 72–82. Jones's argument was echoed by other prominent utility reformers in the pre–World War I era. See, for example, Edward W. Bemis, "Some Present-Day Issues of Public Utility Regulation," *Annals* 57 (Jan. 1915): 62–71; Milo R. Maltbie, "The Distribution of Functions between Local and State Regulation," *Annals* 57 (Jan. 1915): 163–69; and J. Allen Smith, "Municipal vs. State Control of Public Utilities," *National Municipal Review* 2 (Jan. 1913): 24–30.

55. E. Smith, "Municipal Voters' League," 839.

56. This theme is expanded in Nord, *Newspapers and New Politics*, chap. 2. See also Melvin G. Holli, "Urban Reform in the Progressive Era," in *The Progressive Era*, ed. Lewis Gould (Syracuse, N.Y.: Syracuse University Press, 1974), 140; Stanley P. Caine, "The Origins of Progressivism," in *The Progressive Era*, ed. Gould, 24–25.

57. Samuel P. Hays, "The Politics of Reform in Municipal Government in the Progressive Era," *Pacific Northwest Quarterly* 55 (Oct. 1964): 157–69. See also James Weinstein, "Organized Business and the City Commission and Manager Movements," *Journal of Southern History* 28 (May 1962): 166–82.

58. Holli, *Reform in Detroit*, chap. 8; Holli, "Urban Reform."

59. This was a central theme in much of the boss-vs.-reformer literature. See, for example, John M. Allswang, *Bosses, Machines, and Urban Voters: An American Symbiosis* (Port Washington, N.Y.: Kennikat, 1977); Alexander B. Callow, ed., *The City Boss in America: An Interpretive Reader* (New York: Oxford University Press, 1976); Blaine A. Brownell and Warren Stickle, eds., *Bosses and Reformers: Urban Politics in America, 1880–1920* (Boston: Houghton Mifflin, 1973). This was also a theme in most monographic studies of structural reform. See, for example, Paul Boyer, *Urban Masses and Moral Order in America, 1820–1920* (Cambridge, Mass.: Harvard University Press, 1978); Martin J. Schiesl, *The Politics of Efficiency* (Berkeley: University of California Press, 1977); and Kenneth Fox, *Better City Government: Innovation in American Urban Politics, 1850–1937* (Philadelphia: Temple University Press, 1977). A good review essay is Michael Frisch, "Oyez, Oyez, Oyez: The Recurring Case of Plunkett v. Steffens," *Journal of Urban History* 7 (Feb. 1981): 205–18.

60. Roy Lubove, "Frederic C. Howe and the Quest for Community in America," *Historian* 39 (Feb. 1977): 273.

61. Steven Kesselman, *The Modernization of American Reform: Structures and Perceptions* (New York: Garland, 1979).

62. The idea that policy outcomes in the progressive era do not necessarily reveal the intentions or ideologies of reformers is the theme of Richard L. McCormick, "The Discovery that Business Corrupts Politics: A Reappraisal of the Origins of Progressivism," *American Historical Review* 86 (Apr. 1981): 247–74.

PART 2

Communities of Reception

8. A Republican Literature: A Study of Magazine Readers and Reading in Late Eighteenth-Century New York

PRESIDENT George Washington was a subscriber. So were Vice President John Adams, Chief Justice John Jay, and New York mayor Richard Varick. With such a distinguished readership it is little wonder that the publishers of the *New-York Magazine; or, Literary Repository* decided to publish a list of subscribers to their first volume in 1790. Like all eighteenth-century magazine publishers, Thomas and James Swords were proud of their association with gentlemen of character, stature, and literary taste.[1] Yet men such as Washington and Adams were not the only readers of the *New-York Magazine,* as the standard magazine histories seem to suggest.[2] There were women on the list, and barbers, bakers, butchers, and boardinghouse proprietors. These are the forgotten readers of the *New-York Magazine* and of late eighteenth-century magazines in general. Who were these people? How did they make a living? Where did they live? What were they like? Were they different from nonsubscribers? What kinds of material did they read? This chapter seeks to answer those questions. It is, in effect, a magazine readership survey, and its purpose is to contribute to our understanding of the history of reading—especially among the shopkeepers and artisans of New York City—during the first years of the American Republic.

As Carl Kaestle has pointed out, we have learned a great deal since the 1960s about the demographics of simple literacy in the past, but we have only begun to develop a genuine social history of reading—that is, a history of the *uses* of literacy. This is hardly surprising, for as Kaestle says, it "is very difficult to trace printed works to their readers and still more difficult to trace meaning from the text to the reader."[3] This chapter tries to do both, though with more confidence about the former than the latter. It is a study of both the subscribers and the content of the *New-York Magazine* in 1790.

My main argument is that magazine reading in this era seems to have been a more broadly democratic activity than has usually been supposed. At first glance the magazine's content would seem to be evidence of a rather elite audience, and this has been the inference of historians. Yet the subscriber list shows a more varied readership. Considered together, the subscriber list and the content may offer some insight into the social function of journalistic and literary reading in this era. They suggest the importance of reading as a form of participation in the new social order of post-Revolutionary America. Edward Countryman has argued that "radical politics and nascent class consciousness foundered on electoral participation and on the spirit of voluntary association" in the 1780s.[4] In other words, the radicalism of the small shopkeepers and urban artisans lost its urgency as those groups began to participate more fully in a political culture that had once been closed to them. Similarly, the magazine might be viewed as another arena for popular participation, in this case participation in the formerly elite culture of science and education, arts and letters, virtue and honor, cultivation and character. The values of the magazine were traditional; it was the participation of the working class that was new. In short, this was a republican readership and a republican literature.

* * *

Republican was a thoroughly commonplace term in the American political vocabulary of 1790, yet its ubiquity was probably matched by its ambiguity. Historians disagree, rather warmly, over what Americans in the late eighteenth century meant when they talked about republicanism. One stream of scholarship, growing from the pathbreaking work of Bernard Bailyn and J. G. A. Pocock, emphasizes the classical republican tradition—that is, the tradition of Aristotle and Cicero, filtered through Italian Renaissance humanism and the radical Whig thought of the English "country" politicians of the late seventeenth and early eighteenth centuries. In this tradition the basis for republican government was civic virtue, the sacrifice of individual interests to the common good.[5] Another stream of scholarship emphasizes the liberal dimension of American republicanism. Though historians such as Joyce Appleby have rejected the one-dimensional Lockean perspective of Louis Hartz, they still argue that the mainstream of American political thought in the late eighteenth century was liberal—that is, committed to private property and individualism. In this tradition virtue and the sources of human happiness lay largely outside government in a natural economy and self-regulating society.[6] A third stream of scholarship owes much to the classical republican perspective, in that it finds even among the common people of the Revolutionary era a devotion to the ideas of civic virtue and common-wealth. But there are differences of emphasis. Growing more from social history than from the history of political thought, this literature stresses the equal rights or radical egalitarian aspects of American republicanism. His-torians working in this stream are usually more interested in the actual po-litical participation of working-class Americans than they are in abstract political theory.[7]

Of course, *all* of these (and still other) meanings of *republicanism* were current in American thought in the 1790s. As Joyce Appleby says, "It would be surprising if scholars were able to agree upon the meaning of a word that contemporaries themselves used in such disparate contexts." People clearly used the vocabulary of republicanism, but they used new vocabularies as well, and they used the old words in new ways, as circumstances changed.[8] Linda Kerber has suggested that the language and values of classical republicanism remained more meaningful, more vital, for some Americans than others, depending upon their place in the new liberal order that was rapidly emerg-ing. Historians must be alert to how real people shaped political ideas to make sense of their own lives in a complex, modern world.[9]

New York City in 1790, for example, was an enormously complex social, political, and economic universe. At one extreme, the city was still the do-main of the Livingstons, Schuylers, and Stuyvesants—a traditional aristoc-racy that continued to influence public life in the post-Revolutionary era. Furthermore, New York was the American capital in 1789–90, the gathering place for a new aristocracy of founding fathers and federal officials, who at-tended to the business of the country by day and to the balls, dinners, and receptions of New York high society by night. At the other extreme, New York was home to the desperately poor—cartmen, mariners, common laborers; the sick, the helpless, the chronically unemployed.[10] It would be remarkable indeed if these diverse New Yorkers shared the same notions of what it meant to be a citizen of the new republic.

Most of the citizens of New York, however, fell between these extremes, and their story is central to my story about reading in the late eighteenth century. A sample from the 1790 city directory suggests that about two-thirds of the city's heads of household were artisans or shopkeepers. (See table 8.1.) Other historians have come up with roughly comparable figures. Certainly the largest group of working people in New York and in other large cities in this era were artisans—that is, master craftsmen and their journeyman employees.[11]

What it meant to be an artisan (or even a shopkeeper) was changing in 1790. The traditional relationships among master, journeyman, and appren-tice were breaking down. Some masters were becoming retailers, manufac-

Table 8.1. Occupational Status of Subscribers to
New-York Magazine and a Random Sample from the
New York City Directory, 1790

Occupation Category	Subscribers	Random Sample
1. Professional	20.0%	6.6%
2. Merchant	29.1	8.5
3. Shopkeeper	21.5	26.5
4. Artisan	27.9	41.4
5. Nonskilled	1.5	17.0
	100.0%	100.0%
	($N = 265$)	($N = 377$)
Occupation information missing	$N = 33$	$N = 23$

Source: List of subscribers in *New-York Magazine; or, Literary Repository,* vol. 1 (New York: Thomas and James Swords, 1790), iii–vi; *The New-York Directory and Register* (New York: Hodge, Allen, and Campbell, 1789 and 1790); *The New-York Directory and Register* (New York: T. and J. Swords, 1791 and 1792). See also appendix A.

turers, or incipient capitalists. Some journeymen were becoming wageworkers, with little hope of achieving the traditional status of independent master. Many shops were hiring untrained boys, without any commitment to the obligations of apprenticeship. The whole ancient system was shifting, very gradually, with the rising tide of laissez-faire.[12]

But though the economic world was changing, many of the values of the eighteenth-century artisan culture remained strong. In fact, some of these values were reinforced by the experience of the Revolution. During the Revolution and the decade of crisis that preceded it, the artisans and shopkeepers had become active participants in the political culture—first in crowd action, then in electoral politics. That commitment to politics would not subside.[13] Yet political equality and political participation were not the only components of "artisan republicanism," as Sean Wilentz has explained it. The tradesmen of New York and other American cities also embraced an older ideology that tied together a devotion to craft and to commonwealth. The artisans believed in equality and independence but not as ends in themselves, for independence should free men "to exercise virtue, to subordinate private ends to the legislation of the public good."[14] Certainly, the artisans and small shopkeepers of New York City stood for individual initiative, for economic progress, and for the rights of private property. In this sense they were liberals. Yet, as Wilentz puts it, they also stood for something else:

> With a rhetoric rich in the republican language of corruption, equality, and independence, they remained committed to a benevolent hierarchy of skill and

the cooperative workshop. Artisan independence conjured up, not a vision of ceaseless, self-interested industry, but a moral order in which all craftsmen would eventually become self-governing, independent, competent masters. . . . Men's energies would be devoted, not to personal ambition or profit alone, but to the commonwealth; in the workshop, mutual obligation and respect—"the strongest ties of the heart"—would prevail; in more public spheres, the craftsmen would insist on their equal rights and exercise their citizenship with a view to preserving the rule of virtue as well as to protecting their collective interests against an eminently corruptible mercantile and financial elite.[15]

Gordon Wood has argued that the grand achievement of the founders in the 1780s was to move political thought from a classical to a romantic or liberal conception of republicanism. In the classical republican vocabulary *virtue* and *commonwealth* were the key terms. For a republic to survive, individual aspirations must be wedded to the common good. This was the language of 1776. By 1787 the old words had taken on new meanings. The republic devised by Madison and his colleagues was a system that would not depend upon the virtue of the people. In the federalist scheme the traditional vices of republican government—individualism and self-interest—became strengths. The commonweal would emerge automatically in the competition of private interests.[16] While Wood's study brilliantly illuminates the changing political thought of the founding elites, it obscures the continuity, the complexity, and the contradictory nature of the political thought of those men and women of the "middling classes." Urban artisans, especially, felt the steady pull of liberalism, yet they also harbored great misgivings about the new economic order that seemed to lie ahead. For them, the commitment to classical republican values remained strong well into the nineteenth century. Just what sort of commonwealth or republican order they envisioned was not always clear or consistent. What was unmistakably clear, however, was their insistence that they be recognized as full-fledged participants in that order, whatever it may be.[17] The most obvious arena of participation was politics. Another was reading.

* * *

It was into this milieu that the *New-York Magazine* was born. It wasn't the first attempt to start a magazine in New York in the postwar era. Just three years earlier, in 1787, Noah Webster had brought out the *American Magazine.* After only a year, however, he abandoned the project, mainly for financial reasons. "I will now leave writing and do more lucrative business," Webster said. "I am happy to quit New York."[18] Thomas and James Swords hoped for a better fate as they offered to the public the first issue of the *New-York Mag-*

azine in January 1790. Though New York had been devastated economically by the war, the city was bustling again by 1790. The population passed thirty thousand in 1789, and during the 1790s the city climbed to first rank as the commercial metropolis of America.[19] The Swords brothers often complained that the city's prosperity never trickled down to them ("the horizon remains dark and gloomy," they liked to report to their readers). But they did manage to stay in business eight full years—the longest run of any eighteenth-century American magazine.[20]

Part of the reason for the magazine's early success was its association with "a society of gentlemen," a local group of would-be "literary men" and patrons of the arts who began to work with the Swords brothers on the March issue. Their aim was to provide the magazine with "literary support" and editorial direction and to promote "the pen of virtue and morality, science and taste." Clearly, the *New-York Magazine* represented the aspirations for culture and refinement of the American elite. The magazine's price was somewhat aristocratic as well—$2.25 per year, at a time when 50 cents a day was a common wage for a New York workingman.[21] In this sense the *New-York Magazine* was not unlike similar magazines in the United States and Britain. Its model undoubtedly was the *Gentleman's Magazine* of London, the great pioneer of the general interest magazine in English. Like the *Gentleman's*, the *New-York Magazine* was impartial, restrained, stolid—not in the least critical of the culture of "the rich, the well-born, and the able," as subscriber John Adams described the new social elite of New York.[22]

Yet neither the editors nor the "society of gentlemen" viewed the enterprise as elitist. In an "Introductory Essay" published with the April issue, they proclaimed their commitment to the republican ideal of "equal liberty," especially equal access to *knowledge*. Following a eulogy to the democratic science of Benjamin Franklin, the editors described their vision of the purpose of a magazine:

> A well conducted magazine, we conceive must, from its nature, contribute greatly to diffuse knowledge throughout a community, and to create in that community a taste for literature. The universality of the subjects which it treats of will give to every profession, and every occupation, some information, while its variety holds out to every taste some gratification. From its conciseness, it will not require more time for its perusal than the most busy can well spare; and its cheapness brings it within the convenient purchase of every class of society.[23]

Was the *New-York Magazine* the province of the elite, as the magazine's tone suggests, or of "every class of society," as its editors declared? Fortunately, the answer to that question need not be pure guesswork, for the subscribers were listed by name in the 1790 volume.

* * *

In 1790 the *New-York Magazine* had 370 subscribers, a small but respectable number for that time.[24] (Historians have generally assumed that each copy of a newspaper or magazine in this era was read by quite a few people.) About 80 percent of the subscribers lived in New York City (Manhattan). About 5 percent lived in Albany; another 5 percent lived in other New York State towns; and the rest were scattered from Nova Scotia to Antigua. The vast majority of subscribers were men (98 percent), though surely many of their subscriptions were intended for wives and children as well. Seven women were subscribers in their own names. I located 90 percent (269 of 298) of the New York readers in city directories and/or other biographical sources. For 265 of these, I was able to secure information on occupations and street addresses. For comparison, I also drew a random sample of four hundred entries from the 1790 city directory. (The nature and limitations of the city directory are discussed in appendix A.)

The readership of the *New-York Magazine* was indeed more "upscale" than the general population of the city. (See table 8.1.) While nearly 50 percent of the readers were professionals or merchants, only 15 percent of the random sample fell into these two categories. Moreover, the most common professional occupation among the readers was lawyer, while among the general population the most common professional jobs were somewhat lower in prestige: local government official and schoolteacher. The difference between the two groups at the bottom of the scale is even more striking. In the random sample 17 percent fell into the "nonskilled" category. Most of these were cartmen, laborers, and mariners. In the subscriber group only four individuals were classified as "nonskilled": a gardener, a nurseryman, a washer, and a widow. The first two would certainly fall higher on a measure of skill than laborers or cartmen, and they may not even belong in this category. The same might be said of widows. The one widow subscriber, for example, was a Beekman, one of the leading families of the city. The washer also was a woman, and she too may have been a member of a social class higher than her occupation suggests. (The other two women subscribers that I was able to trace were a teacher and a glover.) In short, it might be said that virtually no one from the very bottom of the socioeconomic scale—the truly poor—subscribed to the *New-York Magazine*.[25]

Though the proportions at the top and bottom of the occupational scale for the two groups look quite different, the middle range proportions are much less disparate. About half of the subscribers were shopkeepers or artisans, compared with two-thirds of the random sample. While this is a significant difference, I would argue that 50 percent is still a substantial proportion. If it is important that half the readers of the *New-York Magazine* were merchants and professionals, it is equally important that the other half were artisans and shopkeepers. Both groups deserve a closer look.

Who were the elite readers? Most were merchants. More than one-quarter of the total list of subscribers identified themselves simply as merchants. The range of wealth and income within this category was large. Some "merchants" were doubtless no more than hopeful or pretentious shopkeepers; others were the leading commercial operators of the city and of the nation. Whether large or small, most merchants of that era were somewhat unspecialized, working on commission and handling a variety of goods. For example, one of the *New-York Magazine* subscribers advertised in a local newspaper a stock of Madeira wine, Carolina indigo and rice, China tea, a house and lot on Queen Street, thirteen acres near Harlem, and "a neat post chaise with harness." Another subscriber advertised imported cloth, buttons, buckles, glass, and "continental certificates"—and he was willing to barter for "country produce."[26]

If the prestige of an address reflects status, the merchants in the subscriber group may not have been much more well-to-do than merchants generally. Forty-two percent of the merchant readers held addresses on the most important business streets of the city: Queen (now Pearl), Water, and Hanover Square. But 37 percent of the merchants in the random sample also had addresses on these same streets. In both samples only a scattering of individual merchants lived in the more distant sections of the city—that is, north of what is now Fulton Street or west of Broadway.

Though many of the merchant readers were small-scale operators, some were the leaders of the mercantile elite. The names Beekman, Kip, Livingston, Roosevelt, Van Rensselaer, and Verplank—old families and old money—dot the list.[27] Another subscriber, William Duer, is an example of a new-money man who read the *New-York Magazine*. Duer was perhaps the leading speculator of the day in land, securities, government contracts, and manufacturing ventures. He had made one fortune during the war, and he was hard at work on another in 1790. Besides the big merchants, some of the most prominent lawyers and politicians of the city were subscribers. Egbert Benson, one of the leading conservative assemblymen of New York in the 1780s, was on the list. So was James Duane, former congressman and mayor of New York. And, of course, Washington, Adams, et al. Little wonder that the Swords brothers had such high hopes for their little magazine.[28]

But half the readers were not so wealthy or so prominent. Half were shopkeepers and artisans. Most of the shopkeepers, about 60 percent of them in
both the subscriber group and the random sample, were listed simply as
shopkeepers, storekeepers, or grocers. The others represented a variety of
specialties: taverns, livery stables, bookstores, paint stores, hardware stores,
tobacco shops, and so on. The main street for shopkeeper subscribers was
Broadway, an up-and-coming business and residential street in New York in
1790. Others lived throughout the city. The artisans were a larger and even
more varied group. Altogether, thirty-nine different trades were represented on the subscription list, compared with forty-eight trades in the random
sample.

What kinds of artisans were likely to read the *New-York Magazine*? The
quick answer seems to be: all kinds. The range of trades is striking, with many
crafts represented by a single subscriber. (See appendix B.) The only woman
artisan subscriber, for example, was also the only glover on the list. Yet some
patterns may be discerned. Table 8.2, for example, shows the leading ten artisan occupations for the subscribers and for the random sample. By far, the
three leading trades in the general population were shoemaker, carpenter, and

Table 8.2. Ten Leading Occupations of Artisan Subscribers to *New-York Magazine* and
Artisans in a Random Sample from the New York City Directory, 1790

Subscribers		Random Sample	
Occupation	Percentage of Artisans	Occupation	Percentage of Artisans
1. Carpenter	9.5%	1. Shoemaker	14.7%
2. Printer[a]	9.5	2. Carpenter	11.5
3. Sea captain[a]	6.8	3. Tailor	10.3
4. Barber	5.4	4. Cooper	5.8
5. Cabinetmaker	5.4	5. Ship carpenter	3.8
6. Shoemaker	5.4	6. Hatter	3.2
7. Baker	4.1	7. Blacksmith[b]	2.6
8. Clock/watchmaker	4.1	8. Block maker[b]	2.6
9. Cooper	4.1	9. Chair maker	2.6
10. Tailor	4.1	10. Gold/silversmith	2.6
	58.4%		59.7%
	(N = 43)		(N = 93)
All artisans	100.0%		100.0%
	(N = 74)		(N = 156)

Source: List of subscribers in *New-York Magazine; or, Literary Repository,* vol. 1 (New York: Thomas and James
Swords, 1790), iii–vi; *The New-York Directory and Register* (New York: Hodge, Allen, and Campbell, 1789 and
1790); *The New-York Directory and Register* (New York: T. and J. Swords, 1791 and 1792). See also appendix A.
a. These trades do not appear at all in the random sample.
b. These trades do not appear at all on the subscriber list.

tailor, which account for nearly 37 percent of the artisans in the random sample. These three trades were not the leading trades among the artisan subscribers, however, though they were well represented. The top three trades among the subscribers were carpenter, printer, and sea captain. This is an interesting comparison, for no printers or sea captains turned up at all in the random sample. Obviously, these were not common artisan occupations, yet they were relatively quite common on the *New-York Magazine*'s subscription list. Conversely, two crafts—blacksmith and block maker—appear in the top ten artisan occupations in the random sample but not at all on the subscription list.

Why printers and sea captains (but not blacksmiths and block makers) would subscribe to a magazine seems fairly obvious. Their trades and their lifestyles were clearly more associated with reading. The same might be said for the barbers, whose customers loitered around the shops then just as they do today. But what of the coppersmiths and cutlers, the saddlers and sail makers? The street addresses of the artisans provide a clue. The magazine subscribers were somewhat more likely than other artisans to live and work in the commercial heart of the city. This difference should not be exaggerated, however; the artisan subscribers were spread out among thirty-four different streets in the city. Yet the artisans in the random sample were spread out even more widely on sixty-seven different streets, including some of the newer and less built-up areas around Bowery Lane on what was then the far northeast side of town.

Table 8.3 shows the difference. The artisan subscribers were more concentrated on the same streets as the merchant subscribers: Queen, Water, and Hanover Square. King Street (now Pine) was another prominent street in this same area. Again, this concentration should not be overstated; the artisans from the random sample were also heavily represented on Queen and Water. But the other main streets for them—Fair (now Fulton), Ann, and Chatham (now Park Row)—were several blocks farther north on the outskirts of the commercial center of the city in 1790.

Because little is known about most of the individual artisan subscribers, it is difficult to say what sort of men they were. But at least some of them were clearly men of stature and influence, both within their crafts and in the larger public culture. Some were on their way to becoming manufacturers and capitalists. For example, White Matlock, a brewer on Chatham Street, was vice president of the New York Manufacturing Society, which was headed by the well-known merchant-politician Melancthon Smith. The aim of this society was precisely to move manufacturing from handicraft to factory.[29] On the other hand, other artisan subscribers were just as clearly devoted to the craft tradition. The chairman and deputy chairman of the General Society of

Table 8.3. Five Leading Street Addresses of Artisan Subscribers to *New-York Magazine* and Artisans in a Random Sample from the New York City Directory, 1790

Subscribers		Random Sample	
Occupation	Percentage of Artisans	Occupation	Percentage of Artisans
1. Queen	13.5%	1. Queen	12.8%
2. Hanover Square	8.1	2. Fair	5.1
3. Water	8.1	3. Water	4.5
4. Broadway	5.4	4. Chatham	3.8
5. King	5.4	5. Ann	3.2
	40.5%		29.4%
	(N = 30)		(N = 46)
All artisans	100.0%		100.0%
	(N = 74)		(N = 156)

Source: List of subscribers in *New-York Magazine; or, Literary Repository,* vol. 1 (New York: Thomas and James Swords, 1790), iii–vi; *The New-York Directory and Register* (New York: Hodge, Allen, and Campbell, 1789 and 1790); *The New-York Directory and Register* (New York: T. and J. Swords, 1791 and 1792). See also appendix A.

Mechanics and Tradesmen were both readers of the *New-York Magazine.* Anthony Post was a carpenter; James Bramble was a whitesmith (tinned or galvanized iron). The General Society, founded in 1785, was a revival of the radical mechanics' committee of the 1770s, which had been instrumental in recruiting the city's working class to Revolutionary politics. It was an organization of substantial, ambitious, and politically active master tradesmen. By 1796, for example, Anthony Post owned property valued at £3,500. But it was also a group devoted to the traditions of craft work and to the values of artisan republicanism.[30]

* * *

The content of the *New-York Magazine* did not impress William Loring Andrews, one of the earliest of the few historians who have written about the magazine. His enthusiasm was expended on the copperplate engravings that formed the frontispiece of each issue. Of the rest of the content he wrote: "Aside from the record of marriages and deaths and a few local items of some slight historical importance, there is nothing in the literature of *The New-York Magazine* that, if it had been totally destroyed, would have proved a serious loss to posterity or to the world of letters."[31] In a sense Andrews was right. Except for some early poetry by William Dunlap, the literature of the *New-York Magazine* is of little interest to "the world of letters."[32] But it is of great interest to the social historian of reading, for here we can see what the merchants, shopkeepers, and artisans actually read in 1790.

Through a simple content analysis and a close reading of the 1790 volume, I confirmed that many of the conventional notions about late eighteenth-century American magazines are true of the *New-York Magazine*.[33] The magazine was highly eclectic—in subject matter, in style, and in source of material. In this sense American magazines were like their English counterparts. The prototypical and highly successful English magazine, the *Gentleman's Magazine*, was perhaps most famous for its orderly but miscellaneous character. In fact, largely because of the influence of the *Gentleman's*, *magazine* became almost synonymous with *miscellany*.[34] An article on the history of magazines that appeared in the *New-York Magazine* in 1790 was almost exclusively about the *Gentleman's*. A proper magazine, the article declared, should have two characteristics: It should be "very various and extensive" in its coverage and commentary, and it should unite "utility with entertainment, . . . instruction with pleasure."[35]

Certainly, the *New-York Magazine* took the idea of instruction very seriously. Though few of its articles and essays dealt directly with government or politics, many were highly didactic on the subject of public virtue. In many ways the content of the *New-York Magazine* was very much devoted to what have been called the "didactic arts," those arts and sciences considered useful to the cultivation of virtue and character, the essential ingredients of republican men and women.[36] (See table 8.4.)

While a good deal of the content of the *New-York Magazine* was given over to discussions of specific topics in politics, religion, or science, the largest proportion of the articles fell into a more nebulous area that I have labeled "manners and morals." (See table 8.5.) Many of these pieces were romances—usually sentimental stories of love lost or found, seduction resisted or embraced. Many were simple expositions on virtue—with titles such as "Vanity," "Avarice," "On Idleness," "The Benefits of Temperance," or simply "On Virtue." Many were purely descriptive pieces—travelogues, anecdotes on manners and customs, sundry tales of exotica. Counting all the prose pieces for 1790, about two-thirds were written in descriptive or expository style; one-third were narratives. About one-eighth were set in New York City; seven-eighths were set elsewhere or had no specific locale.

What were these stories and articles like? A closer look at some of the regular features and some of the long-running serials provides some insight. Three of the most frequent contributors to the *New-York Magazine* in 1790 were "Philobiblicus," "Juvenis," and "The Scribbler." They rather nicely represent the range of material in the magazine, from the arcane to the mundane.

"Philobiblicus" falls into the arcane category. He contributed a piece each month on scriptural matters, especially issues in biblical translation. The

Table 8.4. Items Devoted to Various Subject Categories in
New-York Magazine, 1790

Subject Category	Percentage of Items
1. Politics and government	15.3%
2. Manners and morals	46.8
3. Religion	4.9
4. Science and health	3.9
5. Household advice	1.0
6. Humor	4.2
7. Commentary on art, music, and letters	3.9
8. "American Muse" (poetry)	3.9
9. "Intelligence" (news briefs)	3.6
10. "Marriages," "deaths," and other vital statistics	12.6
	100.1%
	(*N* = 308)

Source: *New-York Magazine; or, Literary Repository,* vol. 1 (New York: Thomas and James Swords, 1790). See also appendix A.

Table 8.5. Items Devoted to Various Subcategories of "Manners and Morals" in *New-York Magazine,* 1790

Subcategories of "Manners and Morals"	Percentage of Items
1. Romance (love, seduction, etc.)	24.3%
2. Education	9.7
3. Virtue (morality, wisdom, etc.)	29.2
4. Description (travel, exotica, slice of life, etc.)	36.8
	100.0%
	(*N* = 144)

Source: *New-York Magazine; or, Literary Repository,* vol. 1 (New York: Thomas and James Swords, 1790). See also appendix A.

more subtle the philology, the more complex the etymology, the better "Philobiblicus" liked it. His aim, he said in his first piece, was to be "both instructing and entertaining," particularly through the use of "fine language and elegance of expression."[37]

"Juvenis" was more practical. Virtually all of his many pieces were little homilies on virtue. In a variety of ways he preached a simple sermon, "that happiness results from the constant practice of virtue." On his list of the important virtues were the traditional ones. "The very ideas of justice, truth, benevolence, modesty, humility, mildness, and temperance please and beautify the mind," he wrote.[38]

"The Scribbler" was considerably more down to earth, even earthy, than either "Philobiblicus" or "Juvenis." Writing was his avocation; he was an artisan by occupation, though in what craft he doesn't say. In his first contribution he tells the story of how excited he had been as a young man to see his first piece of writing appear in a newspaper. He began to daydream and to imagine himself a great writer and a great man:

> In my reflections upon it next day, I beheld myself wielding a pen with all the force of a furious and animated combatant, until reaching to supply it with ink, I overturned one of the implements of my profession. The noise brought me to my proper recollection, and, strange metamorphosis! I found myself in my master's workshop, busied in the execution of a design which my extraordinary avocation had destroyed, and surrounded by my fellow apprentices, who were looking at my actions with astonishment, and picking up the remains of the valuable instrument which I had thrown down, and which was broken to pieces. For this piece of mischief I was severely corrected by my master, but the disaster did not prevent me in the prosecution of my favorite hobby horse. I continued to wield the goose-quill, and I every day saw myself rising into consequence by the respectable figure Mr. Scribbler made in the newspapers.[39]

"The Scribbler's" contributions continued to touch on the lives of the "middling classes" of New York City.

The long-running serials in 1790 also reflect the range of material in the *New-York Magazine*. In this category the most arcane may have been the series called "Observations on the Utility of the Latin and Greek Languages," which ran for eight months beginning in April. In this series "T.Q.C." summarized in copious detail all the various arguments supporting the study of the ancient languages—ranging from the needs of Christianity to physiology.[40] Another prominent monthly feature was the serialization of John Adams's *Defense of the Constitutions of Government of the United States,* a book that explored and promoted English constitutional theory as much as American.[41] A third serial that ran for many months was "The History of the Dutchess de C__," a romance of passion, power, intrigue, confinement, cruelty, terror, outrage, and calamity among the rich and wellborn of Europe.[42]

The other material in the magazine shows a similar diversity. For example, many of the articles and stories were aimed at women. Though only seven women were subscribers in their own names, it is clear that the readership was heavily female. The first issue, for example, carried a letter from a local woman praising the editors for launching such an important literary enterprise. She promised that she and all her friends would subscribe, and she hinted that Noah Webster's *American Magazine* had perished largely because the *men* of the city had failed to support it. About 11 percent of the articles in 1790 either had a woman as the main character or had a clearly identified female author, and many more were obviously aimed at and probably written by women. This is clearly true of the romances and sentimental fiction, generally considered at that time, as Linda Kerber has pointed out, to be the province of the woman reader.[43]

Some of the pieces aimed at women were simply conventional reflections on traditional feminine virtues: "How much more pure, tender, delicate, irritable, affectionate, flexible, and patient is woman than man?" Or: "The female thinks not profoundly; profound thought is the power of the man. Women feel more. Sensibility is the power of woman."[44] In their "Introductory Essay" the editors said that they expected their women readers to submit "many a poetic wreath," for poetry "seems peculiarly the province of that sex, whose sweetest ornament is the mild tear that trembles in the eye of sensibility."[45] The magazine also carried advice pieces for women: "On the Choice of a Husband," or "On the Virtue of Acorn Coffee" ("to cure the slimy obstructions in the viscera"), or on how to behave in company (no "sitting cross-legged, straddling, spitting, blowing noses, etc., etc.").[46] Some were parables of seduction and lost virtue, such as the sad story of "Frivola," who became so obsessed with luxury that she ended her wasted life in Europe, the slave of "every species of polite dissipation."[47] The emphasis on the supposed sensibility and sentimentality of the woman reader was characteristic of popular thought in England as well as in America.[48]

Yet some of the articles directed toward women were less conventional. These included tales of women's heroism, calls for women's education, and articles by women sensitive to women's concerns. An example of the latter was a piece criticizing men for always talking about women's vanity.[49] In this the *New-York Magazine* seems to have been similar to other American magazines of the time. Mary Beth Norton found that magazines were often in the forefront of a new approach to women, an approach that emphasized a more active and equal participation of women in family life, household management, and the education of children. This new approach still placed woman's sphere within the home and family. But home and family had now taken on a somewhat larger and more political role in the nurture of the new republic.[50]

Despite all the diversity, several important themes recur. Virtue, for example, was commonly portrayed as *public* virtue. The golden rule was taken very seriously by the contributors to the *New-York Magazine*. "Amongst the number of public virtues we may note love to our country, zeal in promoting the good of society, seeking the good of our neighbor in all our conduct," wrote the author of a piece called "On Virtue." Similarly, even the deeply religious

"Juvenis" stopped far short of arguing that virtue is a private matter between a man and God. If a man is virtuous, he wrote, "he has sacrificed his own interest rather than wrong his neighbor. He has been benevolent to his fellow men. The children of poverty and affliction he has assisted and consoled."[51] Women's virtue was usually portrayed as a more private matter of "morality and piety," but the relationship between women's virtue and the welfare of the community was sometimes suggested—for example, in an essay on women's education by a Philadelphia school girl in the magazine's first issue.[52] In short, the connection between virtue and commonwealth was vividly clear in the pages of the *New-York Magazine*.

Another recurrent theme was suspicion of luxury. On this theme the aphorisms abounded: "Luxury and idleness are similar in their effects—By the former, families are reduced to indigence, and are involved in misery and ruin; by means of the latter, they are prevented from arriving at a comfortable situation in life." The parables and allegories were equally common. In one, "Wealth" and "Poverty" meet each other on life's road at the end of their journeys. In a piece called "On Avarice" the author argued that "the avaricious man regards nothing but his purse; the welfare and prosperity of his country never much employs his thoughts. . . . He is a stranger to public spiritedness." The theme was always that luxury is self-defeating because it is self-serving.[53] "Juvenis" perhaps expressed it most clearly: The virtuous man "has never indulged himself in luxury or any kind of excess, and used every exertion to promote the welfare of society."[54]

A third recurrent theme was the power and democracy of knowledge. In America everyone had a right and a duty to participate in the life of the mind. Some writers put this theme rather bluntly. In a paean to science one writer declared:

> It is indeed questionable whether an ignorant people can be happy, or even exist, under what Americans call a free government. It may be also doubted, whether a truly enlightened people were ever enslaved. Science is so meliorating in its influence upon the human mind, that even he who holds the reins of power, and hath felt its rays, loses the desire of a tyrant, and is best gratified in the sense of public love and admiration. Liberty is a plant which as naturally flourishes under this genial light, as despotism is engendered by the horrors of intellectual darkness.[55]

In more subtle form this theme ran through many of the articles in the *New-York Magazine* in 1790. Women, for example, were urged "to attend to the cultivation of letters"—and not simply because of the obligations of "republican motherhood." One writer advocated education for women partly for their own "happiness." In old age, when their traditional feminine plea-sures had faded, they could take "refuge in the bosom of knowledge."[56] Even "Philobiblicus," the master of erudition, argued that instruction in Latin and Greek should be central even to a "republican education," for in a republic every man should be and could be a scholar.[57]

In this the magazine reflected a widespread belief in America that diffu-sion of knowledge was beneficial for republican government and for the vir-tue of the people. Though classical republican thinkers were sometimes rather skeptical of education for the masses, Americans were almost wholly for it.[58] Benjamin Rush, Noah Webster, Thomas Jefferson, and many others argued passionately that education must be the foundation of republican govern-ment. But they went further than simply praising education. They stressed the broadest possible diffusion of knowledge through universal participation in public schools. As Rush put it, "a free government can only exist in an equal diffusion of literature." To this end Rush proposed not only public schools and state universities but also a wider diffusion of libraries and newspapers. "I consider it possible to convert men into republican machines," he declared in a now-famous quotation. "This must be done if we expect them to per-form their parts properly in the great machine of the government of the state."[59] Of course, these men supported the diffusion of education and knowledge precisely because they believed it would have a conservative, sta-bilizing influence on the nation. The fear of mass education per se, which was widespread in England, never took root in America.[60] In American republi-can ideology everyone had the right and the duty to participate in the life of the mind.

Public virtue, suspicion of luxury, and the power and democracy of knowl-edge—these were republican themes, and they were laden with meaning for eighteenth-century Americans, perhaps especially American artisans. These themes did not appear in every story and article in the *New-York Magazine*. But they were common enough to run like brightly colored threads through the great diversity of material, from heavy political discourse to ethereal ro-mance. This, then, was what the readers of the *New-York Magazine*—the shopkeepers and artisans, as well as the merchants and politicians—were reading in 1790.

* * *

In its first issue in January 1790 the *New-York Magazine* published an article titled "On the Means of Preserving Public Liberty." It is a nice summary of what might be called a republican ideology of magazine and newspaper read-ing. "Information," the article said, had been the mainspring of the Revolution, and it must now be the wellspring of the new republic. The author continued:

> A few enlightened citizens may be dangerous; let all be enlightened, and oppression must cease, by the influence of a ruling majority; for it can never be their interest to indulge a system incompatible with the rights of freemen. Those institutions are the most effectual guards to public liberty which diffuse the rudiments of literature among a people. . . . A few incautious expressions in our constitution, or a few salaries of office too great for the contracted feelings of those who do not know the worth of merit and integrity, can never injure the United States, while literature is generally diffused, and the plain citizen and planter reads and judges for himself. . . . Disseminate science through all grades of people, and it will forever vindicate your rights.[61]

This sentiment was not confined to America. The claim to equal access to knowledge, as well as to political power, was central to the new revolutionary spirit of Europe. The old regimes of both France and England were notoriously fearful of the power of information and reading, as Richard Altick and Robert Darnton have made clear.[62] The American elites were likewise impressed by the power of information, but they tended to be less fearful of reading—perhaps because so much reading matter remained fundamentally supportive of the values of American republicanism. The literature of the *New-York Magazine,* for example, was not a popular, democratic literature produced by or even directed toward the lower classes. This kind of modern mass media would not emerge in the United States until the nineteenth century.[63] Yet neither was this an aristocratic literature, accessible only to the elite. The readership was broader than that. It was instead a kind of republican literature with a republican purpose. It affirmed traditional values while inviting all (except the truly poor) to take part. Like politics, it was an arena in which artisans and shopkeepers could participate in public life—in this case the cultural life—of the new nation. And participation, not social revolution, was what artisan republicanism was all about.

Appendix A: Notes on Method

As far as I have been able to determine, this study is the first readership research based upon the subscription list of an eighteenth-century magazine. The methods that I used were fairly simple. I started with the list of 370 subscribers published in the *New-York Magazine; or, Literary Repository,* vol. 1 (New York: Thomas and James Swords, 1790), iii–vi. The list itself identified 298 of these as residents of New York City. I located information on 265 of these New Yorkers in city directories or, in a few cases, in the biographical sources cited in my footnotes. The directories I used were *The New-York Directory and Register* (New York: Hodge, Allen, and Campbell, 1789 and 1790) and *The New-York Directory and Register* (New York: T. and J. Swords, 1791 and

1792). I also drew a random sample of four hundred entries from the 1790 directory. These two groups—the subscriber census and the random sample—provided the data for the reader analysis.

Of course, some people do not appear in these directories. Women, for instance, appear only if they were heads of households. In my random sample only 7.8 percent were women, and almost all of them were identified by occupation (58 percent) or listed as widows (35 percent). Furthermore, historians have usually assumed that common laborers, especially mariners, were substantially underrepresented and that vagrants and transients were not listed at all. Yet I also found the opposite to be true as well—that is, a few of the wealthy merchants on the subscription list did not appear in the city directories. I identified them from other biographical sources. Since I was able to trace only well-to-do people, not poor people, in these other sources, my survey of subscribers may be even more upwardly biased. On the other hand, because some of the incipient manufacturers in New York in 1790 still sometimes listed themselves as artisans, there is a countervailing downward class bias in the survey as well. Overall, I tend to agree with Carl Kaestle that the New York directories from the 1790s probably provide a fairly reliable representation of the range of occupations in the city. See Carl F. Kaestle, *The Evolution of an Urban School System: New York City, 1750–1850* (Cambridge, Mass.: Harvard University Press, 1973), 31–32. I'm confident partly because I was able to trace all but thirty-three of the New York subscribers. Moreover, if there is an upper-class bias in my survey, that would have a conservative effect upon the conclusions of the study, undercounting those at the lower end of the economic scale. This also gives me some confidence in my suggestion that shopkeepers and artisans made up about 50 percent of the readers of the magazine.

The classification of occupations in table 8.1 and appendix B is based largely upon my own understanding of late eighteenth-century employment, but it does not differ radically from the schemes used by other historians, such as Carl Kaestle and Howard Rock. See also Michael B. Katz, "Occupational Classification in History," *Journal of Interdisciplinary History* 3 (Summer 1972): 63–88. Several of the occupations in the "professional" category (such as clerk and local government official) are perhaps out of place there. Similarly, gardener, nurseryman, and widow may not belong in the "nonskilled" category. But these involve so few individuals that I don't believe that the argument is distorted. Furthermore, the identical classification scheme was used for both the subscriber census and the random sample, so the comparative statements should be fairly reliable.

For the content analysis, I simply classified articles by topic. The unit of analysis was the individual article or story, though certain standard groupings of items were counted only once per issue. These included "American Muse," a collection of poems in each issue; "Intelligence," a monthly collection of short news items; "Marriages" and "Deaths"; and "Congressional Affairs," excerpts from the proceedings of Congress (coded as "politics"). I did not code the copperplate engravings at the beginning of each issue. I did not code advertisements, because in 1790 there were none. Fine distinctions among categories are not important for the argument. The aim was simply to get a general idea of the manifest content of the editorial matter in the magazine (table 8.5).

Appendix B: Occupation List of Subscribers

1. PROFESSIONAL:

attorney	military officer
benevolent society	minister
clerk	physician
college	college student
federal government official	teacher
local government official	

2. MERCHANT:

banker	insurer
broker	merchant

3. SHOPKEEPER:

boardinghouse	porterhouse
bookstore	ship chandler
grocer	store or shopkeeper
ironmonger	tavern
jewelry store	tobacco store
livery stable	vendue master
paint and glass store	

4. ARTISAN:

baker	gold/silversmith
barber	hatter
bookbinder	mason
brewer	mathematical instrument maker
butcher	nail maker
cabinetmaker	pewterer
carpenter	pilot
carver and gilder	printer
chair maker	saddler
chandler	sail maker
clock/watchmaker	sea captain
coach painter	ship carpenter
cooper	ship joiner
copperplate printer	shoemaker
coppersmith	tailor or mantua maker
cutler	tanner or currier
dancing master	type founder
distiller	upholsterer
furrier	weaver
glover	whitesmith

5. NONSKILLED:

gardener	washer
nurseryman	widow

Notes

1. Preface to *New-York Magazine; or, Literary Repository,* vol. 1 (New York: Thomas and James Swords, 1790), viii. Mathew Carey, proprietor of the *American Museum* magazine in Philadelphia, was similarly proud of the respectability and character of his subscribers. See preface to *American Museum,* vol. 2 (Philadelphia: Mathew Carey, 1787).

2. Frank Luther Mott, *A History of American Magazines, 1741–1850,* 5 vols. (Cambridge, Mass.: Belknap, 1930), 1:115–16; James Playsted Wood, *Magazines in the United States,* 3d ed. (New York: Ronald Press, 1971), 26.

3. Carl F. Kaestle, "The History of Literacy and the History of Readers," Program Report 85-2, Wisconsin Center for Education Research, Madison, February 1985, p. 43. Kaestle later expanded this report into chapters 1 and 2 of Carl F. Kaestle et al., *Literacy in the United States: Readers and Reading since 1880* (New Haven, Conn.: Yale University Press, 1991).

4. Edward Countryman, *A People in Revolution: The American Revolution and Political Society in New York, 1760–1790* (Baltimore: Johns Hopkins University Press, 1981), 294.

5. Bernard Bailyn, *The Ideological Origins of the American Revolution* (Cambridge, Mass.: Harvard University Press, 1967); J. G. A. Pocock, *The Machiavellian Moment: Florentine Political Thought and the Atlantic Republican Tradition* (Princeton, N.J.: Princeton University Press, 1975). For reviews of this literature, see Linda Kerber, "The Republican Ideology of the Revolutionary Generation," *American Quarterly* 37 (Fall 1985): 474–95; Robert E. Shalhope, "Republicanism and Early American Historiography," *William and Mary Quarterly* 39 (Apr. 1982): 334–56; and Lance Banning, "Jeffersonian Ideology Revisited: Liberal and Classical Ideas in the New American Republic," *William and Mary Quarterly* 43 (Jan. 1986): 3–19.

6. Louis Hartz, *The Liberal Tradition in America* (New York: Harcourt, Brace and World, 1955); Joyce Appleby, *Capitalism and a New Social Order: The Republican Vision of the 1790s* (New York: New York University Press, 1984); John Patrick Diggins, *The Lost Soul of American Politics: Virtue, Self-Interest, and the Foundations of Liberalism* (New York: Basic, 1984). For a review of this literature, see Joyce Appleby, "Republicanism in Old and New Contexts," *William and Mary Quarterly* 43 (Jan. 1986): 20–34.

7. Eric Foner, *Tom Paine and Revolutionary America* (New York: Oxford University Press, 1976); Gary B. Nash, *The Urban Crucible: Social Change, Political Consciousness, and the Origins of the American Revolution* (Cambridge, Mass.: Harvard University Press, 1979); Dirk Hoerder, *Crowd Action in Revolutionary Massachusetts, 1765–1780* (New York: Academic, 1977).

8. Appleby, "Republicanism," 21; Appleby, "Introduction," 469. See also Robert E. Shalhope, *The Roots of Democracy: American Thought and Culture, 1760–1800* (Boston: Twayne, 1990), chap. 2.

9. Kerber, "Republican Ideology," 492–95.

10. Sidney I. Pomerantz, *New York: An American City, 1783–1803* (New York: Columbia University Press, 1938), 24–25, 460–61; Frank Monaghan and Marvin Lowenthal, *This Was New York: The Nation's Capital in 1789* (Garden City, N.Y.: Doubleday, Doran, 1943), 33–34; Martha J. Lamb and (Mrs.) Burton Harrison, *History of the City of New York: Its Origins, Rise, and Progress,* vol. 3 (New York: A. S. Barnes, 1896), 11. The most detailed account of day-to-day events in New York City during this era is I. N. Phelps Stokes, *The Iconography of Manhattan Island,* vol. 5 (New York: Robert H. Dodd, 1926).

11. Sean Wilentz, *Chants Democratic: New York City and the Rise of the American Working Class, 1788–1850* (New York: Oxford University Press, 1984), 27; Carl F. Kaestle, *The Evolution of an Urban School System: New York City, 1750–1850* (Cambridge, Mass.: Harvard University Press, 1973), 31. For a discussion of my sampling and classification methods, see appendix A.

12. Pomerantz, *New York,* 209–25; Wilentz, *Chants Democratic,* 24–35. See also David Montgomery, "The Working Classes of the Pre-Industrial American City, 1780–1830," *Labor History* 9 (Winter 1968): 3–22.

13. Countryman, *A People in Revolution,* 292–94. See also Staughton Lynd, "The Mechanics in New York Politics, 1774–1785," in *Class Conflict, Slavery, and the United States Constitution: Ten Essays* (Indianapolis: Bobbs-Merrill, 1967); and Alfred F. Young, ed., *The American Revolution: Explorations in the History of American Radicalism* (DeKalb: Northern Illinois University Press, 1976).

14. Wilentz, *Chants Democratic,* 14.

15. Ibid., 102. See also Foner, *Tom Paine.*

16. Gordon S. Wood, *The Creation of the American Republic, 1776–1787* (New York: W. W. Norton, 1972), 606–15. See also Kerber, "Republican Ideology," 494.

17. Wilentz, *Chants Democratic,* 95. See also Howard B. Rock, *Artisans of the New Republic: The Tradesmen of New York City in the Age of Jefferson* (New York: New York University Press, 1979).

18. Webster, quoted in Monaghan and Lowenthal, *This Was New York,* 147. See also Gary Coll, "Noah Webster, Magazine Editor and Publisher," *Journalism History* 11 (Spring–Summer 1984): 26–31.

19. Pomerantz, *New York,* 19–21, 155–59, 199–200; Thomas E. V. Smith, *The City of New York in the Year of Washington's Inauguration, 1789* (New York: Anson D. F. Randolph, 1889), 5–7.

20. Quote from preface to *New-York Magazine,* vol. 2 (New York: Thomas and James Swords, 1791), iv. Little has been written about the *New-York Magazine.* For brief sketches, see Mott, *History of American Magazines,* 114–16; William Loring Andrews, "The First Illustrated Magazine Published in New York," in *The Old Booksellers of New York, and Other Papers* (New York: Author, 1895); Kenneth Scott and Kristin L. Gibbons, eds., *The New-York Magazine Marriages and Deaths, 1790–1797* (New Orleans: Polyauthos, 1975); Mary Rives Bowman, "Dunlap and 'The Theatrical Register' of the *New-York Magazine,*" *Studies in Philology* 24 (July 1927): 413–25. Incidentally, Isaiah Thomas's *Massachusetts Magazine* also survived for eight years.

21. Editorial announcement, *New-York Magazine* 1 (Mar. 1790): unnumbered page. See also Mott, *History of American Magazines,* 34; Pomerantz, *New York,* 216.

22. *New-York Magazine* 1 (May 1790): 256–58; C. Lennart Carlson, *The First Magazine: A History of The Gentleman's Magazine* (Providence, R.I.: Brown University Press, 1938). Adams is quoted in Monaghan and Lowenthal, *This Was New York,* 34.

23. *New-York Magazine* 1 (Apr. 1790): 197. I have modernized eighteenth-century spelling and capitalization.

24. By comparison, the new nation's largest-circulating magazine, the *American Museum,* had about 1,250 subscribers. See the subscription list published with the *American Museum,* vol. 2 (1787). See also Mott, *History of American Magazines,* 101.

25. Some of the thirty-three subscribers whom I couldn't trace may have been from the bottom occupational groups. If table 8.1 is biased, it seems likely that it is biased upward. See appendix A for a discussion of this issue. For a list of subscriber occupations, see appendix B.

26. Smith, *City of New York,* 99. The ads are from Monaghan and Lowenthal, *This Was New York,* 52–53, 71. See also Pomerantz, *New York,* chap. 4.

27. Information on prominent individuals came from several biographical sources, including Margherita Arlina Hamm, *Famous Families of New York,* 2 vols. (New York: G. P. Putnam's Sons, 1901); Lyman Horace Weeks, ed., *Prominent Families of New York,* rev. ed. (New York: Historical Co., 1898); James Grant Wilson, ed., *Memorial History of the City of New York,* vol. 5 (New York: New-York History, 1893).

28. On Duer see Pomerantz, *New York,* 181. On Benson and Duane see Countryman, *A People in Revolution,* passim.

29. Smith, *City of New York,* 108; Pomerantz, *New York,* 197.

30. *The New-York Directory and Register* (New York: Hodge, Allen, and Campbell, 1789), 117; Smith, *City of New York,* 107. On the General Society see Wilentz, *Chants Democratic,* 38–39 and passim. On Anthony Post see Lynd, "The Mechanics," 82, 107–8.

31. Andrews, "First Illustrated Magazine," 60.

32. L. Leary, "Unrecorded Early Verse by William Dunlap," *American Literature* 39 (Mar. 1967): 87–88.

33. For notes on the content analysis method, see appendix A. For a general description of the content of eighteenth-century magazines, see Mott, *History of American Magazines,* chap. 2.

34. Carlson, *First Magazine,* vii, 58. The passion for a wide variety of factual, scientific information in magazines had its counterpart in eighteenth-century European book publishing, most notably the success of the *Encyclopedie* in France. See Robert Darnton, *The Business of Enlightenment: A Publishing History of the Encyclopedie, 1775–1800* (Cambridge, Mass.: Harvard University Press, 1979).

35. *New-York Magazine* 1 (May 1790): 257–58.

36. G. Wood, *Creation of the American Republic,* 104. See also Neil Harris, *The Artist in American Society: The Formative Years, 1790–1860* (New York: G. Braziller, 1966).

37. *New-York Magazine* 1 (Jan. 1790): 4.

38. *New-York Magazine* 1 (Aug. 1790): 442. See also *New-York Magazine* 1 (Feb. 1790): 104–6.

39. *New-York Magazine* 1 (Jan. 1790): 21. See also *New-York Magazine* 1 (Feb. 1790): 104–6.

40. *New-York Magazine* 1 (Apr. 1790): 212–18; 1 (Aug. 1790): 467–69.

41. The serialization of Adams begins in *New-York Magazine* 1 (Jan. 1790): 41–47. On Adams and this book see G. Wood, *Creation of the American Republic,* chap. 14; and Diggins, *Lost Soul,* chap. 3.

42. This tale begins in *New-York Magazine* 1 (Jan. 1790): 10–15. This is a translation of a romance by Madame la Comptesse de Genlis, a popular French writer of sentiment and sensation.

43. *New-York Magazine* 1 (Jan. 1790): 9; Linda K. Kerber, *Women of the Republic: Intellect and Ideology in Revolutionary America* (Chapel Hill: University of North Carolina Press, 1980), 235–36.

44. *New-York Magazine* 1 (June 1790): 335–36.

45. *New-York Magazine* 1 (Apr. 1790): 198.

46. *New-York Magazine* 1 (Jan. 1790): 16–17, 51; 1 (Mar. 1790): 160.

47. *New-York Magazine* 1 (Jan. 1790): 22–23; 1 (Mar. 1790): 160–61; 1 (Nov. 1790): 646–48.

48. Richard D. Altick, *The English Common Reader* (Chicago: University of Chicago Press, 1957), 45.

49. *New-York Magazine* 1 (Sept. 1790): 515–16; 1 (Oct. 1790): 563–65; 1 (Feb. 1790): 90; 1 (Dec. 1790): 694–95.

50. Mary Beth Norton, *Liberty's Daughters: The Revolutionary Experience of American Women, 1750–1800* (Boston: Little, Brown, 1980), 246–50. See also Kerber, "Republican Ideology," 484–85; and Kerber, *Women of the Republic,* 11–12.

51. *New-York Magazine* 1 (Mar. 1790): 152–53; 1 (Aug. 1790): 442.

52. *New-York Magazine* 1 (Jan. 1790): 40–41.

53. Ibid., 28–29; *New-York Magazine* 1 (Mar. 1790): 159, 162; 1 (Jan. 1790): 18; 1 (Feb. 1790): 113.

54. *New-York Magazine* 1 (Aug. 1790): 442.

55. *New-York Magazine* 1 (May 1790): 295.

56. *New-York Magazine* 1 (Feb. 1790): 90.

57. Ibid., 89–90; *New-York Magazine* 1 (Oct. 1790): 585–86.

58. Eugene F. Miller, "On the American Founders' Defense of Liberal Education in a Republic," *Review of Politics* 46 (Jan. 1984): 65–90. See also Eva Brann, *Paradoxes of Education in a Republic* (Chicago: University of Chicago Press, 1979).

59. Benjamin Rush, "A Plan for the Establishment of Public Schools and the Diffusion of Knowledge in Pennsylvania" (1786), reprinted in *Essays on Education in the Early Republic,* ed. Frederick Rudolph (Cambridge, Mass.: Harvard University Press, 1965), 3, 8, 17. See also Daniel Calhoun, *The Intelligence of a People* (Princeton, N.J.: Princeton University Press, 1973), chap. 2.

60. Altick, *English Common Reader,* 3; Carl F. Kaestle, *Pillars of the Republic: Common Schools and American Society, 1780–1860* (New York: Hill and Wang, 1983), 33–34.

61. *New-York Magazine* 1 (Jan. 1790): 24–25.

62. Altick, *English Common Reader,* 3; Robert Darnton, "Reading, Writing, and Publishing in Eighteenth-Century France: A Case Study in the Sociology of Literature," *Daedalus* 100 (Winter 1971): 243–44.

63. David D. Hall, "The Uses of Literacy in New England, 1600–1850," in *Printing and Society in Early America,* ed. William L. Joyce, David D. Hall, Richard D. Brown, and John B. Hench, (Worcester: American Antiquarian Society, 1983); David Paul Nord, "The Evangelical Origins of Mass Media in America, 1815–1835," *Journalism Monographs* 88 (May 1984): 1–30. The same might be said of England, France, and Germany. See Altick, *English Common Reader;* and Darnton, "What Is the History of Books?" *Daedalus* 111 (Summer 1982): 78–79.

9. Readership as Citizenship in Late Eighteenth-Century Philadelphia

IN THE EARLY MORNING darkness of September 8, 1793, the cry of "Fire!" rang out in Philadelphia. One man, awakened by the alarm, hesitated to leave his house to join the bucket brigades. He was momentarily frozen in fear that death lay waiting for him in the streets of the city, for in the autumn of 1793 Philadelphia was gripped by epidemic yellow fever. Quickly, however, he overcame his fear and resolved to do his duty:

> What, thought I, is to become of us at this critical moment, amid the sickness which is now prevailing? I knew, however, that exertions would be necessary, and believed it right for me to turn out and use my efforts, which notwithstanding the numerous probable obstacles at such a juncture, I had no doubt would be in conjunction with a considerable number of the remaining citizens. I prepared myself according to the best of my judgment for the occasion; I bathed my temples and forehead with the proper vinegar, took some in my mouth, and went forward. . . .
>
> While I was occupied handing buckets, I looked at my companions on each side, but did not know them; they might for anything I knew, have come from the gloomy chambers of debilitated friends or relatives; I stayed, however, at my post as long as it appeared necessary, and then went home. After writing the chief part of what precedes, I ate my breakfast. . . .[1]

This man's story is revealing in several ways. It suggests something about the nature of community life in an increasingly impersonal city, a place where strangers, caught up in common disasters, might meet, in bucket lines and elsewhere. It also suggests something about the importance that writing held for this man in his efforts to make sense of his experience: He wrote his narrative, then he ate his breakfast. But the most interesting aspect of the story may not be what it says about civic virtue or about this man's need to write out his thoughts. Perhaps most interesting is that, the next day, he sent his story to a newspaper.

Why would someone send an anonymous personal narrative such as this to a newspaper? Why would someone send *anything* to a newspaper during a catastrophe such as the yellow fever epidemic? Surely the answer is that people sent material to newspapers because they believed other people would profit from reading it or would simply enjoy reading it. A study of the correspondence sent to late eighteenth-century newspapers, therefore, should reveal what some readers thought other readers should read. This is especially true, I believe, of newspaper correspondence submitted during a community crisis, such as the Philadelphia yellow fever epidemic. During this crisis, the newspaper (indeed, a single newspaper, the *Federal Gazette*) became an extraordinarily important medium of public communication. The paper brimmed with information about the fever. And much of this information came not from public officials but from the people of the city—the readers of the newspaper.

This chapter, then, is a study of the civic function of the newspaper during the yellow fever crisis in Philadelphia in 1793. But not only that. The correspondence in the newspaper (and commentary on newspaper reading in contemporary letters and diaries) opens a window on the *readers* of the newspaper as well. These correspondents were readers writing for other readers, and the material they shared with each other is a fascinating collection of evidence for the history of reading.[2] What was the public purpose of reading the newspaper in the late eighteenth-century American city? That is the question that this chapter will explore.

From the beginning, observers saw the role of the newspaper, especially the *Federal Gazette,* as crucial to the public response to the yellow fever epidemic. In his instant history of the epidemic Mathew Carey proclaimed the *Federal Gazette* "of utmost service in conveying to the citizens of the United States authentic intelligence of the state of the disorder, and of the city." Most historians who have written about the yellow fever have followed Carey in assigning to the newspaper the rather simple role of information disseminator.[3] My approach is somewhat different. I am interested in the readers, a very active community of readers, that gathered around the *Federal Gazette* during the fearful autumn of 1793.[4] This reader community included city officials and elite physicians, who sought to commandeer the paper to disseminate their own versions of "authentic intelligence." But it also included ordinary people, passing along rumors, offering folk cures and remedies, speculating on the religious meaning of the disease, sharing their fears and their sorrows. For all of these people, the newspaper was a place for community participation, and readership a form of citizenship.[5]

* * *

[Through newspapers] we keep company with the absent; we are, by their means made acquainted with strangers—we feel, in solitude, a sympathy with mankind.[6]

When the man in the fire bucket line looked to his left and right, he saw strangers. That scene symbolizes Philadelphia's changing community life in 1793. No longer was Philadelphia "a single community," as Sam Bass Warner characterized it in its pre-Revolutionary days.[7] By 1793 Philadelphia had become the metropolis of North America, a complex urban center controlling nearly one-quarter of the export trade of the United States, housing both state and federal governments, and teeming with a population of some fifty-one thousand.[8] The gap between the rich and poor, always wide, was probably growing wider in the 1790s, as rents escalated, as immigration increased, and as an economic system based upon the harsh insecurities of wage labor took root. More than half of the families owned no real property at all, and one-third probably lived at the subsistence level.[9] This class division was increasingly manifest as residential division as well. By 1793 the compact, mixed-class eighteenth-century town was disappearing, as the poor settled on the periphery, reserving the older core wards for the rich. Taken together, these economic and social transformations prompted one contemporary observer to call Philadelphia "one great hotel or place of shelter for strangers."[10]

Yet Philadelphia remained a community. Men still turned out to fight a neighbor's fire and, if necessary, an epidemic. Gary Nash has urged historians of eighteenth-century cities to pay closer attention to the new forms of community life that took root in the rubble of the old. "Rather than nostalgically tracing the *eclipse* of community," he says, "we need to trace the continuously evolving *process* of community." He talks of the growth of working-class taverns and craft organizations, middle- and upper-class benevolent and reform associations, and (his special interest) free black churches and self-help societies. Far from dismissing these formal, structured organizations as mere *Gesellschaft,* Nash assigns to them a leading role in the creation of true urban community, of what he calls "'*Gemeinschaft* of mind'—the mental life of the community."[11]

In other words, the increasing complexity of the modern city required formal structures to build community and to hold it together. For Nash, the most interesting of these formal structures are working-class political movements and voluntary associations—structures that helped groups of urban people fabricate their own "communities within communities."[12] For me, the most interesting of these structures are those that sought to maintain a city-wide sense of community. And these structures have frequently been the institutions of public communication and—for literate people—of print.[13]

As community life in the city became more complex and more formally structured, so did the communication system. In his discussion of the community life of pre-Revolutionary Philadelphia, Sam Bass Warner links community to communication, but in his account communication was almost entirely oral and interpersonal, swirling through the streets, taverns, and families of the city. Though Philadelphia had two newspapers and a prosperous publishing trade by the early 1760s, Warner does not think it necessary to mention printing in his discussion of the city's "communications system."[14] Such an omission would be strikingly inappropriate for the 1790s. The Revolution and its aftermath left Philadelphians with a heightened taste for newspaper reading. By 1794 the city had eight newspapers, four of them dailies. (The first dailies in America appeared in Philadelphia in the 1780s.) These newspapers carried at least ten times as much material as had the city's two weeklies in 1764. Meanwhile, the proportion of space given over to local news, compared with foreign and national news, was growing as well—from 12 percent to 23 percent of the total news space. The circulations of most of these newspapers are unknown, though likely none was more than fifteen hundred. So, newspaper reading was certainly not a universal experience for all classes of Philadelphians in the 1790s. Indeed, some small but considerable proportion of Philadelphians could not read in 1793, though the exact illiteracy rate is also unknown.[15] But newspaper reading was common enough to lead one smug and successful Philadelphia publisher to declare, in verse, that the newspaper was "everyone's hobby horse":

> We say (with deference to the college)
> News Papers are the spring of knowledge;
> The gen'ral source throughout the nation,
> Of every modern conversation.[16]

One such "spring of knowledge" in 1793 was Andrew Brown's *Federal Gazette and Philadelphia Daily Advertiser,* a successful and fairly typical Philadelphia daily. Brown had been the principal of a girls' academy before he launched the *Federal Gazette* in 1788 to plump for the new Constitution, and like many of his fellow republican educators, he held to the belief that in popular knowledge lay the stability of government and the safety of the people. "The foundation of all free governments seems to be a general diffusion of knowledge," he wrote. Like his fellow editors, Brown came to associate the success of newspapers with the progress of republican government and the success of the American experiment. In the self-congratulatory rhetoric that newspaper publishers loved then and still love today, Brown ranked newspapers with schools as "heralds of truth" and "protectors of peace and good order," and he proclaimed his own paper "a faithful guardian of the sacred rights of the community."[17]

For Andrew Brown, the function of the newspaper at the local level was a blend of community booster and community forum. In his first issue he published a list of projects that a proper newspaper should pursue, including "the advancement of agriculture, manufactures, and commerce in and around Philadelphia." This booster spirit remained part of the *Federal Gazette*'s publicly stated mission.[18] At the same time Brown promised that his paper would be open to all correspondents. Though committed to the federal Constitution and the Republican interpretation of it, the *Federal Gazette* was not intended by Brown to be a party paper. He insisted that by "free press" he meant a newspaper "open to writers on both sides of every political or other question."[19] Like several of the other large dailies in Philadelphia in the 1790s (such as John Dunlap's *American Daily Advertiser*), Brown's *Federal Gazette* seemed to make its way more as a community common carrier than as a party organ. In a paean to community building, Brown declared of newspapers: "We keep company with the absent; we are, by their means, made acquainted with strangers—we feel, in solitude, a sympathy with mankind. . . . Men stick to their business, and yet the public is addressed as a town meeting. Yet the gazettes follow us to our closets and give us counsel there."[20]

This is not to suggest that Brown conducted the *Federal Gazette* as a kind of public philanthropy. Not at all. The *Federal Gazette* was a decidedly private business. Even in his public statements Brown made this clear. He seldom failed to remind his readers that his good service to the community warranted their financial support, through subscriptions and advertising.[21] Moreover, there is some evidence from inside the business to suggest that Brown may have been a quintessential private enterpriser. One of his apprentices, Robert Simpson, described him as "a very wicked man" and "a vile monster," who beat his apprentices, fed them scraps, and forced them to work on the Sabbath in order to squeeze from the business as much personal gain as possible. "However he may flourish in this life," Simpson wrote to a runaway apprentice friend, "he will one day or other receive the punishment so justly his due."[22]

The *Federal Gazette,* then, was a private institution but one clothed in public purpose. In 1793, when the yellow fever began to spread, people turned to the newspaper, this newspaper. They turned to it to *get* information; they also turned to it to *give* information. The resentful Robert Simpson may have been correct to assume that Andrew Brown's motives for staying in business during the fever were purely pecuniary. But, regardless of Brown's private motives, Philadelphians seemed to agree that the *Federal Gazette* played a key public role in the community's response to the epidemic.[23] Indeed, many probably agreed entirely with Brown's own boast that "the continued publication of this paper amid scenes of uncommon danger and daily threatening mortality, has been of great use to the public. It has kept whole the general chain of intelligence that must otherwise have been broken."[24] But what was this "chain of intelligence"? What kind of community institution or forum should a newspaper be? What sort of civic function should newspaper publishing and newspaper reading serve? On these questions agreement was less than complete.

* * *

Their burying grounds are like ploughed fields.[25]

The story began quietly in the late summer of 1793. A few cases of an unusually malignant fever appeared near Water Street. The symptoms were severe: fever and chills, a feeble pulse, deep torpor, delirium, a morbid yellowing of the skin and eyes, a fetid black vomit. As their patients died, one by one, the physicians of Philadelphia worried and conferred. The most famous among them, Dr. Benjamin Rush, recalled the visitation of a similar fever in Philadelphia in 1762. On August 19 he was prepared to call this new pestilence by name: the yellow fever. As the death toll mounted, the doctors despaired, for, as Rush wrote to his wife in late August, the disease mocked the best efforts of medicine.[26]

By the end of August panic was building in Philadelphia. Thousands fled. Those who stayed shuttered themselves into their houses. The few who ventured out buried their mouths and noses in vinegar-soaked handkerchiefs. By September the streets of the city were largely abandoned to the carters of the dead and dying. The ordeal lasted through October, and in its course more than four thousand died.[27] The epidemic seemed to crush the survivors as well. In his account of the fever Mathew Carey described case after case of tragedy and terror. He concluded that "while affairs were in this deplorable state, and people at the lowest ebb of despair, we cannot be astonished at the frightful scenes that were acted, which seemed to indicate a total dissolution of the bonds of society."[28]

But the bonds of society were not dissolved. As Carey himself acknowledged, the fever produced scenes of bravery as well as panic, heroism as well as cruelty, community organization as well as chaos.[29] It also produced an incredible rush of communication—the fundamental bond of society. The fever dominated every channel of communication within Philadelphia and between Philadelphia and the outside world, from word-of-mouth rumor to learned medical treatise. But one channel—the newspaper—seems to have taken on a particularly important community role. Nearly everyone, from public officials to letter writers and diarists, seems to have turned to it. Even the doggerel poet of the fever, Samuel Stearns, acknowledged his debt to the newspaper:

> A pestilence, which there did rage
> With rapid force, has swept away
> An hundred people from the stage,
> Within the compass of a day.
> But sometimes less, and sometimes more,
> The daily publications tell,
> Upon that mournful city's shore,
> In that short time, have often fell.[30]

Though the newspaper was in some ways "the source of every modern conversation" during the fever, people had very different ideas of what it should do. Some believed that it should be the voice of authority, a font of what Mathew Carey called "authentic intelligence." Others believed that it should be the conversation of community, a forum for "every observation" on the fever.

✶ ✶ ✶

The hundred tongues of rumor were never more successfully
employed than on this melancholy occasion.[31]

The yellow fever dominated the private conversations of Philadelphians and of those with links to Philadelphia. The surviving letters and diaries overflow with the news.[32] Of course, much of the news was nothing more than rumor, and many of these rumors were printed in newspapers all over the country. This flood of rumors, both private and public, exasperated the authorities of Philadelphia. The public officials and the leading physicians believed that the spread of rumor—especially in the newspapers—contributed mightily to the distress of the city.[33] Letter writers were exasperated as well. Their correspondence is filled with warnings to friends and loved ones not to believe the wild rumors they might hear.[34] But as an antidote to rumor, both private citizens and public authorities turned to the same medium that seemed most recklessly effective in spreading rumor: the newspaper.

The letters and diaries suggest that news spread mainly by word of mouth and letter. "This day's mail brings us dismal accounts indeed from your metropolis," one New Yorker wrote to relatives in Philadelphia. He urged his brother-in-law to write to the family in New York by at least every other post, because "so many dreadful and contradictory reports prevail here that we know not what to believe."[35] As far away as London, stories of the epidemic were circulated by travelers and letters, and anxious relatives waited and worried. Closer to Philadelphia, the distress was all consuming. "My thoughts are full of the subject," a young woman wrote to her father. "It is difficult to disengage them to obtain even that momentary relief that seems necessary to health."[36] But the news was inescapable: "Anxiously did I wait the time for the post to arrive each day, but alas everyday brought more distressing accounts and made me even dread to hear."[37] And as the news was dreadful but inescapable, so was the need to spread it. In a long, clumsy letter to his brother, a young Philadelphia artisan spilled out the story, adding, "I had no expectations when I begun this letter, to have made it so lengthy, but being led on from one thought, to another, it seems almost impossible to stop."[38]

The scene in nearby Germantown provides a glimpse of how the news system worked. Thousands of Philadelphians fled to the outlying towns, especially Germantown, to weather the storm. There they waited, hungry for news. Elizabeth Drinker's diary is filled with reports from the city, usually brought out by traveler or letter. Her entries for these doleful days are replete with the vague attributions of secondhand news: "we have heard this day," "we have an account this morning," "several carriages stopped to talk," "they say they have received a letter or letters," "some say," "it is said." The entries are also filled with skepticism. "The accounts this day from the city are many and various," she writes, but they "are not ascertained." She tells of "hearsays from the city of a great number of funerals," but she hopes that "the number is greatly exaggerated." She mentions rumors that Negroes may have poisoned the wells, but "those are flying reports, and most likely false."[39] Another diarist, Jacob Hiltzheimer, who stayed in Philadelphia, describes the nervous ambivalence of the refugees: "Rode out to Germantown, which is filled with Philadelphians who were anxious to hear the news from the city, but kept their distance when they found we were from there."[40]

Although people depended heavily on private communication for information about the fever, many turned to the newspapers for a kind of authentication of the news. Susanna Dillwyn, for example, describes the scene in

Trenton, which lay on the main road to New York. Everyday the people would rush to read the newspapers dropped off by the northbound stagecoaches. In his letters to Robert Ralston in Wilmington, John Welsh routinely included accounts from the *Federal Gazette*. At first he sent copies of the paper, but in October he arranged with Andrew Brown to start a subscription for Ralston, to be dispatched to Wilmington by post. Even after Ralston's subscription had begun, Welsh continued to cite the newspaper in his letters, once copying an item verbatim. "As you will not have the newspapers till Monday evening," he explained, "I will transcribe a piece out of last evening's." In her diary in late October, Elizabeth Drinker cited the newspaper as her source for the total number dead, and in early November she copied verbatim the *Federal Gazette*'s announcement that the fever was over.[41] The surviving manuscript records suggest that Andrew Brown may have exaggerated little when he said he had learned from people all over the country that they had relied on his newspaper for "the most accurate information" on the fever.[42]

As people turned to newspapers for authoritative information, the authorities moved to gain control of the newspapers, especially the *Federal Gazette,* the only major daily in publication after mid-September.[43] After the first week or so of chaos and panic the public officials and institutional leaders of Philadelphia began to reassert their authority. Their major task was organization—organization of community resources to meet the crisis. But part of their task was communication. Like the people of Philadelphia and the nation, the leadership elites of the city were obsessed with the news. They were obsessed, however, not with reading it but with shaping it.

The first efforts to control the flow of news involved the mayor, Matthew Clarkson, and the prestigious College of Physicians of Philadelphia. In 1793 Philadelphia was home to the best medical minds in America, and the College of Physicians was their temple. Here gathered the leading doctors of the new Republic to honor and advance medical science and themselves.[44] Naturally, the desperate mayor turned to the college for help in confronting the looming catastrophe. The fellows of the college met on August 25 to draft a list of recommendations to be published in the newspapers. Dr. Rush wrote the report, passed it along to the mayor, and two days later it appeared in print.[45]

In the weeks after August 27 Mayor Clarkson (and other public officials) peppered the papers with official information. These communiqués included a variety of public orders (on sanitation, ship inspections, etc.) as well as announcements of "authenticated" fever news. The news ranged from notices of the work of organizations to official statements on the death toll of the week—the latter aimed at dispelling the extravagant rumors of wholesale slaughter. At times the mayor used the press to squelch a specific rumor, such as an erroneous report that the fever had infected the city jail. These pieces were printed verbatim, usually in the form of signed letters, and often with the tag line: "The printers of newspapers in the city are requested to insert the above."[46]

On September 14 Mayor Clarkson called together an extraordinary citizens' committee to supervise the city's response to the epidemic. This committee of volunteers, with Clarkson presiding, stood as virtually the only public authority in Philadelphia at the height of the fever. "The Committee," as it was called, quickly gained a reputation for practicality, efficiency, and quiet heroism. The tasks of the Committee included distribution of provisions to the poor, care of impoverished orphans, and supervision of a makeshift charity hospital located at Bush Hill, the country seat of a local gentleman.[47] The distribution of tangible services to the sick and poor was the Committee's top priority. But distribution of information to the newspapers ranked high as well. Again and again, in its official minutes, the Committee directed its secretary "to hand to the printer of the *Federal Gazette* for publication" a certain report or "to cause the following communication to be printed for the information of our fellow citizens."[48]

An early aim of these official reports was to quash the rumors that admission to Bush Hill was a death sentence. One reader wrote to the *Federal Gazette* in early September to complain about the lack of reliable information about Bush Hill. "We ought at least to have been informed by public authenticity, how it is attended," he said. "This will have at least one wholesome effect—it will stop the gossiping reports of idle people." The Committee was soon able to reply, in official reports to the newspaper, that conditions at Bush Hill were improving daily. The accommodations were now sanitary, the doctors and nurses competent, and the course of treatment salubrious.[49] In early October the Committee turned to the newspaper to attack rumors that all the outlying towns were hostile and unsympathetic to Philadelphia's plight. The Committee ordered dozens of letters published that told of public sympathy and relief campaigns in other cities and states. And, at long last, the Committee used the newspaper in late October to announce officially the end of the epidemic.[50]

Though the College of Physicians faded early in the epidemic as an institutional voice of authority, individual doctors continued to count the dissemination of information among their major duties. Indeed, it sometimes seemed as if the newspaper article was the chief instrument of medical practice in Philadelphia in 1793. The doctors wrote newspaper articles for two somewhat separate reasons: to serve the public and to establish the authority of a particular mode of treatment. In the doctors' minds, of course, these reasons were identical.

Among the physicians of Philadelphia, the leading newspaper writer was Benjamin Rush. Though Rush had composed the College of Physicians' initial report on the fever, he soon grew dissatisfied with his colleagues' timidity in treating it. In early September, Rush discovered his own cure for the yellow fever: heroic purging and copious bleeding. With powerful doses of calomel (a mercury compound) and liberal use of the lancet, Rush believed the fever could be weakened and defeated.[51] Instantly, he turned to the press to publicize his discovery. The first announcement of "Dr. Rush's Directions for Curing and Preventing the Yellow Fever" appeared in the *Federal Gazette* on September 11. From that day forth a day rarely passed without some reference in the newspaper to Dr. Benjamin Rush.

Rush used the newspaper partly to save time. After tending to upward of one hundred patients in a day, Rush spent his evenings answering letters from anxious doctors in the countryside and writing to his family. He could neither see enough patients nor answer enough mail to meet the demands laid upon him. Indeed, he said that merely reading all the letters was nearly beyond his endurance. So, he prescribed in print. At the height of the fever he wrote to his wife: "To save the trouble of writing answers to each of them, I have this evening composed a short account of the origin, symptoms, and treatment of the disease which I shall address to Dr. Rodgers of New York in the form of a letter and publish in Mr. Brown's paper. My postage for letters frequently amounts to 7/6 a day."[52]

But, for Rush, medical practice via newspaper made political as well as practical sense, for Rush believed (or so he said) in a republican medicine. Virulent diseases such as the yellow fever were actually quite simple enough for anyone to understand.[53] His aim, therefore, was "to teach the people to cure themselves by my publications in the newspapers." Cure themselves. This was a recurrent theme in the writings of this lifelong American patriot and republican, who could declare with conviction that "the people rule here in medicine as well as government."[54] In other words, Dr. Rush believed that the yellow fever could be cured by purging, bleeding, and reading the newspaper.

Yet his faith in the people was not equal to his faith in himself. When people disparaged his heroic cures, he pressed on with them, because he knew that he was right, that truth was on his side. And his truth was derived from logic and theory, more than from experimental or empirical (or, one might well add, republican) practice. Though he daily worked himself to exhaustion among the sick and dying, his true research was done in his study, not in the streets and sickrooms of Philadelphia. "I applied myself with fresh ardor to the investigation of the disease before me," he wrote. "I ransacked my library, and pored over every book that treated of the yellow fever."[55] Certainly, Rush believed that he was an experimentalist. He believed that he could see the good results in practice. But, fundamentally, Rush's cure was based on abstract principle and wishful thinking, not on systematic observation and experiment. Thus much of his newspaper writing during the fever consisted of the quotation of authoritative medical sources.[56]

Most of Rush's colleagues abhorred virtually all of his ideas about the epidemic, except his belief in the power and utility of the press. Like Rush, they turned to the newspapers to disseminate their theories and to establish their authority. On the same day that Rush's directions for purging and bleeding appeared in the *Federal Gazette,* Dr. Adam Kuhn published a long piece denouncing emetics and laxatives and favoring mild teas and barks. The next day Rush published a rejoinder. And the floodgates were opened.[57] Almost daily thereafter the *Federal Gazette* was heavily laden with the writings of the physicians of Philadelphia. Most claimed public service and service to the truth as their only motives. In a typical opening Dr. Thomas Ruston wrote: "At a time when the public mind is so much agitated by the prevalence of a very alarming disease, . . . it becomes the duty of every good citizen to step forward, and to contribute his mite, not only to quiet those alarms, but if possible to assist in removing the cause."[58]

Though they spoke of quieting the public alarm, the doctors were equally concerned about the victory of their theories. The rancor and hostility rose with the death toll. And the entire controversy was played out in the newspaper. In support of Dr. Kuhn, Dr. William Currie wrote that Rush's treatment "cannot fail of being certain death. . . . It is time the veil should be withdrawn from your eyes, my fellow citizens!" In support of Dr. Rush, Dr. Robert Annan denounced Currie's "bold ignorance" and declared that such a man "is not fit to be reasoned with."[59] Meanwhile, Rush brooded and fulminated: "They have confederated against me in the most cruel manner and are propagating calumnies against me in every part of the city. Dr. Currie (my old friend) is now the weak instrument of their malice and prejudices. If I outlive the present calamity, I know not when I shall be safe from their persecutions. Never did I before witness such a mass of ignorance and wickedness as our profession has exhibited in the course of the present calamity."[60] Rush believed that the publications of his enemies were killing people by the hundreds. "I was contending," he wrote years later, "with the most criminal ignorance, and the object of the contest was the preservation of a city."[61]

Many readers were dismayed by the doctors' newspaper war. Ebenezer

Hazard expressed a sentiment that is not uncommon in the surviving manuscript letters: "Our physicians differ in sentiment both about the nature of
the disorder and the mode of treating it, and have added to the general distress by publishing their contradictory opinions in the newspapers."[62] Some
readers were unhappy enough to publish their complaints. "A Citizen" wrote
to the *Federal Gazette:* "From such a contrariety of sentiments, what are we
to conclude, or how shall we act? It would be well if those gentlemen would
consider the perturbation, the extreme anxiety and distress, with which those
publications have filled the minds of their fellow citizens."[63] In a few of the
letters the perturbation was palpable. One exasperated reader wrote to Andrew Brown: "For God's sake!—for the sake of those who daily wait for the
publication of the *Federal Gazette,* with anxiety! and for your own sake! let
your readers be no more pestered with disputes about a doctrine, which hath
been a bone of contention for a couple of centuries."[64]

In short, both elite and regular readers turned to the newspaper in the terrible autumn of 1793 for authoritative news, for "authentic intelligence." But
what they sometimes found were rumors, contradictions, and arcane ideological disputes among the doctors. This confusion of authority worried the
would-be authorities very much. But what could be done about it? One approach would be to make the printed word more formally and systematically
the voice of authority. This is precisely what Mathew Carey proposed to city
health officials the next autumn, when it appeared that the fever would visit
Philadelphia once again. He reminded them of the terror that was spread by
false reports and contradictory news in 1793. He then added: "The remedy is
obvious. Let the genuine truth be made known. Let such a respectable body
of men as you are—a body in whom not only our own citizens, but those of
the other states, will place implicit reliance—publish daily, or otherwise as you
may judge proper, a faithful, unvarnished state of the business."[65]

But was a faithful, unvarnished report all that mattered? Was "authentic
intelligence" all that readers expected from their newspaper in the throes of
a crisis like the yellow fever? The evidence suggests that the newspaper played
for its readers a much richer and more complicated role than that.

* * *

Mr. Brown,
As every observation on the present prevailing disorder, founded
on fact, may have its use, you will please publish the following.[66]

The man who wrote that sentence in a letter to the *Federal Gazette* seems
to have been neither a public official nor a doctor. He was merely a citizen of

Philadelphia and a reader of the newspaper. He caught the fever; he recovered; and now he wanted to share his experience and his remedy with others. His personal story was a bit rambling, but his cure was simple: molasses. Over the three-day course of the fever he took about two quarts of molasses, which produced, among other things, "very great discharges of wind, which the disorder seems to generate in great quantities in the stomach, which wind is perhaps the fatal instrument of destruction." He ended his letter with the obvious recommendation: "Perhaps the daily use of molasses in its common form, or mixed with water, might at this time be beneficial."

The sharing of personal experiences and folk remedies was just one of several uses that common readers made of the newspaper, uses that ranged far beyond the domain of official pronouncements and authenticated information. Readers also came to the newspaper to make suggestions to public officials, to thank people, to explain the religious meaning of the fever, to defend the civic honor of Philadelphia, and to try to disarm the terror with humor and satire. Each of these uses suggests the desire—perhaps the compelling need—of readers to participate in the community's response to the epidemic by participating in the newspaper.

Throughout the epidemic, but especially in the early weeks before the doctors' pens were fully mobilized, the newspapers published dozens of letters from readers recommending a fascinating variety of folk cures and preventatives. On the same day that the molasses man told his story, another reader proclaimed "earth bathing" as the "universal remedy." Others liked earth as well. One reader recommended covering sickroom floors with fresh earth; another suggested burying the linens of death beds in the ground for three days. Still other correspondents prescribed smoke, vinegar, camphor, tar, garlic, rue, wormwood, lavender, and pennyroyal. Some proposed cleanliness, temperance, and cheerfulness.[67] And so on. In a rare commercial endorsement one reader said he had tried "quack medicines and nostrums of every kind," but "candor must acknowledge that none has yet appeared to compare with Delany's Aromatic Distilled Vinegar."[68]

Besides recommending cures, these letters often included personal narratives, and they were frequently prefaced by statements asserting every citizen's right and duty to contribute information to the public through the press. For example, the earth bather declared that "every method of prevention and cure for diseases in general, and for this present epidemic in particular, ought to be made known to the public." Another said, "It behooves every friend of humanity, who may possess the smallest knowledge of any means whereby the present unhappy malady may be checked, or prevented from spreading, to publish such useful hints as may have this tendency." All seemed to agree with "A Friend to the Public," who admitted that his cure (tobacco smoke) may not work, but surely "a trial cannot be amiss in this time of public calamity."[69]

Some readers made suggestions to public officials through the newspapers. One letter writer argued that fires in the streets were useless and that the city should ban them. Several days later Mayor Clarkson did just that. Citizens wrote to urge the city to appoint more police guards and to see to it that people who left town left their fire buckets in a public place. The city followed up on those suggestions too. Others offered advice to the Committee. Of course, not all of the advice was equally well taken. One reader wrote that the West Indians had discovered that nothing stops yellow fever better than the firing of cannon. He added that the people of Philadelphia "would cheerfully pay the expense of the powder, and I am sure that General Proctor would with pleasure attend the firing." This nostrum proved instantly unpalatable. Mayor Clarkson quickly moved to ban the shooting of guns in the streets of the city—via a notice in the newspaper, of course.[70]

Readers also used the newspaper to make public their thankfulness. Some offered words of general thanksgiving to the mayor, the Committee, the ministers, and the doctors ("those intrepid sons of Galen") who served the city faithfully and selflessly. "Blessed be the corporation," one writer declared, "for their attention to whatever concerns the health of our city." Others thanked specific people, often their doctors or pastors. Like most letters in the paper, these were usually unsigned. Of those that were signed, the writers ranged from Secretary of the Treasury Alexander Hamilton to lumber merchant James Corkrin to baker Frederick Fraley.[71] Along with their praise and thanks, several letters carried notes of censure for doctors and ministers who forsook their public duties and fled the city. One reader even suggested that the worthy and unworthy be identified publicly—in the newspaper.[72]

For the doctors, the mayor, and the Committee, the fever was purely a problem of medicine and public health. But for many readers of the newspaper the epidemic was an event charged with religious and moral meaning. And they used the newspaper to proclaim this belief. "I have waited with longing expectation," a reader wrote, "in hopes that some able and well-disposed persons would take up their pen, and state their ideas of the real causes of the chastisements of the inhabitants of this city." What were the real causes? "Pride, speculation, and ambition; . . . Playhouses, circus, palaces, carriages, and costly edifices." Sounding a call that would become commonplace, another correspondent declared: "Instead of fleeing from the city during the present visitation of Divine Providence, the inhabitants should give themselves time to reflect, and humble themselves under JEHOVAH's awful rod."[73]

Religious people did not deny the natural origin of the disease, but they saw behind nature the agency of God; and, thus, they saw within the fever a divine commentary on the corruption of community life in Philadelphia.[74]

On the other hand, more readers were defenders than critics of Philadelphia. As news of the epidemic spread, other cities and towns acted, sometimes rather harshly, to repel the refugees as well as the disease itself. These quarantine actions, publicized in the newspapers, aroused a spirit of community pride and solidarity in the readers of the *Federal Gazette*.[75] One blasted the "cruelty and selfishness" of these towns: "Ye unfeeling savages! Ye monsters in the shape of men! 'How can you hope for mercy rendering none?'" Another conceded the need to control the spread of the fever but asked, "Why no expression illustrative of your tender feelings? Are we not your brothers?" Still others urged Philadelphians to come together as a community in defiance of the censorious outside world. "Let New York, Trenton, and Baltimore resolve and re-resolve that we may all perish together," one reader exclaimed. "We are resolving under Providence to live, in spite of all their cruel resolves." Another summed up the feeling quite nicely: "Let us, my fellow citizens, bear in mind that we are members of one common family; that, as such, we ought by no means to desert one another in the moment of our suffering."[76]

When the suffering was most intense, some readers of the *Federal Gazette* tried to break the tension with humor and satire. In late September and early October, Brown published two satiric dialogues sent in by readers. One of them, which tells the story of a Philadelphia man's cold reception in New Jersey, spoofs both the hostility of the surrounding countryside and the doctors' controversy over cures. A farmer greets the man with a pitchfork. "Ho!—Who are you, you yellow-fever looking fellow, and what business have you out of your city?" The man replies that he is perfectly healthy. The farmer is unconvinced. "Why, sir, your breath is pestilence. . . . You are a moving mass of putridity, corruption, plague, poison, and putrefaction." When the farmer refuses to let him stay the night, the Philadelphian asks to buy some meat. "Beef for a man in your situation!—You are, beyond all doubt, raving mad, and lightheaded. If you were in your right senses, you would rather ask for tartar-emetic, jalaps, purges, collery morbus, ippecaanha, doses of Spanish flies, and cartloads of drugs, physics, and medicines of every denomination and description."[77]

The second dialogue also takes place in New Jersey, this time between two farmers, with George telling William of his harrowing trip into the city. Before crossing the Delaware, George had stopped up all his bodily orifices—the two lower ones with a cork and a stout leather string, his ears and nose with putty, and his mouth with a handkerchief. As he crossed the river, he could see that the city was as yellow as a pumpkin patch. In town, people were drop-ping dead in the street, left and right. Yet he made it to the market and sold his eggs for four shillings and his butter for five shillings, nine pence. He would have gotten more, he said, but he couldn't haggle properly through his gag. William was impressed by the scenes of death and devastation but more im-pressed by the high prices. Tomorrow, he said, he would go to Philadelphia.[78]

* * *

> Instead of equipages and a throng of passengers, the voice of levity
> and glee, which I had formerly observed, and which the mildness
> of the season would, at other times, have produced, I found
> nothing but a dreary solitude.[79]

When Charles Brockden Brown's fictional hero Arthur Mervyn enters Philadelphia during the 1793 epidemic, he is struck most forcefully by the eerie isolation that the fever has fastened upon the inhabitants of the city. Mervyn comes into town from the west along Market Street at nightfall:

> The market-place, and each side of this magnificent avenue, were illuminated, as before, by lamps; but between the verge of the Schuylkill and the heart of the city I met not more than a dozen figures; and these were ghost-like, wrapped in cloaks, from behind which they cast upon me glances of wonder and suspi-cion, and, as I approached, changed their course, to avoid touching me. . . . I cast a look upon the houses, which I recollected to have formerly been, at this hour, brilliant with lights, resounding with lively voices, and thronged with busy faces. Now they were closed, above and below; dark, and without tokens of being inhabited. From the upper windows of some, a gleam sometimes fell upon the pavement I was traversing, and showed that their tenants had not fled, but were secluded or disabled.[80]

This theme of isolation runs through all of the fever narratives. Jacob Hiltzheimer wrote in his diary in mid-September that "very few people walk the streets, and if it is known to your friends that any of your family are sick they avoid you." Isaac Heston wrote to his brother that "those who have not removed are afraid to see anybody, even their nearest friends, and keep them-selves close confined in their houses, and this city never wore so gloomy an aspect before." Many years later Robert Simpson recalled the same doleful scene: "It was indeed melancholy to walk the streets, which were completely deserted, except by carts having bells attached to the horses heads, on hear-ing which the dead bodies were put outside on the pavement and placed in the carts by the negroes, who conveyed their charge to the first grave yard, when they returned for another load."[81]

With thousands dying, thousands fleeing, and thousands cowering from the supposed contagion, isolation was inevitable. Yet some people argued that there wasn't isolation enough, that isolation should be imposed upon the city by law as well as by choice. The College of Physicians had recommended that the sick be avoided, and several letters in the *Federal Gazette* in the weeks following urged city officials to enforce this recommendation. One letter writer called for the suspension of *all* social contact—business meetings, church services, sick calls, funerals. Another agreed that there was too much contact, too much talking. All social intercourse should cease, he said, for "the general anxiety for information about the sick has been the speedy means of spreading death and terror around us."[82] And, of course, the newspapers were criticized for spreading fear and rumor.

In spite of hazard, warning, and threat, however, the "anxiety for information" overwhelmed the fear of death. Many people simply would not stop visiting, would not stop talking, would not stop communicating. Throughout the epidemic church services and Quaker meetings continued, even flourished, despite strong sentiment against them. Nervous parishioners smoked their churches and doused themselves with vinegar, but still they came together.[83] And beyond these face-to-face congregations of people, the communication was perhaps even more intense. Day after day the letters flowed and the newspapers circulated. In his account of the fever Dr. Rush made a small but significant point. He said that no one ever believed that the disease could be transmitted by paper; thus people were able to maintain the bonds of written and printed communication.[84] And what a blessing that was, for in this great urban crisis reading and writing were as central to the story and as important to the people as all the nostrums the good doctors could devise.

In a sense the isolation imposed by the yellow fever and the hunger for communication that it generated are only extrapolations, intensifications of the ordinary impact of urban life on the inhabitants of the modern city. In cities people are thrust together yet separated; they are neighbors yet strangers. And much of urban institutional life might be seen as an effort to bridge those gaps. Central to that effort, as I have tried to show, has been reading the newspaper. Newspapers do not bring everyone in the city together. Like other urban institutions, they have often been instruments of division as well as connection. But in America, where literacy rates were high, they have sometimes served as important construction sites for the building of new forms of public community in the modern, impersonal metropolis.[85]

In 1791, two years before the yellow fever crisis, Andrew Brown described the virtue of newspaper reading as sympathy in solitude. That phrase, I think, begins to capture the special role of the newspaper (and perhaps of reading in general) in modern community life. People can be separated yet in communion. But the phrase suggests a more passive reader than the readers I followed through the yellow fever epidemic of 1793. Those readers were active. With notes, letters, discussions, arguments, prayers, and meditations—in the newspaper and out of it—they replenished the texts of public discourse. For those readers, newspaper readership was a form of active citizenship, a way to participate in the ongoing conversation of their community.[86]

Notes

1. *Federal Gazette,* Sept. 9, 1793. All newspapers cited in this chapter were published in Philadelphia. The *Federal Gazette* was the only one to remain in business throughout the yellow fever epidemic of 1793. I have standardized eighteenth-century spelling in all quotations.

2. On the effort to build a history of reading—in other words, to move the historical study of literacy toward the study of actual readers—see Carl F. Kaestle et al., *Literacy in the United States: Readers and Reading since 1880* (New Haven, Conn.: Yale University Press, 1991), chaps. 1–2; David D. Hall, "Readers and Reading in America: Historical and Critical Perspectives," *Proceedings of the American Antiquarian Society* 103 (Aug. 1993): 337–57; Robert Darnton, "First Steps toward a History of Reading," in *The Kiss of Lamourette: Reflections in Cultural History* (New York: W. W. Norton, 1990); and Jonathan Rose, "Rereading the English Common Reader: A Preface to a History of Audiences," *Journal of the History of Ideas* 53 (1992): 47–70.

3. Mathew Carey, *A Short Account of the Malignant Fever, Lately Prevalent in Philadelphia,* 4th ed. (Philadelphia: Mathew Carey, 1794), 22. Accounts of the 1793 yellow fever include John Harvey Powell, *Bring Out Your Dead: The Great Plague of Yellow Fever in Philadelphia in 1793* (1949; rpt., Philadelphia: University of Pennsylvania Press, 1993); and the essays in J. Worth Estes and Billy G. Smith, eds., *A Melancholy Scene of Devastation: The Public Response to the 1793 Philadelphia Yellow Fever Epidemic* (Canton, Mass.: Science History Publications, 1997). See also Charles-Edward A. Winslow, *The Conquest of Epidemic Disease* (Princeton, N.J.: Princeton University Press, 1943), chap. 11; Martin S. Pernick, "Politics, Parties, and Pestilence: Epidemic Yellow Fever in Philadelphia and the Rise of the First Party System," *William and Mary Quarterly,* 3d ser., 29 (1972): 559–86; Richard G. Miller, "The Federal City, 1783–1800," in *Philadelphia: A 300-Year History,* ed. Russell F. Weigley (New York: W. W. Norton, 1982); and Eve Kornfeld, "Crisis in the Capital: The Cultural Significance of Philadelphia's Great Yellow Fever Epidemic," *Pennsylvania History* 51 (1984): 189–205. Broader medical or social histories of the disease include William Coleman, *Yellow Fever in the North: The Methods of Early Epidemiology* (Madison: University of Wisconsin Press, 1987); Margaret Humphreys, *Yellow Fever and the South* (New Brunswick, N.J.: Rutgers University Press, 1992); James C. Riley, *The Eighteenth-Century Campaign to Avoid Disease* (New York: St. Martin's, 1987); and K. David Patterson, "Yellow Fever Epidemics and Mortality in the United States, 1693–1905," *Social Science and Medicine* 34 (1992): 855–65.

4. My understanding of reader communities has been aided by Janice Radway, "Interpretive Communities and Variable Literacies: The Functions of Romance Reading," *Daedalus* 113 (Summer 1984): 49–73; Cathy N. Davidson, *Revolution and the Word: The Rise of the Novel in America* (New York: Oxford University Press, 1986), chap. 1; Norman N. Holland, *The Critical I* (New York: Columbia University Press, 1992); Stanley Fish, *Is There a Text in this Class? The Authority of Interpretive Communities* (Cambridge, Mass.: Harvard University Press, 1980); and the essays in Jane P. Tompkins, ed., *Reader-Response Criticism: From Formalism to Post-Structuralism* (Baltimore: Johns Hopkins University Press, 1980).

5. Many residents of Philadelphia, including slaves and the transient poor, were excluded from this reader community because they could not read or could not read English. Yet even illiterates were sometimes part of oral communities that were linked through literates to the print culture of the city.

6. *Federal Gazette*, Dec. 6, 1791.

7. Sam Bass Warner Jr., *The Private City: Philadelphia in Three Periods of Its Growth* (Philadelphia: University Pennsylvania Press, 1968), 11.

8. Benjamin Davies, *Some Account of the City of Philadelphia* (Philadelphia: Richard Folwell, 1794), 16–18, 80. See also Gary B. Nash and Billy G. Smith, "The Population of Eighteenth-Century Philadelphia," *Pennsylvania Magazine of History and Biography* 99 (1975): 362–68; R. Miller, "The Federal City"; and Susan E. Klepp, *Philadelphia in Transition: A Demographic History of the City and Its Occupational Groups, 1720–1830* (New York: Garland Press, 1989).

9. Richard G. Miller, *Philadelphia—The Federalist City: A Study of Urban Politics, 1789–1801* (Port Washington, N.Y.: Kennikat, 1976), 5–6; John K. Alexander, *Render Them Submissive: Responses to Poverty in Philadelphia, 1760–1800* (Amherst: University of Massachusetts Press, 1980), 12; Billy G. Smith, *The "Lower Sort": Philadelphia's Laboring People, 1750–1800* (Ithaca, N.Y.: Cornell University Press, 1990), chaps. 3–4; Billy G. Smith, "Inequality in Late Colonial Philadelphia: A Note on Its Nature and Growth," *William and Mary Quarterly*, 3d ser., 41 (1984): 629–45; Sharon V. Salinger, "Artisans, Journeymen, and the Transformation of Labor in Late Eighteenth-Century Philadelphia," *William and Mary Quarterly*, 3d ser., 40 (1983): 62–84.

10. R. Miller, *Philadelphia*, 4 (quotation), 6–8.

11. Gary B. Nash, "The Social Evolution of Preindustrial American Cities, 1700–1820: Reflections and New Directions," *Journal of Urban History* 13 (Feb. 1987): 119, 133.

12. Ibid., 119; Gary B. Nash, *Forging Freedom: The Formation of Philadelphia's Black Community, 1720–1840* (Cambridge, Mass.: Harvard University Press, 1988). See also Thomas Bender, *Community and Social Change in America* (New Brunswick, N.J.: Rutgers University Press, 1978), chaps. 1–2.

13. Like Michael Warner, I am interested in how publication was related to public life in the late eighteenth century. While Warner explores the republican discourse itself, I'm concerned with how ordinary readers participated in it. See Warner, *The Letters of the Republic: Publication and the Public Sphere in Eighteenth-Century America* (Cambridge, Mass.: Harvard University Press, 1990). Studies of actual readers in this era include Richard D. Brown, *Knowledge Is Power: The Diffusion of Information in Early America, 1700–1865* (New York: Oxford University Press, 1989); and William J. Gilmore, *Reading Becomes*

a Necessity of Life: Material and Cultural Life in Rural New England (Knoxville: University of Tennessee Press, 1989).

14. S. Warner, *Private City,* 20. See also Carl Bridenbaugh, "The Press and the Book in Eighteenth Century Philadelphia," *Pennsylvania Magazine of History and Biography* 65 (1941): 1–30; Edwin Wolf II, *The Book Culture of a Colonial City: Philadelphia Books, Bookmen, and Booksellers* (New York: Oxford University Press, 1988).

15. Davies, *Some Account,* 83; William F. Steirer Jr., "Philadelphia Newspapers: Years of Revolution and Transition, 1764–1794" (Ph.D. diss., University of Pennsylvania, 1972), 228–29, 310, 347.

16. "The Newspaper," *Pennsylvania Packet,* Sept. 22, 1784.

17. Samuel Magaw, *A Discourse Occasioned by the Mournful Catastrophe, through Fire, Which Destroyed Mr. Andrew Brown, His Wife, and Three Children* (Philadelphia: Ormrod and Conrad, 1797); [Andrew Brown], "An Essay on the Utility of Newspapers" and "To the Public," *Philadelphia Gazette,* Jan. 1, 1794. Brown changed the name of the *Federal Gazette* to the *Philadelphia Gazette* in 1794 to disassociate it from the emerging Federalist Party.

18. *Federal Gazette,* Oct. 1, 1788. Brown reaffirmed this booster role in his inaugural issue of the *Philadelphia Gazette,* Jan. 1, 1794.

19. *Federal Gazette,* Oct. 29, 1788, and Oct. 1 and Nov. 25, 1793.

20. *Federal Gazette,* Dec. 6, 1791. See also Steirer, "Philadelphia Newspapers," 80; and Dwight L. Teeter Jr., "John Dunlap: The Political Economy of a Printer's Success," *Journalism Quarterly* 52 (1975): 3–8, 55.

21. *Federal Gazette,* Oct. 26, 1793; *Philadelphia Gazette,* Jan. 1, 1794.

22. Robert Simpson, Letterbook, 1788–1807, Historical Society of Pennsylvania; Robert Simpson, "Narrative of a Scottish Adventurer," *Journal of the Presbyterian Historical Society* 27 (1949): 48–49. Simpson's wish came true less than three years later. Brown and his family were killed in a house fire. See *American Daily Advertiser,* Feb. 7, 1797, and Magaw, *A Discourse.*

23. Simpson, Letterbook; Powell, *Bring Out Your Dead,* 141–42, 256. Most contemporary accounts of the epidemic mention the importance of the newspapers, especially the *Federal Gazette.* I found only one disparaging comment on the utility of the newspaper in the crisis. It appeared in Benjamin Franklin Bache's paper—in an effort after the epidemic to justify to his readers his own decision to suspend publication. See *General Advertiser,* Nov. 25, 1793. A useful article on the politics of the *Federal Gazette* at the time of the yellow fever epidemic appeared after this chapter was in already in press. See Mark A. Smith, "Andrew Brown's 'Earnest Endeavor': The *Federal Gazette*'s Role in Philadelphia's Yellow Fever Epidemic of 1793," *Pennsylvania Magazine of History and Biography* 120 (1996): 321–42.

24. *Federal Gazette,* Oct. 26, 1793.

25. John Fenno to Joseph Ward, Oct. 8, 1793, in "Letters of John Fenno and John Ward Fenno, 1779–1800; Part 2, 1792–1800," ed. John B. Hench, *Proceedings of the American Antiquarian Society* 91 (1980): 177. The original letters are in the Joseph Ward Collection, Chicago Historical Society.

26. Benjamin Rush to Julia Rush, Sept. 25, 1793, in *Letters of Benjamin Rush,* 2 vols., ed. L. H. Butterfield (Princeton, N.J.: Princeton University Press, 1951), 2:640. See also Nathan

G. Goodman, *Benjamin Rush: Physician and Citizen, 1746–1813* (Philadelphia: University of Pennsylvania Press, 1934), 170–71; Benjamin Rush, *An Enquiry into the Origin of the Late Epidemic Fever in Philadelphia* (Philadelphia: Mathew Carey, 1793); Benjamin Rush, *An Account of the Bilious Remitting Yellow Fever, as It Appeared in the City of Philadelphia, in the Year 1793* (Philadelphia: Thomas Dobson, 1794), 14–15.

27. Rush to Julia Rush, Aug. 25, Aug. 27, and Aug. 29, 1793, in *Letters of Benjamin Rush,* ed. Butterfield, 2:640–45; William Currie, *A Treatise on the Synochus Icteroides; or, Yellow Fever, as It Lately Appeared in the City of Philadelphia* (Philadelphia: Thomas Dobson, 1794), 3; *Minutes of the Proceedings of the Committee, Appointed on the 14th September, 1793, . . . To Attend to and Alleviate the Sufferings of the Afflicted with the Malignant Fever* (Philadelphia: City of Philadelphia, 1848), 137. These minutes were originally printed in 1794 by R. Aitken of Philadelphia. Evans lists thirty-nine titles dealing with the yellow fever in his 1793 and 1794 volumes. See Charles Evans, *American Bibliography,* 14 vols. (New York: Peter Smith, 1941). The most widely circulated contemporary account was Carey, *Short Account of the Malignant Fever.* For mortality rates, see Susan E. Klepp, "Appendix I: 'How Many Precious Souls Are Fled': The Magnitude of the 1793 Yellow Fever Epidemic," in *Melancholy Scene of Devastation,* ed. Estes and Smith.

28. Carey, *Short Account of the Malignant Fever,* 23. See also Sally F. Griffith, "'A Total Dissolution of the Bonds of Society': Community Death and Regeneration in Mathew Carey's *Short Account of the Malignant Fever,*" in *Melancholy Scene of Devastation,* ed. Estes and Smith.

29. Carey, *Short Account of the Malignant Fever,* 25. The heroic organizational response to the fever is a common theme in contemporary accounts. For example, see David Nassy, *Observations on the Cause, Nature, and Treatment of the Epidemic Disorder Prevalent in Philadelphia* (Philadelphia: Parker, 1793), 43–44; Jean Deveze, *An Enquiry into and Observations upon the Causes and Effects of the Epidemic Disease Which Raged in Philadelphia* (Philadelphia: Pierre Parent, 1794); A.J. and R.A. [Absalom Jones and Richard Allen], *A Narrative of the Proceedings of the Black People, during the Late Awful Calamity in Philadelphia* (Philadelphia: William Woodward, 1794), 10; James Hardie, *The Philadelphia Directory and Register,* 2d ed. (Philadelphia: Jacob Johnson, 1794), 219; *Poulson's Town and Country Almanac, for the Year of Our Lord 1795* (Philadelphia: Zachariah Poulson, 1794); *Banneker's Almanac for the Year 1795* (Philadelphia: William Young, 1794).

30. Samuel Stearns, *An Account of the Terrible Effects of the Pestilential Infection in the City of Philadelphia* (Providence, R.I.: William Child, 1793), 5–6.

31. Carey, *Short Account of the Malignant Fever,* 45.

32. This generalization is based upon a reading of published letters and diaries as well as manuscript collections in Philadelphia libraries: The Library Company, the Historical Society of Pennsylvania, the American Philosophical Society, and the College of Physicians of Philadelphia.

33. Carey, *Short Account of the Malignant Fever,* 45–47; Deveze, *An Enquiry,* 10–12; Nassy, *Observations,* 9; Joshua Cresson, *Meditations Written during the Prevalence of the Yellow Fever in the City of Philadelphia in the Year 1793* (London: W. Phillips, 1803), 7. As terrifying rumors spread from Philadelphia, many outlying communities took steps—sometimes violent steps—to turn fleeing Philadelphians away. The *Federal Gazette* reported on many of these actions. For example, see *Federal Gazette,* Sept. 18, Sept. 19, and Oct. 2, 1793.

34. For example, see Susanna Dillwyn to William Dillwyn, Sept. 29, 1793, in Susanna Dillwyn Correspondence, Library Company manuscripts, housed in the Historical Society of Pennsylvania, Philadelphia. Susanna lived in New Jersey; her father, William, in England. Letters to the newspaper made the same plea, and Brown himself warned "our friends in the country" to be slow to believe the rumors they heard. See *Federal Gazette,* Sept. 12 and Oct. 12, 1793.

35. John Depeyster to Charles Willson Peale, Oct. 2 and Oct. 10, 1793, in Sellers Family Papers, American Philosophical Society, Philadelphia. This is a common theme in the surviving letters. For example, several people wrote this same sort of letter to Benjamin Rush. See S. Baynton to Rush, Oct. 3, 1793; John Bayard to Rush, Sept. 9, 1793; Jacob Rush to Rush, Sept. 10, 1793, in Benjamin Rush Papers, vols. 35–36, Historical Society of Pennsylvania.

36. William Dillwyn to Susanna Dillwyn, Nov. 26, 1793; Susanna Dillwyn to William Dillwyn, Sept. 11, 1793, in Susanna Dillwyn Correspondence.

37. Mary Eddy Hosack to Catherine Wistar, Oct. 1, 1793, in Bache Family Papers, American Philosophical Society.

38. Isaac Heston, "Letter from a Yellow Fever Victim, Philadelphia, 1793," ed. Edwin B. Bronner, *Pennsylvania Magazine of History and Biography* 86 (Apr. 1962): 206.

39. *The Diary of Elizabeth Drinker,* 3 vols., ed. Elaine Forman Crane (Boston: Northeastern University Press, 1991), 1:496–500, entries for Aug. 26, Aug. 31, and Sept. 3, 1793. The rumor about the blacks is a particularly interesting and sad one. In fact, the free black people of Philadelphia worked hard during the epidemic to demonstrate their courage and their willingness to serve the city. They were maligned, nonetheless. See Nash, *Forging Freedom,* 121–25; [Jones and Allen], *A Narrative of the Proceedings of the Black People;* and Phillip Lapansky, "'Abigail, a Negress': The Role and the Legacy of African Americans in the Yellow Fever Epidemic," in *Melancholy Scene of Devastation,* ed. Estes and Smith.

40. "Extracts from the Diary of Jacob Hiltzheimer of Philadelphia," *Pennsylvania Magazine of History and Biography* 16 (1892): 417, entry for Oct. 14, 1793.

41. Susanna Dillwyn to William Dillwyn, Sept. 9, 1793, in Susanna Dillwyn Correspondence; John Welsh to Robert Ralston, Sept. 16, Sept. 18, Oct. 14, and Nov. 2, 1793, in Miscellaneous Collections, Historical Society of Pennsylvania; *Diary of Elizabeth Drinker,* 1:523, 524, entries for Oct. 24 and Nov. 3, 1793. See also John Fenno to Joseph Ward, Oct. 8, 1793, in "Letters of John Fenno and John Ward Fenno," 177; Heston, "Letter from a Yellow Fever Victim," 206; and Samuel Massey to Ann Massey, Sept. 15, 1793, Samuel Massey Letters, College of Physicians of Philadelphia.

42. *Federal Gazette,* Oct. 1 and Oct. 26, 1793. At least one letter to the editor also mentioned people in the countryside avidly reading the paper. See *Federal Gazette,* Sept. 26, 1793.

43. John Dunlap's *American Daily Advertiser* and Benjamin Franklin Bache's *General Advertiser* played active roles in the early days of the epidemic, but they suspended publication on Sept. 14 and Sept. 25, respectively, and did not resume until December. The two famous national party papers, John Fenno's *Gazette of the United States* and Philip Freneau's *National Gazette,* were small nondailies that had little yellow fever material. They also suspended publication.

44. Kornfeld, "Crisis in the Capital," 190–91. See also Whitfield J. Bell Jr., *The College of Physicians of Philadelphia: A Bicentennial History* (Canton, Mass.: Science History Publications, 1987), chap. 2.

45. Rush, *An Account,* 21–24; Rush to Julia Rush, Aug. 25, 1793, in *Letters of Benjamin Rush,* ed. Butterfield, 2:641; *Federal Gazette,* Aug. 27, 1793; *American Daily Advertiser,* Aug. 27, 1793. See also Minutes, 1793, in *Records of the College of Physicians* (manuscript volumes), vol. 1, College of Physicians of Philadelphia, passim.

46. *Federal Gazette,* Sept. 1793, nearly every day. An example of an official death toll announcement appeared Sept. 7. The jail item appeared Sept. 19.

47. Most contemporary accounts praise the work of the Committee. For example, see *Federal Gazette,* Nov. 22, 1793; *Banneker's Almanac;* Nassy, *Observations,* 45; Deveze, *An Enquiry.* Deveze, a French West Indian, was the head doctor at Bush Hill.

48. *Minutes of the Proceedings of the Committee, Appointed on the 14th September, 1793,* 47, 89, 103. The Committee also urged Carey to write his instant history of the fever. See Mathew Carey, *Address of M. Carey to the Public* (Philadelphia: Mathew Carey, 1794), 3.

49. *Federal Gazette,* Sept. 11, 17, 19, 23, and 27, and Oct. 2, 1793.

50. *Federal Gazette,* Oct. 1793, nearly every day. Letters about relief efforts, sent to the *Federal Gazette* by the Committee, became very common after the middle of the month. On the end of the epidemic see *Federal Gazette,* Oct. 16, 28, and 29, and Nov. 1, 4, 14, and 22, 1793.

51. *Federal Gazette,* Sept. 12, 1793. Useful accounts of Dr. Rush's cure are Chris Holmes, "Benjamin Rush and the Yellow Fever," *Bulletin of the History of Medicine* 40 (1966): 246–63; Mark Workman, "Medical Practice in Philadelphia at the Time of the Yellow Fever Epidemic, 1793," *Pennsylvania Folklife* 27 (1978): 33–39; and J. Worth Estes, "Introduction: The Yellow Fever Syndrome and Its Treatment in Philadelphia, 1793," and Jacquelyn C. Miller, "Passions and Politics: The Multiple Meanings of Benjamin Rush's Treatment for Yellow Fever," both in *Melancholy Scene of Devastation,* ed. Estes and Smith. See also Goodman, *Benjamin Rush,* chap. 8; Carl Binger, *Revolutionary Doctor: Benjamin Rush, 1746–1813* (New York: W. W. Norton, 1966), chap. 11.

52. Rush to Julia Rush, Oct. 3 and Sept. 11, 1793, in *Letters of Benjamin Rush,* ed. Butterfield, 2:659, 701. The term "7/6" means seven shillings, six pence. See also *Federal Gazette,* Oct. 7, 1793; and Rush, *An Account,* 345. The Rush Papers at the Historical Society of Pennsylvania are filled with letters seeking help and advice.

53. Rush, *An Account,* 329–30; *Federal Gazette,* Sept. 15, 1793; Rush to Julia Rush, Sept. 15, 1793, in *Letters of Benjamin Rush,* ed. Butterfield, 2:664.

54. Benjamin Rush, *The Autobiography of Benjamin Rush: His "Travels through Life" Together with His Commonplace Book for 1789–1813,* ed. George W. Corner (Princeton, N.J.: Princeton University Press, 1948), 97; Rush to Julia Rush, Sept. 29, 1793, in *Letters of Benjamin Rush,* ed. Butterfield, 2:687.

55. Rush, *An Account,* 12–15, 196; Rush, *Autobiography,* 98; Holmes, "Benjamin Rush," 254.

56. *Federal Gazette,* Oct. 11, 22, and 26, 1793. See also Rush to Julia Rush, Oct. 27, 1793, in *Letters of Benjamin Rush,* ed. Butterfield, 2:727. Chris Holmes traced the outcome of Rush's cure for some fifty of his patients and found that most lived, despite the fact that purging and bleeding were probably quite harmful treatments. See Holmes, "Benjamin Rush," 251.

57. *Federal Gazette,* Sept. 11–12, 1793. The doctors' dispute is treated at length in Powell, *Bring Out Your Dead,* 206–15.

58. *Federal Gazette,* Sept. 23, 1793. The *Federal Gazette* carried dozens of items from doctors and testimonials on various doctors' cures. The major articles are reprinted in Rush, *An Account,* 207–42. See also Nassy, *Observations,* 11–13.

59. *Federal Gazette,* Sept. 17 and 21, 1793.

60. Rush to Julia Rush, Sept. 21, 1793, in *Letters of Benjamin Rush,* ed. Butterfield, 2:673.

61. Rush, *Autobiography,* 96–97. See also Rush, *An Account,* 308–9.

62. Ebenezer Hazard to Jedidiah Morse, Sept. 30, 1793, in Simon Gratz Collection, Historical Society of Pennsylvania; John Welsh to Robert Ralston, Sept. 18, 1793, in Miscellaneous Collections, Historical Society of Pennsylvania; Samuel Massey to Ann Massey, Sept. 15, 1793, Samuel Massey Letters, College of Physicians of Philadelphia; James Pemberton, "A Summary Account of a Contagious Fever which Prevailed in Philadelphia," manuscript journal (1793), in College of Physicians of Philadelphia.

63. *Federal Gazette,* Sept. 20–21 and Oct. 3, 1793. See also Rush, *An Account,* 126.

64. *Federal Gazette,* Oct. 10, 1793.

65. Mathew Carey, *Gentlemen, Actuated by a Sincere Regard for the Welfare of Our Common City . . .* (Philadelphia: Mathew Carey, 1794). This is a printed letter sent to the Committee of Health for the City of Philadelphia.

66. *Federal Gazette,* Sept. 24, 1793.

67. *Federal Gazette,* Aug. 23, 26, 27, and 31, and Sept. 2, 9, 13, 14, and 30, 1793.

68. *Federal Gazette,* Sept. 2, 1793. Paid ads for Delany's vinegar had already begun to appear. For example, see *Federal Gazette,* Aug. 30, 1793.

69. *Federal Gazette,* Sept. 24, 11, 27, and 26, 1793.

70. *Federal Gazette,* Aug. 24, Aug. 29, Sept. 4, 12, and 14, and Oct. 14–15, 1793.

71. *Federal Gazette,* Sept. 5, Sept. 11, Oct. 1, 2, 5, 22, and 23, and Nov. 5 and 22, 1793.

72. *Federal Gazette,* Oct. 3 and Nov. 11 and 22, 1793.

73. *Federal Gazette,* Sept. 7, Sept. 25, Oct. 3, 5, 15, and 16, and Nov. 2 and 21, 1793.

74. J. Henry Helmuth, *A Short Account of the Yellow Fever in Philadelphia for the Reflecting Christian,* trans. Charles Erdmann (Philadelphia: Jones, Hoff, and Derrick, 1794), 10–12. See also Elhanan Winchester, *Wisdom Taught by Man's Mortality; or, The Shortness and Uncertainty of Life . . . Adapted to the Awful Visitation of the City of Philadelphia, by the Yellow Fever, in the Year 1793* (Philadelphia: R. Folwell, 1795).

75. On the defensive actions of other towns see *Federal Gazette,* Sept. 15, 18, 19, and 25, 1793.

76. *Federal Gazette,* Sept. 21 and 24, and Oct. 2 and 5, 1793. Another illustration of community boosterism was the widespread hostility that arose against Rush when he announced that the disease was not imported but of local origin. Many people construed this to be a libel on the climate and quality of life in Philadelphia. See *Federal Gazette,* Sept. 18, 1793; Rush to Julia Rush, Oct. 28, 1793, in *Letters of Benjamin Rush,* ed. Butterfield, 2:729; and Rush, *An Enquiry,* 12.

77. *Federal Gazette,* Sept. 28, 1793.

78. *Federal Gazette,* Oct. 2, 1793. In humor and satire the leading paper (before its demise) was Philip Freneau's *National Gazette.* Freneau's paper was thin on fever news, but

it carried several of the editor's own satiric barbs and verses. See Powell, *Bring Out Your Dead*, frontispiece and 239–40. See also *National Gazette*, Sept. 4 and 21, 1793.

79. Charles Brockden Brown, *Arthur Mervyn; or, Memoirs of the Year 1793*, 2 vols. (Port Washington, N.Y.: Kennikat, 1963), 1:140. *Arthur Mervyn* was originally published in two parts in 1799 and 1800.

80. Ibid., 140. See also William L. Hedges, "Benjamin Rush, Charles Brockden Brown, and the American Plague Year," *Early American Literature* 7 (1973): 295–311; and M. Warner, *Letters of the Republic*, chap. 6.

81. "Extracts from the Diary of Jacob Hiltzheimer," 417; Heston, "Letter from a Yellow Fever Victim," 206; Simpson, "Narrative," 50. See also Samuel Massey to Ann Massey, Sept. 12, 1793, Samuel Massey Letters, College of Physicians of Philadelphia; and Carey, *Short Account of the Malignant Fever*, 22. Though many blacks died from the disease, they were thought to be immune; thus they were recruited as nurses and pallbearers. See Kenneth F. Kiple and Virginia, "Black Yellow Fever Immunities, Innate and Acquired, as Revealed in the American South," *Social Science History* 1 (1977): 419–36. See also Klepp, "Appendix I," and Lapansky, "Abigail."

82. *Federal Gazette*, Sept. 14 and 10, 1793. See also Carey, *Short Account of the Malignant Fever*, 92–93.

83. Helmuth, *Short Account of the Yellow Fever*, 40–45; Pemberton, "A Summary Account"; Cresson, *Meditations; Federal Gazette*, Oct. 5, 1793.

84. Rush, *An Account*, 108. Actually, despite Rush's claim, a few people did fear that the disease could be transmitted by paper, and mail from Philadelphia was occasionally smoked in order to disinfect it.

85. I see the urban newspaper as central to what Michael Warner has called (following Jürgen Habermas) the republican public sphere of eighteenth-century America. See Warner, *Letters of the Republic*, chap. 2. I develop the idea of "public community" more fully in a study of a later period of American urban history. See David Paul Nord, "The Public Community: The Urbanization of Journalism in Chicago," *Journal of Urban History* 11 (Aug. 1985): 411–41, which is reprinted as chapter 5 in this book.

86. The verb *replenish* is Norman Holland's, in "Unity Identity Text Self," in *Reader-Response Criticism*, ed. Tompkins, 118. Holland, like Stanley Fish, sees the reader as necessarily the key figure in the creation of meaning. See Holland, *Critical I*, and Fish, *Is There a Text in this Class?*

10. Working-Class Readers: Family, Community, and Reading in Late Nineteenth-Century America

WHO READ NEWSPAPERS, magazines, and books in the late nineteenth century? Were readers different from nonreaders? Were avid readers different from moderate readers? Was reading associated with differences in income, ethnicity, region of residence, schooling, or other family characteristics? Was reading linked to the lifestyles of readers? These kinds of questions are central to an understanding of reading as a social institution during the early years of mass media in America. Yet we do not know the answers. Historians in recent years have made marvelous contributions to our understanding of the extent and characteristics of simple literacy in eighteenth- and nineteenth-century America.[1] But we still have much to learn about the history of reading among the majority of people who could read, particularly in the late nineteenth century, at the dawn of the era of mass communication. Nearly all of the research in the history of newspapers and magazines and much of the research in the history of the popular book has centered on the production, not the consumption, of reading materials. We know a lot about Joseph Pulitzer, Edward Bok, and Horatio Alger; we know little about the readers of the *New York World,* the *Ladies Home Journal,* and *Ragged Dick.*

The central assumption of this chapter is that scholars ought to look more carefully at the history of readers and reading as well as the history of literacy and the publishing trade. Carl Kaestle has made the same point. In a detailed review of the literature in the field, he concluded that the history of literacy and reading is at a turning point:

> Historians of literacy have taught us a great deal in the past twenty years about the consequences of literacy and of print in the early modern West, and they

have assiduously charted trends in signature writing and self-reported literacy for later centuries. Many generalizations have been tested and refined. We can say, indeed, that we know a lot about these matters. Although some historians have also done imaginative work on the uses of literacy in everyday life, we know much less about this important aspect of the subject. Consequently we need research on the functions of printed matter among different reading publics.[2]

The purpose of this chapter is to suggest one way that this task might be done. Specifically, I will offer a description and an analysis of a collection of nineteenth-century data on working-class families that may suggest some partial answers to that deceptively simple question: Who read newspapers and books in late nineteenth-century America?

* * *

Some historians have made remarkable progress in the historical study of book readership. For many years, book and library historians have conducted studies that infer the characteristics and tastes of readers from book sales, from circulation records of libraries, and from the mere existence of libraries and the book trade in particular regions.[3] More recently, historians have studied book ownership and reading behavior more directly through the analysis of probate records and other personal documents left behind by individual readers. Typically, readership studies in this new social history of the book review hundreds, sometimes thousands, of seemingly unrelated estate inventories and then use these individual-level data to generalize about who read what at a particular place and time.[4] Like other practitioners of the "new social history," they have in a sense learned to conduct surveys among the dead.

But these are mainly the well-to-do dead. What about the readers of popular books, magazines, and newspapers? This is an important question for the history of reading, but it is a much more difficult one to answer. Subscriber lists for mass magazines and daily newspapers are virtually nonexistent. Moreover, the reading of mass media has always been a much more ephemeral enterprise than the reading of quality books; people do not usually leave bundles of newspapers or paperbacks in their estates to be inventoried and probated. Yet newspaper and other popular reading is a behavior that has been recorded in some individual-level historical records. One such record is the family cost-of-living budget—a favored form of statistical survey conducted by the newly created bureaus of labor statistics on both state and national levels in the late nineteenth and early twentieth centuries.

* * *

The creation of bureaus of labor statistics was part of the passion of late nineteenth-century reformers for "facts." The transformation of America from an agrarian and commercial nation to an industrial nation brought with it an avalanche of immensely complicated economic and social problems. In their efforts to understand this strange new world, reformers and politicians sought help from the fledgling social sciences. Resolute in their faith in a scientific, factual basis for reform, they hoped to answer the great economic questions of the day through empirical investigations. No question was of greater concern than the so-called labor question—the interlocking problems of labor productivity, unemployment, pay, hours, child labor, labor organization, and social unrest. The first bureau of labor statistics was set up in Massachusetts in 1869, the Federal Bureau of Labor was established in 1884, and by 1891 twenty-seven state bureaus had been organized across the United States.[5]

Carroll D. Wright, who became the first U.S. commissioner of labor after his service as chief of the Massachusetts bureau, was the leading figure in the development of labor statistics from 1873 until his death in 1909. One of Wright's most important contributions to labor statistics was his effort to study empirically the cost of living of working-class families.[6] Wright's cost-of-living surveys gathered detailed information on family size, age, ethnicity, and work patterns; on family income from all sources; and on family expenditures of every sort, from potatoes to life insurance. The original purpose of these surveys was to study consumption and its relation to income, taking into account a variety of other family, industrial, and regional variables. Several of the federal studies were also designed to provide Congress with information during tariff debates.[7] Happily for historians, some of the studies were published in nonaggregated form, thus preserving the raw survey data for posterity and for posterity's computers. Happily for historians of literacy and reading, a variable commonly surveyed was expenditures for newspapers and books.

The most important cost-of-living surveys reported in nonaggregated form were published by Carroll Wright's bureaus in 1875 and in 1890 and 1891.[8] The 1875 study, conducted when Wright was Massachusetts commissioner, was a survey of 397 working-class families in that state. Wright's agents purposely selected the sample to represent a range of occupations; within each occupation the individuals interviewed were selected more or less at random. The interviewers for all of Wright's surveys were persistent and meticulous, though the exact procedures they followed are not fully specified and certainly did not guarantee a random sample in the modern sense of the term.[9] After he became U.S. commissioner of labor, Wright conducted a monumental replication of the Massachusetts survey: a study of the budgets of more than eighty-five hundred families all over the United States and in several foreign countries in selected industries. Though these surveys may be the best sources for historical cost-of-living data, they are by no means the only such sources. Wright conducted other studies, as did several state bureaus.[10]

Several social and economic historians have made use of these historical surveys. The economic historian Jeffrey Williamson used the data to study income elasticity in the nineteenth century. The economic historians Peter Lindert and Michael Haines used the surveys in studies of fertility, child costs, and family life cycles. The social historian John Modell looked into the consumption patterns of native workers compared to Irish immigrants. When this chapter was first published in 1986, no one working in the history of literacy or mass communication had used these cost-of-living surveys to study reading behavior, and little has been done with them since.[11]

* * *

Wright's 1890–91 survey falls in the midst of one of the most extraordinary periods in American economic history. It was an extraordinary era in media history as well. First, this era is aptly remembered as the genesis of the modern mass-circulation newspaper in America. Nationwide, the number of daily newspapers increased 78 percent in the 1880s, and the percentage growth of evening papers—the workingman's paper—was even greater, 112 percent. Over the same decade the circulation of all dailies jumped 135 percent, from 3.6 million to 8.4 million per day. Altogether, more than 4.5 billion copies of newspapers and periodicals were issued in 1890, a tenfold increase from mid-century.[12] Second, the decades of the 1880s and 1890s saw the birth of the modern, mass-circulation national magazine. Lured by the development of cheap paper, the rise of national advertising, and a favorable postal act of 1879, magazine publishers were able for the first time in the 1880s and 1890s to establish a truly national mass medium.[13] Third, the post–Civil War decades constitute the era in which book publishing—including the publication of enormous numbers of cheap books and paperbacks—"came to full flower in the New World."[14] Fourth, this was an era of great growth in the foreign-language press in America. Between 1880 and 1890 the number of newspapers printed in foreign languages increased 45 percent—from 799 to 1,159.[15]

Who was reading these newspapers, magazines, and books in 1890? To find out I turned to the nonaggregated cost-of-living data in the *Seventh Annual Report* of the U.S. Commissioner of Labor (1891).

* * *

My study of working-class readers is based upon a stratified random sample of three hundred cases drawn from the 1891 report. In their original form the data were already stratified by industry and state or country of residence. Because the surveys were designed to generate a factual basis for the congressional tariff debates, the industries studied were major protected industries of the time: bar iron, pig iron, steel, bituminous coal, coke, iron ore, cotton textiles, woolens, and glass. My sample consisted of one hundred families in the cotton textile industry from the leading manufacturing states in each of the three major cotton-milling regions of the United States: New England (Massachusetts and New Hampshire), the mid-Atlantic (New York and Pennsylvania), and the South (Georgia and North Carolina).[16] After a preliminary analysis of three industrial groups, I decided to work only with cotton textile workers. Of the industries surveyed by Wright, cotton milling was the *only* industry well represented across regions and ethnic groups. Because my interest lay with regional, ethnic, and family variations, rather than with industry variations, it seemed logical to limit the analysis to one industry.

Before turning to regional, ethnic, and family variations in reading behavior, it is important to note the overall ubiquity of reading as a working-class activity in this era. About 77 percent of the families in the sample reported at least some spending on newspapers and books, a higher proportion than for any other discretionary expenditure included in Wright's survey.[17] The average (mean) annual expenditure for reading materials was $4.23. By comparison, families spent on the average about half that much for organizational activities, about one-and-one-half times that much for amusements, and twice that much for liquor. This raw figure of $4.23 amounts to about 2.4 percent of the average family's discretionary spending and about 0.75 percent of the family's total expenditures. Interestingly, these proportions do not seem very much less than comparable media expenditures in the twentieth century. Maxwell McCombs found that expenditures for printed media made up about 1.15 percent of consumer spending by all Americans during the period 1929–68.[18] In short, reading was a very widespread (though not universal) activity among these working-class families in late nineteenth-century America.

Who were these working-class readers? What were they like? To seek answers to these questions I looked at the relationships between expenditures for newspapers and books and four categories of family attributes: (1) income,

(2) region of residence, (3) nationality of birth, and (4) family-community ties. I will explore each of these four categories in turn—though, as I will try to show, the real significance lies in their interconnections.

Income

The average annual family income from all sources for the cotton workers in my sample was $667, with 90 percent earning less than $1,000. Wages in cotton manufacturing were low for unskilled and semiskilled operatives, especially women and children, but total family incomes were comparable to the other industries surveyed by Wright.[19] The average pay of husbands in my sample was $354—ranging from $31 to $978 per year. Although the husband was usually the principal wage earner, the children worked in about 52 percent of the families, often earning more, collectively, than their fathers. Only about 18 percent of the wives worked for wages, and their contribution to family income was considerably less than that of either husbands or children. Overall, it seems fair to say that individual wages were low in cotton textile work, but family earnings could range from bare subsistence to a modestly comfortable standard of living.

Income, not surprisingly, was a significant determinate of spending on newspapers and books. Then, as now, when people had more money, they tended to spend it. When the families in the sample are divided into equal thirds according to family income rank (low, middle, and high income), the high-income families spent nearly twice as much on reading materials as the low-income families. (See table 10.1.)

This apparently simple linear relationship, however, was neither simple nor

Table 10.1. Average Expenditure for Newspapers and Books and Average Percentage of Discretionary Spending for Newspapers and Books by Family Income Status, 1891

Income Status	Average Expenditure per Family	Percentage of Discretionary Income
Low	$2.93	2.7%
Middle	4.59	2.6
High	5.17	2.0
Overall	$4.23	2.4

Source: U.S. Commissioner of Labor, *Seventh Annual Report* (1891).
Note: Differences in mean expenditures among income groups are significant at $p < .01$; differences in percentages are not significant.

linear. The simple correlation coefficient between reading expenditures and total family income is only .15, a statistically significant but weak relationship. The weak relationship stems in part from the fact that spending on reading materials did not rise proportionally with family income. In other words, high-income families allotted a smaller proportion of their discretionary expenditures to reading compared with either low-or middle-income families, as table 10.1 shows. Though interesting in some ways, a focus on total family income and reading tends to obscure more than it reveals. Family income patterns mask the influence of other family variables, including region of residence, nationality, and—perhaps most important—who earned the family's income, the father or the children.

Region

On the surface it would seem that region of residence would affect reading expenditures largely through differences in family income. Incomes in cotton textile manufacturing in the South were much lower than in either New England or the mid-Atlantic states.[20] Expenditures on books and newspapers by the southern workers were very low as well. But the influence of region was not purely an income effect. At every level of income the southerners were low spenders on books and newspapers.[21] Overall, the New Englanders in the sample allotted more than 3 percent of their discretionary spending for reading materials; the southerners, by contrast, spent less than half that proportion. (See table 10.2.)

Another way of getting at the effect of "southernness" on reading behavior among these mill workers is to compare readers with nonreaders. For this

Table 10.2. Average Family Income, Average Expenditure for Newspapers and Books, and Average Percentage of Discretionary Spending for Newspapers and Books by Region of Residence, 1891

Region	Family Income	Average Expenditure per Family	Percentage of Discretionary Income
New England	$692	$5.32	3.4%
Mid-Atlantic	805	5.08	2.6
South	504	2.30	1.4
Overall	$667	$4.23	2.4

Source: U.S. Commissioner of Labor, *Seventh Annual Report* (1891).
Note: Differences in means among regions are significant at $p < .01$.

comparison (and some other comparisons described later), I divided the families into three groups: "nonreaders," those who spent nothing on books and newspapers; "low readers," those who spent below the sample median in the proportion of their discretionary income devoted to reading materials; and "high readers," those who spent above the median on that measure. (The median was about 2.5 percent of discretionary spending for newspapers and books.) Table 10.3 displays the result. First, the South shows a significantly higher proportion of nonreaders. But more important than this, few southerners were high readers. That is, few spent a large proportion of their discretionary income on reading. And this holds across income levels. For example, among the fourteen high-income southern families in my sample, only one fell into the category of high reader, compared with more than 40 percent of the forty-eight high-income families in the mid-Atlantic states.

These figures on family reading consumption coincide with what has long been known about the production of reading materials in late nineteenth-century America. The 1890 census reported that per capita production of newspapers and periodicals was much higher in the North than in the South. For the states in my sample, the number of residents per copy of all newspapers and periodicals published was 0.41 for the mid-Atlantic states, 0.53 for New England, and 3.79 for the South. In other words, the North had more copies of newspapers and magazines than people, while the South had nearly four people for each copy.[22] Of course, these are production figures, not circulation figures. But my data on spending suggest that circulation also was much lower among working-class readers in the South.

Though table 10.3 shows most clearly the differences between North and South, it also suggests something about the working-class families in New England as well. More than one-fourth of the New England families in the sample were nonreaders. In other words, though New England had nearly twice the proportion of high readers as the South, it also had—like the

Table 10.3. Cross-Tabulation of Families by Reading Status and Region of Residence, 1891

Reading Status	New England	Mid-Atlantic	South
Nonreaders	26%	9%	35%
Low readers	35	43	44
High headers	40	48	21
	101%	100%	100%
	(N = 98)	(N = 100)	(N = 100)

Source: U.S. Commissioner of Labor, *Seventh Annual Report* (1891).
Note: Chi-square is significant at *p* < .01.

South—a large proportion of people who spent nothing at all on books and newspapers. And, in fact, many of these nonreading families fell into the high-income category. (Nearly 30 percent of the high-income families in New England were nonreaders, compared to only 6 percent in the mid-Atlantic states.) Who were these people? Was their reading behavior similar to that of the southerners? Might their experience shed some light on reading in the South as well as in the North? The answers to these questions are linked to another broad family variable—nationality of birth.

Nationality

At first glance nationality of birth appears to have been unrelated to reading behavior. When all three regions are lumped together, the data show no significant difference in the reading behavior of immigrants versus native-born Americans. Overall, immigrant families earned more income and spent a little more for books and newspapers, but both groups spent about the same proportion of their discretionary incomes: Immigrants spent about 2.4 percent for reading materials; native-born Americans about 2.5 percent. Table 10.4, however, tells a more subtle story. With regional effects controlled, it seems clear that nationality of birth did make a difference. In the North native-born Americans were bigger spenders on reading, despite the fact that their family incomes were less. (This effect is not apparent when all three regions are considered together, because of the contradictory influence of the

Table 10.4. Average Family Income, Average Expenditure for Newspapers and Books, and Average Percentage of Discretionary Spending for Newspapers and Books by Region of Residence and Nationality of Birth, 1891

Region and Nationality	Family Income	Average Expenditure per Family	Percentage of Discretionary Income
New England			
Native	$641	$9.04	5.9%
Immigrant	709	4.05	2.5
Mid-Atlantic			
Native	$738	$5.48	2.8
Immigrant	852	4.79	2.3
South			
Native	$504	$2.30	1.4

Source: U.S. Commissioner of Labor, *Seventh Annual Report* (1891).
Note: Differences in means among regions and among nationalities within New England are significant at $p < .01$.

South, where all the workers were native-born Americans but were low spenders on reading nonetheless.) The difference between immigrants and native-born Americans was sharpest in New England. There immigrant families earned substantially more than native Americans, but they spent less than one-half as much on reading—measured both in dollars *and* in proportion of discretionary spending. Why this striking difference? To answer that question we need to look inside the families themselves.

Total family income is a poor predictor of reading expenditures because it mattered *who* earned the income of the family. The simple correlation between reading expenditures and family income is only .15, but the correlation between reading expenditure and *husband's* income is nearly .40, a fairly strong correlation in this data set. The reason for the difference is that children's income is negatively correlated with reading expenditures; and the higher the family income, the larger the contribution from the children. In low-income families about one-third of the school-age children worked, and the father's pay made up about two-thirds of the family's income. In high-income families, on the other hand, nearly three-fourths of the children worked, and the father's pay made up less than one-half of the family's income. In other words, income status in cotton textile manufacturing in the nineteenth century was a family affair. High income usually meant children at work. And it was the children of immigrants and southerners who seemed to work the hardest.

Table 10.5 shows how the composition of family income affected spend-

Table 10.5. Average Income from Father, Average Income from Children, Percentage of Income from Father, and Percentage of Discretionary Spending for Newspapers and Books by Region of Residence and Nationality of Birth, 1891

Region and Nationality	Father's Income	Children's Income	Percentage of Income from Father	Percentage of Discretionary Income
New England				
Native	$479	$ 49	78%	5.9%
Immigrant	396	190	63	2.5
Mid-Atlantic				
Native	$471	$189	70	2.8
Immigrant	367	280	52	2.3
South				
Native	$235	$197	48	1.4

Source: U.S. Commissioner of Labor, *Seventh Annual Report* (1891).

Note: Differences in means among regions and among nationalities within regions are significant at *p* < .01.

ing on books and newspapers. In general, the higher the proportion of family income supplied by the husband's earnings, the higher the proportion of discretionary spending on reading materials.[23]

In short, an important determinate of family expenditures on reading was the role that children played in earning the family's income. Table 10.6 shows this relationship rather vividly. Families with children working were half as likely to be high readers as families who did not have their children at work.

To some extent the importance of children working helps to explain regional and ethnic differences in reading behavior. As Tables 10.4 and 10.5 suggest, the groups that rank low on proportion of discretionary spending devoted to reading are also the groups that depended most on their children's incomes: southern natives and northern immigrants. But child labor is only part of the story, as table 10.7 makes clear. Even when the children-at-work

Table 10.6. Cross-Tabulation of Families by Reading Status and Whether They Had Children at Work, 1891

Reading Status	No Children Working	Children Working
Nonreaders	23%	24%
Low readers	28	52
High readers	49	25
	100%	101%
	($N = 140$)	($N = 158$)

Source: U.S. Commissioner of Labor, *Seventh Annual Report* (1891).
Note: Chi-square is significant at $p < .01$.

Table 10.7. Average Expenditure for Newspapers and Books and Average Percentage of Discretionary Spending for Newspapers and Books by Region of Residence, Nationality of Birth, and Whether the Family Had Children at Work, 1891

Region and Nationality	No Children Working		Children Working	
	Expenditure	Percentage	Expenditure	Percentage
New England				
Native	$9.17	6.6%	$8.71	4.1%
Immigrant	4.65	3.4	3.18	1.2
Mid-Atlantic				
Native	$5.26	3.0	$5.77	2.7
Immigrant	6.61	3.5	4.00	1.8
South				
Native	$2.46	1.6	$2.20	1.3
Overall	$4.97	3.3	$3.56	1.7

Source: U.S. Commissioner of Labor, *Seventh Annual Report* (1891).
Note: Differences in means among regions, within New England, and overall between children working and no children working are significant at $p < .01$.

factor is controlled, the North-South difference and the native-immigrant difference are still apparent. Perhaps the most interesting of these groups are the native southerners and the New England immigrants.

The reading behavior of southerners was related to a variety of historical forces that made the South a distinctive region in America, even after Civil War and even in the South's nascent industrial sector. Southern cotton manufacturing, for example, was an important industry in the "New South" by 1890, but it stood apart from manufacturing in other regions. The mills were much smaller, more widely scattered, and much more likely to be staffed by native-born American workers.[24] In general, manufacturing was not as closely associated with urbanization in the South as it was in the North. This in itself surely had some impact on reading behavior because in nineteenth-century America both the production of reading materials and basic literacy were closely correlated with population concentration. And illiteracy was much more prevalent in the South than in the North.[25] But population concentration does not fully explain the disparity between the North and the South in either literacy rates or in the consumption of reading materials. Another factor strongly emphasized by Lee Soltow and Edward Stevens is schooling. They argue that school attendance, even in rural areas, was strikingly different between regions and was closely associated with differences in literacy.[26]

On the basis of such aggregate regional comparisons one might easily suppose that school attendance was closely related to reading behavior. My individual-level data, however, suggest otherwise. Certainly, the southerners in my sample were much less likely than the northerners to send their children to school. But nowhere did the fact that people had their children in school make much difference in their expenditures on reading materials. I found no correlations between reading expenditures and proportion of school-age children in school in any region, even when controlling for family income and income of the father.[27] Southern families remained significantly different from northern families, regardless of whether they had their school-age children in school or not. (See table 10.8.)

Perhaps some light can be shed on the reading habits of southern mill workers by comparing them with the most similar group in the North: New England immigrants. As table 10.3 shows, New England had a large proportion of nonreaders. Most of these were immigrants. Among the immigrant families of New England, about 32 percent spent nothing on reading materials—a nonreading rate comparable only to the South. Who were these nonreaders? Half of them, it turns out, were from one particular ethnic group: French Canadians. Among the twenty-one French-Canadian families in the New England sample (21 percent), fully two-thirds spent nothing at all on

Table 10.8. Average Expenditure for Newspapers and Books and Average
Percentage of Discretionary Spending for Newspapers and Books by Region of
Residence and Whether the Family Had School-Age Children in School, 1891

	No Children in School		Children in School	
Region	Expenditure	Percentage	Expenditure	Percentage
New England	$4.26	2.5%	$4.03	2.1%
Mid-Atlantic	4.70	2.5	5.28	2.3
South	2.21	1.4	2.81	1.1

Source: U.S. Commissioner of Labor, *Seventh Annual Report* (1891).
Note: Differences in means among regions are significant at $p < .01$.

books or newspapers. This low spending behavior was not due to poverty.
In my sample the French-Canadian families scored well above average on
family income (mean = $859). But their reading expenditures were extraor-
dinarily low—about $1.29 per year, compared to the overall average of $4.23.
The proportion of discretionary spending on reading was also extremely
low—about 0.7 percent. The issue here is not simply one of language. Foreign language materials, including French publications, were readily available. Yet French Canadians' spending figures are lower than those for any
other ethnic group, including the other foreign language groups. The French
Canadians were low spenders on reading even when their incomes were high.
In fact, more than half of the high-income French Canadians were nonreaders, by far the largest proportion for any ethnic group in the entire sample.

Part of the explanation for the reading behavior of the French Canadians
lies in the composition of their family incomes. The French Canadians had
larger-than-average families, but they also had more than the average proportion of their school-age children at work. Thus the proportion of family income earned by the husband in French-Canadian families was very low, about
45 percent.[28] At the high-income level the father earned only about 31 percent
of the family income, the lowest for any ethnic group in the sample. But the
French Canadians were not the only nationality group to lean heavily on their
children for family income. The Irish, who earned on the average the highest
family income in the sample ($881), were the most dependent on their chil-
dren. Overall, Irish fathers earned only 38 percent of the family's income, even
less than French-Canadian fathers. Yet the Irish scored well above the French
Canadians in expenditures for books and newspapers.[29] In other words, the
reading behavior of the French Canadians, like that of the southerners, cannot be explained solely in terms of income or family earning patterns.

The same might be said of schooling. As with southerners, school attendance does not seem to have been the key factor. French Canadians with

children in school spent a larger proportion of their discretionary incomes on reading materials than did those who did not have their school-age children in school. But in both categories (children in school or not in school), the French Canadians scored the lowest of all ethnic groups in the sample. Just as the southerners maintain their distinctiveness even when school attendance is taken into account, so here too children in school does not seem to have been a key determinant of reading behavior.

Other family structure variables also fail to explain the reading habits of southerners or French Canadians. I tried to discover, for example, if reading behavior was related to family life cycle. Working with these same data, Michael Haines found that the life cycle of a late nineteenth-century family unfolded into fairly regular income and consumption patterns.[30] In my sample, however, age of the family (husband + wife) was not correlated with reading expenditures, with or without controls for income. On the measure of family age, moreover, neither the southerners nor the French Canadians seemed strikingly different from other groups in the sample. The southern parents were a little younger; the French Canadians a little older. On other family life-cycle variables—such as home ownership or whether the wife worked outside the home—the two groups were not significantly different from their neighbors.

So why did they spend so much less for newspapers and books? I think a more subtle cultural influence was at work, an influence that touched southerners and French Canadians in similar ways and that had to do with their new lives in the new industrial communities of late nineteenth-century America.

Community

In the South in the 1880s the poor white workers were new to an industrial system that had not yet acquired a permanent working-class culture. They were rural people, and they often expected to return to the land. Many, in fact, maintained their farming roots while working in nearby mills. They continued to mark time by the traditional seasons of "hog-killin'," "cotton choppin'," and "'tween crops." Those without local roots often lived the same migratory lives as they had lived as sharecroppers. This persistence of traditional lifestyles led progressive-era experts on cotton manufacturing to complain about the improvident, undisciplined, undependable ways of southern mill workers.[31] The historian C. Vann Woodward told the story somewhat more sympathetically: "The whole of this rustic individualism moved to a rural rhythm."[32] In other words, these families were cultural transients.

The French Canadians of New England were similar to the southern mill workers in several ways. Like the southerners, the French Canadians held tenaciously to their traditional ways, adamantly refusing to become part of a larger working-class culture. By 1890 they were recognized as perhaps the most separate and distinctive of the many ethnic groups in the polyglot textile industry of New England.[33] They were extremely clannish about marriage, church, schools, and other group values and behaviors. Because of their proximity to to Quebec, they were able to maintain close ties to their homeland. Their aim was what they called *la survivance:* the perpetuation of their historic and traditional culture. And they were remarkably successful until well into the twentieth century, perhaps more successful than any other American ethnic group.[34] By the 1890s they supported a French-language press in New England, but newspapers were never so important to their lives or to the survival of French-Canadian culture as were the traditional institutions of clan, church, and family.[35] In the expanding American textile industry, in other words, they were strangers—not unlike the native-born mill workers of the South.

Viewed together, the behavior of the southerners and the French Canadians may suggest a connection between reading and a feeling of arrival in a new culture, of involvement with the surrounding community—whether native or immigrant. If this is true and reading is connected to community involvement, there should be some relationship between reading expenditures and expenditures on other community-related activities. And there is some evidence that this was the case.

The interplay between family and community during the process of industrialization and urbanization has long fascinated historians. In a classic essay Herbert Gutman suggested that the American working class, both native and immigrant, was only gradually and with much travail brought into the clock-and-machine culture of the nineteenth century. Over many decades, as they adjusted to new work routines and to the lifestyles of industry and city, workingmen and their families clung to preindustrial habits and behaviors.[36] Thomas Bender describes this process of adjustment in terms of *Gemeinschaft* and *Gesellschaft,* Ferdinand Tönnies's terms for traditional interpersonal community and modern contractual society. Bender argues that *Gemeinschaft* was not replaced by *Gesellschaft* but rather the two forms of social experience came to coexist in nineteenth-century America. Traditional family and community behaviors continued to flourish side by side with the institutions of the modern marketplace society.[37]

Some family historians have used census records and other historical data to try to test ideas such as these about family responses to changing environments. John Modell, for example, using data from Wright's 1875 and 1890–91 surveys, found that both American and Irish families increased what he calls their "prudential" expenditures, for such things as organization memberships and insurance. Yet, at the same time, "indulgent" expenditures on liquor and tobacco, which he views as a preindustrial cultural response to crisis, also remained high. In this and other ways individual families exhibited traits of both industrial and preindustrial cultures.[38]

My data offer some evidence that reading was an activity associated with more modern community activities (*Gesellschaft*) than with traditional activities of family and clan (*Gemeinschaft*). I studied four categories of expenditures that touch on the lifestyle of the family in the community: family amusements, church and charities, insurance, and organizations. It seems to me that the first two of these categories suggest more traditional family and clan (*Gemeinschaft*) interests; the latter two suggest more of a connection with the formal, contractual (*Gesellschaft*) community.

The relationship between these four categories of expenditures and spending on newspapers and books is not exactly overwhelming, but it is clear. The partial correlation (controlling for income) is .27 between reading and insurance expenses and .21 between reading and organization expenses. This is not a terribly strong correlation, but it is a statistically significant one. On the other hand, the partial correlations between reading and amusements and reading and church and charity are negligible and insignificant. Table 10.9 shows these relationships somewhat more vividly than the partial correlations, because the relationships are not altogether linear. In spending on amusements and church (*Gemeinschaft* expenditures) nonreaders were not significantly different from readers in my sample. In spending on insurance and organizations (*Gesellschaft* expenditures), on the other hand, nonreaders were quite different indeed. On the average they spent less than half the amount spent by even the moderate readers. And these relationships between readers and nonreaders hold *within* regions as well.

Embedded within these figures are the southerners and the French Canadians. (See table 10.10.) Their experience suggests what the figures might mean. Of the four categories of discretionary spending that I studied, the southerners' chief expenditure was for family amusements; the French Canadians' primary commitment was to church and charity.[39] In the more *Gesellschaft* categories, on the other hand, both groups fell well below the sample means.

Historians of the mass media have speculated that the popular newspapers and periodicals of the late nineteenth century helped to integrate the newcomer into the brave new world of modern urban and industrial life.

Table 10.9. Average Expenditure for Amusements, Church and Charity, Organizations, and Insurance by Family Reading Status, 1891

Reading Status	Amusements	Church and Charity	Organizations	Insurance
Nonreaders	$5.08	$ 9.06	$1.03	$4.00
Low readers	5.54	11.61	2.71	8.78
High readers	5.89	11.45	3.25	9.68
Overall	$5.56	$11.60	$2.51	$8.00

Source: U.S. Commissioner of Labor, *Seventh Annual Report* (1891).
Note: Differences in means among reading status groups are significant for organizations and insurance at $p < .01$; insignificant for amusements and church and charity.

Table 10.10. Average Expenditure for Amusements, Church and Charity, Organizations, and Insurance for Southerners and French Canadians, 1891

Ethnic Group	Amusements	Church and Charity	Organizations	Insurance
Southerners	$6.73	$ 6.18	$1.82	$1.74
French Canadians	6.66	14.24	1.30	5.09
Overall	$5.56	$11.60	$2.51	$8.00

Source: U.S. Commissioner of Labor, *Seventh Annual Report* (1891).
Note: Differences in means between each ethnic group and the overall sample (except for amusements) are significant at $p < .01$.

These new mass media may have helped to build new communities among the ashes of the old.[40] My data lend some support to this association of working-class reading and modern community life. Though reading was a common activity for all groups in my sample of working-class families, the more avid readers seem to have been more at home with the institutions of the modern industrial community.

* * *

This study of the family budgets of cotton textile workers in 1890 mainly confirms the expected—that reading was related to income, region, nationality, and community life. But I hope it also contributes to an understanding of how these general categories of family life may have been interconnected.

First, the analyses suggest that reading expenditures were sensitive to who in the family earned the income. Regardless of family income, a very important factor in expenditures on books and newspapers was children at work. The more the family depended on children's income, the less it spent on reading. This could be merely the negative side of commitment to schooling, but I did not find this to be the case. Although children at work was always related to low-level reading expenditures, children in school was not.

Second, my data clearly show the expected regional variations in reading expenditures, with the South scoring extremely low on actual dollars spent on books and newspapers and low on proportion of discretionary spending for reading materials. Though the southern workers were more likely than the northern workers to have their young children at work and much less likely to have them in school, these variables did not seem to be the keys to southernness. No matter what controls I introduced, southern reading expenditures remained low and quite distinctive.

Third, I looked at nationality, comparing the southerners and the southern work experience to a northern ethnic group with similar reading behavior: the French Canadians. For both groups, family work patterns were important. Both depended heavily on income from their working children, and neither group showed much concern for schooling. Yet, even with these factors controlled, the distinctiveness remained.

To explain this distinctiveness I looked at the similar cultural experiences of the southerners and the French Canadians. Though they were extraordinarily different in many ways, both groups shared a fundamental similarity. They were cultural sojourners—*in* but not *of* the emerging modern communities of industrial America. Their commitments lay more with *Gemeinschaft* institutions, such as family and church, and less with *Gesellschaft* institutions, such as organizations and insurance companies. And, finally, I have argued that the consumption of newspapers and books seems to have been tied more to this latter *Gesellschaft* world.

Notes

1. For example, see Kenneth A. Lockridge, *Literacy in Colonial New England: An Enquiry into the Social Context of Literacy in the Early Modern West* (New York: W. W. Norton, 1974); Harvey J. Graff, *The Literacy Myth: Literacy and Social Structure in the Nineteenth-Century City* (New York: Academic, 1979; Lee Soltow and Edward Stevens, *The Rise of Literacy and the Common School in the United States: A Socioeconomic Analysis to 1870* (Chicago: University of Chicago Press, 1981); Harvey Graff, ed., *Literacy and Social Development in the West* (Cambridge: Cambridge University Press, 1982).

2. Carl F. Kaestle, "The History of Literacy and the History of Readers," Program Report 85-2, Wisconsin Center for Education Research, Madison, February 1985, pp. 43–44. Kaestle later expanded this report into chapters 1 and 2 of Carl F. Kaestle et al., *Literacy in the United States: Readers and Reading since 1880* (New Haven, Conn.: Yale University Press, 1991).

3. For example, see James D. Hart, *The Popular Book: A History of America's Literary Taste* (New York: Oxford University Press, 1950); John David Marshall, ed., *Approaches to Library History* (Tallahassee, Fla.: Journal of Library History, 1966); Michael H. Harris and Donald G. Davis, eds., *American Library History: A Bibliography* (Austin: University of Texas Press, 1978).

4. Michael H. Harris, "Books on the Frontier: The Extent and Nature of Book Ownership in Southern Indiana, 1800–1850," *Library Quarterly* 42 (1972): 416–30; Michael H. Harris, *A Guide to Research in American Library History,* 2d ed. (Metuchen, N.J.: Scarecrow, 1974); Joseph F. Kett and Patricia A. McClung, "Book Culture in Post-Revolutionary Virginia," *Proceedings of the American Antiquarian Society* 94 (1984): 97–147.

5. Wendell D. MacDonald, "The Early History of Labor Statistics in the United States," *Labor History* 13 (1972): 267–78.

6. James Leiby, *Carroll Wright and Labor Reform: The Origin of Labor Statistics* (Cambridge, Mass.: Harvard University Press, 1960); S. N. D. North, "The Life and Work of Carroll Davidson Wright," *Quarterly Publications of the American Statistical Association* 11 (1908–9): 447–66.

7. George J. Stigler, "The Early History of Empirical Studies of Consumer Behavior," *Journal of Political Economy* 42 (1954): 95–113, reprinted in George Stigler, *Essays in the History of Economics* (Chicago: University of Chicago Press, 1965); U.S. Department of Agriculture, *Studies of Family Living in the United States and Other Countries: An Analysis of Material and Method,* by Faith M. Williams and Carle C. Zimmerman, Miscellaneous Publication No. 23 (Washington, D.C.: Government Printing Office, 1935).

8. Massachusetts Bureau of the Statistics of Labor, *Sixth Annual Report,* Public Document No. 31, Mar. 1875; U.S. Commissioner of Labor, *Sixth Annual Report* (1890); U.S. Commissioner of Labor, *Seventh Annual Report* (1891).

9. Carroll D. Wright describes his methods in "A Basis for Statistics of Cost of Production," *Proceedings of the American Statistical Association* 2 (1890–91): 157–77. John Modell checked the internal consistency of Wright's methods and results and found them fairly sound. Michael Haines tested Wright's survey data against data from the 1890 census. He found some differences in some areas, such as age distributions, but overall he found the survey data fairly representative. See John Modell, "Patterns of Consumption, Acculturation, and Family Income Strategies in Late Nineteenth-Century America," in *Family and Population in Nineteenth-Century America,* ed. Tamara K. Hareven and Maris Vinovskis (Princeton, N.J.: Princeton University Press, 1978); Michael R. Haines, "Industrial Work and the Family Life Cycle, 1889–1890," *Research in Economic History* 4 (1979): 289–356.

10. For example, see U.S. Commissioner of Labor, *Seventh Annual Report* (1891); and Illinois Bureau of Labor Statistics, *Third Biennial Report,* pt. 2 (1884).

11. Jeffrey Williamson, "Consumer Behavior in the Nineteenth Century: Carroll D. Wright's Massachusetts Workers in 1875," *Explorations in Entrepreneurial History* 2d ser., 4 (1966–67): 98–135; Peter Lindert, "Child Costs and Economic Development," in *Population Change and Economic Growth in Developing Countries,* ed. Richard A. Easterlin (Chicago: University of Chicago Press, 1980); Haines, "Industrial Work"; Modell, "Patterns of Consumption." See also John F. McClymer, "Late Nineteenth-Century American Working-Class Living Standards," *Journal of Interdisciplinary History* 17 (1986): 379–98. For an example of how the data have been used in literacy studies, see Lawrence C.

Stedman, Katherine Tinsley, and Carl F. Kaestle, "Literacy as a Consumer Activity," in Kaestle et al., *Literacy in the United States,* chap. 5.

12. U.S. Census Office, *Report on Manufacturing Industries in the United States at the Eleventh Census: 1890,* pt. 3: Selected Industries, "Printing and Publishing" (1895), 651–52.

13. Frank Luther Mott, *A History of American Magazines, 1885–1905,* vol. 4 (Cambridge, Mass.: Belknap, 1957).

14. John Tebbel, *A History of Book Publishing in the United States,* vol. 2: *The Expansion of an Industry, 1865–1919* (New York: R. R. Bowker, 1975), 1.

15. Census Office, "Printing and Publishing," 651–52.

16. In fact, the analysis is based upon a sample of 298. Because of a coding error, I ended up with only 98 cases in the New England subsample. The error did not affect the randomness of the sample and therefore should not have affected the analysis. After this chapter was first published in 1986, the data contained in the U.S. Commissioner of Labor's *Seventh Annual Report* were put into machine-readable form and deposited into the Inter-University Consortium for Political and Social Research, Ann Arbor, Michigan. See Kaestle et al., *Literacy in the United States,* 167.

17. "Discretionary expenditures" are those over which the family exercised some significant choice. Specifically, I defined (and computed) "discretionary expenditures" as total family spending minus expenditures for food, rent, utilities, taxes, and medical care.

18. Maxwell E. McCombs, "Mass Media in the Marketplace," *Journalism Monographs* 24 (1972): 98–99.

19. Commissioner of Labor, *Seventh Annual Report,* 856–77.

20. U.S. Census Office, *Report on Manufacturing Industries in the United States at the Eleventh Census: 1890,* pt. 3: Selected Industries, "Cotton Manufacturing," (1895), 174.

21. This statement is based on an analysis of variance, with income as a covariate.

22. Census Office, "Printing and Publishing," 660.

23. This relationship (shown in table 10.5) also holds in partial correlation analysis, within regions and across regions, with and without controls for family income. On the composition of family income see Claudia Goldin, "Family Strategies and the Family Economy in the Late Nineteenth Century: The Role of Secondary Workers," in *Philadelphia: Work, Space, Family, and Group Experience in the Nineteenth Century,* ed. Theodore Hershberg (New York: Oxford University Press, 1981); and Greg Hoover, "Supplemental Family Income Sources: Ethnic Differences in Nineteenth-Century Industrial America," *Social Science History* 9 (1985): 293–306.

24. Census Office, "Cotton Manufacturing," 171–73, 186–93; Melvin Thomas Copeland, *The Cotton Manufacturing Industry of the United States,* Harvard Economic Studies, vol. 8 (Cambridge, Mass.: Harvard University Press, 1912), 32–53.

25. Census Office, "Printing and Publishing," 660; Soltow and Stevens, *Rise of Literacy,* 164–66, 194–95.

26. Soltow and Stevens, *Rise of Literacy,* 160–61, 170, 189.

27. Stedman, Tinsley, and Kaestle found a correlation between reading expenditures and children in school. See Stedman, Tinsley, and Kaestle, "Literacy as a Consumer Activity," 168. See also David L. Angus, "The Social and Economic Correlates of School At-

tendance among the Children of Textile Workers, 1890," *Journal of the Midwest History of Education Society* 10 (1982): 1–6.

28. Compare table 10.5. See also Copeland, *Cotton Manufacturing Industry,* 120.

29. See also Modell, "Patterns of Consumption," 239–40.

30. Haines, "Industrial Work," 318–20.

31. Copeland, *Cotton Manufacturing Industry,* 41. See also David L. Carlton, *Mill and Town in South Carolina, 1880–1920* (Baton Rouge: Louisiana State University Press, 1982).

32. C. Vann Woodward, *Origins of the New South, 1877–1913* (Baton Rouge: Louisiana State University Press, 1951), 223.

33. Copeland, *Cotton Manufacturing Industry,* 120–21.

34. George French Theriault, *The Franco-Americans in a New England Community: An Experiment in Survival* (New York: Arno, 1980), reprint of a Ph.D. dissertation, Harvard University, 1951. A recent study of French Canadians in Massachusetts, published long after this chapter was written, sees them as somewhat more assimilationist. See John F. Mc-Clymer, "Carroll D. Wright, L'Abbé Jean-Baptiste Primeau, and French-Canadian Families," in *The Human Tradition in the Gilded Age and Progressive Era,* ed. Ballard C. Campbell (Wilmington, Del.: SR Books, 2000).

35. Theriault, *Franco-Americans,* 518. See also Census Office, "Printing and Publishing," 653.

36. Herbert G. Gutman, "Work, Culture, and Society in Industrializing America, 1815–1919," *American Historical Review* 78 (1973): 531–88. See also Herbert G. Gutman, *Work, Culture, and Society in Industrializing America: Essays in American Working-Class and Social History* (New York: Alfred A. Knopf), 1976.

37. Thomas Bender, *Community and Social Change in America* (New Brunswick, N.J.: Rutgers University Press, 1978), 17–18, 117, and 142.

38. Modell, "Patterns of Consumption," 211–17.

39. On southern mill workers and amusements see Copeland, *Cotton Manufacturing Industry,* 41. On French Canadians and their close connection to church and parish life, see Theriault, *Franco-Americans,* 326–27.

40. Michael Schudson, *Discovering the News: A Social History of American Newspapers* (New York: Basic, 1978), chap. 3; Gunther Barth, *City People: The Rise of Modern City Culture in Nineteenth-Century America* (New York: Oxford University Press, 1980), chap. 3; David Paul Nord, "The Public Community: The Urbanization of Journalism in Chicago," *Journal of Urban History* 11 (Aug. 1985): 411–41. That article appears as chapter 5 in this book.

11. Reading the Newspaper: Strategies and Politics of Reader Response, Chicago, 1912–17

> Shambaugh, Iowa
> Jan. 5, 1915
> Herald Editors:
> My subscription to your paper expires Jan. [15].
> Please stop the paper as I am American born
> protestant and have no further use for a paper
> in which Rome has the directing hand.
> > Yours sincerely,
> > R. E. Young

> Harvard, Ill.
> Feb. 19, 1915
> [no greeting]
> I will not sign for your Paper again until you
> can tell me why you are so down on us
> *Catholics*, Why you don't think we ought to
> have a Liberty of Conscience as well as the
> Protestants.
> > H. P. Donovan[1]

NEWSPAPER STORIES, like poems, do not have fixed meanings. Meaning occurs not in the text but in the reading of it. As these two letters to the editor of the *Chicago Herald* suggest, people can and do read their newspapers in strikingly different ways. Reading the newspaper, like reading a poem or story, is not a transmission of meaning from text to reader but rather a *transaction* between text and reader. It involves the reader in *replenishing* the text, in *making sense* with it; it involves the reader's seeing the text through the lenses of *interpretive strategies* provided by *interpretive communities;* it involves the *codes* and *canons* of culture. These terms and the concepts they name—drawn from reader-response literary criticism—are as useful for the study of journalism as of poetry.[2]

But in other ways, reading a newspaper is not at all like reading a poem. Two differences are particularly important. First, journalism is a genre with its own peculiar codes and conventions, and readers develop certain expectations of it. Yet the most characteristic convention of modern journalism— a style of relativism that journalists call objectivity—can be both puzzling and annoying to even the most faithful reader. Second, journalism is always intensely political. Of course, this might be said—is said—of all literature. But journalism is not merely literature with a political strain or subtext to it. It is, quite literally, the literature of politics, the literature through which ordinary political activity is conducted, day by day. The study of readers reading the news, therefore, has several virtues. It casts light on the nature of journalism. How readers read the newspaper suggests what the newspaper is. It also casts light on the nature of reading. How readers negotiate the conventions of a genre and how they set their readings into the explicit political contexts of journalism may suggest ways of thinking about the more subtle conventions and politics of reading in general.

This chapter is about reader response to journalism during an important transitional period in the history of the American newspaper: the early years of the twentieth century. It is a study of how some readers responded to the *Chicago Tribune* and the *Chicago Herald* in the years between 1912 and 1917. The study is based on manuscript letters sent by readers to the editor of those two papers, James Keeley, and on his replies.[3] These conversations between reader and editor provide a window on newspaper readers and reading in those days. The surviving letters are not a random sample of reader response; they cannot tell us what proportion of readers responded in what specific ways. But they can suggest to us how some readers read, across a broad range of response. They can give us what we now need most in our effort to construct a history of readership: a glimpse into the past of some actual readers reading their newspapers.[4]

Specifically, the letters suggest three themes about newspaper readership:

First, the letters illustrate how readers engaged the text of their newspapers. Not unexpectedly, the range of reader response was vast. At one extreme, some readers took on the text of the newspaper directly and seriously; at the other extreme, some strayed so far from the text that it was impossible even for the editors at the time to follow their winding trails of thought. Most revealing perhaps are the letters that fall between these extremes. These show how the text cued readers to respond in certain conventional ways and how readers made sense of the news by linking one event or idea to another. The notions of *cuing* and *linking* are key elements in a taxonomy of newspaper reader response that I will develop in this chapter.

Second, the letters suggest that some readers did not understand (or did not agree with) the new methodology of "objectivity" that editors such as James Keeley were developing in the early years of the twentieth century. These editors, a new generation for a new century, were proudly inventing the modern American newspaper, but their readers did not always appreciate their efforts. Keeley and his readers often found themselves talking past one another, frustrated by one another's understanding of truth, facts, bias, and impartiality. As a result, reader and editor sometimes held dramatically differently notions of what journalism should be and what a newspaper should do. In a sense they were working from divergent epistemologies of journalism. Some readers simply did not believe that a newspaper story should be open to multiple interpretations—that it should "mean" like a poem. But Keeley did.

Third, the letters suggest that readers responded to the newspaper according to interpretive strategies made available to them by interpretive communities and that those communities were sometimes overtly political. In other words, most reader response was determined neither by the text nor by idiosyncrasy. As Jonathan Culler has put it, "Meaning is not an individual creation but the result of applying to the text operations and connections which constitute the institution of literature." In other words, some of Keeley's readers read in a similar way because they brought to their reading a similar repertoire of "conventions and norms" for reading a newspaper.[5] And often these interpretive communities were inspired by formal political organizations and interest groups. In a famous phrase from the literature on political power, E. E. Schattschneider defined political organization as "the mobilization of bias."[6] This linking of *bias* with formal *organization* is a key idea for understanding reader response in the realm of the newspaper, for teaching readers how to read their papers is often political work of the utmost urgency. So it was in Chicago in the early twentieth century.

I will unfold my argument in five parts. The first part is a sketch of the editor and his readers and the collection of letters they together left behind. The next three parts develop my three themes about newspaper reading, with particular emphasis on the methodology of journalism and the mobilization of bias. The last part sets the Chicago case into a larger argument about the history of newspaper reading and reading in general.

* * *

In publishing a newspaper you endeavor to print what the people
want to read.
—James Keeley[7]

James Keeley spoke those words to the journalism students at the University of Notre Dame in November 1912. He judged this address to be his most
thoughtful statement on the nature of what he liked to call "the modern
newspaper." The modern newspaper, he said, must be more than a mirror,
more than a simple news-gathering machine. Keeley was propelled to fame
and authority on the *Tribune* by his obsession with getting the news. As a pure
newsman, he was ruthless and peerless. The *Tribune,* he had said in his days
as managing editor, "had no friends and wanted none."[8] By 1912, however,
he had come to believe that a newspaper must be oriented less to the news
and more to the readers. It must have great variety; it must be balanced and
impartial; and most of all it "must enter into the everyday life of its readers."[9]

To this end Keeley began to promote the idea of "personal service."
Though the *Tribune* remained an intensely political paper and an editorial
organ of the Republican Party (Bull Moose in 1912), its expanding circulation under Keeley grew more from its combination of nonpartisan news and
popular features, a combination that would make the *Tribune* the great success story of Chicago journalism in the twentieth century. During Keeley's
tenure as managing editor and editor (1898–1914), the *Tribune* added a variety of new features: advice to the lovelorn, help for the working girl, recipes
and cooking tips, health information, guidance for investments and household economy. Keeley aimed to get readers involved in the newspaper. A *Tribune* ad read: "What Shall I Do? Ask the *Tribune.*" And readers did. By 1912
the paper was receiving thirty-five hundred letters a week, most of them generated by these new "personal service" features. Also by 1912 the *Tribune* had
gained supremacy in the morning field in Chicago, with a circulation of some
230,000 daily and 300,000 Sunday, a circulation that cut across class lines,
from prominent businessmen to waterfront roustabouts.[10]

In 1914 Keeley left the *Tribune* to take over one of its chief morning rivals,
the *Chicago Record-Herald,* which he combined with the failing *Inter Ocean*
and renamed the *Herald.* Even more than the *Tribune,* the *Herald* became a
laboratory for Keeley's idea of personal service journalism. The *Herald* could
not compete with the *Tribune* on news, and it didn't try. Its forte was reader-
oriented features and family fare—a formula that helped to boost circulation to more than 200,000 daily (300,000 Sunday) by July 1914. On the *Herald,*

as on the *Tribune*, Keeley was intensely interested in reader response. In addition to the letters to columnists, the *Herald* carried the usual letters to the editor as well as "Editorials by the Laity." And the *Herald* solicited reader letters constantly. "What Do *You* Think?" the paper asked its readers. "The Herald wants to hear from its big family often."[11]

"Family" is a good label for Keeley's image of a newspaper's readership, for he had the kind of love/hate relationship with his readers that one might expect of a happy but harried family man with 200,000 close relatives. On the one hand, as an enthusiastic marketer of popular culture, he seemed genuinely to believe in the native genius of American public opinion. In his speeches he routinely referred to reader letters as a source of inspiration and ideas. He told the students at Notre Dame that he was "constantly profiting and learning" from the letters. Even the scornful letters, the barbs, were wise in their way. "The little stickers are there to prick us into activity," he told the Michigan Press Association, "to keep us on the jump, to stir our emotions, awaken our enterprise, jar dormant brain cells into activity."[12]

On the other hand, the letters often baffled and exasperated him. In his Michigan talk he called the letters "Thorns on the Journalistic Rose" (the title of his speech that evening). He explained: "Now, with your kind permission, I will open my letter file and let you see what kind of a villain stands before you: A traitor, a crook, a thief who should be in the penitentiary, an ass, a knave, a man who has been bought with British gold and German geldt, a foe to his church and a paid advocate of that, a bought hireling of the trusts and an anarchist who has no respect for the rights of property, an all-around unhung scoundrel who is a disgrace to the human race." These letters are especially interesting because they were aimed at Keeley himself (or at the generalized figure of the editor), not at the public via the convention of "letters to the editor." In other words, these really were letters to the editor, not little essays. They were readers speaking directly to—often shouting at—Keeley. Sometimes he replied to these correspondents, occasionally with heavy sarcasm; often he dismissed them as "the 'bugs' who help to maintain the postal service through their contributions to the waste-paper basket."[13]

But Keeley did not throw the letters away. He saved them—the lunatic letters along with the serious, principled letters of argumentation. On the more odd and outrageous specimens he scrawled "Bug" at the top of the page and had them deposited not in the wastepaper basket but in the "Bug file" that he began to keep in the early years of the century. He also saved many of the more polite and sweetly reasonable letters from his readers. And, of equal interest, he saved some of his replies. Clearly, Keeley was fascinated by the vagaries of reader response. Indeed, he sometimes said that in retirement he would write a book on the newspaper business and would depend on the letters to try to see (and to show) the newspaper through the eye of the reader. But he never wrote the book, and the letters now lie in repose in the manuscripts department of the Chicago Historical Society.[14]

* * *

Herrin, Ill.
July 9—[19]14
The Editor of the Chicago Herald,
   Sir I am not a writer of any Discriptian, or Speller either, I am
only a plain grocery clerk hard working man every day.
R. D. Pool[15]

Keeley should have written the book. The readers' letters (and his replies) do shed light on the newspaper business. More important, they illuminate the readers themselves. Better than letters submitted for publication, manuscript letters suggest a diversity of purpose and style. Even this small remnant of the fat files that Keeley once held reveals a striking range of reader response. The published letters in the *Tribune*'s "Voice of the People" column and the *Herald*'s "Editorials by the Laity" and "Letters from *Herald* Readers" do not exhibit such great range. They had their quirks, of course. But, like letters to the editor today, they typically discussed the major issues of the day that had usually been suggested in the news columns.[16] The reader response displayed in the manuscript letters was more diverse and often perversely idiosyncratic, but it was not random. It can be described and classified in logical and useful ways. The reader's purpose in writing is one obvious criterion of classification. Perhaps more important for the study of reader response is the criterion that I will call *orientation to the text*.

One way to classify reader purpose is to identify the audience to whom the reader was writing. Published letters to the editor almost always were intended for the public, for other readers. Some of the manuscript letters in the Keeley collection fall into that category. Most of the letters, however, were addressed to the editor as editor. Their purpose was to speak directly to the person in charge of the paper. They were personal, not open, letters. Still other letters were quite introspective, almost reflexive—as if the readers were speaking to themselves. Their goal was not to harangue either the public or the editor; it was self-expression: thoughts addressed to no one in particular.

These three reader purposes—to speak to the public, to the editor, or to the self—interacted with another dimension of reader response: orientation to the text. Some letter writers were self-oriented. Their letters were either wholly unrelated to the text of the newspaper, or they were cued by the text but then took off down their own idiosyncratic paths. Other letter writers were text-oriented. They engaged the text directly, but they certainly were not compelled or constrained by it. They replenished the text in their own peculiar ways: They added information, they added context, they inferred, they linked. Of course, reality is messier than this crude taxonomy suggests; these labels at best define continua, not discrete categories, of response. But they serve an analytical purpose, I believe, especially the ideas of *cuing* and *linking,* which I will argue are important, perhaps necessary, styles of response to the texts of journalism.

At one extreme on the continuum of orientation to the text was the reader who was oriented to the text not at all: the utterly self-absorbed. This includes the classic characters of editorial page lore: the crackpot and the lunatic. The Keeley collection has its share. "I have a message for the Jews of Chicago if you will see that they get it," a Michigan writer began. "I am that messiah that the Jews are looking for to bring Salvation to the world." Another reader had a white feather that gave him the power to send people (including Keeley) to heaven. "I will be in the asylum at Elgin 15 years the thirteenth of next month," the letter explained; "that is a long time for a sane man." Another warned of "the Catholic Black Hand operating upon the heads of Protestant people in the city of Chicago, with telepathy, osteopathy and xoneopathy. Also upon the heads of Republican politicians." Some wrote so regularly that Keeley knew their labyrinthine tales by heart. In a note attached to one long letter from another mental patient, Keeley penciled, "Miss G., File. She's an old correspondent."[17] Not all the self-absorbed were crazy. Dozens of letters in the files simply promoted individual readers' plans, schemes, and scams—ranging from news scoops for sale ("bid high") to pleas for publicity ("We are two young athletic women and we expect to walk from Chicago to New York in the very near future").[18] They had only one thing in common: They were oblivious to the text of the newspaper.

Of more relevance for understanding reader response are those letter writers who were cued by the text—that is, prompted but not at all guided by it. This describes a large and fascinating category of letters in the Keeley collection. Some of these are so close to the extreme of total self-absorption that it is impossible to figure out why the cue triggered the response it did. The response was idiosyncratic, yet somehow the text cued it. For example, the collection contains several clippings with cryptic messages for Keeley scrawled on them. One said, "Keeley has slipped up on Hearst in the dark. Refer to Tribune July 8, 1906." But when an assistant editor checked the reference, he could make no sense of what the writer had in mind about Hearst. Another writer enclosed a clipping of a political cartoon with a note that declared, "If the doctor may scatter his microbes pray why not the politician. Is the Political microbe less desirable than the microbe of fear sown in the thought of the inocent reader." In a note to Keeley across the top of the page, an editor wrote: "What's this guy driving at?"[19]

Usually, it is easier to understand how the cue worked, to see what a writer was driving at. For example, the newspaper text often prompted the reader to think of another special text: the Bible. Several letters were battles over textual authority, with the reader challenging the newspaper with a direct quotation from the Bible. "Sir: Your Ed is disgraceful, contemptible, rotten," began a letter in response to an editorial on women's suffrage. "Does not the 1st chap of Genesis, 3rd verse say '& Thy (woman's) desire shall be to *thy Husband and he shall rule over thee.*'" Another writer saw in the news of the day the fulfillment of biblical prophesy—and of his own. He noted, with obvious glee, the untimely deaths of editors and the failures of newspapers around the country. "It is believed now," he prophesied, "that the time is very near for the total destruction of all the daily papers who do not publish all news according to the commandments or holy will of Jesus Christ."[20]

For other readers, newspaper stories did not necessarily cue up a specific Bible passage, but they did trigger a pat religious response. Many letters in the files were sent by Protestants complaining about the "Romanized paper" that the *Tribune* or *Herald* had become. I will discuss the political context of these anti-Catholic letters more fully later in this chapter. Here I am concerned with the simple responses, the knee-jerk reactions, the standard stereotypes of religious intolerance. "A lot of your readers are sick of the Papal stuff you are handing out so lavishly," a reader wrote about a story on the pope's peace mission in Europe. "Let the Pope stick to his beads and holy water and keep out of the political game." Another sent in a clipping on a speech by James Cardinal Gibbons and asked, "Why publish this 'bunk' from the Catholic official Press Bureau? Give 'Prince' Gibbons a rest in his old age." A few letters exhibit the same sort of conventional, hostile response to stories about Jews. Even the atheists could take offense. For instance: "I buy a daily newspaper to acquaint myself with the current events of the day and not to be told on the front page, or elsewhere, of said paper, that 'Jesus has risen,' or similar information regarding the supernatural."[21]

The newspaper cued pat political responses as well. The mere mention of Teddy Roosevelt, for example, could induce agitated tirades against this "most detestable and unscrupulous politician in history." Other writers defended Roosevelt—or William Jennings Bryan or Woodrow Wilson or whomever. "A Union Man" was outraged even to receive a solicitation to subscribe to the *Tribune:* "I am in receipt of your folder you send me yesterday, and beg to inform you that your scabby sheets are not welcome in my house. . . . If the officers of my union would find me Guilty of useing any part of your scabby paper in my toilet, I would be subject to a $100 fine at the next meeting." Responding to a crime story, a black reader wrote: "What on earth, heaven or hell makes you so hateful? Why do you have such an antipathy for negroes? . . . Since you have taken chg. of the Tribune, you *always* and *invariably* make much of *anything* that these thieving police say vs. the negro. You're wrong Mr. Keeley—and you will see it—if you don't see it sooner—when the 'roll is called up yonder.'"[22]

When the war began in August 1914, items in the paper regularly cued standard nationalist responses—some pro-German, some pro-Allies. "We got it from both sides," Keeley complained in the autumn of 1914. To one pro-British reader who complained of pro-German "piffle," Keeley replied, "If I print something that does not please the Germans, I, metaphorically, am kicked from dawn till dusk. If a German point of view is given, ditto."[23]

Cuing was a fairly simple response: An item in the paper triggered a conventional religious, political, or ideological reaction. Somewhat more complex is the response I call *linking*. By linking I mean the strategy of making sense of one event or story by linking it to others, by stringing various news items together into a curriculum of meaning. The genre of journalism begs for linking, for it is almost by definition incoherent. It is a daily sampling of a rushing flow of occurrences and observations, which has no beginning and no end. Readers must find (create, actually) coherence through connection, interpolation, and inference. In a word, they link. Both cuing and linking are logical responses to the terse, uncontextualized texts of journalism.[24]

The most vivid form of linking is the detection of conspiracies. Conspiracies serve wonderfully well to make sense of the flow of news, and Keeley's correspondents detected many. To some readers Keeley himself appeared to be the agent of a pro-Catholic conspiracy. Many letter writers believed that he was Irish, that his name was really Kelly, and that that fact explained everything. "A Despiser of Bigotry and Hypocrisy" wrote, "Everyone knows that that Irish invertebrate Kelley is responsible for the paper's editorial Catholic slop. You filthy vulture!"[25] Others discerned Irish/Catholic conspiracies within local and state government and read the news accordingly. A small news item announcing the appointment of Finley Bell as secretary of the Legislative Reference Bureau in Springfield prompted "One Who Knows" to send in an exposé of a Jesuit scheme to seize America for Catholicism: "Mr. Bell's appointment is another proof, that if proof were wanting, that Governor Dunne is bent upon constructing a *Papist machine* that will be serviceable in his Presidential Aspirations and that the Secretary in the Legislative Reference Bureau will be one of his spies." Another reader cited several acts of the governor, the mayor, and the local Board of Education, all reported in the newspaper, that illustrated the tightening grip of Catholic power.[26] These news items were not linked in the newspaper; they were linked in the reading of it.

Sometimes conspiracies were revealed to readers by what was *not* in the paper. A story about a murder committed by a Catholic priest prompted a reader to think about all the similar stories he had not seen in the *Tribune*. "I suppose the inference to be drawn is that Catholic priests heretefor have not been guilty of crime." That he doubted.[27]

Of course, not all conspiracies were Catholic. Readers also made sense of the news by linking stories into patterns of political or business skullduggery. For example, stories about municipal water waste and the possibility of the city's metering water inspired this diatribe:

> Waste of City Water is all rubbish and Bulls Manure on the Public. People should have plenty water to wash the soil off their Bodies and get rid of the Political Scum. . . . Now, Mr. Jim Keeley, being an old advertiser of your new Paper and a Subscriber, take *a whack* at *this dam* lot of *Millionaire Democratic City Hall Land Speculators,* who have been soaking honorable owners of Real Estate and busting honest small business men and ruining the lives of Chicago Natives, that even now this rotten Element wants to deprive them of the free use of water—O let the Bloody revolution come.

Another unhappy reader wrote from Iowa:

> It has now been my ill fortune to read your editorials for three months. If these have ever contained one line in sympathy with progress or humanity it has escaped my notice. Your sentiments are a thousand years behind the mental stage attained by the troglodytes or the cave men. I feel that in this comparison apologies are due the two latter classes. . . . I feel some curiosity as to whether the Chicago Street RR Company has subsidized you to oppose municipal bus lines; but it is really of little importance since the Herald is always on the side of the corporations anyhow, as opposed to the interest of the common people.

Another reader explicated the *Tribune*'s gentle treatment of Roosevelt:

> Is it not a fact that the Tribune Co. is owned and controlled by the McCormicks of the Harvester Trust? Is it not a fact that one of the McCormicks is a son-in-law of John D. Rockefeller? Is it not a fact that Geo. W. Perkins is a director of the Steel Trust? Is it not a fact that Geo. W. Perkins spent over half a million dollars to nominate Roosevelt, J. Pierpont Morgan's hired man? Is it not a fact that the Harvester trust sells its products for much less money in foreign countries than in these United States? Is it not a fact that Roosevelt has always discountenanced proceedings against the Harvester Trust?

And on and on.[28]

Many other linking strategies run through the letters as well. A reader linked an item on the public responsibility of railroads with the *Tribune*'s lease of public land from the Board of Education. Another linked the break-down of sexual morality with the economic oppression of families. Another linked a story on the newspaper publisher Victor Lawson's real estate tax problems with his own father's tax problems. One reader even managed to link the rise of insanity to the *Tribune*'s editorial support of high tariffs:

> I see on the front page of your paper a colum on the growth of insanity in Chi-cago in my humble opinion the Tribune is to blame to a certain extent for this increase of insanity I have a brother at the present writing out in dunning asylim he went there from drinking whiskey. Now Mr. Editor let me remind you that in the British Isles I never knew of a man evenly haveing the shakes from drink & the reason in my opinion is because the drink is pure & not adulterated. The tribune is a strong advocate of a high protective tariff & a high protective tariff means adulterated food and adulterated food is helping to drive people insane.[29]

These readers were oriented to the text of the newspaper, but the text alone was insufficient. In their reading they drew upon conventional religious, political, and personal themes and strategies of meaning making. In writing their letters, they hoped to discern or create order in what they had read. For some, it was the world that was disordered and perplexing. One reader wrote to say nothing more than that the endless flow of bad news in the paper was giving her "mental nausea." She had nothing to ask, nothing to demand, nothing to proclaim. She simply wanted to speak. "There are many others who think the same as I do," she said. "You may not give this a thought, or hold it up for ridicule. Any way, I feel better for having relieved my mind."[30] For others, it was the journalism itself that was perplexing. Either they could not quite understand how journalism worked (its methodology), or they thought they understood it perfectly well—sometimes with the help of po-litical interest groups.

* * *

Chicago
September 19, 1913
Why cannot men of the standard that write these articles be
allowed to tell the truth?
Mrs. Anna Parker Saylor[31]

Like Anna Saylor, James Keeley believed that newspapers should tell the truth. He said so in his 1912 address to the journalism students at Notre Dame.

But Keeley's understanding of "truth" differed from Mrs. Saylor's. In his list of the virtues of good journalism, only once did Keeley mention truth, and then he meant *accuracy:*

> If I were an instructor in a newspaper school, my pupils would put in many hours of simply writing lists of names from dictation. They would have to devote more time to learning to tell the truth, from initials to debates, than in the study of history and literature. . . . Study history and literature for the foundation such studies give, for the polish that will come from perusal of the masterworks of the ages. But more important, and I know in some circles I shall be held heretical, is the simple art of getting Mr. Brown's initials correctly, the gift of accurately condensing what the gifted and often long winded orator said, the faculty of not mixing dates and facts.

The virtues of news reporting also included "impartiality" and "fairness," Keeley said. "Accuracy, however, is the keynote."[32]

Keeley's description of good journalistic method reflected a trend across the newspaper industry in that era: an embrace of impartiality and facticity. Since the mid-1890s big-city newspapers had been under steady fire for sensationalism, for dramatizing and puffing the news, and for pandering to politicians and advertisers. Press critics routinely raised the same question that Mrs. Saylor pressed upon Keeley. In his famous 1911 series in *Collier's* on "The American Newspaper," Will Irwin said that people everywhere were asking it: "Why don't our newspapers tell the truth?" The theme of the First National Newspaper Conference, organized by the sociologist Edward A. Ross in 1912, was a variant of the same nagging question: "Are newspaper and magazine writers free to tell the truth?"[33] But what is truth? Critics and editors knew then, as they know now, that truth is elusive, complex, even hypothetical. Irwin said it as well as anyone in his opening piece for *Collier's:* "When Pilate asked: 'What is truth?' he expressed the eternal quandary of the news editor. Truth, absolute truth, is a hypothesis. No man, from a cub reporter writing a dog-fight to a star writing a political convention, but puts into his work a point of view."[34]

For press critics and editors, the key issue was not truth at all but independence and, sometimes, impartiality. At the National Newspaper Conference, for example, the speakers focused more on the word *free* in their theme than on the word *truth:* "Are newspaper and magazine writers *free.* . . ." At least one speaker, Melville Stone of the Associated Press, took the question precisely this way, titling his talk, "Can the Impartiality of the News-Gathering and News-Distributing Agencies Be Fairly Challenged?"[35] Most of the remedies proposed by press reformers focused on independence and impartiality, not truth: endowed newspapers, professionalism, ethical codes, education for journalism, licensing of journalists, and government regulation.[36] Though they usually resisted the remedies, editors and publishers often agreed with their critics' definition of the problem. When a leading New York editor asked, in an *Atlantic Monthly* article, "Is an Honest Newspaper Possible?" he meant an *independent* newspaper. [37]

Keeley thought it was. Like many editors of his era, he believed that a newspaper should be independent, that his newspaper was independent, and that its independence was demonstrated daily by its impartiality, fairness, and openness to both sides of controversy. He also believed in the authority of facts. Facts could speak. Keeley did not believe that facts spoke the pure, unambiguous truth. He did believe that facts could be separated from opinions and value judgments and that a newspaper could and should stick closely to lean, terse reporting of facts. Then the readers could pronounce their own judgments upon them. As he told the Notre Dame students, "The day of 'fine writing' is past," and getting the plain facts right is more important than history and literature.[38] This turn to impartiality and facticity—to what by the 1920s would be called "objectivity" in journalism—was the central thrust of the reform and modernization of the American newspaper in the early years of the twentieth century.[39]

Some readers, however, were skeptical. They wanted the truth to be told, and they did not believe that impartiality and simple factual accuracy provided a satisfactory substitute for truth. For years, Keeley argued with his readers over both of these issues: facticity and impartiality. Despite Keeley's private replies and public preachments, some readers continued to see these modern trends in journalism for what they really were: creeping relativism. They didn't like it, and they complained.

In other words, some readers clearly expected facts to speak truth, pure and simple. Often, they phrased their critiques of the slant of the news in the language of fact. "Is it not a fact . . ." was a recurrent refrain in the letters. The recitation of lists of facts was a common pattern. "Facts, you know, are very stubborn," one writer warned the editor. "They are like Banco's ghost that was always bobbing up when least expected."[40] When the war began, the flow of confused and angry letters increased dramatically, many taking issue with what to the writers seemed simple matters of fact. Keeley saw it differently, and in his replies he lectured his objectivist readers on the peculiar nature of objectivity in modern journalism. To one complainant he wrote: "I am under the impression that the Herald printed all the 'facts' to which you refer as they became public. It seems to me that what you really wish is not more facts, but an expression of judgment upon the facts. That task the

Herald must decline, owing to their complexity and because each side practically denies the truth of everything the other says." As the battle of journalism methodology heated up along with the war, the relativist editor wrote sarcastically to one carping positivist: "You say you know what is true and what is false in the news that we print. Come to Chicago and the Herald will pay you more money in a month than you can make in your own town in a year. You are the man the whole country, yes, the whole world, is looking for. Telegraph me when you [can] start and I will reserve a room for you at my club, meet you at the depot and see that you are well taken care of in every respect." "Would that we editors had the omniscience of our critics," he mused to the Michigan Press Association, "the unerring instinct which can pick out lies and truths."[41]

Keeley also debated with his readers the virtues of impartiality and balance. Some readers professed to believe in fairness and impartiality; they understood that modern journalistic objectivity meant balance. They simply demanded more of it for their side. "I have often wondered why people can't be fair in politics," one reader lamented. His complaint? Negative items in the *Herald* about Wilson and the Democrats were insufficiently balanced by criticisms of William Howard Taft and the Republicans. Another asked only for simple "justice" for Bryan: "Some day I hope this city will be able to support an independent newspaper that will treat men and issues without bias but in the meantime I am forced to read the 'Herald' as the lesser of evils and try to consider the source of such disgusting attacks as you have maintained from the start on our foremost citizen." Another detected imbalance in fallen-clergy stories:

> Enclosed is a clipping from your Romanized paper. Personally it is no difference to me whether it is a Protestant minister or a Roman Catholic priest goes wrong, however the world would be better did neither go astray. But why do you refer to Hans Schmidt as the 'one time' priest? Has he been excommunicated? If so why did you not publish such excommunication for the benefit of your readers? You do not follow this policy with Protestant ministers, but refer to them as Rev. Richeson *the Baptist* preacher etc. etc. even on the day of their execution.[42]

Specimens of unadulterated special pleading, such as these, went directly to the "Bug file," without reply.

But Keeley sometimes took offense when readers assumed that the "bias" they perceived in the paper sprang from willful dishonesty. And he replied. Bias to some readers was balance to him, as he explained to one grumpy correspondent:

Yes, I received your two letters and filed them. They are too long for publication and, frankly, one of them is, if you will pardon my saying it, so extravagant not only [in] its claims regarding Mr. Bryan, but [in] its criticisms of newspapers, that I could not very well print it. I really do not know where you got
your information about newspapers who disagree with your point of view,
being controlled by money devils, etc., but believe such a broad allegation is
not true. . . . I do not object to criticism. I would be an ass if I did, because it is
the fundamental part of my business to criticise and also to praise. Neither does
the Herald claim to be omniscient. It makes mistakes. Its point of view, of
course, cannot be universally accepted. What I do try to do is to strike the happy medium between conservatism and radicalism.[43]

For Keeley, striking "the happy medium" was a fundamental principle of
modern journalism. For some readers, it was a pusillanimous outrage. This
comes through most clearly in the stream of anti-Catholic letters in the Keeley
collection. For many Protestant readers, Keeley's "impartiality" in publishing religious news was inexplicable and inexcusable. They wanted *no* Catholic news—or at least very little. "No doubt you are aware," one letter began, "that a considerable majority of your readers are Protestants. It seems
to me you should cater to that majority, by keeping your columns as clear as
possible of Catholicism. It is an imposition on most of your readers to put
that damnable rot before their eyes." Others sent in clippings with notes saying the stories were of interest to no one—except Catholics. Another suggested a Protestant boycott: "You may not realize it, but the day is not far distant
when Chicago must have a purely Protestant Daily Paper."[44]

In short, these readers wanted their newspaper to tell the truth—that is,
their truth. And their hunger for truth was not sated by the modern journalistic diet of impartiality, balance, fairness, and factual accuracy. Either they
did not understand what Keeley was trying to do, or they understood all too
well. In either case they resisted it.

* * *

[Jan. 9, 1914]
The wonderful growth of "The Menace" has been a eye opener.
R. S. Forhes[45]

Sometimes readers canceled their subscriptions to the *Tribune* or the *Herald* because they believed Editor James Keeley was a Catholic foreigner who
had made their newspaper an organ of Catholic propaganda. Keeley hated
this. To R. E. Young—the letter writer quoted in the epigraph that begins this
chapter—he wrote: "I regret exceedingly that you have decided to cease taking the Herald and my regret is based on the reasons you give for your ac-

tion. I too am of the same faith as you. Born in London, I came to America when fifteen years of age and became a citizen on my twenty first birthday, just as early as possible. I cannot imagine what has given you the impression you have. Will you not be good enough to let me know?"[46]

This reply was disingenuous. By January of 1915 Keeley knew perfectly well what lay behind Mr. Young's letter. Keeley knew that nativism and anti-Catholicism were resurgent in America; his proclamation of his own Protestant non-Irishness suggests that he knew the score. Moreover, he had been receiving letters like Young's for several years at both the *Tribune* and the *Herald*.[47] He also knew that anti-Catholic organizations had specifically targeted the daily newspaper press. These groups were struggling to expose a pro-Catholic conspiracy to take over the country, and they saw the press as a co-conspirator. Thus one of their aims was to teach Protestants how to read their newspapers—or, to use reader R. S. Forhes' metaphor, how to *see*. The readers of the *Chicago Tribune* and the *Chicago Herald* were a diverse lot who read their papers through their own eyes. But sometimes those eyes had been opened by the efforts of organized political interest groups.

In late December 1913, for example, news stories began to appear in the *Tribune* about the teaching of "sex hygiene" in the public schools. These stories were straightforward reports on school board meetings, where board members debated the propriety of continuing the "personal purity" lectures that had been tried out that school year. The lectures were by no means briefs for birth control; rather they aimed to deliver the facts of life, of reproduction, of the dangers of disease, and so on. Despite the purported "scientific" approach of the lectures, two trustees opposed them ardently, and on Jan. 7 the board voted to cancel the program.[48] Also on Jan. 7 the paper carried a letter from Joseph Medill Patterson, a member of the *Tribune*'s ownership family, declaring that opposition to sex education came mainly from Catholics and arguing for what he called a compromise. Let the lectures continue, he said, but give parents—especially Catholic parents—the option to have their children excused from them. "I do not want to enforce my beliefs on Catholic children," he concluded. "Equally I do not want Catholic beliefs enforced on my children."[49]

These news stories and Patterson's letter set off a storm of reader response. Many of the letters—especially those published in the paper—were even-tempered, reasonable, and tightly focused on the issue at hand. Patterson's critics denied that the issue of sex education was sectarian, Catholic versus Protestant; many non-Catholic parents also opposed the program. They argued, as critics of sex education often do today, that teaching about sex in a purely factual way, in order to avoid controversial moral messages, carried a moral message anyway: that sex could be separated from morality. And they insisted that *not* teaching a subject so closely tied to personal morality was not a case of forcing anyone's beliefs on anyone.[50]

Many other readers, however, quickly strayed from the subject of sex education. They were cued by this specific issue to launch into wide-ranging diatribes against Catholics and their relationship to the public schools. For example, one man wrote to praise Patterson's letter, which he interpreted as a general attack on Catholic influence in public education. He told of an acquaintance who claimed to have heard a secret lecture delivered a few years earlier by Archbishop John Ireland in St. Paul. Ireland supposedly told his members (and the writer quoted him directly): "'The public school system is the most damnable institution conceived in the mind of man, and it is losing us sixty thousand members every year & unless we do away with it, it will do away with us. We must get control of the politics of the country, then we'll do away with it. . . . Do you know that in forty eight hours we can put two hundred thousand' (or three hundred thousand, I forget which he said) 'armed & drilled men in the field & force our demands.'"[51]

This bogus quotation from Ireland illustrates two persistent figments in the paranoid fancy of anti-Catholic nativism. One was the fear of an armed Catholic uprising, often portrayed as a bloody war of extermination of Protestant heretics. The other was the fear of a Catholic plot to destroy or capture the public schools.[52] Both of these standard themes—especially the fear of school subversion—turned up again and again in the letters to the *Tribune*.

The relationship of Catholics to public education had long been a spring of interreligious controversy in America. In the nineteenth century American Catholics had steadily withdrawn from the public schools, which they viewed as nurseries of Protestantism. Meanwhile, many Protestants abhorred what they imagined to be going on in the separate system of Catholic parochial schools, which they viewed as nurseries of un-Americanism. By the early twentieth century the public school issue had become a central theme of organized anti-Catholic politics.[53] In large cities such as Chicago, where the political power of Catholics and Catholic ethnic groups was great and growing, many Protestants feared that the public schools were slipping from their grasp. Thus the flood of letters cued by the "sex hygiene" controversy was not surprising.

Nor was it spontaneous or idiosyncratic. Identical themes of Catholic power in the schools heated the rhetoric of organized anti-Catholic politics in Chicago in 1913–14. For example, around the time of the "sex hygiene" controversy, a printed broadside circulated in Chicago titled "The Warning! Catholicizing Public Schools." The flyer—which at least one reader sent to Keeley—described case after case of Chicago public school teachers drilling their pupils in Catholic dogma. It also included a string of incendiary quotations ("Education must be controlled by Catholic authorities even to war and bloodshed") attributed to various priests and Catholic periodicals. Near the end of the sheet was a list of "Books for Every American Home," available at a local bookstore. It was the classic anti-Catholic syllabus, including *Convent Horror, Maria Monk,* and *The Priest, the Woman, and the Confessional.* And, finally, at the foot of the page, in boldface type, appeared this appeal: "**Read the MENACE.**"[54]

The *Menace.* This was a name that James Keeley knew well by January 1914. References to the *Menace* cropped up again and again in Keeley's correspondence from readers, and he remarked on its influence in at least one of his speeches. The menace of the title was Catholicism, and the *Menace* was interested in little else. This little four-page weekly was founded in 1911 in Aurora, Missouri, by Wilbur Franklin Phelps, a country editor and sometime progressive. The Reverend Theo. C. Walker was editor. The paper's themes were drawn from the traditional inventory of anti-Catholic nativism, with particular and fearsome emphasis on secret plots and conspiracies: to undermine democratic government, to subvert the public schools, to wage war on heretics. This hysterical screed, belabored week after week, was immensely popular across the country. Within three years of its founding the *Menace* boasted a national circulation of more than a million.[55] Some of these readers, as Keeley was often reminded, were also readers of the *Chicago Tribune.*

For the most part, the influence of the *Menace* on reader response to the *Tribune's* "sex hygiene" coverage must be inferred. Some of the reader letters mentioned the *Menace;* most simply laid out interpretations and made linkages congruent with those of the *Menace.*[56] But when the *Menace* turned its artillery on the newspapers themselves, its influence on reader response was direct and unmistakable. In late 1913 the *Menace* published an item called "Rules To Be Followed by 'Cub' Reporters on all Daily Papers," supposedly a set of guidelines that the Catholic conspiracy had been able to impose upon American journalism. The guidelines listed, in two columns, the "news" and then the "space" to be allotted to it. A brief sampling:

NEWS	SPACE
Pope sneezes	One half column—front page.
Protestant minister goes wrong	Full page—front page, if possible get large photograph.
Patriotic orders federate	No mention.
Irish Catholic club formed	Two columns.
Priest attacks fourteen-year-old girl	No mention.
Catholics demand public school funds	Two columns.
Ammunition explodes in priest's house	No mention.

The guidelines also declared: "Same rules apply to City and Associated Press Associations. Refer all matter to Catholic censor before publication." At the end the *Menace* editor added, "Cut this out, send it to the daily newspaper you subscribe for, and ask them why this rule is followed."

Many readers of the *Chicago Tribune* did just that, and the yellowed clippings still reside in the Keeley collection. Though the "Rules" on their face were phony, some readers took them seriously. "A *True* American" sent in the clipping with a one-sentence letter: "Dear Sir—Will you please state in your columns of the Daily Paper *why* you follow these enclosed Rules." Another wrote: "Please find enclosed slip and I as an old time reader of your paper I would like you to answer me. I am a Prodastant and a Mason and I beleave in the constitution of our Country given us by our fore Fathers. Church and State separate and as I think and hope you are a loyal Citizen, why do you cater to the Roman Church an Enemy to our Constitution." Keeley replied: "While you do not definitely say so I judge from the context of your letter that you believe the 'Space Rules to be followed by "Cub" Reporters on all Daily Papers' are true, i.e., that these alleged rules are in force in the office of The Chicago Tribune. Neither they nor anything in any way approximating them are in existence or have been promulgated verbally or by word of mouth in this office. . . . The 'rules' are a fake and a fraud." By January 1914 Keeley's replies to the *Menace* clippings had become routine. On a sheet of note paper attached to one, he scrawled quickly to his secretary, "Usual Answer."[57]

Other readers sent in a broadside with a similar message titled "The Daily Press of the United States Sold Out to the Roman Catholic Hierarchy." It described in detail how newspapers had been bribed and turned into "Catholic ad sheets." At the end it said, "As soon as you get this circular send it in to your newspaper, with a nice letter, stating that you know the statements set forth to be absolutely true and ask for an explanation." With growing exasperation Keeley replied to one reader: "As you say you have been 'a reader of The Tribune for a long time' you ought to know that the circular you send has no bearing whatever on the conduct of this paper."[58]

Some readers who sent in the *Menace* clippings were confused and skeptical. They thought they detected in the *Tribune*'s news columns evidence for the *Menace*'s claims, but they weren't sure. They wrote for guidance and clarification from their editor. For example, one writer said he had "considered the Tribune too broad and democratic to bow to Rome and her Rum soaked Priests." Yet several recent stories in the paper about a fallen priest, compared with coverage of a Protestant minister gone bad, led him to believe that "the inclosed clipping must have some truth in it." Another reader also mentioned, in light of the *Menace's* guidelines, the stories about the two fallen clergymen. Now he was too perplexed and troubled to know what to think. He had received guidance from the *Menace;* now he needed it from the *Tribune:* "I have been a reader of the Tribune for many years and I have always thot it was a great paper. During the last year I have read a paper called the Menace. It is a terrible paper and I often wonder if it is really true. If the priesthood is as bad as they claim I think that your great paper should help them in there cause to expose such rotteness. If this Menace is not true it should be stopped."[59] Here was a reader who simply wanted his newspaper to tell the truth.

A few readers were more than skeptical; they knew the *Menace* lied. A Catholic reader damned the *Tribune* for not attacking the *Menace,* "the worst Reptile ever printed in this our country *America."* With more measured tone but with equal fervor, the president of the Federation of German Catholic Societies of Illinois, J. A. Bauer, sought help from Keeley in resisting the new flood tide of anti-Catholicism and the resurgence of the old "historical falsehoods" of conspiracies, secret armies, and so on. At the head of Bauer's list of the new brokers of bigotry stood the *Menace.*[60]

In 1913–14 both Catholics and Protestants perceived a mobilization of bias at work in American journalism—aimed at both the writing and the reading of it. Many Catholics feared that "a small number of plotting editors" on fanatical papers like the *Menace* were deceiving America. "Not the Catholic Church but those men are the real menace of the nation," J. A. Bauer wrote. Meanwhile, many Protestant readers of the *Tribune* believed with the *Menace* that a Catholic mobilization of bias was under way in the daily press. In response to the Patterson letter and its aftermath, one reader wrote:

> I was absolutely amused at the seemingly spontaneous but really *machine made* indignation in the replies 'The Tribune' received & published, seemingly from local residents, but inspired by the local Viceroy of the King-God whose permanent abiding place is over the Alps, and who, baffled or challenged in every Catholic country in Europe, can apparently and as opportunely enforce his views amongst the putrescent protestants of America—*and thus defeat a policy that would destroy the sex hygiene teachings of the Confessional*—as if his throne were on the banks of the Wabash instead of upon the Tiber.[61]

In short, both sides were paranoid. But on the issue of mobilization of bias, both were also correct. Both sides had indeed launched organized political efforts to influence not only the content of the newspapers but the readers' reading of it.[62]

* * *

> You are herewith sentenced to Death as a british spy and traitor to
> our beloved Country. Your buildings will be blown up. Everyone of
> your family will be killed.
>
> [unsigned][63]

James Keeley's readers never killed him, though murder is not an unknown form of reader response in the history of American journalism.[64] Readers have always taken their journalism seriously. And they have always taken it actively, making sense of it in whatever way they can, and acting upon it. With its pose of impartiality, objectivity, and simple facticity on the one hand, yet its vital and direct link to political power on the other hand, it is little wonder that journalism has sometimes driven its readers to violence—or at least to their writing tables. Surely, journalism is the branch of literature where the active reader is most likely to be found.

But what does it mean to say a reader is "active"? What does it mean to say, as Stanley Fish said so strikingly, that literature is in the reader, not in the text?[65] By the 1980s the idea of the active reader had become a commonplace—a kind of all-purpose postmodern cliché—in literary studies, cultural studies, and mass communication research. Mass communication research, with its traditional interest in empirical audience studies, discovered the active reader (and the passive text) as early as the 1940s in the classic political communication surveys conducted by Paul Lazarsfeld and other sociologists, a research tradition that culminated in the "limited effects" model of mass media influence.[66] In the early 1960s the social psychology wing of media studies, led by Raymond Bauer, discovered an "obstinate audience," an audience "impervious to influence," and thereby gave birth to the tradition of audience research in the 1970s and '80s called "uses and gratifications." This approach found a nearly sovereign audience, a set of rugged individualist readers and viewers almost entirely immune to the content of the media message.[67] The active reader also became the central figure in reader-response literary criticism and in some strains of the "new historicism" in literary studies.[68] Even critical cultural studies, which had traditionally emphasized the constraints imposed by dominant hegemonic ideologies, turned to the study of "polysemy" (multiple sign/meaning) and "oppositional decoding" of texts—in other words, active meaning making by readers.[69] Clearly, the postmodern moment had arrived: The interpretation, not the text, was the thing.

But wait! Though readers were proclaimed to be more than insouciant victims injected with meaning by the hypodermic needles of literature, mass media, or journalism, does that fact make them free? Is activity necessarily agency? Other strains of research in literature and communication—critical theory, deconstruction, semiotics—have answered that question with a resounding no. Scholars in these fields see reader response as occurring within a linguistic/cultural system, a system of ideological constraint, a system not at all of the reader's own making. For these theorists, the turn to interpretation did not reveal an autonomous and empowered reader but rather a reader wholly dependent upon (indeed, created by) the patterns of language and culture—or perhaps even a reader who is the creature of the multinational media conglomerate.[70]

These disparate notions of reader "activity" might seem to be rooted in rather different conceptions of human nature and human agency. On one side seems to stand the autonomous individual, the idiosyncratic mind, the Cartesian "I." On the other side floats a fictive Nietzschean "I," the child of language, the creature of culture, entirely suspended in webs of interpretation and intertextuality. To some degree these positions do involve different philosophical stances, but philosophy is not the key to the difference. Both positions grow from a postpositivist, social-constructionist sensibility; both stress the interpretation more than the text. I see the difference more as an artifact of methodology, of differing levels of analysis. Observed at the individual level, human beings appear diverse, idiosyncratic, free. Raise the observation to a higher level of abstraction, and they become more comparable, more predictable, more constrained. This apparent change in human nature is produced not by a change in reality or even philosophy but by a change in methodology, a change in perspective.

In other words, it is possible to conceive of readers as *both* active and passive, both free and bound, both creative and constrained—not a little of each but a lot of both. It depends on how we look at them—or, more properly, where we look for them, in what social context. Individuals not only look different in the different contexts that touch their lives; they are different. They are, simultaneously, the shapers and the shaped. The idea that context and level of analysis are crucial to understanding reader response has produced an interesting convergence in several streams of readership/audience research. For example, here are three voices from quite diverse fields of study. First, Norman Holland, a psychoanalytic literary critic:

> We respond to poems and stories and movies both individually and culturally, not either one way or the other. We can understand that we do have codes and systems of belief. These codes and canons do speak through us, but their presence does not require that we disappear. Rather they require us to run them. These codes both enable and limit us as we live imperfectly in this imperfect world. They enable us to do some things, but our very doing limits us from other things.

Carl Kaestle, a social historian:

> People act individually to develop identities, choose allegiances, form beliefs, and conduct their day-to-day lives, but they do so within the constraints of cultural inheritances and economic relationships. Some of these constraints act systematically and are rooted in the social structure. Applying this model of agency and constraints to the world of reading, we can acknowledge the unpredictable responses of individuals within an analysis of how social forces shape the content of reading material and the distribution of literacy skills.

Frank Biocca, a mass communication researcher:

> We can see that the concept of active audience defined as cognitive independence, personal freedom, and imperviousness to influence appears strangely to be both bloated and seemingly anemic and thin. . . . Should we be surprised when, as social scientists, we behold perception, choice, reflection, and even selection? And if in the shopping aisles of media fare our active citizen chooses his or her banalities in pink, blue, or red boxes, should we pronounce them free, active, and "impervious to influence"?[71]

These three scholars have different notions of what psychological, social, or economic factors are important. But they share the conviction that what is needed is not more philosophy, not more theory about audience activity or passivity, but rather more empirical research, research that links different levels of analysis, research that links actual readers not only to texts but to social contexts in which the readers lived and the texts were read.

Some students of reader (and viewer) response to journalism have taken up the challenge to observe and listen to "active readers" as they make sense of the daily flow of news. Through focus groups, unstructured interviews, and other interpretive social science methods, William Gamson, Justin Lewis, and others have tried to explore in more subtle ways the manifold strategies that ordinary people use to interpret the newspapers they read and the television news they watch. For example, Gamson's "peer-group conversations" with working-class Bostonians reveal a fascinating variety of themes and frames and codes that readers employ to impose meaning on the bewildering river of news that flows over them. Their responses are often curious but not unintelligible. They draw on personal experience and, more important, on religious, political, and cultural themes and conventions. In short, they make sense in context.[72]

If context is the key, then history is a vital laboratory for the study of reader response, for history is the discipline of context, of the rich specificity of time and place. But the historian, whose readers have fallen silent, faces a task considerably more daunting than the task of the media sociologist because the experience of most readers in the past can never be recovered. Yet historical readership research is possible. Some readers have left behind a residue of their reading: diaries, memoirs, private libraries, marginalia in books, expenditure data, family letters, letters to editors. The work of building a genuine social history of reading is well under way—at least a history of the reading of books.[73] The reading of journalism, however, is even more difficult to trace in the past because journalism is so ephemeral and the reading of it so commonplace and unremarkable and therefore so commonly unremarked upon in the historical record. Yet it is precisely this commonness that makes the history of journalism readership central to the broader social history of reading in everyday life.[74]

So I return to the question: What does it mean to say that a reader is active? What does it mean to say that a reader of *journalism* is active? Reformulated as a historical (contextualized) question, it becomes: What did it mean to be an active reader of the *Chicago Tribune* and the *Chicago Herald* in 1912–17?

My study of reader letters has suggested a threefold answer. First, though the readers' letters were enormously diverse and often quite idiosyncratic, discernible patterns of response ran through most of them. Often, newspaper stories cued readers to think of religious texts or political ideas; often, readers linked one story with others to impose a meaningful order on the oddly disjointed curriculum of news. Like readers of journalism today, these letter writers necessarily brought to the task of reading a repertoire of interpretive strategies of response. Second, some of these strategies were related to the readers' notion of what a newspaper should be and do—that is, to their understanding of the methodology of journalism and the conventions of the genre. In this era of substantial change in journalistic method, the readers' understanding was sometimes at odds with the editor's, and the resulting reader-editor conversation sheds light on how readers read their newspapers in the early twentieth century. Third, the readers' strategies for reading were often highly political but not simply political in a general ideological way. They grew directly from the organized efforts of political interest groups. In short, the letters reveal a wonderfully active community of readers but an activity rooted in the social and political institutions of time and place.

Do these patterns of reader response in the Keeley correspondence transcend Chicago, 1912–17? I think so. The enduring conventions of American journalism—the never-ending curriculum of news, the standard methods of news reporting, and so on—have placed upon readers in other times and places similar interpretive burdens and opportunities. Readers must always learn to navigate these conventions, to make sense of the news as best they can. And when journalistic conventions change, readers sometimes find themselves unusually perplexed and grumpy—though some degree of perplexity and grumpiness may be the universal predicament of the newspaper reader. One element of American journalism, however, has never changed: its fundamental political character. If journalism is the literature of politics, we may expect to find in any time and any place that the building of interpretive communities of newspaper readers is seldom left to chance. Of course, similar arguments have been made about the politics of reading in other streams of literature. Readers are always taught *how* to read as well as taught *to* read.[75] But nowhere is this political reading instruction—this mobilization of bias—more organized, more systematic, or more ardent than in the reading of newspaper journalism.

Notes

1. R. E. Young letter, Jan. 5, 1915, folder 5; H. P. Donovan letter, Feb. 19, 1915, folder 5; in the James Keeley Papers, Chicago Historical Society.

2. These terms (and others like them) appear in the essays in Charles R. Cooper, ed., *Researching Response to Literature and the Teaching of Literature: Points of Departure* (Norwood, N.J.: Ablex, 1985); and Jane Tompkins, ed., *Reader-Response Criticism: From Formalism to Post-Structuralism* (Baltimore: Johns Hopkins University Press, 1980). For a lucid discussion of reader response, see Norman N. Holland, *The Critical I* (New York: Columbia University Press, 1992).

3. Reader letters form the bulk of the Keeley Papers. The collection consists of six folders and includes a few family letters, a speech text, and some office memos, as well as the reader letters. All letters cited in this article are from the Keeley Papers. Almost all incoming letters are addressed to Keeley or "Editor"; a few are addressed to other editors or to no one. I have retained original spelling, capitalization, and punctuation, except for a few places where a comma or other punctuation mark seemed needed for clarity.

4. This chapter is a contribution to a new social history of reading based upon evidence of actual reader response in the past. It is an attempt to do in the realm of journalism the kind of empirical "history of audiences" suggested by Roger Chartier, Robert Darnton, David D. Hall, Carl Kaestle, Jonathan Rose, and other social historians. See, for example, Roger Chartier, *The Order of Books: Readers, Authors, and Libraries in Europe between the Fourteenth and Eighteenth Centuries* (Stanford, Calif.: Stanford University Press, 1994); Robert Darnton, "First Steps toward a History of Reading," in *The Kiss of Lamourette: Reflections in Cultural History* (New York: W. W. Norton, 1990); David D. Hall, "Readers and Reading in America: Historical and Critical Perspectives," *Proceedings of the American Antiquarian Society* 103 (Oct. 1993): 337–57, reprinted in David D. Hall, *Cultures of Print: Essays in the History of the Book* (Amherst: University of Massachusetts Press, 1996); Carl F. Kaestle et al., *Literacy in the United States: Readers and Reading since 1880* (New Haven, Conn.: Yale University Press, 1991); Jonathan Rose, "Rereading the English Common

Reader: A Preface to a History of Audiences," *Journal of the History of Ideas* 53 (Jan.–Mar. 1992): 47–70.

5. Jonathan Culler, *The Pursuit of Signs: Semiotics, Literature, Deconstruction* (Ithaca, N.Y.: Cornell University Press, 1981), 54, 127–30. The term *interpretive community* is usually attributed to Stanley Fish. See Fish, *Is There a Text in This Class? The Authority of Interpretive Communities* (Cambridge, Mass.: Harvard University Press, 1980), pt. 2. See also Janice Radway, "Interpretive Communities and Variable Literacies: The Functions of Romance Reading," *Daedalus* 113 (Summer 1984): 52–53; and Holland, *Critical I*, 190–91. Holland, my favorite reader-response critic, speaks of interpretive communities in terms of cultural "canons" or sometimes the "schemata" of cognitive psychology. On the application of the idea of interpretive community to mass media, see Thomas R. Lindhof, "Media Audiences as Interpretive Communities," in *Communication Yearbook*, no. 11, ed. James Anderson (Newbury Park, Calif.: Sage, 1988).

6. E. E. Schattschneider, *The Semisovereign People: A Realist's View of Democracy in America*, 2d ed. (Hinsdale, Ill.: Dryden, 1975), 69. See also Jeffrey C. Isaac, *Power and Marxist Theory: A Realist View* (Ithaca, N.Y.: Cornell University Press, 1987), pt. 1; and Roger W. Cobb and Charles D. Elder, *Participation in American Politics: The Dynamics of Agenda-Building*, 2d ed. (Baltimore: Johns Hopkins University Press, 1983).

7. James Keeley, *Newspaper Work: An Address Delivered before the Students in the Course of Journalism at Notre Dame University, Nov. 26, 1912* (n.p., n.d.), pamphlet in library of the Chicago Historical Society, p. 2.

8. James W. Linn, *James Keeley, Newspaperman* (Indianapolis: Bobbs-Merrill, 1937), 5, 91, 194–95. For other accounts of Keeley's career on the *Chicago Tribune*, see Peter Clark Macfarlane, "Explaining Keeley," *Collier's* 51 (June 1913): 5–6, 25–27; and Lloyd Wendt, *Chicago Tribune: The Rise of a Great American Newspaper* (Chicago: Rand McNally, 1979), chap. 15.

9. Keeley, *Newspaper Work*, 4.

10. Ibid., 4–7; Wendt, *Chicago Tribune*, chaps. 15–16. The *Tribune*'s chief competitors were Victor Lawson's *Chicago Record-Herald* and William Randolph Hearst's *Chicago Examiner*. Though all appealed to broad multiclass audiences, the *Record-Herald* and the *Tribune* were more middle class, the *Examiner* more working class.

11. *Chicago Herald*, Aug. 1914.

12. Keeley, *Newspaper Work*, 1; Keeley, speech to the Michigan Press Association, galley proof, folder 6, Keeley Papers. See also Keeley, speech to the Illinois Press Association, quoted in Linn, *James Keeley*, 214.

13. Keeley, Michigan Press speech.

14. Both Keeley and his biographer, James Linn, speak of thousands of reader letters. The Chicago Historical Society collection, however, contains fewer than three hundred. They are a mix of "bug" letters, ordinary reader letters, and a handful of family letters. I know of no other surviving letters.

15. R. D. Pool letter, July 9, 1914, folder 4, Keeley Papers.

16. In political science and mass communication research, there is a small but long-flowing stream of research on *published* letters to the editor. This research has raised two main questions (both different from mine): Do letters to the editor reflect general public opinion? And how are letters related to the news and editorial content of the newspapers?

Research on the first question has produced mixed findings. Some researchers have found letter writers to be quite different from the general public; some have found similarities. See, for example, H. Schuyler Foster Jr. and Carl J. Friedrich, "Letters to the Editor as a Means of Measuring the Effectiveness of Propaganda," *American Political Science Review* 31 (Apr. 1937): 71–79; William D. Tarrant, "Who Writes Letters to the Editor?" *Journalism Quarterly* 34 (Fall 1957): 501–2; David L. Grey and Trevor R. Brown, "Letters to the Editor: Hazy Reflections of Public Opinion," *Journalism Quarterly* 47 (Autumn 1970): 450–56, 471; Emmett H. Buell Jr., "Eccentrics or Gladiators? People Who Write about Politics in Letters to the Editor," *Social Science Quarterly* 56 (Dec. 1975): 440–49; Thomas J. Volgy, Margaret Krigbaum, Mary Kay Langan, and Vicky Moshier, "Some of My Best Friends Are Letter Writers: Eccentrics and Gladiators Revisited," *Social Science Quarterly* 58 (Sept. 1977): 321–27; and David B. Hill, "Letter Opinion on ERA: A Test of the Newspaper Bias Hypothesis," *Public Opinion Quarterly* 45 (Fall 1981): 384–92. Research on the the second question has tended to find letter writers cued by news or editorials in the paper. See Foster and Friedrich, "Letters to the Editor"; Grey and Brown, "Letters to the Editor"; Hal Davis and Galen Rarick, "Functions of Editorials and Letters to the Editor," *Journalism Quarterly* 41 (Winter 1964): 108–9; and Richard V. Ericson, Patricia M. Baranek, and Janet B. Chan, *Negotiating Control: A Study of News Sources* (Toronto: University of Toronto Press, 1989), 339, 375. Researchers have reported some evidence of cueing in the reverse direction: Reader letters sometimes cue editors and editorial writers. See David Pritchard and Dan Berkowitz, "How Readers' Letters May Influence Editors and News Emphasis: A Content Analysis of 10 Newspapers, 1948–1978," *Journalism Quarterly* 68 (Autumn 1991): 388–95; and Ericson, Baranek, and Chan, *Negotiating Control*, 340.

17. H. Zollinger letter, Apr. [1915], folder 5; William O'Brien letter, June 30, 1915, folder 5; Jno. Wurster letter, June 25, 1913, folder 2; James Keeley memo, n.d., folder 5, Keeley Papers.

18. Julio Carneiro letter, [Jan. 31, 1916], folder 6; William Florance letter, Feb. 17, 1915, folder 5; Danny Digger and Ted Harrington letter, Nov. 16, 1912, folder 2, Keeley Papers.

19. Marked-up clipping from *Chicago Herald*, Aug. 26, 1915, along with unsigned, undated office memo, folder 5; unsigned letter, Jan. 17, 1914, with clipping from *Chicago Tribune*, Jan. 17, 1914, folder 3, Keeley Papers.

20. Unsigned letter, June 15, [1914], folder 4; Samuel George Priddle letter, May 10, 1914, folder 4, Keeley Papers.

21. J. M. Alford letter, Feb. 8, 1915, and clipping, folder 5; unsigned letter, [Feb. 18, 1915], and clipping, folder 5; unsigned letter, [1916], folder 6; D. E. Kenyon letter, Jan. 12, 1915, folder 5, Keeley Papers.

22. "Progressive Republican but Not a Roosevelt Maniac" letter, June 12, 1912, folder 2; William H. Hart letter, Mar. 27, 1912, folder 2; R. P. Pool letter, Jan. 7, 1915, folder 5; F. A. Wells letter, Apr. 20, 1915, folder 5; "A Union Man" letter, Oct. 12, 1912, folder 2; Eugene Gray letter, [Nov. 27, 1911], folder 1, Keeley Papers.

23. Keeley described this letter and his reply in his Michigan Press speech.

24. For similar discussions in current social research on reader response to journalism, see the studies cited in note 72. I am indebted to James Carey for the wonderfully apt idea of journalism as a "curriculum." See James W. Carey, "The Dark Continent of American Journalism," in *Reading the News*, ed. Robert Karl Manoff and Michael Schudson (New York: Pantheon, 1986), 151.

25. Keeley, quoted in Linn, *James Keeley,* 213; and "Justice" letter, Jan. 18, 1912, folder 2; unsigned postcard, Mar. 14, 1913, folder 2, both in Keeley Papers.

26. "One Who Knows" letter, Aug. 26, 1913, folder 2; F. R. Phillips letter, Dec. 11, 1913, folder 3; illegible signature letter, Apr. 12, 1913, folder 2, Keeley Papers.

27. R. S. Forhes, [Jan. 9, 1914], folder 3, Keeley Papers.

28. "Very Old Subscriber" letter, June 12, 1914, folder 4; A. C. Palmer letter, Jan. 23, 19[13], folder 5; I. F. Strauss letter, July 1, 1912, folder 2, Keeley Papers.

29. "A Subscriber" letter, Sept. 15, 1913, folder 2; unsigned letter, June 1, 1912, folder 2; illegible signature letter, Jan., 1914, folder 3; "A Working Man That Knows a Little about High Protective Tariff," Sept. 5, 1913, folder 2, Keeley Papers.

30. Mrs. J. A. Skinner letter, Oct. 27, [1914], folder 4, Keeley Papers.

31. Anna Parker Saylor letter, Sept. 19, 1913, folder 2, Keeley Papers.

32. Keeley, *Newspaper Work,* 27–29.

33. Will Irwin, "The American Newspaper: VII—The Reporter and the News," *Collier's* 47 (Apr. 22, 1911): 21; "The First National Newspaper Conference," *Outlook* 101 (Aug. 17, 1912): 847. See also Marion Tuttle Marzolf, *Civilizing Voices: American Press Criticism, 1880–1950* (New York: Longman, 1991), 62–63. The Irwin series was reprinted in facsimile as Will Irwin, *The American Newspaper: A Series First Appearing in COLLIER'S, January–July, 1911,* with comments by Clifford F. Weigle and David G. Clark (Ames: Iowa State University Press, 1969).

34. Irwin, "The American Newspaper: I—The Power of the Press," *Collier's* 46 (Jan. 21, 1911): 18.

35. "First National Newspaper Conference," 847. See also James Edward Rogers, *The American Newspaper* (Chicago: University of Chicago Press, 1909); and Hamilton Holt, *Commercialism and Journalism* (Boston: Houghton Mifflin, 1909).

36. These and other themes of press criticism from this era are summarized in Marzolf, *Civilizing Voices,* chaps. 3–5.

37. Article by "A New York Editor," "Is an Honest Newspaper Possible?" *Atlantic Monthly* 102 (Oct. 1908): 441.

38. Keeley, *Newspaper Work,* 27–28. See also Marzolf, *Civilizing Voices,* 40–46.

39. Michael Schudson, *Discovering the News: A Social History of American Newspapers* (New York: Basic, 1978), 120–22; Gaye Tuchman, "Objectivity as Strategic Ritual: An Examination of Newsmen's Notions of Objectivity," *American Journal of Sociology* 77 (Jan. 1972): 660–77.

40. Anna Parker Saylor letter, Sept. 19, 1913, folder 2; I. F. Strauss letter, July 1, 1912, folder 2; "A Subscriber" letter, Sept. 15, 1913, folder 2, Keeley Papers.

41. Keeley, Michigan Press speech, Keeley Papers.

42. F. A. Wells letter, Apr. 20, 1915, folder 5; C. M. Dolan letter, June 10, 1915, folder 5; Frank Day letter, Dec. 15, 1913, folder 3, Keeley Papers.

43. Keeley reply to R. D. Pool, Jan. 9, 1915, folder 5, Keeley Papers.

44. C.I.K. letter, Dec. 5, 1914, folder 4; J. M. Alford letter, Dec. 21, 1913, folder 3; illegible signature letter, [Jan. 9, 1914], folder 3; H. B. Green letter, Oct. 31, 1914, folder 4; F. R. Phillips letter, Dec. 11, 1913, folder 3, Keeley Papers.

45. R. S. Forhes letter, [Jan. 9, 1914], folder 3, Keeley Papers.

46. Keeley reply to R. E. Young, Jan. 9, 1915, folder 5, Keeley Papers.

47. On the resurgence of anti-Catholic nativism in this era, see John Higham, *Strangers in the Land: Patterns of American Nativism, 1860–1925* (New York: Atheneum, 1969), chap. 7; Timothy Walch, *Catholicism in America* (Malabar, Fla.: Robert E. Krieger, 1989), 66–70; and David H. Bennett, *The Party of Fear: From Nativist Movements to the New Right in American History* (Chapel Hill: University of North Carolina Press, 1988), 179–82.

48. *Tribune*, Dec. 30, 1913, and Jan. 1 and 8, 1914.

49. Joseph Medill Patterson letter, *Tribune*, Jan. 7, 1914.

50. See "Voice of the People" letters, in *Tribune*, Jan. 8–10, 1914. Some of the manuscript letters are also tightly focused on the "sex hygiene" issue. For example, see Charles Day Moore letter, Jan. 6, 1914, folder 3; and E. B. Newell letter, Jan. 8, 1914, folder 3, Keeley Papers.

51. D. E. Russell letter, Jan. 10, 1914, folder 3, Keeley Papers.

52. Barbara Welter, "From Maria Monk to Paul Blanshard: A Century of Protestant Anti-Catholicism," in *Uncivil Religion: Interreligious Hostility in America*, ed. Robert N. Bellah and Frederick E. Greenspahn (New York: Crossroad, 1987), 53–55; James Hennesey, *American Catholics: A History of the Roman Catholic Community in the United States* (New York: Oxford University Press, 1981), 221–22. Ireland was an unlikely villain to smear with this quotation. A leader of the American Catholic liberals in the late nineteenth century, he promoted a firm commitment to "Americanism," including an accommodation with the public schools. See Andrew Greeley, *The Catholic Experience: An Interpretation of the History of American Catholicism* (Garden City, N.Y.: Doubleday, 1967), chap. 6.

53. The school issue had two political manifestations: campaigns to preserve the non-Catholic (i.e., Protestant) character of public schooling; and campaigns to require mandatory *public* schooling of *all* children, which actually became state law in Oregon in 1922. See James W. Sanders, *The Education of an Urban Minority: Catholics in Chicago, 1833–1965* (New York: Oxford University Press, 1977), chap. 2; and David B. Tyack, "The Perils of Pluralism: The Background of the Pierce Case," *American Historical Review* 74 (Oct. 1968): 74–98, reprinted in *Modern American Catholicism, 1900–1965: Selected Historical Essays*, ed. Edward R. Kantowicz (New York: Garland, 1988). See also John Tracy Ellis, *The Life of James Cardinal Gibbons*, 2 vols. (Milwaukee: Bruce Publishing, 1952), 1:635–707; and James H. Moynihan, *The Life of Archbishop John Ireland* (New York: Harper, 1953), 73–103.

54. "The Warning! Catholicizing Public Schools" (n.p., [1913]), broadside flyer in folder 2, Keeley Papers. The *Menace* itself carried similar school stories, similar book lists, and identical quotations attributed to Catholic sources. See, for example, *Menace*, Aug. 5, 1911, Feb. 10, 1912, Sept. 13, 1913, and Jan. 15, 1914.

55. See, *Menace*, 1913–14, passim. A good statement of purpose appeared on Nov. 25, 1911. Each week the *Menace* trumpeted its growing circulation. For background on the *Menace*, see Higham, *Strangers in the Land*, 180–81; Walch, *Catholicism in America*, 67; Hennesey, *American Catholics*, 221–22.

56. Thomas Burke Grant letter, [Jan. 9, 1914], folder 3; R. S. Forhes letter, [Jan. 9, 1914], folder 3. See other letters in folder 3 passim, Keeley Papers. For examples of the *Menace* on public schools, see issues cited in note 54.

57. "A True American" letter, Dec. 1913, folder 3; Chas. M. Leavitt letter, Dec. 13, 1913, folder 3; Keeley reply to Leavitt, Dec. 16, 1913, folder 3; Keeley memo ("Usual Answer") attached to L. F. Diddie letter, Jan. 2, [1914], folder 3, Keeley Papers. The Keeley Papers also

hold a *typed* version of the *Menace*'s "Rules," origin unknown. See also "Romanizing the Press," in *Menace*, Mar. 23, 1912.

58. "The Daily Press of the United States Sold Out to the Roman Catholic Hierarchy" (n.p., [1914]), broadside flyer in folder 3; Keeley reply to R. Evans, Jan. 6, 1914, folder 3, Keeley Papers.

59. L. F. Diddie letter, Jan. 2, [1914], folder 2; "A Subscriber" letter, Feb. 2, 1914, folder 3, Keeley Papers. The *Menace* regularly carried stories about the murder case of Father Hans Schmidt in New York, which several *Tribune* readers mentioned in their letters. See, for example, *Menace*, Nov. 1, 1913, and Jan. 17, 1914.

60. H. P. Donovan letter, Feb. 19, 1915, folder 5; J. A. Bauer letter, Jan. 8, 1914, folder 3, Keeley Papers.

61. J. A. Bauer letter, Jan. 8, 1914, folder 3; Thomas Burke Grant letter, [Jan. 9, 1914], folder, Keeley Papers. Powerful Catholic groups did seek to have the *Menace* barred from the mails. See *Menace*, Feb. 17, 1912.

62. David Brion Davis has remarked that paranoid politics are usually rooted, in some way, in reality. Most conspiratorialists in American history "were responding to highly disturbing events; and their perceptions, even when wild distortions of reality, were not necessarily unreasonable interpretations of available information. Collective beliefs in conspiracy have usually embodied or given expression to genuine social conflict." See his introduction to his edited collection *The Fear of Conspiracy: Images of Un-American Subversion from the Revolution to the Present* (Ithaca, N.Y.: Cornell University Press, 1971), xiv. See also Bennett, *Party of Fear,* 9; and Richard Hofstadter, *The Paranoid Style in American Politics* (New York: Knopf, 1965).

63. Unsigned postcard, [1917], folder 6, Keeley Papers.

64. John C. Nerone, *Violence against the Press: Policing the Public Sphere in U.S. History* (New York: Oxford University Press, 1994). Before the nineteenth century, when imaginative literature was more overtly political, poetry and fiction often generated the kind of violent response that I am associating here with journalism. See Jane P. Tompkins, "The Reader in History: The Changing Shape of Literary Response," in *Reader-Response Criticism,* ed. Tompkins.

65. Stanley E. Fish, "Literature in the Reader: Affective Stylistics," *New Literary History* 2 (Autumn 1970): 123–62, reprinted in *Reader-Response Criticism,* ed. Tompkins.

66. Paul F. Lazarsfeld, Bernard Berelson, and Hazel Gaudet, *The People's Choice* (New York: Harper and Row, 1944); Elihu Katz and Paul F. Lazarsfeld, *Personal Influence* (New York: Free Press, 1955); Joseph T. Klapper, *The Effects of Mass Communication* (Glencoe, Ill.: Free Press, 1960).

67. Raymond A. Bauer, "The Obstinate Audience," *American Psychologist* 19 (May 1964): 319–28; Jack M. McLeod and Lee B. Becker, "The Uses and Gratifications Approach," in *Handbook of Political Communication,* ed. Dan Nimmo and Keith Sanders (Beverly Hills, Calif.: Sage, 1981); Jay G. Blumler and Elihu Katz, eds., *The Uses of Mass Communications: Current Perspectives on Gratifications Research* (Beverly Hills, Calif.: Sage, 1974). Useful literature reviews included Janice Peck, "The Power of Media and the Creation of Meaning: A Survey of Approaches to Media Analysis," in *Progress in Communication Sciences,* vol. 9, ed. Brenda Dervin and Melvin J. Voigt (Norwood, N.J.: Ablex, 1989); and Klaus Bruhn Jensen, "When Is Meaning? Communication Theory, Pragmatism, and Mass Me-

dia Reception," in *Communication Yearbook*, no. 14, ed. James Anderson (Newbury Park, Calif.: Sage, 1991).

68. For example, see the essays in Jeffrey N. Cox and Larry Reynolds, eds., *New Historical Literary Study: Essays on Reproducing Texts, Representing History* (Princeton, N.J.: Princeton University Press, 1993); Elizabeth A. Flynn and Patrocinio P. Schweickart, eds., *Gender and Reading: Essays on Readers, Texts, and Contexts* (Baltimore: Johns Hopkins University Press, 1986); James L. Machor, ed., *Readers in History: Nineteenth-Century American Literature and the Contexts of Response* (Baltimore: Johns Hopkins University Press, 1993); and H. Aram Veeser, ed., *The New Historicism* (New York: Routledge, 1989). For a critical perspective, see Brook Thomas, *The New Historicism and Other Old-Fashioned Topics* (Princeton, N.J.: Princeton University Press, 1991).

69. David Morley, "Active Audience Theory: Pendulums and Pitfalls," *Journal of Communication* 43 (Autumn 1993): 13–19, reprinted in *Defining Media Studies: Reflections on the Future of the Field*, ed. Mark R. Levy and Michael Gurevitch (New York: Oxford University Press, 1994); Justin Lewis, "The Meaning of Things: Audiences, Ambiguity, and Power," in *Viewing, Reading, Listening: Audiences and Cultural Reception*, ed. Jon Cruz and Justin Lewis (Boulder, Colo.: Westview, 1994); Stuart Hall, "Encoding/Decoding Television Discourse," in *Culture, Media, Language*, ed. Stuart Hall et al. (London: Hutchinson, 1980); John Fiske, "Television: Polysemy and Popularity," in *Critical Perspectives on Media and Society*, ed. Robert K. Avery and David Eason (New York: Guilford, 1991); Horace M. Newcomb, "On the Dialogic Aspects of Mass Communication," in *Critical Perspectives*, ed. Avery and Eason; Linda Steiner, "Oppositional Decoding as an Act of Resistance," in *Critical Perspectives*, ed. Avery and Eason; and Janice Radway, *Reading the Romance: Women, Patriarchy, and Popular Literature* (Chapel Hill: University of North Carolina Press, 1984). For a literature review, see Tamar Liebes, "On the Convergence of Theories of Mass Communication and Literature Regarding the Role of the 'Reader,'" in *Progress in Communication Sciences*, vol. 9, ed. Dervin and Voigt.

70. Raymond Williams, *Television: Technology and Cultural Form* (London: Fontana, 1974); Daniel C. Hallin, "The American News Media: A Critical Theory Perspective," in *Critical Theory and Public Life*, ed. John Forester (Cambridge, Mass.: MIT Press, 1985); Mike Budd, Robert M. Entman, and Clay Steinman, "The Affirmative Character of U.S. Cultural Studies," *Critical Studies in Mass Communication* 7 (June 1990): 169–84; Thomas Streeter, "Polysemy, Plurality, and Media Studies," *Journal of Communication Inquiry* 13 (Summer 1989): 88–106; Culler, *Pursuit of Signs;* Umberto Eco, *The Role of the Reader: Explorations in the Semiotics of Texts* (Bloomington: Indiana University Press, 1979); Christopher Norris, *What's Wrong with Postmodernism: Critical Theory and the Ends of Philosophy* (Baltimore: Johns Hopkins University Press, 1990); Herbert I. Schiller, *Culture, Inc.: The Corporate Takeover of Public Expression* (New York: Oxford University Press, 1989). Holland, in *The Critical I*, lucidly reviews the deconstruction and semiotic approaches to literary analysis.

71. Holland, *Critical I*, 232; Kaestle et al., *Literacy in the United States*, 51; Frank A. Biocca, "Opposing Conceptions of the Audience: The Active and Passive Hemispheres of Mass Communication Theory," in *Communication Yearbook*, no. 11, ed. Anderson, 75.

72. William A. Gamson, *Talking Politics* (New York: Cambridge University Press, 1992); William A. Gamson, "A Constructionist Approach to Mass Media and Public Opinion,"

Symbolic Interaction 11 (1988): 161–74; Justin Lewis, *The Ideological Octopus: An Exploration of Television and Its Audience* (New York: Routledge, 1991); W. Russell Neuman, Marion R. Just, and Ann N. Crigler, *Common Knowledge: News and the Construction of Political Meaning* (Chicago: University of Chicago Press, 1992). See also David Morley, *Television, Audiences, and Cultural Studies* (New York: Routledge, 1992); and Ien Ang, *Living Room Wars: Rethinking Media Audiences for a Postmodern World* (New York: Routledge, 1996).

73. For American examples, see Richard D. Brown, *Knowledge Is Power: The Diffusion of Information in Early America, 1700–1865* (New York: Oxford University Press, 1989); William J. Gilmore, *Reading Becomes a Necessity of Life: Material and Cultural Life in Rural New England* (Knoxville: University of Tennessee Press, 1989); Ronald J. Zboray, *A Fictive People: Antebellum Economic Development and the American Reading Public* (New York: Oxford University Press, 1993); Cathy N. Davidson, *Revolution and the Word: The Rise of the Novel in America* (New York: Oxford University Press, 1986); and the essays in Cathy N. Davidson, ed., *Reading in America: Literature and Social History* (Baltimore: Johns Hopkins University Press, 1989); and Machor, *Readers in History.*

74. Some, but not much, research has been done in the history of readers of journalism. See, for example, the other chapters in part 2 of this volume. See also Thomas C. Leonard, *News for All: America's Coming of Age with the Press* (New York: Oxford University Press, 1995), chap. 1; David Henkin, *City Reading: Written Words and Public Spaces in Antebellum New York* (New York: Columbia University Press, 1998), chap. 5; and Ronald J. Zboray and Mary Saracino Zboray, "Political News and Female Readership in Antebellum Boston and Its Region," *Journalism History* 22 (Spring 1996): 2–14.

75. Jane Tompkins, *Sensational Designs: The Cultural Work of American Fiction, 1790–1860* (New York: Oxford University Press, 1985), 27; Tompkins, "Reader in History," 226. See also David Paul Nord, "A Plea for *Journalism* History," *Journalism History* 15 (Spring 1988): 8–15; and Michael Denning, *Mechanic Accents: Dime Novels and Working-Class Culture in America* (London: Verso, 1987), chap. 4.

12. Readers Love to Argue about the News—But Not in Newspapers

DURING THE Persian Gulf War the computer bulletin boards lit up like the skies over Baghdad. These electronic networks link computer users who share special interests. One academic field alone may have hundreds of them, many with worldwide reach. With the war on, they filled up with news, rumors, arguments, counterarguments, and assorted harangues, screeds, diatribes, and prayers. Like newspapers, they became instruments of international political communication—but with a difference. On an electronic bulletin board every subscriber is a reporter and editor as well as a reader. Readers are by necessity active participants in the process of journalism.

Of course, these readers also used television and newspapers for news and information. But the need to participate, to discuss, was strong. It always is. Journalism has always been a participatory activity, perhaps especially in America. Democratic people need news; they also need discussion.

When Alexis de Tocqueville visited the United States in 1831–32, he was struck by how Americans participated in their journalism, including their newspapers. In *Democracy in America* he virtually defined American newspapers in terms of democratic participation. "Newspapers make associations, and associations make newspapers . . . ," he wrote. "We should underrate their importance if we thought they just guaranteed liberty; they maintain civilization." Newspapers maintain civilization, Tocqueville believed, by making collective action possible in a large polity. They permit many people to think the same thoughts and to feel the same feelings, simultaneously. Newspapers thrive in a democracy not because they provide information cheaply but because people need them "to communicate with one another and to act together."

If Tocqueville could visit the United States today, he would be impressed by our newspapers, pleased by our electronic bulletin boards, but perhaps somewhat surprised and disappointed by the separation between the two. The separation between information and participation—between the professional mass media and the new interpersonal, interactive media—is wide and growing. Tocqueville would have expected the reverse, that the vastly improved communications technologies of the twentieth century would have made audience participation in the mass media more common rather than less.

Many newspaper editors today also deplore this separation. They seek to bridge it by supplementing their news stories (which are typically based on official and expert sources) with feature stories about common people, person-on-the-street reaction stories, poll stories, and so on. Though commendable and sometimes entertaining, these efforts rarely contribute much to democratic participation. They tend to be snippets of opinion, slivers of feeling. In times of crisis they certainly help us feel part of a larger community, but they rarely help us think seriously about public life and public policy.

The problem is that they rely too much on feeling and opinion and not enough on discussion and argumentation—on genuine participation in the journalistic process. They serve a communal function but not a political one. It was different in Tocqueville's America. The newspapers of that era were better democratic institutions than our newspapers and broadcast media today.

*   *   *

Tocqueville observed the American press at a critical democratic moment. For him, the most important tool of American democratic participation was the voluntary association. For every purpose—business, education, religion, social reform—Americans formed groups and organizations. And they founded newspapers to support them. There were about nine hundred newspapers in the United States when Tocqueville visited in 1831; by 1840 the census counted 1,631. Many of these papers were local partisan weeklies. Others were religious or reform papers linked in some way to voluntary associations or interests. These papers tied together scattered communities of believers— religious, moral, and political. In addition to "the news," they were filled with essays and letters and commentaries, often submitted by ordinary readers.

In this proliferation of associational newspapers Tocqueville thought he saw the future of democratic communication in America. Alas, he did not. Instead, in the decade after Tocqueville's visit a new form of "democratic" newspaper emerged: the penny press. These popular papers took the path of democratization via commercialization; that is, they were developed as a cheap consumer good to be sold in the marketplace along with other new products of the industrial revolution. The participatory nature of the press was largely lost. Instead of an active group of readers directly involved in the process of journalism, the readers of the popular commercial press became an audience. Instead of participants, they became spectators.

Our daily newspapers today are descendants of the penny press, not of Tocqueville's associational press. Associational newspapers live on but mainly outside the mainstream of American journalism. Groups and individuals still seek access to the mainstream press, of course, but in ways quite different from the way they participated in the press of Tocqueville's time. Now they must provide "news," or reactions to the news, or representative feelings or opinions about the news. Except in letters to the editor and op-ed essays, there is little democratic participation in the press—that is, sustained political discussion by the people, by the readers of the newspaper.

Critics often complain that "the people" are too ignorant or complacent to engage in serious political discussion. This may be true of many people, but it is patently untrue of large numbers of people, perhaps especially of newspaper readers. The popularity of computer bulletin boards, radio talk shows, and letters to the editor, as well as the ubiquity of voluntary associations in America, suggest that the populists, not the elitists, are right. The people are political, and they have things to say.

* * *

But intelligent argumentation is not easy. People need models, they need access, and they need training. I think newspapers should give them all three. To do so would produce more interesting (and saleable) newspapers, as well as more a effective democracy.

Models

Researchers who study journalism sometimes say that newspapers tell people not what to think but what to think about—the agenda-setting influence of the press. It strikes me that the press may be most successful in yet another way, in telling people *how* to think. By their preference for event reporting and their reliance on the brief quotation of official and expert sources, newspapers teach their readers that event orientation and source reporting are the natural attributes of journalism. Small wonder, then, that individuals and groups who seek access to the press usually do so by creating events and by providing punchy quotations.

It could be otherwise. Even in ordinary source reporting, newspapers could be much more attuned to discussion and participation. Rather than merely juxtaposing the opinions of officials and experts, reporters could try harder to put these sources into conversation with each other. Sources could be pressed more than they usually are to provide arguments and evidence, not just generalizations. And they could be forced to deal more directly and fully with what other sources have said. (Television news talk shows have this sort of format, but they rarely give their sources enough time to develop their arguments and counterarguments.)

Beyond better conventional source reporting, newspapers could also provide interpretive reporting more rooted in argumentation. For example, when an issue arises, such as war in the Persian Gulf or PCB pollution at home, newspapers might assign reporters "disciplinary" rather than "institutional" beats. In other words, reporters could be assigned to cover history, technology, geology, rhetoric, religion, and economics, rather than city hall, the Pentagon, or the EPA. The point is to restructure ordinary reporting to reflect the need for systematic argument as well as for information.

Newspapers might also demonstrate to their readers how discussion and argumentation can be done in daily journalism by letting their reporters do more of it. Here are three ways:

- First, permit reporters to do more essays and "first-person" magazine-style pieces; let readers see that their reporters have minds at work.
- Second, from time to time have two reporters write the same story from different perspectives, just to remind the readers that omniscience and objectivity are unattainable.
- Third, mix together news stories and commentaries. Put editorials into sidebar boxes right next to the stories they comment on. Encourage reporters to write commentaries to go with their news stories. If an editor or another reporter disagrees, give him or her a sidebar box too.

In short, let's give readers models of journalism that illustrate argumentation and discussion, that value the interchange of ideas as well as the dissemination of news.

Access

Newspapers should throw open more of their pages to the writings of their readers. Letters to the editor already provide access for readers, but in most papers the space allotted is small, the letters short, the selection haphazard. They are chosen much as quotes are chosen for news stories—to represent opinion, not to provide argument and participation. More space should be provided for unsolicited letters, but also individuals and group representatives should be recruited to write and be given the space to develop their ideas. General calls for letters on specific topics should be issued routinely. But newspapers should also invite specific local people to write columns and even series of columns. If other people complain about the writers, the complainers should be invited to write as well. When issues loom on the horizon, editors should arrange ahead of time for essays. Scrambling at deadline for a few "reaction" quotes is a poor way to involve people in the analysis of the news.

Newspaper staffers should also engage these letter writers in conversation. Encourage reporters to write replies to critical letters, explaining how and why they did a story as they did. Keep the discussion going.

Beyond these extensions of the op-ed tradition, newspapers should also extend the review tradition of newspaper journalism to all aspects of public and quasi-public policy. Why should a high school play or concert be criticized in a formal review but not last night's meeting of the planning commission? Newspapers should invite interested readers to write reviews on every aspect of public business. And then they should invite officials to review the reviews. Every day's paper should be filled with these sorts of exchanges.

Training

But can readers write useful and interesting argumentative essays, columns, and reviews? Perhaps not. But then let's train them. People already have been trained to provide news. Newspapers overflow with news and quotations provided by organization leaders and PR people. Why not train them for argumentation? First, newspapers should make it clear to the various interest groups they deal with that from now on they want arguments, not just news and opinion. Get out the message: A good essay will more likely be published than the announcement at a phony news conference. Second, newspapers should publish, in the paper and in booklet form, models and guidelines for groups and individuals seeking press access. Third, newspapers should routinely hold evening and weekend writing workshops for representatives of groups and for any other readers who want to learn how to participate in the press. In other words, newspapers should consort and conspire with their best readers just as they do with their best sources.

* * *

Tocqueville believed that newspapers were central to democracy because political discussion and association building were central to newspapers. Insofar as newspapers have abandoned the role of public forum in favor of merely reporting the news, they have abdicated their fundamental democratic purpose. The gap that began to grow in the 1830s between the associational function and the information function of the press—between participation and news—has long been a deep wound in American democracy. It should be healed.

Afterword: Newspapers, Readers, and Communities Today

IN 1991, WHEN I WROTE the little essay that appears as chapter 12 in this book, I was fascinated by the journalistic possibilities of the Internet. The computer bulletin boards that were springing up in the early 1990s seemed poised to fulfill the communal promise of media that Alexis de Tocqueville imagined so long ago. They permitted, as Tocqueville might have said, many people to think, to feel, and to act together. Since 1991, of course, the Internet has inflated like the big bang, and the incipient bulletin boards have exploded into millions of listservs, discussion groups, chat rooms, interactive Web sites, and e-mail networks, where anyone can post just about anything to anyone or even everyone. In this new media universe, it seems, every reader is a journalist.

So, where does that leave the newspaper? In the early 1990s I saw little evidence that newspapers were much interested in the new communications technology. That has changed dramatically. Today, though newspapers have not abandoned ink and paper and are not likely to do so anytime soon, virtually all operate online editions as well, all of which seek to exploit the technological virtues of the Internet to do in new and better ways what newspapers have always done: provide information and promote discussion. Indeed, the new communications technologies—archivable, searchable, linkable, capacious, and wonderfully interactive—seem ideally suited to both traditional functions of the newspaper: information and forum.

Newspapers still gather and report the news as they have always done, but the nearly limitless capacity of the Web means more news, more information, more background, more documents, more data, more everything. Newspapers also engage their readers more imaginatively than they did or could in the early 1990s. They are increasingly reader friendly, shaped by reader polls and focus groups, and packed with "news you can use." They also exploit the interactive quality of online publication to solicit reader feedback, to personalize news and information, and to organize topic-specific discussion groups. Today even the most obtuse and obdurate ink-stained publisher is entranced by the electronic glow.

Yet the separation that I wrote about in 1991, between the information function and the forum function of the press, between news and democratic participation, still characterizes the American newspaper, on line as well as on paper. Certainly, some change has occurred. Reform movements such as civic journalism (along with new competitive pressures) have inspired editors and publishers to ponder more seriously the nature of their local community and their newspaper's place in it.

Civic engagement, community conversation, even the name Alexis de Tocqueville have become fashionable catchphrases in the vocabularies of editors and publishers sensitized to a new readerly style of newspaper management. But the forces of both commerce and technology are more centrifugal than centripetal, more individualizing than communal—and they are very powerful. Vastly more fragmenting of audiences than even cable television, the new Web technology allows newspaper sites to target not just niche audiences but individuals, producing for each reader "The Daily Me," as it has been called. The interactive nature of the Web makes discussion groups so inexpensive to run that community conversations are easily fragmented into thousands of separate, nonintersecting streams of narrowly focused chat. In other ways too, the commercial imperative still drives the modern press to serve the consumer more than the citizen, the individual more than the community. And neither individualized information nor fragmented chatter adds up to the kind of democratic argumentation that I envisioned—with the help of Jefferson, Garrison, Tocqueville, Christopher Lasch, and others— back in 1991.

It could be otherwise. Technology and commerce, though relentless, are not inexorable. If the stories I tell in the chapters of this book have a moral, that is it. Technology and commerce have always had a powerful influence on print culture and therefore on American culture more generally. But more powerful, more historically important, have been the choices that people have made. In the earliest days of the American newspaper, John Campbell chose one model of newspaper and community; James Franklin chose another. In the early Republic nationalizers in the federal government chose to subsidize the broad circulation of newspapers. In the 1830s James Gordon Bennett chose to found one kind of newspaper, William Lloyd Garrison another. In the 1870s Wilbur Storey chose to use the latest printing technology to create an individualized cornucopia of news; Melville Stone chose to use the same technology to fashion a more communal media experience, a public community. From Philadelphia in the 1790s to Chicago in the 1910s, editors and publishers made newspapers for their own purposes; readers remade them for theirs.

Are we living today at the dawn of the greatest revolution in communications technology since Gutenberg? I don't know. I do know that real revolutions flow from our choices, not from our technology. Every age could have been otherwise. That is one lesson, perhaps the only lesson, that history has to teach.

Index

DAVID PAUL NORD is a professor of journalism and American studies and an adjunct professor of history at Indiana University. He is the author of *Newspapers and New Politics: Midwestern Municipal Reform, 1890–1900* and many articles and book chapters on the history of readers and reading, religious publishing, and journalism. He has served as acting editor of the *Journal of American History* and as a volume editor of *A History of the Book in America,* a multivolume project of the American Antiquarian Society and Cambridge University Press.

The History of Communication

Composed in 10.5/13 Minion
by Jim Proefrock
at the University of Illinois Press
Manufactured by Thomson-Shore, Inc.

University of Illinois Press
1325 South Oak Street
Champaign, IL 61820-6903
www.press.uillinois.edu